UnitedHealth **Foundation**

UnitedHealth Foundation
P.O. Box 1459 Minneapolis, MN 55440-1459

July, 2002

W9-AGK-877

Dear Colleague,

We at UnitedHealth Foundation are once again pleased to provide our nation's physicians with a complimentary copy of the BMJ Publishing Group's increasingly relevant publication, *Clinical Evidence*. This marks the fifth edition that we have been privileged to distribute. *Clinical Evidence* is an international resource that benefits from considerable input by clinical experts from the USA.

We are particularly excited to present you with this new edition of *Clinical Evidence* called *Clinical Evidence Concise*. As the pace of clinical and evidence-based health research has intensified, the BMJ Publishing Group noted that both the content and size of *Clinical Evidence* was expanding. Given that the goal is to provide useful information in a convenient and easy to access format, the growing size of *Clinical Evidence* was becoming an issue. As such, we think the BMJ's decision to provide this concise version of *Clinical Evidence*, supplemented by the enclosed CD-ROM containing the full text, was the right decision to support medical professionals in the practice of the best possible care to their patients. Of course, as a recipient of the UnitedHealth Foundation distribution, you continue to have free access to CE-Online. To make use of this feature go to *www.clinicalevidence.com*. Once there, register as a recipient of UHF distribution.

Our goal at the UnitedHealth Foundation is to provide support for the medical decisions that lead to the best possible health care for the American people. We think that the new format will assist you in providing quality medical care that meets the high standards for which we all strive.

Sincerely,

William W. McGuire, M.D.
Chairman
UnitedHealth Foundation

7 ISSUE

JUNE 2002

clinical
evidence

concise

The international source of the
best available evidence for
effective health care

BMJ
Publishing
Group

Editorial Office
BMJ Publishing Group, BMA House, Tavistock Square, WC1H 9JR, United Kingdom.
Tel: +44 (0)20 7387 4499 • Fax: +44 (0)20 7383 6242 • www.bmjpg.com

Subscription prices
Clinical Evidence and *Clinical Evidence Concise* with companion CD-ROM are both published six monthly (June/December) by BMJ Publishing Group. The annual subscription rates for both publications are:

Personal: £75 • US$110 • Can$160
Institutional: £160 • US$240 • Can$345
Student/nurse: £35 • US$50 • Can$75

The combined rates, for both formats, are:

Personal: £110 • US$165 • Can$235
Institutional: £220 • US$330 • Can$475
Student/nurse: £60 • US$90 • Can$130

All individual subscriptions (personal, student, nurse) include online access at no additional cost.

Institutional subscriptions are for full print/concise versions only. Institutions may purchase online site licences separately. The Publishers offer discounts for any society or organisation buying bulk quantities for their members/specific groups. For further information visit the subscription pages of our website www.clinicalevidence.com or contact Miranda Lonsdale at mlonsdale@bmjgroup.com (UK and rest of the world) or Diane McCabe at ussales@bmjgroup.com (North and South America).

All subscriptions from countries outside the Americas to be directed to BMJ Publishing Group, PO Box 299, London, WC1H 9TD, UK.
Tel: +44 (0)20 7383 6270 • Fax: +44 (0)20 7383 6402 • CEsubscriptions@bmjgroup.com

All subscriptions from countries in North and South America to BMJ-Clinical Evidence, PO Box 512, Annapolis Jct, MD 20701-0512, USA.
Tel: +1 800 373 2897/+1 240 646 7000 • Fax: +1 240 646 7005 • clinevid@pmds.com

Alternatively, you can visit our website to order online at www.clinicalevidence.com.

Rights
For information on translation rights or the availability of foreign language editions of *Clinical Evidence*, please contact Daniel Raymond-Barker at draymond-barker@bmjgroup.com.

British Library Cataloguing in Publication Data. A catalogue record for this book is available from the British Library. ISSN 1475-9225 ISBN 0-7279-17102.

Legal Disclaimer
Care has been taken to confirm the accuracy of the information presented and to describe generally accepted practices. However, the authors, editors, and publishers are not responsible for errors or omissions or for any consequences from application of the information in this book and make no warranty, express or implied, with respect to the contents of the publication.

Categories presented in *Clinical Evidence* indicate a judgement about the strength of the evidence available and the relative importance of benefits and harms. The categories do not indicate whether a particular treatment is generally appropriate or whether it is suitable for individuals. The numbers needed to treat (NNTs) presented for one trial cannot be compared directly with NNTs in another trial.

Printed by Quebecor World, Kingsport, Tennessee, USA
Designed by Pete Wilder, The Designers Collective Limited, London, UK

Acknowledgements

The BMJ Publishing Group thanks the following people and organisations for their advice and support: The Cochrane Collaboration, and especially Iain Chalmers, Mike Clarke, Phil Alderson, Peter Langhorne and Carol Lefebvre; the NHS Centre for Reviews and Dissemination, and especially Jos Kleijnen and Julie Glanville; the NHS, and especially Tom Mann, Sir John Patteson, Ron Stamp, Veronica Fraser, Muir Gray and Ben Toth; the British National Formulary, and especially Dinesh Mehta, Eric Connor and John Martin; the Health Information Research Unit at McMaster University, and especially Brian Haynes and Ann McKibbon; the UnitedHealth Foundation, and especially Dr Reed Tuckson and Yvette Krantz; the clinicians, epidemiologists, and members of patient support groups who have acted as peer reviewers. The BMJ Publishing Group values the ongoing support it has received from the global medical community for *Clinical Evidence*. In addition to others, we wish to acknowledge the efforts of the UnitedHealth Foundation who have provided educational funding to support the wide dissemination of this valuable resource to many physicians and health professionals in the USA. It is hoped that the use of this material will continue to provide expert guidance for good patient outcome. We are grateful to the clinicians and patients who spare time to take part in focus groups, which are crucial to the development of *Clinical Evidence*. Finally, we would like to acknowledge the readers who have taken the time to send us their comments and suggestions.

The BMJ Publishing Group would also like to acknowledge Martin Dawes, Anna Donald, Fiona Godlee, Trisha Greenhalgh, David Jewell, Tim Wilson, and Jeremy Wyatt for their valuable assistance in the development of *Clinical Evidence Concise*.

Contents

Welcome to Clinical Evidence Concise

ABOUT CLINICAL EVIDENCE CONCISE AND COMPANION CD-ROM

Clinical Evidence Concise is an index of the summary information from each chapter in *Clinical Evidence* Issue 7. *Clinical Evidence* summarises the current state of knowledge and uncertainty about the prevention, treatment, and diagnosis of clinical conditions, based on thorough searches and appraisal of the literature. It is neither a textbook of medicine nor a set of guidelines. It describes the best available evidence, and if there is no good evidence it says so.

Clinical Evidence Concise contains evidence relating to hundreds of therapeutic or preventative interventions, derived from thousands of original studies, and presents it in 352 pages. For each condition, interventions are categorised according to whether they have been found to be effective or not. The supporting information behind the summaries, including clinical questions, full evidence details, figures, tables, and appendices, is featured on the accompanying CD-ROM. Also included is a quantified, referenced, and up-to-date background section for each condition.

Clinical Evidence was first published in print format in June 1999 and contained 63 topics over 600 pages. Since then, existing topics have been regularly updated and new topics added. New issues are released every 6 months. The June 2002 issue contains 158 topics over 1817 pages. Our aim is to expand until there are about 400 therapeutic topics, when we hope to provide evidence for 80% of the clinical questions that arise in practice.

The larger volume of information is easily coped with by electronic sources (*Clinical Evidence* is available online at www.clinicalevidence.com, on CD-ROM, and on handheld platforms), but presents major difficulties for a paper book. The 400 topics would cover at least 4000 pages!

Making summaries involves discarding detail, and users of *Clinical Evidence Concise* need to be aware of the limitations of the evidence that is presented. It is not possible to make global statements that are both useful and apply to every patient or clinical context. For example, when stating that we found evidence that a drug is beneficial, we mean that there is evidence that the drug has been shown to deliver more benefits than harms, when assessed in at least one subgroup of people, using at least one outcome at a particular point in time. It does not mean that the drug will be effective in all people given that treatment or that other outcomes will be improved, or even that the same outcome will be improved at a different time after the treatment.

MEASURE OF TREATMENT EFFECTS

The dilemma is how to present summaries that are useful but not misleading. *Clinical Evidence Concise* presents, whenever possible, estimates of the size of the benefit by stating the mean number needed to treat (NNT) that was measured in an illustrative trial. Although this gives some indication of the treatment effect, it does not tell the reader what the NNT will be for their particular patient sitting in front of them. At one extreme, if the patient is at very low risk of the outcome in question then the NNT will probably be much larger and, conversely, if the patient is at very high risk of the outcome the NNT will probably be lower. We have not corrected the NNTs for the different baseline risks in the population studied in different trials, because the methods for such a correction are not robust. However, this means that the NNTs in one trial (say, for amoxicillin versus placebo) cannot easily be compared with the NNTs in another trial (say, for erythromycin versus placebo). The NNTs stated in the text should probably be interpreted as optimistic estimates of the treatment effect, because controlled trials often secure better compliance with treatment and more favourable outcomes than occur in the real world. The 95% confidence interval results for NNTs and numbers needed to harm (NNHs), which reflect the range of uncertainty relating to a particular NNT and NNH, are available on the accompanying CD-ROM.

In future versions of *Clinical Evidence Concise* we may present results in a different format. We have experimented with providing statements with no numerical information at all, with a batch of absolute and relative risks, or with just the odds ratio. Although the odds ratio is probably the most "transportable" statistic, it had little support among the practical clinicians who helped evaluate our pilots. The version we have chosen is a pragmatic compromise between academic rigour and practical utility. Your suggestions on improvements are welcome and will be read with interest.

USING CLINICAL EVIDENCE CONCISE AND COMPANION CD-ROM

Clinical Evidence Concise is intended to be used as a first point of call when trying to decide what the options for treatment might be. A detailed exploration of the evidence will require looking up the detail on the CD-ROM, the full print version, or *Clinical Evidence* online. The electronic versions link, whenever possible, to abstracts of the original research in PubMed or published online versions. In this way, *Clinical Evidence* is also designed to act as a pointer connecting the clinician rapidly to the relevant original evidence.

INDEX PAGE

Each topic on the CD-ROM contains an index page listing interventions within their assigned categories of whether they have been found to be effective or not. The interventions are hyperlinked to the full text, which contains the question, a summary statement, benefits, harms, and a comment.

CATEGORISATION

We have developed these categories of effectiveness from one of the Cochrane Collaboration's first and most popular products, *A guide to effective care in pregnancy and childbirth.*[1] The categories we now use are explained in the table below.

TABLE	Categorisation of treatment effects in *Clinical Evidence*
Beneficial	Interventions for which effectiveness has been demonstrated by clear evidence from RCTs, and for which expectation of harms is small compared with the benefits.
Likely to be beneficial	Interventions for which effectiveness is less well established than for those listed under "beneficial".
Trade off between benefits and harms	Interventions for which clinicians and patients should weigh up the beneficial and harmful effects according to individual circumstances and priorities.
Unknown effectiveness	Interventions for which there are currently insufficient data or data of inadequate quality.
Unlikely to be beneficial	Interventions for which lack of effectiveness is less well established than for those listed under "likely to be ineffective or harmful".
Likely to be ineffective or harmful	Interventions for which ineffectiveness or harmfulness has been demonstrated by clear evidence.

Fitting interventions into these categories is not always straightforward. First, the categories represent a mix of several hierarchies: the level of benefit (or harm), the level of evidence (RCT or observational data), and the level of certainty around the finding (represented by the confidence interval). Second, much of the evidence that is most relevant to clinical decisions relates to comparisons between different interventions rather than to comparison with placebo or no intervention; where necessary, we have indicated the comparisons in brackets. Third, interventions may have been tested, or found to be effective, in only one group of people, such as those at high risk, and we have indicated this where possible. Perhaps the most difficult problem has been trying to maintain consistency across different topics; we are working on ways to improve this.

You may notice that interventions within each category are usually listed alphabetically in *Clinical Evidence Concise*, which differs from the CD-ROM and full text versions. This is to avoid the implication that interventions listed first are more effective than those listed last. We would value your feedback on the presentation of interventions in future issues.

REFERENCES
Full references to the individual studies cited in *Clinical Evidence Concise* are available on the CD-ROM. References cited in the definition, incidence/prevalence, aetiology/risk factors, and prognosis sections are numbered in the text but are available in full as hyperlinks from the equivalent section on the CD-ROM.

TOPIC GLOSSARY
Topics may contain glossary listings; these are available in full on the CD-ROM and can be accessed from the index page of each topic or as hyperlinks from the equivalent section on the CD-ROM. Terms with corresponding CD-ROM definitions will be flagged up with a symbol **Ⓖ**.

MAIN GLOSSARY
Words and terms that are used throughout *Clinical Evidence* are listed in the main glossary on the CD-ROM. One example is the use of the word "significant" which, when used without qualification, is being used in the statistical sense; however, the term "clinically significant" indicates a finding that is clinically important.

TABLES AND FIGURES
The presence of figures and tables on the CD-ROM are flagged up in a similar way with the use of **Ⓕ** for figures and **Ⓣ** for tables.

FUTURE DESIGN
The design of *Clinical Evidence Concise* will change progressively over the next few years. We will perform evaluation studies ourselves to measure the relevance of the material to the questions that are being asked in practice, the ease of use, and to check that the message extracted from the summary corresponds closely with that intended. If you have any comments, suggestions or detect any errors, please let us know at cefeedback@bmjgroup.com.

For more information on any of our methods or processes, please visit our website at www.clinicalevidence.com.

Please refer to the CD-ROM for more information about *Clinical Evidence*. For instructions on how to install your CD-ROM refer to Appendix 3.

REFERENCES
1. Enkin M, Keirse M, Renfrew M, et al. *A guide to effective care in pregnancy and childbirth*. Oxford: Oxford University Press, 1998.

Acute atrial fibrillation

Gregory YH Lip, Sridhar Kamath and Bethan Freestone

What are the effects of interventions to control heart rate?

LIKELY TO BE BENEFICIAL

Digoxin
Two RCTs have found that digoxin versus placebo significantly reduces ventricular rate in the short term in people with atrial fibrillation.

Diltiazem
One RCT in people with atrial fibrillation or atrial flutter found that intravenous diltiazem (a calcium channel blocker) versus placebo significantly reduced heart rate over 15 minutes. Another RCT in people with acute atrial fibrillation or atrial flutter found that intravenous diltiazem versus intravenous digoxin significantly reduced heart rate within 5 minutes.

Timolol
One small RCT found that intravenous timolol (a β blocker) versus placebo significantly reduced ventricular rate within 20 minutes.

Verapamil
RCTs in people with atrial fibrillation or atrial flutter have found that intravenous verapamil (a calcium channel blocker) versus placebo significantly reduces heart rate. One RCT found no significant difference in rate control or measures of systolic function with intravenous verapamil versus intravenous diltiazem in people with atrial fibrillation or atrial flutter, but verapamil caused hypotension in some people.

What are the effects of interventions for conversion to sinus rhythm?

UNKNOWN EFFECTIVENESS

DC cardioversion *New*
We found no RCTs of DC cardioversion in acute atrial fibrillation. It may be unethical to conduct RCTs.

Timolol
One small RCT found that intravenous timolol (a β blocker) versus placebo increased conversion to sinus rhythm, but the difference was not significant.

UNLIKELY TO BE BENEFICIAL

Digoxin
RCTs found no significant difference in conversion to sinus rhythm with digoxin versus placebo.

What are the effects of interventions to prevent embolism?

UNKNOWN EFFECTIVENESS

Antithrombotic treatment prior to cardioversion *New*
We found no RCTs of aspirin, heparin, or warfarin as thromboprophylaxis prior to cardioversion in acute atrial fibrillation.

▶

Acute atrial fibrillation

DEFINITION Acute atrial fibrillation is the sudden onset of rapid, irregular, and chaotic atrial activity, and the 48 hours after that onset. It includes both the first symptomatic onset of persistent atrial fibrillation **G** and episodes of paroxysmal atrial fibrillation. It is sometimes difficult to distinguish episodes of new onset atrial fibrillation from newly diagnosed atrial fibrillation. Atrial fibrillation within 72 hours of onset is sometimes called recent onset atrial fibrillation. By contrast, chronic atrial fibrillation **G** is a more sustained form of atrial fibrillation, which in turn can be described as paroxysmal **G**, persistent, or permanent atrial fibrillation **G**. If the atrial fibrillation recurs intermittently, with sinus rhythm between recurrences and with spontaneous recurrences/termination, then it is designated as paroxysmal atrial fibrillation. More sustained atrial fibrillation, which can be successfully reverted back to sinus rhythm (cardioversion) is designated persistent atrial fibrillation. If cardioversion is inappropriate, then atrial fibrillation is designated as permanent atrial fibrillation. In this review we have excluded episodes of atrial fibrillation that arise during or soon after cardiac surgery, and we have excluded the management of chronic atrial fibrillation.

INCIDENCE/ PREVALENCE We found limited evidence of the incidence or prevalence of acute atrial fibrillation. Extrapolation from the Framingham study[1] suggests an incidence in men of 3/1000 person years at age 55 years, rising to 38/1000 person years at 94 years. In women, the incidence was 2/1000 person years at age 55 years and 32.5/1000 person years at 94 years. The prevalence of atrial fibrillation ranged from 0.5% for people aged 50–59 years to 9% in people aged 80–89 years. Among acute emergency medical admissions in the UK, 3–6% have atrial fibrillation and about 40% were newly diagnosed.[2,3] Among acute hospital admissions in New Zealand, 10% (95% CI 9% to 12%) had documented atrial fibrillation.[4]

AETIOLOGY/ RISK FACTORS Paroxysms of atrial fibrillation are more common in athletes.[5] Age increases the risk of developing acute atrial fibrillation. Men are more likely to develop atrial fibrillation than women (38 years' follow up from the Framingham Study, RR after adjustment for age and known predisposing conditions 1.5).[6] Atrial fibrillation can occur in association with underlying disease (both cardiac and non-cardiac) or can arise in the absence of any other condition. Epidemiological surveys have found that risk factors for the development of acute atrial fibrillation include ischaemic heart disease, hypertension, heart failure, valve disease, diabetes, alcohol abuse, thyroid disorders, and disorders of the lung and pleura.[1] In a UK survey of acute hospital admissions with atrial fibrillation, a history of ischaemic heart disease was present in 33%, heart failure in 24%, hypertension in 26%, and rheumatic heart disease in 7%.[3] In some populations, the acute effects of alcohol explain a large proportion of the incidence of acute atrial fibrillation.

PROGNOSIS We found no evidence about the proportion of people with acute atrial fibrillation who develop more chronic forms of atrial fibrillation (e.g. paroxysmal, persistent, or permanent atrial fibrillation). Observational studies and placebo arms of RCTs have found that more than 50% of people with acute atrial fibrillation revert spontaneously within 24–48 hours, especially atrial fibrillation associated with an identifiable precipitant such as alcohol or myocardial infarction. We found little evidence about the effects on mortality and morbidity of acute atrial fibrillation where no underlying cause is found. Acute atrial fibrillation during myocardial infarction is an independent predictor of both short term and long term mortality.[7] Onset of atrial fibrillation reduces cardiac output by 10–20% irrespective of the underlying ventricular rate[8,9] and can contribute to heart failure. People with acute atrial fibrillation who present with heart failure have worse prognosis. Acute atrial fibrillation ▶

is associated with a risk of imminent stroke.[10–13] One case series used transoesophageal echocardiography in people who had developed acute atrial fibrillation within the preceding 48 hours; it found that 15% had atrial thrombi.[14] An ischaemic stroke associated with atrial fibrillation is more likely to be fatal, have a recurrence, and leave a serious functional deficit among survivors, than a stroke not associated with atrial fibrillation.[15]

Cardiovascular disorders

Acute myocardial infarction

Search date October 2001
Nicolas Danchin, Edoardo De Benedetti and Philip Urban

What treatments improve outcomes in acute myocardial infarction?

BENEFICIAL

Angiotensin converting enzyme inhibitors
One overview and one systematic review in people within 36 hours of acute myocardial infarction have found that angiotensin converting enzyme inhibitors versus placebo significantly reduce mortality (NNT about 200) at 30 days. The overview also found that angiotensin converting enzyme inhibitors significantly increase persistent hypotension and renal dysfunction. The question of whether angiotensin converting enzyme inhibitors should be offered to everyone presenting with acute myocardial infarction or only to people with signs of heart failure remains unresolved.

Aspirin
One systematic review in people with acute myocardial infarction has found that aspirin significantly reduces mortality (NNT 40), reinfarction (NNT 100), and stroke (NNT 300) at 1 month.

β Blockers
Two systematic reviews and one subsequent RCT have found that β blockers versus control given within hours of infarction significantly reduce both mortality and reinfarction. One RCT in people receiving thrombolytic treatment found that immediate versus delayed treatment with metoprolol significantly reduced rates of reinfarction and recurrent chest pain at 6 days, but had no significant effect on mortality in the short term or at 1 year. One RCT comparing carvedilol versus placebo in people with recent myocardial infarction and left ventricular ejection fraction ≤ 40% receiving thrombolytic treatment found no significant difference in the combined endpoint of all cause mortality and hospital admission for any cardiovascular event, although mortality and recurrent non fatal myocardial infarction were significantly lower with carvedilol.

Primary percutaneous transluminal coronary angioplasty (performed in specialist centres)
Two systematic reviews have found that primary percutaneous transluminal coronary angioplasty versus primary thrombolysis significantly reduces mortality (NNT about 48) and reinfarction at 30 days. However, the trials were conducted mainly in specialist centres and the effectiveness of percutaneous transluminal coronary angioplasty versus thrombolysis in less specialist centres remains to be defined.

Thrombolytic treatment
One overview of RCTs in people with acute myocardial infarction and ST elevation or bundle branch block on their initial electrocardiogram has found that prompt thrombolytic treatment (within 6 h of the onset of symptoms) versus placebo significantly reduces short term mortality (NNT 56). The overview found that thrombolytic treatment versus control significantly increased the risk of stroke (NNH 250) or major bleeding (NNH 143). Meta-analysis of RCTs comparing different types of thrombolytic agents versus each other have found no significant difference in mortality.

◀ **LIKELY TO BE BENEFICIAL**

Nitrates
One systematic review (prior to the introduction of thrombolysis) has found that nitrates versus placebo significantly reduced the risk of mortality. Two RCTs (after the introduction of thrombolysis) comparing nitrates versus placebo found no significant difference in mortality.

LIKELY TO BE INEFFECTIVE OR HARMFUL

Calcium channel blockers
One systematic review has found that verapamil versus placebo has no significant effect on mortality, and one RCT has found that nifedipine versus placebo may increase mortality.

Which treatments improve outcomes for cardiogenic shock after acute myocardial infarction?

BENEFICIAL

Early invasive cardiac revascularisation
One RCT has found that early invasive cardiac revascularisation❻ versus initial medical treatment alone significantly reduces mortality after 6 and 12 months (NNT 8). A second RCT found similar results, although the difference was not significant.

UNKNOWN EFFECTIVENESS

Early cardiac surgery; positive inotropes and vasodilators; pulmonary artery catheterisation; ventricular assistance devices and cardiac transplantation
We found no evidence from RCTs about the effects of these interventions.

Intra-aortic balloon counterpulsation
One abstract of an RCT comparing intra-aortic balloon counterpulsation❻ plus thrombolysis versus thrombolysis alone found no significant difference in mortality after 6 months.

UNLIKELY TO BE BENEFICIAL

Thrombolysis
Subgroup analysis of people with cardiogenic shock after acute myocardial infarction from one RCT comparing thrombolysis versus no thrombolysis found no significant difference in mortality after 21 days.

DEFINITION | **Acute myocardial infarction:** The sudden occlusion of a coronary artery leading to myocardial cell death. **Cardiogenic shock:** Defined clinically as a poor cardiac output plus evidence of tissue hypoxia that is not improved by correction of reduced intravascular volume.[1] When a pulmonary artery catheter is used, cardiogenic shock may be defined as a cardiac index❻ below 2.2 litres/minute/m^2 despite an elevated pulmonary capillary wedge pressure ($\geq$ 15 mm Hg).[1-3]

INCIDENCE/ PREVALENCE | **Acute myocardial infarction:** One of the most common causes of mortality in both developed and developing nations. In 1990, ischaemic heart disease was the leading cause of death worldwide, accounting for about 6.3 million deaths. The age standardised incidence varies among and within countries.[4] Each year, about 900 000 people in the USA ▶

experience an acute myocardial infarction and about 225 000 of them die. About half of these people die within 1 hour of symptoms and before reaching a hospital emergency room.[5] Event rates increase with age for both sexes and are higher in men than in women, and in poorer than richer people at all ages. The incidence of death from acute myocardial infarction has fallen in many Western countries over the past 20 years. **Cardiogenic shock:** Cardiogenic shock occurs in about 7% of people admitted to hospital with acute myocardial infarction.[6] Of these, about half have established cardiogenic shock at the time of admission to hospital, and most of the others develop it during the first 24–48 hours of their admission.[7]

AETIOLOGY/ RISK FACTORS **Acute myocardial infarction:** See aetiology/risk factors under primary prevention, p 17. The immediate mechanism of acute myocardial infarction is rupture of an atheromatous plaque causing thrombosis and occlusion of coronary arteries and myocardial cell death. Factors that may convert a stable plaque into an unstable plaque (the "active plaque") have yet to be fully elucidated; however, shear stresses, inflammation, and autoimmunity have been proposed. The changing rates of coronary heart disease in different populations are only partly explained by changes in the standard risk factors for ischaemic heart disease (particularly fall in blood pressure and smoking). **Cardiogenic shock:** Cardiogenic shock after acute myocardial infarction usually follows a reduction in functional ventricular myocardium, and is caused by left ventricular infarction (79% of people with cardiogenic shock), more often than by right ventricular infarction (3% of people with cardiogenic shock).[8] Cardiogenic shock after acute myocardial infarction may also be caused by cardiac structural defects, such as mitral valve regurgitation due to papillary muscle dysfunction (7% of people with cardiogenic shock), ventricular septal rupture (4% of people with cardiogenic shock), or cardiac tamponade following free cardiac wall rupture (1% of people with cardiogenic shock). Major risk factors for cardiogenic shock after acute myocardial infarction are previous myocardial infarction, diabetes mellitus, advanced age, hypotension, tachycardia or bradycardia, congestive heart failure with Killip class II–III**G**, and low left ventricular ejection fraction (ejection fraction < 35%).[7,8]

PROGNOSIS **Acute myocardial infarction:** Acute myocardial infarction may lead to a host of mechanical and cardiac electrical complications, including death, ventricular dysfunction, congestive heart failure, fatal and non-fatal arrhythmias, valvular dysfunction, myocardial rupture, and cardiogenic shock. **Cardiogenic shock:** Mortality rates for people in hospital with cardiogenic shock after acute myocardial infarction vary between 50–80%.[2,3,6,7] Most deaths occur within 48 hours of the onset of shock**G**.[9] People surviving until discharge from hospital have a reasonable long term prognosis (88% survival at 1 year).[10]

Cardiovascular disorders

What are the effects of interventions?

BENEFICIAL*

Advice on cholesterol lowering diet

Systematic reviews have found that advice on cholesterol lowering diet (i.e. advice to lower total fat intake or increase the ratio of polyunsaturated to saturated fatty acid) leads to a small reduction in blood cholesterol concentrations in the long term ($\geq$ 6 months).

Advice on diet and exercise supported by behaviour treatment for the encouragement of weight loss

Systematic reviews and subsequent RCTs have found that a combination of advice on diet and exercise supported by behaviour therapy is probably more effective than either diet or exercise advice alone in the treatment of obesity, and might lead to sustained weight loss.

Advice from physicians and trained counsellors to quit smoking

Systematic reviews have found that simple, one off advice from a physician during a routine consultation is associated with 2% of smokers quitting smoking and not relapsing for 1 year (NNT 40). Advice from trained counsellors (who are neither doctors nor nurses), increases quit rates compared with minimal intervention.

Advice on reducing sodium intake to reduce blood pressure

Systematic reviews have found that salt restriction significantly reduces blood pressure in people with hypertension, and have found limited evidence that salt restriction is effective in preventing hypertension. One RCT found limited evidence that advice on restricting salt intake was less effective than advice on weight reduction in preventing hypertension.

Buproprion as part of a smoking cessation programme

One systematic review of antidepressants used as part of a smoking cessation programme has found that buproprion increases quit rates at 1 year (NNT 8).

Counselling people at high risk of disease to quit smoking

Systematic reviews and subsequent RCTs have found that antismoking advice improves smoking cessation in people at higher risk of smoking related disease.

Counselling pregnant women to quit smoking

Two systematic reviews have found that antismoking interventions in pregnant women increase abstinence rates during pregnancy (NNT about 16) and reduce the risk of low birthweight babies. Interventions without nicotine replacement were as effective as nicotine replacement in healthy non-pregnant women.

Exercise advice to women over 80 years

One RCT found that exercise advice delivered in the home by physiotherapists increased physical activity and reduced the risk of falling in women over 80 years.

Nicotine replacement in smokers who smoke at least 10 cigarettes daily

One systematic review and one subsequent RCT have found that nicotine replacement is an effective additional component of cessation strategies in smokers who smoke at least 10 cigarettes daily. We found no clear evidence ▶

that any method of delivery of nicotine is more effective than others. We found limited evidence from three RCTs with follow up of 2–6 years that the additional benefit of nicotine replacement therapy on quit rates reduced with time.

LIKELY TO BE BENEFICIAL*

Advice from nurses to quit smoking
One systematic review has found that advice to quit smoking versus no advice significantly increased the rate of quitting at 1 year.

Counselling sedentary people to increase physical activity
We found weak evidence from systematic reviews and subsequent RCTs that counselling sedentary people increases physical activity compared with no intervention. Limited evidence from RCTs suggests that consultation with an exercise specialist rather than a physician may increase physical activity at 1 year.

UNKNOWN EFFECTIVENESS*

Physical exercise to aid smoking cessation
One systematic review found limited evidence that exercise might increase smoking cessation.

LIKELY TO BE INEFFECTIVE OR HARMFUL*

Acupuncture for smoking cessation
One systematic review has found no significant difference in rates of smoking cessation at 1 year with acupuncture versus control.

Anxiolytics for smoking cessation
One systematic review found no significant difference in quit rates with anxiolytics versus control.

*In terms of producing the intended behavioural change

DEFINITION	Cigarette smoking, diet, and level of physical activity are important in the aetiology of many chronic diseases. Individual change in behaviour has the potential to decrease the burden of chronic disease, particularly cardiovascular disease. This topic focuses on the evidence that specific interventions lead to changed behaviour.
INCIDENCE/ PREVALENCE	In the developed world, the decline in smoking has slowed and the prevalence of regular smoking is increasing in young people. A sedentary lifestyle is becoming increasingly common and the prevalence of obesity is increasing rapidly.

Search date June 2001

Robert McKelvie

What are the effects of treatments?

BENEFICIAL

Angiotensin converting enzyme inhibitors

Systematic reviews and RCTs have found that angiotensin converting enzyme inhibitors versus placebo significantly reduce mortality, admission to hospital for heart failure, and ischaemic events. Relative benefits are similar in different groups of people, but absolute benefits are greater in people with severe heart failure. RCTs in people with asymptomatic left ventricular systolic dysfunction have found that angiotensin converting enzyme inhibitors versus placebo significantly delay the onset of symptomatic heart failure (NNT 11) and reduce cardiovascular events over 40 months.

Angiotensin II receptor blockers

RCTs found that angiotensin II receptor antagonists versus placebo significantly reduced mortality at 12 weeks. RCTs found no significant difference with angiotensin II receptor blockers versus angiotensin converting enzyme inhibitors in mortality, functional capacity, and symptoms.

β Blockers (in non-black people)

Systematic reviews have found strong evidence that adding a β blocker to an angiotensin converting enzyme inhibitor significantly decreases mortality and admission to hospital. Subgroup analysis in black people found no significant effect on mortality.

Digoxin (improves morbidity in people already receiving diuretics and angiotensin converting enzyme inhibitors)

One large RCT in people already receiving diuretics and angiotensin converting enzyme inhibitors found that digoxin versus placebo significantly reduces the number of people admitted to hospital for worsening heart failure at 37 months (NNT 13), but did not significantly reduce mortality.

LIKELY TO BE BENEFICIAL

Exercise

Systematic reviews have found that prescribed exercise training improves functional capacity and quality of life. One subsequent RCT has found that exercise training versus no exercise training significantly reduces fatal or non-fatal cardiac events (NNT 2), hospital readmission for heart failure (NNT 5), and mortality at 12 months (NNT 4).

Implantable cardiac defibrillators (in people with heart failure and cardiac arrest)

One large RCT in people with heart failure who had experienced a cardiac arrest has found that an implantable cardiac defibrillator versus an antiarrhythmic drug (mainly amiodarone) significantly reduces mortality at 1–3 years.

◀ **Multidisciplinary interventions**

One systematic review has found that multidisciplinary approaches to nutrition, patient counselling, and education versus usual care significantly reduce hospitalisations, but do not significantly reduce mortality. Analysis by each intervention found that only follow up by a multidisciplinary team reduced hospitalisations, whereas telephone contact plus improved coordination of primary care had no significant effect.

Spironolactone in severe heart failure

One RCT in people with severe heart failure taking diuretics, angiotensin converting enzyme inhibitors, and digoxin has found that adding spironolactone versus placebo significantly reduces mortality after 2 years (NNT 9).

UNKNOWN EFFECTIVENESS

Amiodarone

Systematic reviews have found weak evidence suggesting that amiodarone versus placebo may reduce mortality.

Anticoagulation

We found no RCTs of anticoagulation in people with heart failure. We found conflicting evidence from two large retrospective cohort studies.

Antiplatelet agents

We found no RCTs of antiplatelet agents in people with heart failure. Retrospective analyses have included too few events to establish or exclude a clinically important effect of antiplatelet agents.

Prophylactic use of implantable cardiac defibrillators in people with arrythmia

Two RCTs in people at high risk of arrhythmia found conflicting evidence of the effects of prophylactic implantation of implantable cardiac defibrillators versus usual medical treatment.

Treatments for diastolic heart failure

We found no RCTs in people with diastolic heart failure.

UNLIKELY TO BE BENEFICIAL

Calcium channel blockers

One systematic review has found no significant difference in mortality with second generation dihydropyridine calcium channel blockers versus placebo. RCTs comparing other calcium channel blockers versus placebo found no evidence of benefit.

LIKELY TO BE INEFFECTIVE OR HARMFUL

Non-amiodarone antiarrhythmic drugs

Evidence extrapolated from one systematic review in people treated after a myocardial infarction suggests that other antiarrhythmic drugs (apart from β blockers) may increase mortality.

Positive inotropes (ibopamine, milrinone, vesnarinone)

RCTs found that positive inotropic drugs (other than digoxin) versus placebo significantly increased mortality over 6–11 months (NNH about 17–25). ▶

◄ DEFINITION   Heart failure occurs when abnormality of cardiac function causes failure of the heart to pump blood at a rate sufficient for metabolic requirements or maintains cardiac output only with a raised filling pressure. It is characterised clinically by breathlessness, effort intolerance, fluid retention, and poor survival. It can be caused by systolic or diastolic dysfunction and is associated with neurohormonal changes.[1] Left ventricular systolic dysfunction (LVSD) is defined as a left ventricular ejection fraction below 0.40. It can be symptomatic or asymptomatic. Defining and diagnosing diastolic heart failure can be difficult. Recently proposed criteria include: (1) clinical evidence of heart failure; (2) normal or mildly abnormal left ventricular systolic function; and (3) evidence of abnormal left ventricular relaxation, filling, diastolic distensibility, or diastolic stiffness.[2] The clinical utility of these criteria is limited by difficulty in standardising assessment of the last criterion.

INCIDENCE/ PREVALENCE   Both the incidence and prevalence of heart failure increase with age. Studies of heart failure in the USA and Europe found that under 65 years of age the incidence is 1/1000 men a year and 0.4/1000 women a year. Over 65 years, incidence is 11/1000 men a year and 5/1000 women a year. Under 65 years the prevalence of heart failure is 1/1000 men and 1/1000 women; over 65 years the prevalence is 40/1000 men and 30/1000 women.[3] The prevalence of asymptomatic LVSD is 3% in the general population.[4–6] The mean age of people with asymptomatic LVSD is lower than that for symptomatic individuals. Both heart failure and asymptomatic LVSD are more common in men.[4–6] The prevalence of diastolic heart failure in the community is unknown. The prevalence of heart failure with preserved systolic function in people in hospital with clinical heart failure varies from 13–74%.[7,8] Less than 15% of people with heart failure under 65 years have normal systolic function, whereas the prevalence is about 40% in people over 65 years.[7]

AETIOLOGY/ RISK FACTORS   Coronary artery disease is the most common cause of heart failure.[3] Other common causes include hypertension and idiopathic dilated congestive cardiomyopathy. After adjustment for hypertension, the presence of left ventricular hypertrophy remains a risk factor for the development of heart failure. Other risk factors include cigarette smoking, hyperlipidaemia, and diabetes mellitus.[4] The common causes of left ventricular diastolic dysfunction are coronary artery disease and systemic hypertension. Other causes are hypertrophic cardiomyopathy, restrictive or infiltrative cardiomyopathies, and valvular heart disease.[8]

PROGNOSIS   The prognosis of heart failure is poor, with 5 year mortality ranging from 26–75%.[3] Up to 16% of people are readmitted with heart failure within 6 months of first admission. In the USA it is the leading cause of hospital admission among people over 65 years of age.[3] In people with heart failure, a new myocardial infarction increases the risk of death (RR 7.8, 95% CI 6.9 to 8.8); 34% of all deaths in people with heart failure are preceded by a major ischaemic event.[9] Sudden death, mainly caused by ventricular arrhythmias, is responsible for 25–50% of all deaths, and is the most common cause of death in people with heart failure.[10] The presence of asymptomatic LVSD increases an individual's risk of having a cardiovascular event. One large prevention trial found that for a 5% reduction in ejection fraction the risk ratio for mortality was 1.20 (95% CI 1.13 to 1.29), for hospital admission for heart failure it was 1.28 (95% CI 1.18 to 1.38), and for development of heart failure it was 1.20 (95% CI 1.13 to 1.26).[4] The annual mortality of patients with diastolic heart failure varies in observational studies (1.3–17.5%).[7] Reasons for this variation include age, the presence of coronary artery disease, and variation in the partition value used to define abnormal ventricular systolic function. The annual mortality for left ventricular diastolic dysfunction is lower than that found in patients with systolic dysfunction.[11]

Peripheral arterial disease

Search date May 2001

Sonia Anand and Mark Creager

What are the effects of treatments for chronic peripheral arterial disease?

BENEFICIAL

Antiplatelet treatment

One systematic review and one subsequent RCT have found strong evidence that antiplatelet agents versus control treatments significantly reduce the rate of major cardiovascular events over an average of about 2 years (NNT about 53). Systematic reviews have found that antiplatelet agents versus control treatments significantly reduce the risk of arterial occlusion over 19 months and the risk of revascularisation procedures. The balance of benefits and harms is in favour of treatment for most people with symptomatic peripheral arterial disease, because as a group they are at much greater risk of cardiovascular events.

Exercise

Systematic reviews in people with chronic stable claudication have found that regular exercise three times a week for 30 minute sessions versus no exercise significantly improves total walking distance and maximal exercise time after 3–12 months.

LIKELY TO BE BENEFICIAL

Cilostazol

Four RCTs in people with intermittent claudication⊙ have found that cilostazol versus placebo significantly improves initial claudication distance⊙ and absolute claudication distance⊙ measured on a treadmill and significantly reduces the proportion of people with symptoms that do not improve.

Percutaneous transluminal angioplasty (transient benefit only)

Two small RCTs in people with mild to moderate intermittent claudication found limited evidence that angioplasty versus no angioplasty significantly improved walking distance after 6 months but found no significant difference after 2 or 6 years.

Smoking cessation (based on observational studies)

One systematic review has found observational evidence that continued cigarette smoking by people with intermittent claudication is associated with progression of symptoms, poor prognosis after bypass surgery, amputation, and need for reconstructive surgery. Another systematic review found no good evidence from controlled studies about the effects of advice to stop smoking.

UNKNOWN EFFECTIVENESS

Bypass surgery

We found limited evidence from small RCTs about the effects of bypass surgery for people with debilitating symptomatic peripheral arterial disease. However, there is consensus that surgery is effective.

▶

◀ **Pentoxifylline**

Systematic reviews of small RCTs of variable quality in people with intermittent claudication have found that pentoxifylline versus placebo increases the walking distance by a small amount. One RCT with a high withdrawal rate found no significant difference in walking distance between pentoxifylline versus placebo in people with intermittent claudication.

DEFINITION   Peripheral arterial disease arises when there is significant narrowing of arteries distal to the arch of the aorta. Narrowing can arise from atheroma, arteritis, local thrombus formation, or embolisation from the heart or more central arteries. This topic includes treatment options for people with symptoms of reduced blood flow to the leg that are likely to arise from atheroma. These symptoms range from calf pain on exercise (intermittent claudication), to rest pain, skin ulceration, or ischaemic necrosis (gangrene) in people with critical ischaemia.

INCIDENCE/   Peripheral arterial disease is more common in people aged over 50 years
PREVALENCE   than young people, and is more common in men than women. The prevalence of peripheral arterial disease of the legs (assessed by non-invasive tests) is about 3% in people under the age of 60 years, but rises to over 20% in people over 75 years.[1] The overall annual incidence of intermittent claudication is 1.5–2.6/1000 men a year and 1.2–3.6/1000 women a year.[2]

AETIOLOGY/   Factors associated with the development of peripheral arterial disease
RISK FACTORS include age, gender, cigarette smoking, diabetes mellitus, hypertension, hyperlipidaemia, obesity, and physical inactivity. The strongest association is with smoking (RR 2.0–4.0) and diabetes (RR 2.0–3.0).[3] Acute limb ischaemia may result from thrombosis arising within a peripheral artery or embolic occlusion.

PROGNOSIS   The symptom of intermittent claudication can resolve spontaneously, remain stable over many years, or progress rapidly to critical limb ischaemia. The incidence of critical limb ischaemia in Denmark and Italy in 1990 was 0.25–0.45/1000 people a year.[4,5] About 15% of people with intermittent claudication eventually develop critical leg ischaemia, which endangers the viability of the limb. Coronary heart disease is the major cause of death in people with peripheral arterial disease of the legs. Over 5 years, about 20% of people with intermittent claudication have a non-fatal cardiovascular event, myocardial infarction, or stroke.[6] The mortality rate of people with peripheral arterial disease is two to three times higher than that of age and sex matched controls. Overall mortality after the diagnosis of peripheral arterial disease is about 30% after 5 years and 70% after 15 years.[6]

Cardiovascular disorders

Primary prevention

Search date July 2001

*Charles Foster, Cindy Mulrow, Michael Murphy, Andy Ness,
Julian Nicholas, Michael Pignone and Cathie Sudlow*

What are the effects of interventions in asymptomatic people?

LIKELY TO BE BENEFICIAL

Eating more fruit and vegetables

Observational studies have found that consumption of fruit and vegetables reduces ischaemic heart disease and stroke. The size and nature of any real effect is uncertain.

Physical activity

Observational studies have found that moderate to high physical activity significantly reduces coronary heart disease and stroke. They also found that sudden death soon after strenuous exercise was rare, more common in sedentary people, and did not outweigh the benefits.

Smoking cessation

Observational studies have found a strong association between smoking and overall mortality and ischaemic vascular disease. Several large cohort studies have found that the increased risk associated with smoking falls after stopping smoking. The risk can take many years to approach that of non-smokers, particularly in those with a history of heavy smoking.

TRADE OFF BETWEEN BENEFITS AND HARMS

Anticoagulant treatment (warfarin)

One RCT found that the benefits and harms of oral anticoagulation among individuals without symptoms of cardiovascular disease were finely balanced, and that net effects were uncertain.

Antiplatelet treatment (aspirin)

We found insufficient evidence to identify which asymptomatic individuals would benefit overall and which would be harmed by regular treatment with aspirin.

UNKNOWN EFFECTIVENESS

Antioxidants (other than β carotene)

Observational studies found insufficient evidence on the effects of vitamin C, vitamin E, copper, zinc, manganese, or flavonoids. Two RCTs found no significant difference in mortality after about 6 years with vitamin E supplements versus placebo.

LIKELY TO BE INEFFECTIVE OR HARMFUL

β Carotene

RCTs found no evidence that β carotene supplements are effective, and have found that they may be harmful. ▶

◄

What are the effects of interventions aimed at lowering blood pressure?

BENEFICIAL

β Blockers in high risk people

Systematic reviews have found that β blockers versus placebo significantly decrease the risk of fatal and non-fatal stroke, cardiac events, and total mortality. The biggest benefit is seen in people with the highest baseline risk. Systematic reviews have found no significant difference in mortality or morbidity with β blockers versus diuretics.

Diuretics in high risk people

Systematic reviews have found that diuretics versus placebo significantly decrease the risk of fatal and non-fatal stroke, cardiac events, and total mortality. The biggest benefit is seen in people with the highest baseline risk. Systematic reviews have found no significant difference in mortality or morbidity with diuretics versus β blockers.

LIKELY TO BE BENEFICIAL

Angiotensin converting enzyme inhibitors in high risk people

One systematic review and one unblinded RCT found no significant difference in mortality or morbidity with angiotensin converting enzyme inhibitors versus β blockers or diuretics.

α Blockers in high risk people

One RCT found no significant difference in coronary heart disease outcomes with α blockers versus diuretics, but found that α blockers significantly increased cardiovascular events, particularly congestive cardiac failure at 4 years.

Dietary salt restriction

We found no RCTs of the effects of salt restriction on mortality or morbidity. One systematic review has found that a low salt diet versus a usual diet may lead to modest reductions in blood pressure, with more benefit in people older than 45 years than in younger people❶.

Fish oil supplementation

We found no RCTs examining the effects of fish oil supplementation on morbidity or mortality. One systematic review has found that fish oil supplementation in large doses of 3 g a day modestly lowers blood pressure.

Low fat, high fruit and vegetable diet

We found no systematic review and no RCTs examining the effects of low fat, high fruit and vegetable diet on morbidity or mortality of people with raised blood pressure. One RCT found that a low fat, high fruit and vegetable diet versus control diet modestly reduced blood pressure.

Physical activity

We found no RCTs examining the effects of exercise on morbidity or mortality. One systematic review has found that aerobic exercise versus no exercise reduces blood pressure.

Potassium supplementation

We found no RCTs examining the effects of potassium supplementation on morbidity or mortality. One systematic review has found that a daily potassium supplementation of about 60 mmol (2 g, which is about the amount contained in 5 bananas) reduces blood pressure by small amounts.

►

Primary prevention

Reduced alcohol consumption

We found no RCTs examining the effects of reducing alcohol consumption on morbidity or mortality. One systematic review in moderate drinkers (25–50 drinks/wk) found inconclusive evidence regarding effects of alcohol reduction on blood pressure.

Smoking cessation

Observational studies have found that smoking is a significant risk factor for cardiovascular disease. We found no direct evidence specifically in people with hypertension that stopping smoking decreases blood pressure.

Weight loss

We found no RCTs examining the effects of weight loss on morbidity and mortality. One systematic review and additional RCTs have found that modest weight reduction in obese people with hypertension may lead to modest reductions in blood pressure in obese people with hypertension.

TRADE OFF BETWEEN BENEFITS AND HARMS

Calcium channel blockers

We found limited evidence from one systematic review that calcium channel antagonists reduce coronary heart disease and heart failure less than diuretics or β blockers. Observational studies suggest that short and intermediate acting dihydropyridine calcium channel blockers, such as nifedipine and isradipine, may increase cardiovascular morbidity and mortality.

Drug treatment in low risk people

Systematic reviews have found that drug treatment reduces the risk of fatal and non-fatal stroke, cardiac events, and total mortality, with the greatest benefit seen in those with the highest baseline risk. The balance between benefits and harms in people at low risk is less clear.

UNKNOWN EFFECTIVENESS

Calcium supplementation

We found no RCTs examining the effects of calcium supplementation on morbidity or mortality. We found insufficient evidence on the effects of calcium supplementation specifically in people with hypertension. One systematic review in people with and without hypertension found that calcium supplementation may reduce systolic blood pressure by small amounts.

Magnesium supplementation

We found no RCTs examining the effects of magnesium supplementation on morbidity or mortality. We found limited and conflicting evidence on the effect of magnesium supplementation on blood pressure in people with hypertension and normal magnesium concentrations.

◀ *What are the effects of interventions aimed at lowering cholesterol?*

LIKELY TO BE BENEFICIAL

Cholesterol reduction in high risk people

Systematic reviews have found that reducing cholesterol concentration in asymptomatic people lowers the rate of cardiovascular events. RCTs have found that the magnitude of the benefit is related to an individual's baseline risk of cardiovascular events, and to the degree of cholesterol lowering, rather than to the individual's absolute cholesterol concentration.

Low fat diet

Systematic reviews and RCTs have found that combined use of cholesterol lowering diet and lipid lowering drugs reduces cholesterol concentration more than lifestyle interventions alone.

DEFINITION Primary prevention in this context is the long term management of people at increased risk but with no evidence of cardiovascular disease. Clinically overt ischaemic vascular disease includes acute myocardial infarction, angina, stroke, and peripheral vascular disease. Many adults have no symptoms or obvious signs of vascular disease, even though they have atheroma and are at increased risk of ischaemic vascular events because of one or more risk factors (see aetiology below).

INCIDENCE/ PREVALENCE In the USA, about 42% of all deaths are from vascular disease. Acute myocardial infarction and its sequelae remain the most common single cause of death.

AETIOLOGY/ RISK FACTORS Identified major risk factors for ischaemic vascular disease include increasing age, male sex, raised low density lipoprotein cholesterol, reduced high density lipoprotein cholesterol, raised blood pressure, smoking, diabetes, family history of cardiovascular disease, obesity, and sedentary lifestyle. For many of these risk factors, observational studies show a continuous gradient of increasing risk of cardiovascular disease with increasing levels of the risk factor, with no obvious threshold level. Although by definition event rates are higher in high risk people, of all ischaemic vascular events that occur in the population, most occur in people with intermediate levels of absolute risk because there are many more of them than there are people at high risk (see appendix 1 on CD).[1]

PROGNOSIS A study carried out in Scotland found that about half of people who suffer an acute myocardial infarction die within 28 days, and two thirds of acute myocardial infarctions occur before the person reaches hospital.[2] The benefits of intervention in unselected people with no evidence of cardiovascular disease (primary prevention) are small because in such people the baseline risk is small. However, absolute risk of ischaemic vascular events varies dramatically, even among people with similar levels of blood pressure or cholesterol. Estimates of absolute risk can be based on simple risk equations or tables (see appendix 1 on CD).[3,4]

Secondary prevention of ischaemic cardiac events

Search date July 2001

Cathie Sudlow, Eva Lonn, Michael Pignone, Andrew Ness and Chararyit Rihal

What are the effects of treatments?

BENEFICIAL

Angiotensin converting enzyme inhibitors in people with left ventricular dysfunction

One systematic review has found that in people who have had a myocardial infarction and have left ventricular dysfunction, angiotensin converting enzyme inhibitors versus placebo significantly reduce mortality (NNT 17), hospitalisation for congestive heart failure (NNT 28), and recurrent non-fatal myocardial infarction (NNT 43) after 2 years treatment.

Angiotensin converting enzyme inhibitors in high risk people without left ventricular dysfunction

One large RCT in people without left ventricular dysfunction found that ramipril versus placebo significantly reduced the combined outcome of cardiovascular death, stroke, and myocardial infarction after about 5 years (NNT 26).

Amiodarone in selected high risk people

Two systematic reviews have found that amiodarone versus placebo significantly reduces the risk of sudden cardiac death (NNT 59), and reduces mortality (NNT 71) at 1 year in people at high risk of death after myocardial infarction.

Anticoagulants in the absence of antiplatelet treatment

One systematic review has found that high or moderate intensity oral anticoagulants given alone significantly reduce the risk of serious vascular events in people with coronary artery disease, but are associated with substantial risk of haemorrhage.

Antiplatelet treatment

One systematic review has found that prolonged antiplatelet treatment versus placebo or no antiplatelet treatment reduces the risk of serious vascular events in people at high risk of ischaemic cardiac events. It found that, for prolonged use, aspirin 75–150 mg daily is as effective as higher doses, but found insufficient evidence that doses below 75 mg daily are as effective. It found no clear evidence that any alternative antiplatelet regimen is superior to aspirin in the long term secondary prevention of vascular events, but found that clopidogrel is at least as effective and as safe as aspirin.

β Blockers

Systematic reviews in people after myocardial infarction have found that long term β blockers reduce all cause mortality (NNT 48), coronary mortality, recurrent non-fatal myocardial infarction (NNT 56), and sudden death (NNT 63). About 25% of people suffer adverse effects.

Cardiac rehabilitation

One systematic review has found that cardiac rehabilitation including exercise reduces the risk of major cardiac events.

◀ **Cholesterol lowering drugs**

Systematic reviews and large subsequent RCTs have found that lowering cholesterol in people with a previous cardiovascular event substantially reduces the risk of overall mortality, cardiovascular mortality, and non-fatal cardiovascular events.

Exercise alone

One systematic review has found that exercise alone versus usual care significantly reduces mortality.

Percutaneous revascularisation in people with stable coronary artery disease

One systematic review has found that in people with stable coronary artery disease, coronary percutaneous transluminal angioplasty versus medical treatment significantly improves angina pectoris and exercise tolerance. The review found no evidence that percutaneous transluminal angioplasty reduced mortality, myocardial infarction, or need for later angioplasty. RCTs have found that percutaneous transluminal angioplasty is associated with increased risk of emergency coronary artery bypass grafting and of myocardial infarction during and soon after the procedure.

Intracoronary stents (better than coronary percutaneous transluminal angioplasty)

One systematic review has found that intracoronary stents versus coronary percutaneous transluminal angioplasty significantly reduce angiographic restenosis and the need for repeat vascularisation. No significant difference in mortality or myocardial infarction was found, but crossover rates from PTA to stent were high.

Surgical revascularisation

RCTs performed up to the mid-1980s have found that coronary artery bypass grafting versus medical treatment carried a greater risk of death in the first year, but reduced the risk of death from coronary artery disease at 5 and 10 years. Greatest benefit occurred in people with more severe disease (multivessel disease, left ventricular dysfunction, or myocardial infarction). There was no evidence of increased protection against subsequent myocardial infarction. One more recent RCT, using modern techniques and with optimal background medical treatment, has found surgical revascularisation versus non-invasive treatment reduced mortality at 1 and 2 years.

LIKELY TO BE BENEFICIAL

Blood pressure lowering in people at high risk of ischaemic coronary events

We found no direct evidence of the effects of blood pressure lowering in people with established coronary heart disease. Observational studies, and extrapolation of primary prevention trials of blood pressure reduction, support the lowering of blood pressure in those at high risk of ischaemic coronary events. The evidence for benefit is strongest for β blockers, although not specifically in people with hypertension. The target blood pressure in these people is not clear. Angiotensin converting enzyme inhibitors and β blockers are discussed separately above.

▶

Secondary prevention of ischaemic cardiac events

◀ **Coronary artery bypass grafting versus percutaneous revascularisation for multivessel disease (less need for repeat procedures)**

We found no RCTs specifically in people with multivessel disease. One systematic review primarily in people with low to medium risk has found no significant difference with percutaneous transluminal angioplasty versus coronary artery bypass grafting in mortality, the risk of myocardial infarction, and the quality of life. RCTs have found that coronary artery bypass grafting versus percutaneous transluminal angioplasty reduces the need for repeat procedures but is more invasive.

Eating more fish (particularly oily fish)

RCTs have found that advising people with coronary heart disease to eat more fish (particularly oily fish) significantly reduces mortality at 2 years (NNT about 30).

Mediterranean diet

One RCT has found that advising people with coronary artery disease to eat more bread, fruit and vegetables, fish, and less meat, and to replace butter and cream with rapeseed margarine significantly reduces mortality at 2 years (NNT 25).

Psychosocial treatment

One systematic review of mainly poor quality RCTs found that psychological treatments versus usual treatment may decrease rates of myocardial infarction or cardiac death in people with coronary heart disease.

Smoking cessation

We found no RCTs of the effects of smoking cessation on cardiovascular events in people with coronary heart disease. Moderate evidence from epidemiological studies indicates that people with coronary heart disease who stop smoking rapidly reduce their risk of recurrent coronary events or death. Treatment with nicotine patches seems safe in people with coronary heart disease.

Stress management

One systematic review of mainly poor quality RCTs found that stress management may decrease rates of myocardial infarction or cardiac death in people with coronary heart disease.

UNKNOWN EFFECTIVENESS

Adding anticoagulants to antiplatelet treatment

One systematic review found no evidence that the addition of low intensity oral anticoagulation (target international normalised ratio < 1.5) to aspirin produces additional benefit. The effects of adding a more intensive anticoagulant regimen (target international normalised ratio 2–3) are uncertain.

Vitamin C

Pooled analysis of three small RCTs found no evidence that vitamin C versus placebo provided any substantial benefit.

Vitamin E

Pooled analysis of four large RCTs found no evidence that vitamin E versus placebo given for 1.3–4.5 years altered cardiovascular events and all cause mortality.

Hormone replacement therapy

RCTs found no clear evidence that hormone replacement therapy versus placebo reduces major cardiovascular events in postmenopausal women with established coronary artery disease.

▶

◀ **UNLIKELY TO BE BENEFICIAL**

Advice to eat less fat
RCTs found no strong evidence that low fat diets reduced mortality at 2 years.

Sotalol
One RCT found limited evidence that sotalol versus placebo significantly increased mortality within 1 year.

LIKELY TO BE INEFFECTIVE OR HARMFUL

β Carotene
Large RCTs found no evidence of benefit with β carotene, and one RCT found evidence of a significant increase in mortality. Four large RCTs of β carotene supplementation in primary prevention found no cardiovascular benefits, and two of the RCTs raised concerns about increased mortality.

Class I antiarrhythmic agents
One systematic review has found that class I antiarrhythmic agents versus placebo given after myocardial infarction significantly increase the risk of cardiovascular mortality and sudden death.

Short acting dihydropyridine calcium channel blockers
One systematic review found no benefit from calcium channel blockers in people after myocardial infarction or with chronic coronary heart disease. Diltiazem and verapamil may reduce rates of reinfarction and refractory angina in people after myocardial infarction who do not have heart failure.

DEFINITION Secondary prevention in this context is the long term management of people with a prior acute myocardial infarction, and of people at high risk of ischaemic cardiac events for other reasons, such as a history of angina or coronary surgical procedures.

INCIDENCE/ PREVALENCE Coronary artery disease is the leading cause of mortality in developed countries and is becoming a major cause of mortality and morbidity in developing countries. There are pronounced international, regional, and temporal differences in death rates. In the USA, the prevalence of overt coronary artery disease approaches 4%.[1]

AETIOLOGY/ RISK FACTORS Most ischaemic cardiac events are associated with atheromatous plaques that can cause acute obstruction of coronary vessels. Atheroma is more likely in elderly people, in those with established coronary artery disease, and in those with risk factors (such as smoking, hypertension, high cholesterol, diabetes mellitus).

PROGNOSIS Almost 50% of those who suffer an acute myocardial infarction die before they reach hospital. Of those hospitalised, 7–15% die in hospital and another 7–15% die during the following year. People who survive the acute stage of myocardial infarction fall into three prognostic groups, based on their baseline risk❶:[2–4] high (20% of all survivors), moderate (55%), and low (25%) risk. Long term prognosis depends on the degree of left ventricular dysfunction, the presence of residual ischaemia, and the extent of any electrical instability. Further risk stratification procedures include evaluation of left ventricular function (by echocardiography or nuclear ventriculography) and of myocardial ischaemia (by non-invasive stress testing).[4–8] Those with low left ventricular ejection fraction, ischaemia, or poor functional status may be evaluated further by cardiac catheterisation.[9]

Stroke management

Search date May 2001

Gord Gubitz and Peter Sandercock

What are the effects of medical treatments for acute ischaemic stroke?

BENEFICIAL

Aspirin

One systematic review in people with ischaemic stroke confirmed by computerised tomography scan has found that aspirin versus placebo within 48 hours of stroke onset significantly reduces death or dependency at 6 months (NNT 77) and significantly increases the number of people making a complete recovery (NNT 91). We found indirect evidence that aspirin should not be delayed if a computerised tomography scan is not available within 48 hours: results from two large RCTs found no significant difference in further stroke or death with aspirin versus placebo in people who were subsequently found to have haemorrhagic rather than ischaemic stroke.

Stroke units

One systematic review has found that specialist stroke rehabilitation units versus conventional care in general medical wards significantly reduce death and severe disability after 1 year (NNT 16).

TRADE OFF BETWEEN BENEFITS AND HARMS

Thrombolytic treatment

One systematic review has found that thrombolysis versus placebo significantly reduces the risk of death and dependency in the long term (NNT 24), but significantly increases the risk of death from intracranial haemorrhage (NNH 23) in the short term.

UNLIKELY TO BE BENEFICIAL

Neuroprotective agents (calcium channel antagonists, γ-aminobutyric acid agonists, lubeluzole, glycine antagonists, N-methyl-D-aspartate antagonists)

RCTs have found that, compared with placebo, calcium channel antagonists, lubeluzole, γ-aminobutyric acid agonists, glycine antagonists, or N-methyl-D-aspartate🅖 antagonists do not significantly improve clinical outcomes.

LIKELY TO BE INEFFECTIVE OR HARMFUL

Acute reduction in blood pressure

Systematic reviews found insufficient evidence of benefit with antihypertensives versus placebo, but found that acute blood pressure reduction may increase mortality and cause adverse neurological outcomes.

Immediate systemic anticoagulation

One systematic review comparing systemic anticoagulants (unfractionated heparin, low molecular weight heparin, heparinoids, or specific thrombin inhibitors) versus usual care without systemic anticoagulants has found no significant difference in death or dependence after 3–6 months. Immediate systemic anticoagulation significantly reduces the risk of deep venous thrombosis ▶

◀ (NNT 3) and symptomatic pulmonary embolus (NNT 333), but increases the risk of intracranial haemorrhage (NNH 108) or extracranial haemorrhage (NNH 109) up to 14 days. One RCT in people with acute ischaemic stroke and atrial fibrillation found no significant difference with low molecular weight heparin versus aspirin in recurrent ischaemic stroke within 14 days.

What are the effects of surgical treatments for intracerebral haematomas?

UNKNOWN EFFECTIVENESS

Evacuation

We found that the balance between benefits and harms has not been clearly established for the evacuation of supratentorial haematomas. We found no evidence from RCTs on the role of evacuation or ventricular shunting in people with infratentorial haematoma whose consciousness level is declining.

DEFINITION Stroke is characterised by rapidly developing clinical symptoms and signs of focal, and at times global, loss of cerebral function lasting more than 24 hours or leading to death, with no apparent cause other than that of vascular origin.[1] Ischaemic stroke is stroke caused by vascular insufficiency (such as cerebrovascular thromboembolism) rather than haemorrhage.

INCIDENCE/ PREVALENCE Stroke is the third most common cause of death in most developed countries.[2] It is a worldwide problem; about 4.5 million people die from stroke each year. Stroke can occur at any age, but half of all strokes occur in people over 70 years old.[3]

AETIOLOGY/ RISK FACTORS About 80% of all acute strokes are caused by cerebral infarction, usually resulting from thrombotic or embolic occlusion of a cerebral artery.[4] The remainder are caused either by intracerebral or subarachnoid haemorrhage.

PROGNOSIS About 10% of all people with acute ischaemic strokes will die within 30 days of stroke onset.[5] Of those who survive the acute event, about 50% will experience some level of disability after 6 months.[6]

Stroke prevention

Search date September 2001

Gord Gubitz, Gregory Lip, Cathie Sudlow and Peter Sandercock

Cardiovascular disorders

What are the effects of preventive interventions in people with prior stroke or transient ischaemic attack?

BENEFICIAL

Antiplatelet treatment

One systematic review has found that prolonged antiplatelet treatment versus placebo or no antiplatelet treatment significantly reduces serious vascular events, stroke, or mortality over about 3 years unless there is a clear contraindication. It has also found that aspirin 75–150 mg daily is as effective as higher doses. We found no good evidence that any other antiplatelet agents are superior to aspirin for secondary prevention of vascular events. One systematic review has found that clopidogrel or the combination of aspirin and dipyridamole are safe and effective alternatives to medium dose aspirin. One systematic review found that ticlopidine or clopidogrel versus aspirin reduced the odds of a vascular event, but found substantial uncertainty about the size of effect.

Blood pressure reduction

One systematic review and subsequent RCTs have found that blood pressure reduction versus placebo reduces recurrent stroke risk over 2–4 years in people with and without hypertension. We found no clear evidence of differences in effectiveness between different antihypertensive drugs, but RCTs suggest that more intensive treatment produces greater reductions in the risk of stroke and other vascular outcomes.

Carotid endarterectomy in people with severe symptomatic carotid artery stenosis

One systematic review in people with a recent carotid territory transient ischaemic event or non-disabling ischaemic stroke has found that carotid endarterectomy versus control treatment significantly reduces the risk of major stroke or death (NNT 15).

Cholesterol reduction in people who also have coronary heart disease

RCTs have found that reducing total cholesterol by about 21% with a statin reduces the relative odds of stroke by 24%.

UNKNOWN EFFECTIVENESS

Carotid angioplasty

RCTs found insufficient evidence about the effects of carotid angioplasty versus best medical treatment.

Carotid endarterectomy in people with severe asymptomatic carotid artery stenosis

Systematic reviews in people with no carotid territory transient ischaemic event or minor stroke within the past few months found limited evidence suggesting that carotid endarterectomy© versus medical treatment may significantly reduce the risk of perioperative stroke or death or subsequent ipsilateral stroke over 3 years (NNT 37–52). However, as the risk of death without surgery in asymptomatic people is relatively low, the balance of benefits and harms from surgery remains unclear.

◀ **Cholesterol reduction in people without coronary heart disease**

RCTs found inconclusive evidence of the effects of cholesterol reduction in people with no history of coronary heart disease.

LIKELY TO BE INEFFECTIVE OR HARMFUL

Oral anticoagulation in people with prior cerebrovascular ischaemia who are in normal sinus rhythm

One systematic review found no significant difference with anticoagulation versus placebo in death or dependency, mortality, or recurrent stroke at about 2 years, but found a significantly increased risk of fatal intracranial haemorrhage (NNH 49).

What are the effects of preventive interventions in people with atrial fibrillation and prior stroke or transient ischaemic attack?

BENEFICIAL

Oral anticoagulation

Systematic reviews have found that adjusted dose warfarin versus placebo significantly reduces the risk of stroke. Systematic reviews have also found that warfarin versus aspirin significantly reduces the risk of stroke in people with previous stroke or transient ischaemic attack (NNT 7).

Aspirin in people with contraindications to anticoagulants

Systematic reviews have found that aspirin versus placebo reduces the risk of stroke, but found that aspirin is less effective than anticoagulants. These findings support the use of aspirin in people with atrial fibrillation and contraindications to anticoagulants.

What are the effects of preventive interventions in people with atrial fibrillation but no other major risk factors for stroke?

LIKELY TO BE BENEFICIAL

Oral anticoagulation

One systematic review has found that warfarin versus placebo significantly reduces fatal and non-fatal ischaemic stroke (NNT 25), provided there is a low risk of bleeding and careful monitoring. The people in the review had a mean age of 69 years. One overview in people less than 65 years old has found no significant difference in the annual stroke rate with warfarin versus placebo.

Aspirin in people with contraindications to anticoagulants

One systematic review found that aspirin versus placebo significantly reduced the risk of stroke (NNT 45), but another found no significant difference. These findings support the use of aspirin in people with atrial fibrillation and contraindications to anticoagulants.

▶

Stroke prevention

DEFINITION Prevention in this context is the long term management of people with a prior stroke or transient ischaemic attack, and of people at high risk of stroke🅖 for other reasons such as atrial fibrillation. **Stroke:** See definition under stroke management, p 23. **Transient ischaemic attack:** Similar to a mild ischaemic stroke except that symptoms last for less than 24 hours.[1]

INCIDENCE/ PREVALENCE See incidence/prevalence under stroke management, p 23.

AETIOLOGY/ RISK FACTORS See aetiology under stroke management, p 23. Risk factors for stroke include prior stroke or transient ischaemic attack, increasing age, hyper-tension, diabetes, cigarette smoking, and emboli associated with atrial fibrillation, artificial heart valves, or myocardial infarction. The relation with cholesterol is less clear; an overview of prospective studies among healthy middle aged individuals found no association between total cholesterol and overall stroke risk.[2] However, one review of prospective observational studies in eastern Asian people found that cholesterol was positively associated with ischaemic stroke but negatively associated with haemorrhagic stroke.[3]

PROGNOSIS People with a history of stroke or transient ischaemic attack are at high risk of all vascular events, such as myocardial infarction, but are at particular risk of subsequent stroke (about 10% in the first year and about 5% per year thereafter).[4,5] People with intermittent atrial fibrillation treated with aspirin should be considered at similar risk of stroke, compared to people with sustained atrial fibrillation treated with aspirin (rate of ischaemic stroke per year, intermittent v sustained, 3.2% v 3.3%).[6]

What are the effects of treatments?

TRADE OFF BETWEEN BENEFITS AND HARMS

Oral anticoagulants in people with deep vein thrombosis

One RCT found that combined warfarin plus intravenous unfractionated heparin versus warfarin alone for initial treatment significantly reduced recurrence of proximal deep vein thrombosis within 6 months (NNT 8). One systematic review and two subsequent RCTs have found no significant difference between long term low molecular weight heparin❻ versus oral anticoagulation in recurrent thromboembolism, major haemorrhage❻, or mortality. Systematic reviews have found that longer versus shorter duration of anticoagulation is associated with significantly fewer deep vein thrombosis recurrences. One non-systematic review found limited evidence that longer versus shorter duration of warfarin was associated with a significantly increased risk of major haemorrhage, but another non-systematic review found no significantly increased risk of major haemorrhage. The absolute risk of recurrent venous thromboembolism decreases with time, but the relative risk reduction with treatment remains constant. Harms of treatment, including major haemorrhage, continue during prolonged treatment. Individual people have different risk profiles. It is likely that the optimal duration of anticoagulation will vary between people.

Oral anticoagulants in people with pulmonary embolism

We found no direct evidence about the optimum intensity and duration of anticoagulation in people with pulmonary embolism. The best available evidence requires extrapolation of results from studies of people with proximal deep vein thrombosis (see above).

Unfractionated and low molecular weight heparin in people with deep vein thrombosis

Systematic reviews have found that low molecular weight heparin is at least as effective as unfractionated heparin in reducing the incidence of recurrent thromboembolic disease, and have found that short term low molecular weight heparin versus unfractionated heparin is associated with a significantly decreased risk of major haemorrhage.

Unfractionated and low molecular weight heparin in people with pulmonary embolism

One small RCT found that heparin plus warfarin versus no anticoagulation significantly reduced mortality in people with pulmonary embolism at 1 year (NNT 4). The combined results of two RCTs in people with pulmonary embolism found no significant difference in mortality or new episodes of thromboembolism with low molecular weight heparin versus unfractionated heparin.

Warfarin plus heparin in people with isolated calf vein thrombosis

One RCT found that, in isolated calf vein thrombosis, warfarin plus intravenous unfractionated heparin versus heparin alone (international normalised ratio❻ 2.5–4.2) significantly reduced the rate of proximal extension at 1 year. One unblinded RCT found no significant difference between shorter versus longer courses of anticoagulation in recurrent thromboembolism. ▶

Cardiovascular disorders

Computerised decision support in oral anticoagulation management

We found no RCTs of computerised decision support◉ versus usual management of oral anticoagulation that used clinically important outcomes (major haemorrhage or death). One systematic review and two subsequent RCTs have found that computerised decision support in oral anticoagulation improves time spent in the target international normalised ratio range. Another subsequent RCT found no significant difference between computerised decision support and standard manual support in the time spent in the target international normalised ratio range. A subsequent RCT of initiation of warfarin found no significant difference between computerised decision support versus usual care in the time taken to reach therapeutic levels of anticoagulation.

DEFINITION	**Venous thromboembolism** is any thromboembolic event occurring within the venous system, including deep vein thrombosis and pulmonary embolism. **Deep vein thrombosis** is a radiologically confirmed partial or total thrombotic occlusion of the deep venous system of the legs sufficient to produce symptoms of pain or swelling. **Proximal deep vein thrombosis** affects the veins above the knee (popliteal, superficial femoral, common femoral, and iliac veins). **Isolated calf vein thrombosis** is confined to the deep veins of the calf and does not affect the veins above the knee. **Pulmonary embolism** is radiologically confirmed partial or total thromboembolic occlusion of pulmonary arteries, sufficient to cause symptoms of breathlessness, chest pain, or both. **Post-thrombotic syndrome** is oedema, ulceration, and impaired viability of the subcutaneous tissues of the leg occurring after deep vein thrombosis. **Recurrence** refers to symptomatic deterioration because of a further (radiologically confirmed) thrombosis, after a previously confirmed thromboembolic event, where there had been an initial, partial, or total symptomatic improvement. **Extension** refers to a radiologically confirmed new, constant, symptomatic intraluminal filling defect extending from an existing thrombosis.
INCIDENCE/ PREVALENCE	We found no reliable study of the incidence/prevalence of deep vein thrombosis or pulmonary embolism in the UK. A prospective Scandinavian study found an annual incidence of 1.6–1.8/1000 people in the general population.[1,2] One postmortem study estimated that 600 000 people develop pulmonary embolism each year in the USA, of whom 60 000 die as a result.[3]
AETIOLOGY/ RISK FACTORS	Risk factors for deep vein thrombosis include immobility, surgery (particularly orthopaedic), malignancy, smoking, pregnancy, older age, and inherited or acquired prothrombotic clotting disorders.[4] Evidence for these factors is mainly observational. The oral contraceptive pill is associated with death due to venous thromboembolism (ARI with any combined oral contraception: 1–3/million women per year).[5] The principal cause of pulmonary embolism is a deep vein thrombosis.[4]
PROGNOSIS	The annual recurrence rate of symptomatic calf vein thrombosis in people without recent surgery is over 25%.[6,7] Proximal extension develops in 40–50% of people with symptomatic calf vein thrombosis.[8] Proximal deep vein thrombosis may cause fatal or non-fatal pulmonary embolism, recurrent venous thrombosis, and the post-thrombotic syndrome. One observational ▶

study published in 1946 found 20% mortality from pulmonary emboli in people in hospital with untreated deep vein thrombosis.[9] One non-systematic review of observational studies found that, in people after recent surgery who have an asymptomatic calf vein deep vein thrombosis, the rate of fatal pulmonary embolism was 13–15%.[10] The incidence of other complications without treatment is not known. The risk of recurrent venous thrombosis and complications is increased by thrombotic risk factors.[11]

Unstable angina

Search date July 2001

Madhu Natarajan

What are the effects of treatments?

BENEFICIAL

Aspirin

One systematic review has found that aspirin versus placebo significantly reduces the risk of death, myocardial infarction, and stroke at 6 months (NNT 20).

Low molecular weight heparins added to aspirin

One systematic review has found that adding low molecular weight heparin to aspirin significantly reduces death and myocardial infarction in the first 30 days after an episode of unstable angina.

LIKELY TO BE BENEFICIAL

Intravenous glycoprotein IIb/IIIa inhibitors

RCTs have found a significant reduction in death and myocardial infarction with intravenous glycoprotein IIb/IIIa inhibitors added either to unfractionated heparin alone or to unfractionated heparin plus aspirin. This evidence was collected in the context of high rates of early percutaneous angiography.

Unfractionated heparin added to aspirin

Two systematic reviews have found that adding unfractionated heparin to aspirin reduces death or myocardial infarction during treatment, but one of the reviews found no significant difference at 12 weeks.

TRADE OFF BETWEEN BENEFITS AND HARMS

Hirudin

RCTs have found that hirudin versus unfractionated heparin in people also taking aspirin significantly reduces rates of death or myocardial infarction at the end of 72 hours treatment (NNT 112). The benefit of hirudin diminishes once the infusion stops. Hirudin significantly increases major bleeds requiring transfusion, but not life threatening bleeds or haemorrhagic strokes.

Ticlopidine

One large RCT has found that ticlopidine versus conventional treatment (without aspirin) significantly reduces death or non-fatal myocardial at 6 months (NNT 16), but is associated with reversible neutropenia.

UNKNOWN EFFECTIVENESS

β Blockers; nitrates

We found insufficient evidence of the effects of these interventions.

Routine early invasive treatment for all people with unstable angina

Three RCTs have found that routine early invasive treatment versus early conservative treatment significant reduces symptoms and promotes early discharge, but does not significantly reduce mortality.

◀ **UNLIKELY TO BE BENEFICIAL**

Calcium channel blockers

One systematic review has found no significant difference with calcium channel blockers versus placebo or versus standard treatment in mortality or myocardial infarction.

LIKELY TO BE INEFFECTIVE OR HARMFUL

Oral glycoprotein IIb/IIIa inhibitors

One RCT has found no significant difference between oral glycoprotein IIb/IIIa inhibitors versus aspirin in mortality, myocardial infarction, and recurrent ischaemia after 90 days. One RCT has found that orbofiban in addition to aspirin versus placebo significantly increased mortality at 30 days.

DEFINITION Unstable angina is distinguished from stable angina, acute myocardial infarction, and non-cardiac pain by the pattern of symptoms (characteristic pain present at rest or on lower levels of activity), the severity of symptoms (recently increasing intensity, frequency, or duration), and the absence of persistent ST elevation on a resting electrocardiogram. Unstable angina includes a variety of different clinical patterns: angina at rest of up to 1 week's duration; angina increasing in severity to moderate or severe pain; non-Q wave myocardial infarction; and post-myocardial infarction angina continuing for longer than 24 hours.

INCIDENCE/ PREVALENCE In industrialised countries the annual incidence of unstable angina is about 6/10 000 people in the general population.

AETIOLOGY/ RISK FACTORS Risk factors are the same as for other manifestations of ischaemic heart disease: older age, previous atheromatous cardiovascular disease, diabetes mellitus, smoking cigarettes, hypertension, hypercholesterolaemia, male sex, and a family history of ischaemic heart disease. Unstable angina can also occur in association with other disorders of the circulation, including heart valve disease, arrhythmia, and cardiomyopathy.

PROGNOSIS In people taking aspirin the incidence of serious adverse outcomes (such as death, acute myocardial infarction, or refractory angina requiring emergency revascularisation) is 5–10% within the first 7 days and about 15% at 30 days. Between 5% and 14% of people with unstable angina die in the year after diagnosis, with about half of these deaths occurring within 4 weeks of diagnosis. No single factor identifies people at higher risk of an adverse event. Risk factors include severity of presentation (e.g. duration of pain, rapidity of progression, evidence of heart failure), medical history (e.g. previous unstable angina, acute myocardial infarction, left ventricular dysfunction), other clinical parameters (e.g. age, diabetes), electrocardiogram changes (e.g. severity of ST segment depression, deep T wave inversion, transient ST elevation), biochemical parameters (e.g. troponin concentration), and change in clinical status (e.g. recurrent chest pain, silent ischaemia, haemodynamic instability).

Acute gastroenteritis in children

Search date October 2001

Jacqueline Dalby-Payne and Elizabeth Elliott

What are the effects of treatments?

BENEFICIAL

Intravenous fluids (as effective as oral rehydration solutions)

One systematic review in children with mild to moderate dehydration found no significant difference with intravenous fluids versus oral rehydration solutions in duration of diarrhoea, time spent in hospital, or weight gain at discharge. One RCT in children with severe dehydration found that intravenous fluids versus oral rehydration solutions significantly increased the duration of diarrhoea and reduced weight gain at discharge, and were associated with more adverse effects.

Oral rehydration solutions (as effective as intravenous fluids)

See intravenous fluids above.

LIKELY TO BE BENEFICIAL

Lactose-free feeds (for duration of diarrhoea)

One systematic review has found that lactose-free feeds versus lactose-containing feeds reduce the duration of diarrhoea in children with mild to severe dehydration. Subsequent RCTs found conflicting results.

Loperamide (reduces duration of diarrhoea, but adverse effects are unclear)

Two RCTs have found that, in children with mild to moderate dehydration, loperamide versus placebo significantly reduces the duration of diarrhoea. Another RCT found no significant difference with loperamide versus placebo in the duration of diarrhoea. We found insufficient evidence about adverse effects.

UNKNOWN EFFECTIVENESS

Clear fluids for rehydration (other than oral rehydration solutions)

We found no systematic review or RCTs on "clear fluids" (water, carbonated drinks, and translucent fruit juices) versus oral rehydration solutions for treatment of mild to moderate dehydration caused by acute gastroenteritis.

DEFINITION
Acute gastroenteritis is characterised by rapid onset of diarrhoea with or without vomiting, nausea, fever, and abdominal pain.[1] In children, the symptoms and signs can be non-specific.[2] Diarrhoea is defined as the frequent passage of unformed liquid stools.[3]

INCIDENCE/ PREVALENCE
Worldwide, about 3–5 billion cases of acute gastroenteritis occur in children under 5 years of age each year.[4] In the UK, acute gastroenteritis accounts for 204/1000 general practitioner consultations in children under 5 years of age each year.[5] Gastroenteritis leads to hospital admission in 7/1000 children under 5 years of age per year in the UK[5] and 13/1000 in the USA.[6] In Australia, gastroenteritis accounts for 6% of all hospital admissions in children under 15 years of age.[7]

AETIOLOGY/ RISK FACTORS
In developed countries, acute gastroenteritis is predominantly caused by viruses (87%), of which rotavirus is most common;[8–11] bacteria cause most of the remaining cases, predominantly Campylobacter, Salmonella, Shigella, and *Escherichia coli*. In developing countries, bacterial pathogens are more frequent, although rotavirus is also a major cause of gastroenteritis.

◀ PROGNOSIS   Acute gastroenteritis is usually self limiting but if untreated can result in morbidity and mortality secondary to water and electrolyte losses. Acute diarrhoea causes 4 million deaths per year in children under 5 years of age in Asia (excluding China), Africa, and Latin America, and over 80% of deaths occur in children under 2 years of age.[12] Although death is uncommon in developed countries, dehydration secondary to gastroenteritis is a significant cause of morbidity and need for hospital admission.[6,7,13]

Acute otitis media

Search date June 2001

Paddy O'Neill

What are the effects of treatments?

Ibuprofen

One RCT in children receiving antibiotic treatment found that ibuprofen versus placebo significantly reduced earache assessed by parental observation after 2 days (NNT 5).

Paracetamol

One RCT in children receiving antibiotic treatment found that paracetamol versus placebo significantly reduced earache assessed by parental observation after 2 days (NNT 6).

Antibiotics

Systematic reviews have found conflicting evidence about antibiotics versus placebo in acute otitis media. The most recent review found that antibiotics versus placebo significantly reduced the proportion of children still in pain at 2–7 days (NNT 17) and reduced the risk of developing contralateral acute otitis media. However, it found that antibiotics significantly increased the risk of vomiting, diarrhoea, or rashes (NNH 17). Another systematic review found no clear evidence favouring any particular antibiotic.

One RCT found that immediate versus delayed antibiotic treatment significantly reduced the number of days of earache, ear discharge, and amount of daily paracetamol used after the first 24 hours of illness but found no difference in daily pain scores. It also found a significant increase in diarrhoea with immediate versus delayed antibiotic treatment.

One systematic review and two subsequent RCTs have found that 10 day courses of antibiotics versus 5 day courses significantly reduce treatment failure, relapse, or re-infection at 8–10 days, but found no significant difference at 20–30 days.

What are the effects of preventive interventions?

Xylitol chewing gum or syrup

One RCT found that xylitol syrup or chewing gum versus control significantly reduced the incidence of acute otitis media. It found no significant difference with xylitol lozenges versus control gum. More children taking xylitol versus control withdrew because of abdominal pain or other unspecified reasons.

Long term antibiotic prophylaxis

One systematic review (945 people) has found that long term antibiotic prophylaxis versus placebo significantly reduces recurrence of acute otitis media after 1 month (NNT 9). However, one subsequent RCT (194 children) found no ▶

◀ significant difference with antibiotic prophylaxis versus placebo in preventing recurrence. We found insufficient evidence on which antibiotic to use, for how long, and how many previous episodes of acute otitis media justify the starting of preventive treatment.

DEFINITION Otitis media is an inflammation in the middle ear. Subcategories include acute otitis media (AOM), recurrent AOM, and chronic suppurative otitis media. AOM presents with systemic and local signs, and has a rapid onset. The persistence of an effusion beyond 3 months without signs of infection defines otitis media with effusion (also known as "glue ear"). Chronic suppurative otitis media is characterised by continuing inflammation in the middle ear causing discharge (otorrhoea) through a perforated tympanic membrane.

INCIDENCE/ AOM is common and has a high morbidity and low mortality. In the UK,
PREVALENCE about 30% of children under 3 years old visit their general practitioner with AOM each year and 97% receive antimicrobial treatment.[1] By 3 months of age, 10% of children have had an episode of AOM. It is the most common reason for outpatient antimicrobial treatment in the USA.[2]

AETIOLOGY/ The most common bacterial causes for AOM in the USA and UK are
RISK FACTORS *Streptococcus pneumoniae*, *Haemophilus influenzae*, and *Moraxella catarrhalis*. Similar pathogens are found in Colombia.[3] The incidence of penicillin resistant *S pneumoniae* has risen, but rates differ between countries. The most important risk factors for AOM are young age and attendance at daycare centres such as nursery schools. Other risk factors include being white; male sex; a history of enlarged adenoids, tonsillitis, or asthma; multiple previous episodes; bottle feeding; a history of ear infections in parents or siblings; and use of a soother or pacifier. The evidence for an effect of environmental tobacco smoke is controversial.[1]

PROGNOSIS In about 80% of children the condition resolves in about 3 days without antibiotic treatment. Serious complications are rare but include hearing loss, mastoiditis, meningitis, and recurrent attacks.[1] The World Health Organization estimates that each year 51 000 children under the age of 5 years die from complications of otitis media in developing countries.[4]

Asthma in children

Search date June 2001

Duncan Keeley

What are the effects of treatments for acute asthma in children?

BENEFICIAL

Oxygen

One prospective cohort study and clinical experience support the need for oxygen in acute asthma.

Oral corticosteroids

One systematic review has found that oral corticosteroids (prednisone or prednisolone) versus placebo within 45 minutes of an acute asthma attack significantly reduces hospital admission.

Metered dose inhaler plus spacer devices for delivery of β_2 agonists (as effective as nebulisers)

One systematic review in children with acute but not life threatening asthma who were old enough to use a spacer, has found no significant difference in hospital admission rates with a metered dose inhaler plus a spacer versus nebulisation for delivering β_2 agonists (fenoterol, salbutamol, or terbutaline) or β agonist (orciprenaline**G**). Children using metered dose inhaler with spacer may have shorter stays in emergency departments, less hypoxia, and lower pulse rates compared to children receiving β_2 agonist by nebulisation.

Ipratropium bromide added to β_2 agonists

One systematic review has found that in children with mild to severe asthma exacerbations, multiple doses of ipratropium bromide plus a β_2 agonist (fenoterol or salbutamol**G**) versus a β_2 agonist alone significantly reduce hospital admissions (NNT 13) and improve lung function. In children with mild to moderate asthma exacerbations, a single dose of ipratropium bromide plus a β_2 agonist (fenoterol, salbutamol, or terbutaline) versus a β_2 agonist alone significantly improves lung function for up to 2 hours, but does not significantly reduce hospital admissions.

High dose inhaled corticosteroids

One systematic review in children with acute moderately severe asthma has found no consistent difference in hospital admissions or forced expiratory volume in 1 second between initial treatment with high dose inhaled corticosteroids versus oral corticosteroids. One subsequent RCT found that inhaled versus oral corticosteroids significantly improved lung function. One RCT in children with severe attacks found that oral corticosteroids versus inhaled corticosteroids improved lung function and reduced hospital admissions.

LIKELY TO BE BENEFICIAL

Intravenous theophylline

We found conflicting evidence from one systematic review and from one large subsequent RCT on the effects of intravenous theophylline. Treatment was frequently stopped because of adverse effects.

▶

◀ *What are the effects of single agent prophylaxis in childhood asthma?*

Inhaled corticosteroids

One systematic review has found that prophylactic inhaled corticosteroids (betamethasone, beclometasone, budesonide, flunisolide, or fluticasone) versus placebo significantly improve symptoms and lung function. Two systematic reviews of studies with long term follow up and a subsequent long term RCT have found no evidence of growth retardation in children with asthma treated with inhaled corticosteroids. Shorter term studies found reduced growth velocity.

One RCT found no significant difference in symptoms with inhaled beclomethasone versus theophylline.

RCTs have found that inhaled corticosteroids (beclometasone, budesonide, or fluticasone) versus inhaled long acting β_2 agonists (salmeterol) or inhaled nedocromil improve symptoms and lung function.

What are the effects of additional treatments in childhood asthma inadequately controlled by standard dose inhaled corticosteroids?

Increased dose of inhaled corticosteroid

One RCT in children taking beclometasone comparing the addition of a second dose of inhaled corticosteroid (beclometasone) versus placebo found no significant difference in lung function, symptom scores, or exacerbation rates, but found significant reduction of growth velocity at 1 year.

Long acting β_2 agonists

One RCT in children taking beclometasone comparing the addition of a long acting β_2 agonist (salmeterol) versus placebo found that salmeterol significantly increased peak expiratory flow rates in the first few months of treatment but found no increase after 1 year. A second RCT in children taking inhaled corticosteroids found that the addition of salmeterol versus placebo increased morning peak expiratory flow rates and symptom free days at 3 months.

Oral leukotriene receptor antagonists

One crossover RCT in children with persistent asthma who had been taking inhaled corticosteroids (budesonide) for at least 6 weeks found that the addition of a leukotriene receptor antagonist (montelukast) versus placebo significantly improved lung function and decreased the proportion of days with asthma exacerbations over 4 weeks.

Oral theophylline

One small RCT found that addition of theophylline versus placebo to previous treatment significantly increased the proportion of symptom free days and significantly reduced the use of additional β agonist (orciprenaline) and additional corticosteroid (beclometasone or prednisolone) over 4 weeks.

▶

What are the effects of treatments for acute wheezing in infancy?

UNKNOWN EFFECTIVENESS

β_2 Agonists delivered by nebuliser or metered dose inhaler/spacer

We found conflicting evidence from RCTs. Transient hypoxia may be caused by nebulised bronchodilators, particularly with air driven nebulisers, and seems less likely when using metered dose inhalers/spacers (see bronchiolitis, p 41).

Inhaled ipratropium bromide

One systematic review found limited and conflicting evidence on the effects of ipratropium bromide.

Oral corticosteroids

One RCT found no evidence that oral corticosteroids improved outcomes in infants with acute wheezing.

What are the effects of prophylaxis in wheezing infants?

UNKNOWN EFFECTIVENESS

Inhaled corticosteroids

We found weak and conflicting evidence on the effects of prophylaxis with inhaled corticosteroids in wheezing infants.

Inhaled sodium cromoglicate; oral theophylline

We found insufficient evidence in infants of the effects of these interventions.

DEFINITION **Childhood asthma** is characterised by chronic or recurrent cough and wheeze. The diagnosis is confirmed by demonstrating reversible airway obstruction in children old enough to perform peak flow measurements or spirometry. Diagnosing asthma in children requires exclusion of other causes of recurrent respiratory symptoms. **Wheezing in infancy** may be caused by acute viral infection (see bronchiolitis, p 41), episodic viral associated wheeze, or asthma. These are not easy to distinguish clinically.

INCIDENCE/ Surveys have found increasing prevalence of wheeze and shortness of
PREVALENCE breath, and diagnosed asthma in children. The increase is more than can be explained by an increased readiness to diagnose asthma. One questionnaire study from Aberdeen, Scotland, surveyed 2510 children aged 8–13 years in 1964 and 3403 children in 1989. Over the 25 years, prevalence of wheeze rose from 10–20%; episodes of shortness of breath from 5–10%; and diagnosis of asthma from 4–10%.[1] One prospective cohort study (826 neonates reviewed at 3 and 6 years of age) found that 34% had experienced at least one wheezing illness before age 3, 14% wheezed before age 3 years and were still wheezing at age 6, and 15% had a wheezing illness in the past year at age 6 but had not wheezed before age 3.[2]

AETIOLOGY/ Asthma is more common in children with a personal or family history of
RISK FACTORS atopy. Precipitating factors include infection, house dust mites, allergens from pet animals, exposure to tobacco smoke, and anxiety.

PROGNOSIS A historical cohort study of wheezing in the first year of life found that 14% of children with one attack and 23% of children with four or more attacks (recalled at age 5 years) had experienced at least one wheezing illness in the past year at age 10.[3]

Attention deficit hyperactivity disorder in children

Search date June 2001

Carol Joughin, Paul Ramchandani and Morris Zwi

What are the effects of treatments?

LIKELY TO BE BENEFICIAL

Dexamfetamine

Limited evidence from systematic reviews suggests that dexamfetamine versus placebo significantly improved some behavioural outcomes but increased anorexia and appetite disturbance. Another systematic review could not draw firm conclusions about the effects of dexamfetamine versus methylphenidate.

Methylphenidate

RCTs have found that methylphenidate versus placebo significantly reduces core symptoms, but may disturb sleep and appetite. The review could not draw firm conclusions about the effects of methylphenidate versus dexamfetamine or versus tricyclic antidepressants. The review also found that methylphenidate versus psychological/behavioural treatment improves symptoms in the medium term, but the clinical importance of these findings is unclear.

Methylphenidate plus behavioural treatment

One systematic review found inconsistent results for combination treatments (medication plus psychological/behavioural treatment) versus placebo. A second systematic review has found that combination treatments versus psychological/behavioural treatments❻ alone significantly improve attention deficit hyperactivity disorder symptoms.

UNKNOWN EFFECTIVENESS

Clonidine

Limited evidence from one systematic review suggests that clonidine versus placebo reduces core symptoms, but the clinical importance of these findings is unclear.

Psychological/behavioural treatment

One systematic review of two small RCTs found insufficient evidence about the effects of psychological/behavioural treatment versus standard care. One large subsequent RCT found no significant difference between psychological/behavioural treatment versus standard care in behaviour rating scales.

DEFINITION   Attention deficit hyperactivity disorder is "a persistent pattern of inattention and/or hyperactivity and impulsivity that is more frequent and severe than is typically observed in individuals at a comparable level of development" (DSM-IV).[1] Inattention, hyperactivity, and impulsivity are commonly known as the core symptoms❻ of attention deficit hyperactivity disorder. Symptoms must be present for at least 6 months, observed before the age of 7 years, and "clinically significant impairment in social, academic, or occupational functioning" must be evident in more than one setting. The symptoms must not be better explained by another disorder such as an anxiety disorder❻, mood disorder, psychosis, or autistic disorder.[1] The World Health Organization's International Statistical Classification of ▶

Attention deficit hyperactivity disorder in children

Diseases and Related Health Problems (ICD-10)[2] uses the term "hyperkinetic disorder" for a more restricted diagnosis. It differs from the DSM-IV classification[3] as all three problems of attention, hyperactivity, and impulsiveness must be present, more stringent criteria for "pervasiveness" across situations must be met, and the presence of another disorder is an exclusion criterion.

INCIDENCE/ PREVALENCE

Prevalence estimates of attention deficit hyperactivity disorder vary according to the diagnostic criteria used and the population sampled. DSM-IV prevalence estimates among school children range from 3–5%,[1] but other estimates vary from 1.7–16%.[4,5] No objective test exists to confirm the diagnosis of attention deficit hyperactivity disorder, which remains a clinical diagnosis. Other conditions frequently coexist with attention deficit hyperactivity disorder. Oppositional defiant disorder**ⓖ** is present in 35% (95% CI 27% to 44%) of children with attention deficit hyperactivity disorder, conduct disorder**ⓖ** in 26% (95% CI 13% to 41%), anxiety disorder in 26% (95% CI 18% to 35%), and depressive disorder**ⓖ** in 18% (95% CI 11% to 27%).[6]

AETIOLOGY/ RISK FACTORS

The underlying causes of attention deficit hyperactivity disorder are not known.[6] There is limited evidence that it has a genetic component.[7–9] Risk factors also include psychosocial factors.[10] There is increased risk in boys compared to girls, with ratios varying from 3 : 1[6] to 4 : 1.[3]

PROGNOSIS

More than 70% of hyperactive children may continue to meet criteria for attention deficit hyperactivity disorder in adolescence, and up to 65% of adolescents may continue to meet criteria for attention deficit hyperactivity disorder in adulthood.[5] Changes in diagnostic criteria cause difficulty with interpretation of the few outcome studies. One cohort of boys followed up for an average of 16 years found a ninefold increase in antisocial personality disorder and a fourfold increase in substance misuse disorder.[7]

What are the effects of treatments?

UNKNOWN EFFECTIVENESS

Routine antibiotics

We found no evidence about children with bronchiolitis alone. One unblinded RCT in children with bronchiolitis and uncomplicated pneumonia (crackles on auscultation or consolidation on a chest radiograph) found no significant difference in clinical scores with routine use of antibiotics versus placebo, but may not have been sufficiently powered to exclude a clinically important effect.

Bronchodilators

Systematic reviews have found that inhaled bronchodilators versus placebo significantly improve overall clinical scores in the short term, but have found no evidence that bronchodilators reduce admission rates or produce a clinically important improvement in oxygen saturation.

Corticosteroids

One systematic review and eight additional RCTs have found limited and conflicting evidence on the effects of corticosteroids.

Respiratory syncytial virus immunoglobulins (RSV Ig) or palivizumab (monoclonal antibody)

RCTs found insufficient evidence on the effects of immunoglobulin treatment.

Ribavirin

One systematic review in children admitted to hospital with respiratory syncytial virus bronchiolitis has found no significant difference in mortality, the risk of respiratory deterioration, or length of hospital stay with ribavarin versus placebo, but found that ribavirin significantly reduced the duration of ventilation. One small subsequent RCT found no significant difference with ribavarin versus placebo in hospital stay, oxygen needs, recurrence of disease, or admission rates, but may have been too small to exclude a clinically important difference.

What are the effects of preventive interventions?

BENEFICIAL

Respiratory syncytial virus immunoglobulins (RSV Ig) in children at high risk

One systematic review has found that in children born prematurely, in children with bronchopulmonary dysplasia, and in children with a combination of risk factors, prophylactic respiratory syncytial virus immunoglobulin (RSV Ig) or palivizumab (monoclonal antibody) reduces admission rates to hospital and intensive care units.

UNKNOWN EFFECTIVENESS

Nursing interventions (cohort segregation⊙, handwashing, gowns, masks, gloves, and goggles) in children admitted to hospital

We found no RCTs about the effects of these interventions.

▶

DEFINITION Bronchiolitis is a virally induced acute bronchiolar inflammation that is associated with signs and symptoms of airway obstruction. Diagnosis is based on clinical findings. Clinical manifestations include fever, rhinitis (inflammation of the nasal mucosa), tachypnoea, expiratory wheezing, cough, rales, use of accessory muscles, apnoea (absence of breathing), dyspnoea (difficulty in breathing), alar flaring (flaring of the nostrils), and retractions (in-drawing of the intercostal soft tissues on inspiration). The disease severity🛈 of bronchiolitis may be classified clinically as mild, moderate, or severe.

INCIDENCE/ PREVALENCE Bronchiolitis is the most common lower respiratory tract infection in infants, occurring in a seasonal pattern with highest incidence in the winter in temperate climates,[1] and in the rainy season in warmer countries. Each year in the USA, about 21% of infants have lower respiratory tract disease and 6–10/1000 infants are admitted to hospital for bronchiolitis (1–2% of children under 12 months of age).[2] The peak rate of admission occurs in infants aged between 2–6 months.[3]

AETIOLOGY/ RISK FACTORS Respiratory syncytial virus is responsible for bronchiolitis in 70% of cases. This figure reaches 80–100% in the winter months. However, in early spring parainfluenza virus type 3 is often responsible.[1]

PROGNOSIS **Morbidity and mortality:** Disease severity is related to the size of the infant, and proximity and to the frequency of contact with infective infants. Children at increased risk of morbidity and mortality are those with congenital heart disease, chronic lung disease, history of premature birth, hypoxia, and age less than 6 weeks.[4] Other factors associated with a prolonged or compli-cated hospital stay include a history of apnoea or respiratory arrest, pulmo-nary consolidation, as shown on a chest radiograph, and (in North America) native American or Inuit race.[5] The risk of death within 2 weeks is high for children with congenital heart disease (3.4%) or chronic lung disease (3.5%) compared with other groups combined (0.1%).[4] Rates of admission to intensive care units (ICU) (range 31% to 36%) and need for mechanical ventilation (range 11% to 19%) are similar among all high risk groups.[4] The percentage of these children needing oxygen supplementation is also high (range 63% to 80%).[4] In contrast, mortality in children with bronchiolitis but without these risk factors is less than 1%, and rates of ICU admission and ventilation in such children are markedly lower (15% and 8%).[6] **Long term prognosis:**
Information on long term prognosis varies among studies. One small pro-spective study of two matched cohorts (25 children with bronchiolitis; 25 children without) found no evidence that bronchiolitis requiring outpatient treatment is associated with an increased risk of asthma in the long term.[7] Possible confounding factors include variation in illness severity, smoke exposure, and crowding.[8] We found one prospective study in 50 randomly selected infants admitted with bronchiolitis, followed up by questionnaire for 5 years and a visit in the fifth year. It found a doubling of asthma incidence compared with the general population, although there was large (30%) loss to follow up and no matched control group.[9]

Search date February 2002

Kate Ackerman and David Creery

Child health

What are the effects of treatments for non-submersion out of hospital cardiorespiratory arrest?

LIKELY TO BE BENEFICIAL

Bystander cardiopulmonary resuscitation

It is widely accepted that cardiopulmonary resuscitation should be undertaken in children who have arrested. Placebo controlled trials would be considered unethical. One systematic review of observational studies has found that children who received bystander cardiopulmonary resuscitation versus no bystander cardiopulmonary resuscitation were more likely to survive to hospital discharge.

UNKNOWN EFFECTIVENESS

Airway management and ventilation; direct current cardiac shock; standard dose intravenous adrenaline (epinephrine)

Although we found no direct evidence to support their use, widespread consensus based on indirect evidence and extrapolation from adult data holds that these interventions should be universally applied to children who have arrested. Placebo controlled trials would be considered unethical.

High dose intravenous adrenaline (epinephrine); intravenous bicarbonate; intravenous calcium; training parents to perform cardiopulmonary resuscitation

We found no RCTs or prospective cohort studies on the effects of these interventions in children who have arrested in the community.

Intubation versus bag-mask ventilation

One controlled clinical trial found no significant difference with endotracheal intubation versus bag-mask ventilation in survival or neurological outcome.

DEFINITION Non-submersion out of hospital cardiorespiratory arrest in children is a state of pulselessness and apnoea occurring outside of a medical facility and not caused by submersion in water.[1]

INCIDENCE/ We found 12 studies (3 prospective, 9 retrospective) reporting the inci-
PREVALENCE dence of non-submersion out of hospital cardiorespiratory arrest in children❶.[2–13] Eleven studies reported the incidence in both adults and children, and eight reported the incidence in children.[2–9,11–13] Incidence of arrests in the general population ranged from 2.2–5.7/100 000 people a year (mean 3.1, 95% CI 2.1 to 4.1). Incidence of arrests in children ranged from 6.9–18.0/100 000 children a year (mean 10.6, 95% CI 7.1 to 14.1).[8] One prospective study (300 children) found that about 50% of out of hospital cardiorespiratory arrests occurred in children under 12 months, and about two thirds occurred in children under 18 months.[11]

AETIOLOGY/ We found 26 studies reporting the causes of non-submersion pulseless
RISK FACTORS arrests❸ in a total of 1574 children. The commonest causes of arrest were undetermined causes as in sudden infant death syndrome❸ (39%), trauma (18%), chronic disease (7%), and pneumonia (4%)❶.[1,3–12,14–28]

Cardiorespiratory arrest

PROGNOSIS   We found no systematic review that investigated non-submersion arrests alone. We found 27 studies (5 prospective, 22 retrospective; total of 1754 children) that reported only on out of hospital arrest.[1–12,14–28] The overall survival rate following out of hospital arrest was 5% (87 children). Nineteen of these studies (1140 children) found that of the 48 surviving children, 12 (25%) had no or mild neurological disability and 36 (75%) had moderate or severe neurological disability. We found one systematic review (search date 1997), which reported outcomes after cardiopulmonary resuscitation for both in hospital and out of hospital arrests of any cause, including submersion in children.[29] Studies were excluded if they did not report survival. The review found evidence from prospective and retrospective observational studies that out of hospital arrest of any cause in children carries a poorer prognosis than arrest within hospital (132/1568 children [8%] survived to hospital discharge after out of hospital arrest v 129/544 children [24%] after in hospital arrests). About half of the survivors were involved in studies that reported neurological outcome. Of these, survival with "good neurological outcome" (i.e. normal or mild neurological deficit) was higher in children who arrested in hospital compared with those who arrested elsewhere (60/77 surviving children [78%] in hospital v 28/68 [41%] elsewhere).[29]

What are the effects of treatments?

LIKELY TO BE BENEFICIAL

Biofeedback training (short term benefit only)

RCTs found that biofeedback plus conventional treatment (laxatives alone or laxatives plus dietary advice and toilet training) versus conventional treatment alone significantly improved defaecation dynamics and reduced rates of soiling after 3–7 months. Two of the RCTs found no significant difference after 1 year.

Medical treatment plus toilet training

One small RCT found short term benefit from the addition of toilet training to medical treatment (enemas and laxatives).

Osmotic laxatives

RCTs comparing different osmotic laxatives found limited evidence that laxatives may soften stools and increase stool frequency after 2 weeks.

TRADE OFF BETWEEN BENEFITS AND HARMS

Cisapride

RCTs in an outpatient setting found that cisapride versus placebo significantly improved stool frequency and symptoms of constipation after 8–12 weeks of treatment. We found no evidence in primary care settings. Cisapride has been withdrawn in several countries because of suspected adverse cardiac effects.

UNKNOWN EFFECTIVENESS

Increased fibre intake; stimulant laxatives, especially mineral oil

We found no RCTs in children on the effects of these interventions.

DEFINITION   Constipation is characterised by infrequent bowel evacuations, hard, small faeces, or difficult or painful defecation. The frequency of bowel evacuation varies from person to person.[1] Encopresis is defined as involuntary bowel movements in inappropriate places at least once a month for 3 months or more, in children aged 4 years and older.[2]

INCIDENCE/ PREVALENCE   Constipation with or without encopresis is common in children. It accounts for 3% of consultations to paediatric outpatient clinics and 25% of paediatric gastroenterology consultations in the USA.[3] Encopresis has been reported in 1.5% of children at school entry. The peak incidence is at 2–4 years of age.

AETIOLOGY/ RISK FACTORS   No cause is discovered in 90–95% of children with constipation. Low fibre intake and a family history of constipation may be associated factors.[4] Psychosocial factors are often suspected, although most children with constipation are developmentally normal.[3] Chronic constipation can lead to progressive faecal retention, distension of the rectum, and loss of sensory and motor function. Organic causes for constipation are uncommon, but include Hirschsprung's disease (1/5000 births; male : female 4 : 1; constipation invariably present from birth), cystic fibrosis, anorectal physiological abnormalities, anal fissures, constipating drugs, dehydrating metabolic conditions, and other forms of malabsorption.[3]

▶

Constipation

◄ **PROGNOSIS**   Childhood constipation can be difficult to treat and often requires prolonged support, explanation, and medical treatment. In one long term follow up study of children presenting under the age of 5 years, 50% recovered within 1 year and 65–70% recovered within 2 years; the remainder required laxatives for daily bowel movements or continued to soil for years.[3] It is not known what proportion continue to have problems into adult life, although adults presenting with megarectum or megacolon often have a history of bowel problems from childhood.

What are the effects of treatments in different settings?

BENEFICIAL

Nebulised steroids versus placebo in paediatric assessment units🅖
RCTs in children given humidified oxygen have found that nebulised steroids versus placebo significantly reduce poor responses after 2–5 hours, and reduce admissions to hospital (NNT 4). They found no significant difference in re-attendance to any medical practitioner or institution after 1 week.

Nebulised steroids versus placebo in hospital
RCTs have found that nebulised steroids versus placebo significantly improve symptoms after 2 hours (NNT 2), reduce hospital stay, and reduce further medical attendance within 3 days of discharge.

Systemic steroids versus placebo in paediatric assessment units
RCTs have found that a single dose of oral or intramuscular steroids versus placebo significantly improves symptoms within 5 hours, reduces admissions to hospital (NNT 2), and reduces re-attendance to any medical practitioner or institution within 1 week of discharge (NNT 12).

Systemic versus nebulised steroids in paediatric assessment units
RCTs have found no significant difference with systemic dexamethasone versus nebulised budenoside in improvement in symptoms or re-attendance after discharge, but has found that dexamethasone significantly reduces the number of children admitted to hospital.

Systemic steroids versus placebo in hospital
RCTs have found that systemic steroids versus placebo significantly improve symptoms after 12–24 hours (NNT 7) and significantly reduce the length of hospital stay.

LIKELY TO BE BENEFICIAL

Nebulised adrenaline (epinephrine) versus placebo in hospital
One small RCT has found that nebulised adrenaline (epinephrine) versus placebo significantly improves symptoms within 30 minutes, but found no significant difference after 2 hours. Two small RCTs found no significant difference with nebulised adrenaline (epinephrine) versus placebo, but they may have been too small to exclude a clinically important difference.

Nebulised adrenaline (epinephrine) versus placebo in paediatric assessment units
One small RCT in children with stridor at rest has found that nebulised adrenaline (epinephrine) versus placebo significantly improves symptoms within 30 minutes. Symptoms returned to pre-intervention severity after 2 hours in a third of children.

UNKNOWN EFFECTIVENESS

High versus low dose systemic steroid regimens in hospital; inhalation of humidified air/oxygen in hospital; nebulised adrenaline (epinephrine) versus steroids in hospital
We found insufficient evidence on the effects of these interventions.

▶

Croup

◀ **Systemic versus nebulised steroids in hospital; treatment in primary care settings**

We found no RCTs on the effects of these interventions.

DEFINITION   Croup is an acute clinical syndrome characterised by a harsh, barking cough, inspiratory stridor, and hoarse voice, caused by laryngeal or tracheal obstruction. Mild fever and rhinorrhoea may also be present. The most important differential diagnoses are acute epiglottitis, inhalation of a foreign body, and bacterial tracheitis. The RCTs in this review excluded children with previous upper airway abnormalities, previous prolonged intubation, severe croup (cyanosis with impaired consciousness), and recent treatment with steroids. The conclusions of the review should not be applied to children with these clinical features.

INCIDENCE/   Croup occurs in about 3% of children aged under 6 years per year,[1] and
PREVALENCE   causes 2–3% of hospital admissions in young children in the UK.[2] One retrospective Belgian study of 5–8 year olds found that 16% of children had suffered from croup, and 5% had experienced recurrent croup (3 or more episodes).[3]

AETIOLOGY/   Croup is believed to be mainly viral in origin, but atopy plays a part in some
RISK FACTORS   children. The most common virus isolated is parainfluenza types 1, 2, or 3. Other viruses include influenza, adenovirus, respiratory syncytial virus, and rhinovirus.

PROGNOSIS   Fewer than 2% of children with croup are admitted to hospital in the UK.[1] Of those admitted, only 1–2% require intubation. Mortality is low: of 208 children who were given artificial airways over a 10 year period, two died.[4] Symptoms of upper airway obstruction can be extremely distressing to the child and to the family.

Depression in children and adolescents

Search date May 2001

Philip Hazell

Child health

What are the effects of treatments?

BENEFICIAL

Cognitive therapy (in mild to moderate depression)

One systematic review in children and adolescents with mild to moderate depression has found that cognitive behavioural therapy❺ versus non-specific supportive therapies significantly improves symptoms.

LIKELY TO BE BENEFICIAL

Interpersonal therapy in adolescents (in mild to moderate depression)

Two RCTs found that interpersonal therapy❺ versus clinical monitoring or waiting list control significantly increased the number of adolescents who recovered over 12 weeks.

UNKNOWN EFFECTIVENESS

Electroconvulsive therapy; long term effects of psychological or pharmacological treatments; St John's Wort

We found no RCTs in children and adolescents about the effects of these interventions.

Family therapy; group treatments other than cognitive behavioural therapy; lithium; monoamine oxidase inhibitors

We found insufficient evidence in children and adolescents about the effects of these interventions.

Selective serotonin reuptake inhibitors and related drugs

Two RCTs found conflicting evidence on the effects of fluoxetine versus placebo. One small RCT found no significant difference in symptoms with venlafaxine plus psychotherapy versus placebo plus psychotherapy. We found no RCTs on the effects of other serotonin reuptake inhibitor drugs.

UNLIKELY TO BE BENEFICIAL

Tricyclic and heterocyclic antidepressants in adolescents

Systematic reviews comparing tricyclic antidepressants versus placebo in adolescents found no significant difference in failure to recover from depression, but found significantly improved depression severity scores.

LIKELY TO BE INEFFECTIVE OR HARMFUL

Tricyclic and heterocyclic antidepressants in children

Systematic reviews in prepubertal children found no significant difference with tricyclic antidepressants versus placebo in failure to recover from depression or depression severity scores.

DEFINITION See definition under depressive disorders, p 170. Compared with adult depression, depression in children and adolescents may have a more insidious onset, may be characterised more by irritability than sadness, and occurs more often in association with other conditions such as anxiety, conduct disorder, hyperkinesis, and learning problems.[1]   ▶

Depression in children and adolescents

INCIDENCE/ PREVALENCE	Estimates of prevalence of depression among children and adolescents in the community range from 2–6%.[2,3] Prevalence tends to increase with age, with a sharp rise around onset of puberty. Pre-adolescent boys and girls are affected equally by the condition, but depression is seen more frequently among adolescent girls than boys.[4]
AETIOLOGY/ RISK FACTORS	Uncertain, but may include childhood events and current psychosocial adversity.
PROGNOSIS	See prognosis under depressive disorders, p 170. In children and adolescents, the recurrence rate of depressive episodes first occurring in childhood or adolescence is 70% by 5 years, which is similar to the recurrence rate in adults.[5] Young people experiencing a moderate to severe depressive episode may be more likely than adults to have a manic episode within the next few years.[4] Trials of treatment for child and adolescent depression have found high rates of spontaneous remission (as much as two thirds of people in some inpatient studies).

Search date September 2001

Yadlapalli Kumar and Rajini Sarvananthan

Child health

What are the effects of treatments?

UNKNOWN EFFECTIVENESS

H₂ antagonists

One small RCT found that cimetidine versus placebo significantly improved clinical or endoscopic features of gastro-oesophageal reflux complicated by oesophagitis over 12 weeks (NNT 2).

Feed thickeners

We found no clear evidence about the effects of feed thickeners. One small RCT found no significant difference in regurgitation reported by parents with carob flour thickened feeds versus placebo thickened feeds. Another small RCT found that carob flour versus traditional formula thickened with rice flour significantly reduced gastro-oesophageal reflux symptoms and episodes of vomiting.

Proton pump inhibitors; surgery (fundoplication)

We found no RCTs on the effects of these interventions.

Sodium alginate

One small RCT found that sodium alginate versus placebo for 8 days significantly reduced episodes of regurgitation reported by parents.

LIKELY TO BE INEFFECTIVE OR HARMFUL

Cisapride

One systematic review found no significant difference with cisapride versus placebo in clinical symptoms. Cisapride is not widely licensed for use in children and has been withdrawn or its use restricted in several countries because of an association with heart rhythm abnormalities.

Left lateral positioning; prone positioning

Small RCTs have found that prone or left lateral positioning versus supine positioning improves oesophageal pH variables, but both positions are associated with sudden infant death syndrome.

DEFINITION
Gastro-oesophageal reflux disease (GORD) is the passive transfer of gastric contents into the oesophagus due to transient or chronic relaxation of the lower oesophageal sphincter.[1] A survey of 69 children (median age 16 months) with GORD attending a tertiary referral centre found that presenting symptoms were recurrent vomiting (72%), epigastric and abdominal pain (36%), feeding difficulties (29%), failure to thrive (28%), and irritability (19%).[2] Over 90% of children with GORD have vomiting before 6 weeks of age.[1] Rare complications of the condition include oesophagitis with haematemesis and anaemia, respiratory problems (such as cough, apnoea and recurrent wheeze), and failure to thrive.[1] A small comparative study (40 children) suggested that, when compared with healthy children, infants with GORD had slower development of feeding skills and had problems affecting behaviour, swallowing, food intake, and mother–child interaction.[3]

INCIDENCE/ PREVALENCE
Gastro-oesophageal regurgitation is considered a problem if it is frequent and persistent.[1] Regurgitation occurs in 18% of the general infant population.[4] In a study comparing the prevalence of GORD in children with ▶

respiratory dysfunction (62 children) to a control group (387 children), the prevalence of excessive gastro-oesophageal reflux, diagnosed by pH metric criteria, was 42% and 8%, respectively.[5]

AETIOLOGY/ RISK FACTORS   Risk factors for GORD include immaturity of the lower oesophageal sphincter, chronic relaxation of the sphincter, increased abdominal pressure, gastric distension, hiatus hernia, and oesophageal dysmotility.[1] Premature infants and children with severe neurodevelopmental problems or congenital oesophageal anomalies are particularly at risk.

PROGNOSIS   Regurgitation is considered benign, and most cases resolve spontaneously by 12–18 months of age.[6] However, with GORD caused by hiatus hernia, 30% of cases persist until the age of 4 years.[7]

Search date September 2001

Teresa Kilgour and Sally Wade

What are the effects of treatments?

LIKELY TO BE BENEFICIAL

Whey hydrolysate milk

One RCT found limited evidence that replacing cow's milk formula with whey hydrolysate formula⊙ significantly reduced crying recorded in a parental diary.

TRADE OFF BETWEEN BENEFITS AND HARMS

Dicycloverine

One systematic review found limited evidence that dicycloverine (dicyclomine)⊙ versus placebo reduced crying in infants with colic. One RCT found that dicycloverine (dicyclomine) versus placebo significantly reduced the proportion of infants with colic (NNT 3). RCTs found that dicycloverine versus placebo increased drowsiness, constipation and loose stools, but the difference did not reach significance. Case reports of harms in infants have included breathing difficulties, seizures, syncope, asphyxia, muscular hypotonia, and coma.

UNKNOWN EFFECTIVENESS

Casein hydrolysate milk

RCTs found insufficient evidence about the effects of replacing cow's milk formula with casein hydrolysate hypoallergenic formula⊙.

Cranial osteopathy *New*

We found no RCTs about the effects of cranial osteopathy⊙ in infants with colic.

Herbal tea

One small RCT found that herbal tea (containing extracts of chamomile, vervain, licorice, fennel, and balm mint in a sucrose solution) versus sucrose solution significantly improved symptoms of colic rated by parents at 7 days (NNT 3).

Infant massage *New*

One RCT found no significant difference with massage versus a crib vibrator in colic related crying or parental rating of symptoms of infantile colic.

Low lactose (lactase treated) milk

RCTs found no significant difference in outcomes with low lactose treated milk versus untreated milk.

Reduction of stimulation of the infant

One RCT found limited evidence that advice to reduce stimulation (by not patting, lifting, or jiggling the baby, or by reducing auditory stimulation) versus an empathetic interview significantly reduced crying after 7 days in infants under 12 weeks (NNT 2).

Soya based infant feeds

One small RCT found that soya based infant feeds⊙ versus cow's milk significantly reduced the duration of crying.

Spinal manipulation *New*

Two RCTs found inconclusive results about the effects of spinal manipulation⊙. ▶

◀ **Sucrose solution**

One small crossover RCT found limited evidence that sucrose solution versus placebo significantly improved symptoms of colic as rated by parents.

UNLIKELY TO BE BENEFICIAL

Increased carrying

One RCT found no significant difference in daily crying time with carrying the infant, even when not crying, for at least an additional 3 hours a day versus a general advice group (to carry, check baby's nappy, feed, offer pacifier, place baby near mother, or use background stimulation such as music). The "advice to carry" group carried their babies for 4.5 hours daily compared with 2.6 hours daily in the general advice group.

Simethicone (activated dimeticone)

RCTs found no significant difference with simethicone (activated dimeticone)🅖 versus placebo in the presence of colic when rated by carers, or in improvement as rated by parental interview, 24 hour diary, or behavioural observation. One poor quality RCT found that simethicone versus placebo significantly reduced the number of crying attacks on days 4–7 of treatment.

DEFINITION	Infantile colic is defined as excessive crying in an otherwise healthy baby. The crying typically starts in the first few weeks of life and ends by 4–5 months. Excessive crying is defined as crying that lasts at least 3 hours a day, for 3 days a week, for at least 3 weeks.[1]
INCIDENCE/ PREVALENCE	Infantile colic causes one in six families to consult a health professional. One systematic review of fifteen community based studies found a wide variation in prevalence, which depended on study design and method of recording.[2] The two best prospective studies identified by the review yielded prevalence rates of 5% and 19%.[2] One RCT (89 breast and formula fed infants) found that, at 2 weeks of age, the prevalence of crying more than 3 hours a day was 43% among formula fed infants and 16% among breast fed infants. The prevalence at 6 weeks was 12% (formula fed) and 31% (breast fed).[3]
AETIOLOGY/ RISK FACTORS	The cause of infantile colic is unclear and, despite its name, might not have an abdominal cause. It may reflect part of the normal distribution of infantile crying. Other possible explanations are painful gut contractions, lactose intolerance, gas, or parental misinterpretation of normal crying.[1]
PROGNOSIS	Infantile colic improves with time. One study found that 29% of infants aged 1–3 months cried for more than 3 hours a day, but by 4–6 months of age the prevalence had fallen to 7–11%.[4]

Search date November 2001
Anna Donald and Vivek Muthu

Child health

What are the effects of preventive interventions? New

BENEFICIAL

Live combined measles, mumps, and rubella (MMR) vaccine; live monovalent measles vaccine

Large cohort studies, large cross-sectional time series, and population surveillance data from different countries have all found that combined measles, mumps, and rubella (MMR)🄖 and live monovalent measles vaccination🄖 programmes reduce the risk of measles infection to near zero, especially in populations in which vaccine coverage🄖 is high.

We found no RCTs comparing the effects of MMR versus no vaccination or placebo on measles infection rates. Such trials are likely to be considered unethical because of the large body of whole-population evidence finding benefit from vaccination.

Unlike live monovalent measles vaccine, MMR additionally vaccinates against mumps and rubella, which themselves cause serious complications (mumps causes orchitis, pancreatitis, infertility, meningoencephalitis, deafness, and congenital fetal abnormalities; rubella causes deafness, blindness, heart defects, liver, spleen and brain damage, and stillbirth).

One systematic review, one RCT, one large population based survey, and one population based study found no evidence of MMR being associated with acute developmental regression🄖 compared with placebo or no vaccine. Large cross-sectional time series have consistently found no evidence of MMR or live monovalent measles vaccine being associated with autism🄖.

One large, long term population surveillance study and one population based case control study found no evidence that either the monovalent measles vaccine or MMR was associated with inflammatory bowel disease. One large cohort study and two population based case control studies found no association of inflammatory bowel disease with the monovalent vaccine.

One systematic review and one additional RCT have found that MMR and monovalent measles vaccine are associated with a small and similar risk of self limiting fever within 3 weeks of vaccination compared with 100% risk of acute fever in people with measles.

DEFINITION   Measles is an infectious disease caused by a ribonucleic acid (RNA) paramyxomavirus. The illness is characterised by an incubation period of 10–12 days; a prodromal period of 2–4 days with upper respiratory tract symptoms; Koplik's spots on mucosal membranes and high fever followed by further fever; and a widespread maculopapular rash that persists for 5–6 days.[1]

INCIDENCE/   Measles incidence varies widely according to vaccination coverage. World-
PREVALENCE   wide, there are an estimated 30 million cases of measles each year,[2] but an incidence of only 0–10/100 000 people in countries with widespread vaccination programmes, such as the USA, UK, Mexico, India, China, Brazil, and Australia.[3] In the USA, before licensure of effective vaccines, greater than 90% of people were infected by the age of 15 years, whereas after licensure in 1963, incidence fell by about 98%.[1] Mean annual incidence in Finland was 366/100 000 in 1970,[4] but declined to about ▶

zero by the late 1990s.[5] Similarly, annual incidence declined to about zero in Chile, the English speaking Caribbean, and Cuba during the 1990s with introduction of vaccination programmes.[6,7]

AETIOLOGY/
RISK FACTORS
Measles is spread through airborne droplets and is documented for up to 2 hours in closed areas following the presence of an infected person. Measles is highly contagious. As with other infectious diseases, other risk factors include overcrowding, low herd immunity⊙, and immunosuppression. People with immunosuppression, children of less than 5 years of age, and adults of more than 20 years of age have a higher risk of severe complications and death, although these also occur in healthy people (see prognosis below).[1] Newborn babies have a lower risk of measles than older infants because of the persistence of protective maternal antibodies, although in recent US outbreaks, maternal antibody protection was lower than expected.[1]

PROGNOSIS
The World Health Organization estimated that in the year 2000, measles caused 777 000 deaths and a burden of disease of 27.5 million disability adjusted life years.[8] **Disease in healthy people:** In developed countries, most prognostic data come from the pre-vaccination era and from subsequent outbreaks in non-vaccinated populations. In the USA, measles is complicated in about 30% of reported cases. From 1989–1991 in the USA, measles resurgence among young children (< 5 years) who had not been immunised led to 55 622 cases with more than 11 000 hospital admissions and 125 deaths.[1] Measles complications include diarrhoea (8%), otitis media (7%), pneumonia (6%), death (0.1–0.2%), acute encephalitis (about 0.1% followed by death in 15% and permanent neurological damage in about 25%), seizures (with or without fever in 0.6–0.7%), idiopathic thrombocytopenia (1/6000 reported cases), and subacute scerlosing pan-encephalitis causing degeneration of the central nervous system and death 7 years after measles infection (range 1 month to 27 years; 0.5–1.0/100 000 reported cases).[1,9] Measles during pregnancy results in higher risk of premature labour, spontaneous abortion, and low birth weight infants. An association with birth defects remains uncertain.[1] **Disease in malnourished or immunocompromised people:** In malnourished or immunocompromised people, particularly those with vitamin A deficiency, measles case fatality can be as high as 25%. Worldwide, measles is a major cause of blindness and causes 5% of deaths in young children (< 5 years).[1,10]

What are the effects of treatments?

BENEFICIAL

Enuresis alarm (in the long term)

One systematic review has found that significantly more children achieve 14 consecutive dry nights with enuresis alarms versus no treatment, and that 31–61% of children were still dry at 3 months. The review found that children using an alarm were 9 times less likely to relapse than children taking desmopressin. One RCT found that significantly more children achieved 4 weeks of dryness with alarm plus intranasal desmopressin (40 μg) versus alarm alone.

Desmopressin (intranasal)

One systematic review has found that intranasal desmopressin versus placebo significantly reduces bedwetting by at least one night/week, and increases the chance of attaining 14 consecutive dry nights.

LIKELY TO BE BENEFICIAL

Indometacin

One small RCT found that indometacin (indomethacin) versus placebo significantly increased the number of dry nights in children aged over 6 years with primary nocturnal enuresis.

Laser acupuncture *New*

One RCT found no significant difference in the number of wet nights in children aged over 5 years with laser acupuncture versus intranasal desmopressin.

TRADE OFF BETWEEN BENEFITS AND HARMS

Tricyclic drugs

One systematic review has found that tricyclic drugs (imipramine, desipramine) versus placebo significantly increase the chance of attaining 14 consecutive dry nights. It found no significant difference with imipramine versus an alarm during the treatment period but found that children using an enuresis alarm had fewer wet nights per week after the treatment had stopped.

UNKNOWN EFFECTIVENESS

Age to start treatment

We found no RCTs on the best age to start treatment in children with nocturnal enuresis. Anecdotal experience suggests that reassurance is sufficient below the age of 7 years.

Carbamazepine

One small RCT found that carbamazepine versus placebo significantly increased the number of dry nights in nocturnal enuresis caused by detrusor instability in children aged over 7 years.

Dry bed training (in the long term)

One systematic review has found that significantly more children achieved 14 consecutive dry nights with dry bed training versus no treatment, but found no significant difference in the proportion of dry nights in the long term. ▶

Nocturnal enuresis

◀ **Standard home alarm clock (in the long term)**

One RCT found that significantly more children achieved 14 consecutive dry nights with standard home alarm clock versus waking after 3 hours' sleep, but found no significant difference in the proportion of dry nights at 3 months.

Ultrasound *New*

We found no RCTs on use of ultrasound. One small controlled trial found that ultrasound versus control significantly increased the proportion of dry nights for up to 12 months.

DEFINITION	Nocturnal enuresis is the involuntary discharge of urine at night in the absence of congenital or acquired defects of the central nervous system or urinary tract in a child aged 5 years or older.[1] Disorders that have bedwetting as a symptom (termed "nocturnal incontinence") can be excluded by a thorough history, examination, and urinalysis. "Monosymptomatic" nocturnal enuresis is characterised by night time symptoms only and accounts for 85% of cases. Nocturnal enuresis is defined as primary if the child has never been dry for a period of more than 6 months, and secondary if such a period of dryness preceded the onset of wetting.
INCIDENCE/ PREVALENCE	Between 15% and 20% of 5 year olds, 7% of 7 year olds, 5% of 10 year olds, 2–3% of 12–14 year olds, and 1–2% of people aged 15 years and over wet the bed twice a week on average.[2]
AETIOLOGY/ RISK FACTORS	Nocturnal enuresis is associated with several factors, including small functional bladder capacity, nocturnal polyuria, and arousal dysfunction. Linkage studies have identified associated genetic loci on chromosomes 8q, 12q, 13q, and 22q11.[3–6]
PROGNOSIS	Nocturnal enuresis has widely differing outcomes, from spontaneous resolution to complete resistance to all current treatments. About 1% of adults remain enuretic. Without treatment, about 15% of children with enuresis become dry each year.[7]

Recurrent idiopathic epistaxis (nosebleeds)

Search date February 2002

Gerald McGarry

What are the effects of treatments?

UNKNOWN EFFECTIVENESS

Antiseptic cream versus cautery

One small RCT found no significant difference with chlorhexidine/neomycin cream versus silver nitrate cautery in reduction of nose bleeds after 8 weeks. Some children found the smell and taste of the antiseptic cream unpleasant. All children found cautery painful despite the use of local anaesthesia.

Antiseptic cream versus other creams/ointments; cautery versus no treatment

We found no RCTs about the effects of these interventions.

Cautery plus antiseptic cream versus antiseptic cream alone

One small RCT found insufficient evidence about the effects of silver nitrate cautery plus chlorhexidine/neomycin cream versus antiseptic cream alone.

DEFINITION
Recurrent idiopathic epistaxis is recurrent, self limiting, nasal bleeding in children for which no specific cause has been identified. There is no consensus on how frequent or severe recurrences need to be.

INCIDENCE/ PREVALENCE
A cross sectional study of 1218 children (aged 11–14 years) found that 9% had frequent episodes of epistaxis.[1] It is likely that most epistaxis in children is not brought to the attention of health professionals, and that only the most severe episodes are considered for treatment.

AETIOLOGY/ RISK FACTORS
In children, most epistaxis occurs from the anterior part of the septum in the region of Little's area.[2] Initiating factors include local inflammation, mucosal drying, and local trauma (including nose picking).[2] Epistaxis caused by other specific local (e.g. tumours) or systemic factors (e.g. clotting disorders) is not considered here.

PROGNOSIS
Recurrent epistaxis is less common in adolescents over 14 years and many children "grow out" of this problem.

Reducing pain during blood sampling in infants

Search date January 2002

Linda Franck and Ruth Gilbert

What are the effects of interventions to reduce pain during blood sampling in infants?

BENEFICIAL

Automated devices versus manual lancets *New*

RCTs in preterm and term infants have found that automated devices versus manual lancets for heel puncture are less painful, cause less bruising, and reduce the time needed to obtain a sample.

Oral sucrose for heel puncture

Systematic reviews and additional RCTs have found that oral sucrose versus water or no treatment significantly reduces pain responses (particularly the duration of crying).

Venepuncture versus heel puncture

RCTs have found that venepuncture versus heel puncture significantly reduces pain responses (particularly crying) during blood sampling, and also reduces the need for repeat punctures.

LIKELY TO BE BENEFICIAL

Holding in term infants

RCTs found that crying was reduced in infants held during heel puncture.

Oral glucose for heel puncture and venepuncture

RCTs have found that oral glucose versus water or versus no treatment significantly reduces pain responses (particularly the duration of crying).

Oral sucrose for venepuncture

RCTs have found that oral sucrose versus water or no treatment significantly reduces pain responses (particularly the duration of crying).

Other sweeteners for heel puncture *New*

RCTs have found that other sweeteners (hydrogenated glucose❻ or an artificial sweetener, 10 parts cyclamate and 1 part saccharin) versus water significantly reduce pain scores and the percentage of time spent crying.

Pacifiers for heel puncture and venepuncture

RCTs in term and preterm infants have found that pacifiers❻ given prior to heel puncture versus no treatment reduce pain responses. One RCT in term infants having venepuncture found that pacifiers versus water or versus no treatment significantly reduced pain responses.

Rocking

One RCT found limited evidence that rocking by the examiner versus no intervention reduced pain in neonates undergoing heel puncture. Another RCT found no significant difference in pain response with simulated rocking by a mechanical device versus water given before heel puncture.

Topical lidocaine–prilocaine emulsion for venepuncture

RCTs found limited evidence that lidocaine–prilocaine emulsion (EMLA) versus placebo reduced pain responses to venepuncture.

▶

◀ **Topical tetracaine (amethocaine) for venepuncture**

RCTs found that tetracaine (amethocaine) versus placebo reduced pain scores and the number of infants who cried during venepuncture.

Tucking arms and legs in preterm infants

RCTs found limited evidence that pain responses were reduced by tucking the arms and legs into a mid-line flexed position during heel puncture.

UNKNOWN EFFECTIVENESS

Holding plus sucrose versus holding alone for heel puncture

One RCT found that sucrose did not appear to increase the benefit of holding.

Multiple doses of sweet solution

One small RCT found no significant difference with multiple versus single doses of sucrose in pain scores for heel puncture.

Oral glucose or sucrose versus any topical anaesthesia

One RCT found insufficient evidence about the effects of oral sucrose versus EMLA in term infants having heel puncture. We found no RCTs about the effects of oral glucose versus topical anaesthesia.

Other sweeteners for venepuncture *New*

We found no RCTs of other sweeteners for venepuncture.

Swaddling

RCTs found no significant difference in pain responses from swaddling or positioning.

Warming prior to heel puncture *New*

One RCT in term infants found no benefit of warming prior to heel puncture.

UNLIKELY TO BE BENEFICIAL

Topical anaesthetics for heel puncture

Systematic reviews and additional RCTs have found no evidence of reduced pain responses, particularly crying, in infants who received either lidocaine or lidocaine plus prilocaine cream (EMLA) versus placebo prior to heel puncture.

Breast milk

RCTs found no evidence that breast milk or breastfeeding versus water reduced pain responses or crying in neonates undergoing heel puncture.

Oral sucrose plus pacifier versus pacifier or sucrose alone

One RCT in preterm infants found no significant difference in pain score between a pacifier dipped in sucrose versus a pacifier alone.

Oral sucrose versus oral glucose for venepuncture

One RCT found no significant difference in pain scores between sucrose and glucose for venepuncture.

Pacifier plus music versus pacifier alone for heel puncture

One RCT in preterm infants found no significant difference in pain score with pacifiers plus music versus pacifiers alone during heel puncture.

Prone position

One RCT found no significant difference in pain score with prone position versus side or supine position during heel puncture.

▶

Reducing pain during blood sampling in infants

◄ **LIKELY TO BE INEFFECTIVE OR HARMFUL**

Manual lancets *New*

RCTs in preterm and term infants have found that manual lancets versus automated devices for heel puncture are more painful, cause more bruising, and increase the time taken to obtain a sample.

Prior stressful handling☉

One RCT found that handling (as if being prepared for a lumbar puncture) versus no handling significantly increased pain and crying for up to 2 minutes after heel puncture (NNH 5).

DEFINITION   Methods of sampling blood in infants include heel puncture, venepuncture, and arterial puncture. Heel puncture involves lancing of the lateral aspect of the infant's heel, squeezing the heel, and collecting the pooled capillary blood. Venepuncture involves aspirating blood through a needle in a peripheral vein. Arterial blood sampling is not discussed in this review.

INCIDENCE/   Almost every infant in the developed world undergoes heel puncture to
PREVALENCE   screen for metabolic disorders (e.g. phenylketonuria). Many infants have repeated heel punctures or venepunctures to monitor blood glucose or haemoglobin. Preterm or ill neonates receiving intensive care may have 1–21 painful procedures a day.[1–3] Heel punctures comprise 61–87% and venepuncture comprise 8–13% of the invasive procedures performed on ill infants. Analgesics are rarely given specifically for blood sampling procedures, but 5–19% of infants receive analgesia for other indications.[2,3] In one study, comfort measures were provided during 63% of venepunctures and 75% of heel punctures.[3]

AETIOLOGY/   Blood sampling in infants can be difficult to perform, particularly in preterm
RISK FACTORS   or ill infants. Young infants may have increased sensitivity and more prolonged responses to pain than older age groups.[4] Factors that may affect the infant's pain responses include postconceptional age, previous pain experience, and procedural technique.

PROGNOSIS   Pain caused by blood sampling is associated with acute behavioural and physiological deterioration.[4] Other adverse effects of blood sampling include bleeding, bruising, haematoma, and infection. Extremely rarely, heel puncture can result in cellulitis, osteomyelitis, calcaneal spurs, and necrotising chondritis.[5–7]

Search date November 2001

David Creery and Angelo Mikrogianakis

What are the effects of interventions to reduce the risk of sudden infant death syndrome? New

BENEFICIAL

Advice to avoid prone sleeping

One non-systematic review of observational studies and 11 additional observational studies found that campaigns involving advice to encourage non-prone sleeping positions were followed by a reduced incidence of sudden infant death syndrome (SIDS). RCTs are unlikely to be conducted.

LIKELY TO BE BENEFICIAL

Advice to avoid tobacco smoke exposure

One non-systematic review of observational studies and three additional observational studies found that campaigns to reduce a number of SIDS risk factors, which included tobacco smoke exposure, were followed by a reduced incidence of SIDS. RCTs are unlikely to be conducted.

UNKNOWN EFFECTIVENESS

Advice to avoid bed sharing

One observational study found that a campaign to reduce a number of SIDS risk factors, which included advice to avoid bed sharing, was followed by a reduced incidence of SIDS. RCTs are unlikely to be conducted.

Advice to avoid over heating or over wrapping

One non-systematic review of observational studies and one additional observational study found that campaigns to reduce a number of SIDS risk factors, which included over wrapping❻, were followed by a reduced incidence of SIDS. RCTs are unlikely to be conducted.

Advice to avoid soft sleeping surfaces; advice to promote soother use

We found no evidence on the effects of these interventions in the prevention of SIDS.

Advice to breast feed

One non-systematic review of observational studies and and two additional observational studies found that campaigns to reduce a number of SIDS risk factors, which included advice to breast feed, were followed by a reduced incidence of SIDS. RCTs are unlikely to be conducted.

DEFINITION   Sudden infant death syndrome (SIDS) is the sudden death of an infant aged under 1 year that remains unexplained after review of the clinical history, examination of the scene of death, and postmortem.

INCIDENCE/   The incidence of SIDS has varied over time and among nations (incidence
PREVALENCE   per 1000 live births of SIDS in 1996: Netherlands 0.3; Japan 0.4; Canada 0.5; England and Wales 0.7; USA 0.8; and Australia 0.9.[1]

AETIOLOGY/   By definition, the cause of SIDS is not known. Observational studies have
RISK FACTORS   found an association between SIDS and a number of risk factors including prone sleeping position❻,[2,3] prenatal or postnatal exposure to tobacco,[4] ▶

Sudden infant death syndrome

soft sleeping surfaces,[5,6] hyperthermia/over wrapping❶,[7,8] bed sharing (particularly with mothers who smoke),[9,10] lack of breast feeding,[11,12] and soother use❻.[7,13]

PROGNOSIS Although by definition prognosis is not applicable for an affected infant, the incidence of SIDS is increased in the siblings of that infant.[14,15]

Search date May 2001

James Larcombe

Child health

What are the effects of preventive interventions?

LIKELY TO BE BENEFICIAL

Immunotherapy

One systematic review in premature and in low birth weight neonates has found that intravenous immunoglobulins◍ versus placebo significantly reduce the occurrence of serious infections, including urinary tract infections, over 1 month (NNT 24). One RCT has found that pidotomid (an immunotherapeutic agent) versus placebo significantly reduces urinary tract infection recurrence in children.

Prophylactic antibiotics after first or subsequent urinary tract infection

Two small RCTs found limited evidence that prophylactic antibiotic treatment (co-trimoxazole◍ or nitrofurantoin) versus placebo significantly reduced the number of recurrent urinary tract infections at 12 months. We found no RCTs assessing the long term effects or optimum duration of prophylaxis.

UNLIKELY TO BE BENEFICIAL

Surgical correction of minor functional anomalies

We found no RCTs. One observational study suggested that children with minor anomalies do not develop renal scarring and therefore may not benefit from surgery.

Surgical correction of moderate to severe vesicoureteric reflux (similar benefits to medical management)

One systematic review and one subsequent RCT found that, although surgery abolished reflux, there was no significant difference between surgical versus medical management (prophylactic antibiotic treatment) in preventing recurrence or complications from urinary tract infections after 6 months to 5 years.

Which children benefit from diagnostic imaging?

UNLIKELY TO BE BENEFICIAL

Routine diagnostic imaging in all children with first urinary tract infection

One systematic review of descriptive studies found no evidence of benefit from routine diagnostic imaging of all children with a first urinary tract infection. We found indirect evidence suggesting that children at increased risk of morbidity may benefit from investigation.

What are the effects of treatment of acute infection?

BENEFICIAL

7–10 days of antibiotics (better than shorter courses)

Two RCTs have found that antibiotic treatment for 7 days or longer versus a single dose or 1 day course significantly increases cure (eradication of causative organism) after 4 days.

▶

◄ **LIKELY TO BE BENEFICIAL**

Oral (rather than intravenous) antibiotics for acute treatment of children 2 years or younger with normal renal tracts or mild vesicoureteric reflux

One RCT in children under the age of 2 years with an uncomplicated first urinary tract infection found no significant difference between oral versus intravenous antibiotics in mean duration of fever, re-infection, or renal scarring.

UNKNOWN EFFECTIVENESS

Giving early empirical antibiotic treatment instead of awaiting the results of microscopy or culture

We found no RCTs on the effects of delaying treatment while results of microscopy or culture are awaited. Five retrospective studies found that medium to long term delays (4 days to 7 years) in treatment may be associated with an increased risk of renal scarring, but we found inconclusive evidence that shorter delays cause harm.

Oral (rather than intravenous) antibiotics for the acute treatment of children 2 years or younger with moderate or severe vesicoureteric reflux

One RCT found weak evidence from a post hoc subgroup analysis in children with grade III–IV reflux⊙ that oral versus intravenous treatment may increase renal scarring at 6 months.

DEFINITION   Urinary tract infection is defined by the presence of a pure growth of more than 10^5 colony forming units of bacteria per mL. Lower counts of bacteria may be clinically important, especially in boys and in specimens obtained by urinary catheter. Any growth of typical urinary pathogens is considered clinically important if obtained by suprapubic aspiration. In practice, three age ranges are usually considered on the basis of differential risk and different approaches to management: children under 1 year; young children (1–4, 5, or 7 years, depending on the information source); and older children (up to 12–16 years). Recurrent urinary tract infection is defined as a further infection by a new organism. Relapsing urinary tract infection is defined as a further infection with the same organism.

**INCIDENCE/   Boys are more susceptible before the age of 3 months; thereafter the
PREVALENCE**   incidence is substantially higher in girls. Estimates of the true incidence of urinary tract infection depend on rates of diagnosis and investigation. At least 8% of girls and 2% of boys will have a urinary tract infection in childhood.[1]

**AETIOLOGY/   The normal urinary tract is sterile. Contamination by bowel flora may result in
RISK FACTORS** urinary infection if a virulent organism is involved or if the child is immuno-suppressed. In neonates, infection may originate from other sources. *Escherichia coli* accounts for about three quarters of all pathogens. *Proteus* is more common in boys (about 30% of infections). Obstructive anomalies are found in 0–4% and vesicoureteric reflux in 8–40% of children being investigated for their first urinary tract infection.[2] Although vesicoureteric reflux is a major risk factor for adverse outcome, other as yet unidentified triggers may also need to be present.

PROGNOSIS   After first infection, about half of girls have a further infection in the first year and three quarters within 2 years.[3] We found no figures for boys, but a review suggests that recurrences are common under 1 year of age but rare subsequently.[4] Renal scarring occurs in 5–15% of children within 1–2 years of their first urinary tract infection, although 32–70% of these scars are noted at the time of initial assessment.[2] The incidence of renal scarring rises ►

with each episode of infection in childhood.[5] An RCT comparing oral versus intravenous antibiotics found retrospectively that new renal scarring after a first urinary tract infection was more common in children with vesicoureteric reflux than in children without reflux (logistic regression model: AR of scarring 16/107 [15.0%] with reflux v 10/165 [6%] without reflux; RR 2.47, 95% CI 1.17 to 5.24).[6] A study (287 children with severe vesicoureteral reflux treated either medically or surgically for any urinary tract infection) evaluated the risk of renal scarring with serial DMSA**G** scintigraphy over 5 years. It found that younger children (under 2 years) were at greater risk of renal scarring than older children regardless of treatment allocation for the infection (AR for deterioration in DMSA scan over 5 years 21/86 for younger children v 27/201 for older children; RR 1.82, 95% CI 1.09 to 3.03).[7] Renal scarring is associated with future complications: poor renal growth; recurrent adult pyelonephritis; impaired glomerular function; early hypertension; and end stage renal failure.[8–11] A combination of recurrent urinary infection, severe vesicoureteric reflux, and the presence of renal scarring at first presentation is associated with the worst prognosis.

Digestive system disorders

Search date November 2001

John Simpson and William Speake

What are the effects of treatments? New

BENEFICIAL

Adjuvant antibiotics (in adults)

One systematic review and one subsequent RCT in people with simple or complicated appendicitis❻ undergoing appendicectomy have found that prophylactic antibiotics versus no antibiotics significantly reduce wound infections and intra-abdominal abscesses.

Adjuvant antibiotics (in children with complicated appendicitis)

Subgroup analysis from one systematic review has found that antibiotics versus no antibiotics significantly reduce the number of wound infections.

LIKELY TO BE BENEFICIAL

Laparoscopic surgery versus open surgery (in children)

One systematic review has found that laparoscopic surgery versus open surgery significantly reduces the number of wound infections and the length of hospital stay, but found no significant difference in postoperative pain, time to mobilisation, or numbers of intra-abdominal abscesses. One subsequent RCT in children found no significant difference with laparoscopic surgery versus open surgery in length of hospital stay, time to return to normal activity, or numbers of wound infections.

TRADE OFF BETWEEN BENEFITS AND HARMS

Antibiotics versus surgery

One RCT found that conservative treatment with antibiotics versus appendicectomy significantly reduced both postoperative pain and postoperative morphine consumption. However, it found that 35% of people following conservative management were readmitted within 1 year with acute appendicitis and subsequently had an appendicectomy.

Laparoscopic surgery versus open surgery (in adults)

One systematic review has found that laparoscopic surgery versus open surgery significantly reduces the number of wound infections, pain on the first postoperative day, the duration of hospital stay, and the time taken to return to work, but significantly increases the number of postoperative intra-abdominal abscesses.

UNKNOWN EFFECTIVENESS

Adjuvant antibiotics (in children with simple appendicitis)

Subgroup analysis from one systematic review has found no significant difference in the number of wound infections with antibiotics versus no antibiotics. One subsequent RCT in children found no significant difference with antibiotic prophylaxis versus no antibiotic prophylaxis in wound infections, but the RCT may have been too small to exclude a clinically important difference.

Surgery versus no treatment

We found no RCTs of surgery versus no surgery.

▶

◀ **DEFINITION**   Acute appendicitis is acute inflammation of the vermiform appendix.

INCIDENCE/   The incidence of acute appendicitis is falling, although the reason for this
PREVALENCE   is unclear. The reported lifetime risk of appendicitis in the USA is 8.7% in
males and 6.7% in females,[1] and there are about 60 000 cases reported
annually in England and Wales. Appendicitis is the commonest surgical
emergency requiring operation.

AETIOLOGY/   The aetiology of appendicitis is uncertain although various theories exist.
RISK FACTORS Most relate to luminal obstruction, which prevents escape of secretions and
inevitably leads to a rise in intraluminal pressure within the appendix. This
can lead to subsequent mucosal ischaemia, and the stasis provides an ideal
environment for bacterial overgrowth. Potential causes of the obstruction are
faecoliths, often due to constipation, lymphoid hyperplasia, or caecal
carcinoma.[2]

PROGNOSIS   The prognosis of untreated appendicitis is unknown, although spontaneous
resolution has been reported in at least 1/13 (8%) episodes.[3] The recurrence of appendicitis following conservative management,[4] and recurrent
abdominal symptoms in certain patients,[5] suggests that chronic appendicitis
and recurrent acute or subacute appendicitis may also exist.[6] The standard
treatment for acute appendicitis is appendicectomy. The mortality from
acute appendicitis is less than 0.3%, rising to 1.7% following perforation.[7]
The most common complication of appendicectomy is wound infection
occurring in between 5% and 33% of cases.[8] Intra-abdominal abscess
formation occurs less frequently in 2% of appendicectomies.[9] A perforated
appendix in childhood does not appear to have subsequent negative consequences on female fertility.[10]

Anal fissure

Search date May 2001

Marion Jonas and John Scholefield

What are the effects of treatments for chronic anal fissure?

BENEFICIAL

Botulinum A toxin-haemagglutinin (botulinum A toxin-hc)

RCTs have found that botulinum A toxin-hc⊙ injection versus placebo injection or versus topical glyceryl trinitrate significantly improves fissure healing after 2 months.

Botulinum A toxin-hc plus topical isosorbide trinitrate

One RCT has found that botulinum A toxin-hc injection plus topical isosorbide trinitrate versus botulinum A toxin-hc injection alone significantly improves healing at 6 weeks (NNT 3).

Internal anal sphincterotomy

One systematic review has found that internal anal sphincterotomy⊙ and anal stretch⊙ heal 70–95% of fissures. Six RCTs in the review found no significant difference in non-healing with internal anal sphincterotomy versus anal stretch.

LIKELY TO BE BENEFICIAL

Anal advancement flap

One RCT found no significant difference with anal advancement flap⊙ versus anal sphincterotomy in fissure healing or patient satisfaction.

Topical glyceryl trinitrate

RCTs have found that topical glyceryl trinitrate⊙ ointment versus placebo improves fissure healing. Fissures may recur after stopping topical glyceryl trinitrate treatment.

TRADE OFF BETWEEN BENEFITS AND HARMS

Anal stretch

One systematic review of RCTs and observational studies found that internal anal sphincterotomy and anal stretch healed 70–95% of fissures. Six RCTs in the review found no significant difference with anal stretch versus internal anal sphincterotomy in persistence of fissure, but four observational studies in the review found that anal stretch significantly reduced fissure healing. Anal stretch versus internal anal sphincterotomy significantly increased flatus incontinence.

DEFINITION   Anal fissure is a split or tear in the lining of the distal anal canal. It is a very painful condition often associated with fresh blood loss from the anus and perianal itching. "Acute" fissures typically respond within 6 weeks to increased intake of fibre and water. Fissures persisting for longer than 6 weeks are generally defined as chronic. Acute anal fissures have sharply demarcated, fresh mucosal edges, and often with granulation tissue at the base. The margins of a chronic fissure are indurated, there is less granulation tissue, and muscle fibres of the internal anal sphincter may be seen at the base.

▶

Digestive system disorders

INCIDENCE/ PREVALENCE Anal fissures are common in all age groups but we found no evidence to quantify the incidence.

AETIOLOGY/ RISK FACTORS Low intake of dietary fibre may be a risk factor for the development of acute anal fissures.[1] People with anal fissure often have raised resting anal canal pressures with anal spasm.[2,3] Men and women are equally affected. Up to 11% of women develop anal fissures after childbirth.[4]

PROGNOSIS Placebo controlled studies found that 70–90% of untreated "chronic" fissures did not heal during the study.[5,6]

Colonic diverticular disease

Search date June 2001

John Simpson and Robin Spiller

What are the effects of treatments?

LIKELY TO BE BENEFICIAL

Rifaximin (for uncomplicated diverticular disease)

One RCT has found that glucomannan plus oral rifaximin versus glucomannan plus placebo significantly increases the number of people with uncomplicated diverticular disease who are symptom free after 12 months' treatment.

UNKNOWN EFFECTIVENESS

Bran and ispaghula husk (for uncomplicated diverticular disease)

Two small RCTs found no consistent effect of bran or ispaghula husk versus placebo on symptom relief in uncomplicated diverticular disease.

Dietary fibre supplements (to prevent the complications of diverticular disease)

We found no RCTs of advice to consume a high fibre diet or of dietary fibre supplementation to prevent complications in people with diverticular disease.

Elective surgery (for uncomplicated diverticular disease) *New*

We found no RCTs in people with uncomplicated diverticular disease.

Lactulose (for uncomplicated diverticular disease)

One RCT found no significant difference with lactulose versus a high fibre diet in the number of people who considered themselves to be "much improved" (not defined) at 12 weeks.

Medical treatment (for acute diverticulitis)

We found no RCTs of medical treatment versus placebo. One RCT comparing different oral antibiotics found no significant difference in clinical cure in people with a clinical diagnosis of acute diverticulitis that did not need surgery.

Methylcellulose (for uncomplicated diverticular disease)

One small RCT found no significant difference with methylcellulose versus placebo in mean symptom score at 3 months.

Surgery (for acute diverticulitis)

We found no RCTs of surgery versus no surgery or versus medical treatment. One RCT comparing acute resection versus no acute resection (involving a transverse colostomy) of the sigmoid colon found no significant difference between treatments in mortality rates. A second RCT comparing primary versus secondary sigmoid colonic resection found no significant difference in mortality rates, although primary resection was associated with significantly lower rates of postoperative peritonitis and emergency re-operation.

DEFINITION Colonic diverticula are mucosal out pouchings through the large bowel wall. They are often accompanied by structural changes (elastosis of the taenia coli, muscular thickening, and mucosal folding). They are usually multiple and occur most frequently in the sigmoid colon.

INCIDENCE/ PREVALENCE In the UK, the incidence of diverticulosis❸ increases with age: about 5% of people are affected in their fifth decade of life and about 50% by their ninth decade.[1] Diverticulosis is common in developed countries, although there ▶

is a lower prevalence of diverticulosis in western vegetarians consuming a high roughage diet.[2] Diverticulosis is almost unknown in rural Africa and Asia.[3]

AETIOLOGY/
RISK FACTORS
There is an association between low fibre diets and diverticulosis of the colon.[3] Prospective observational studies have found that both physical activity and a high fibre diet are associated with a lower risk of developing diverticular disease🅖.[4,5] One case control study found an association between the ingestion of non-steroidal anti-inflammatory drugs and the development of severe diverticula complications including pericolic abscess, generalised peritonitis, bleeding, and fistula formation.[6] People in Japan, Singapore, and Thailand develop diverticula that affect predominantly the right side of the colon.[7]

PROGNOSIS
Symptoms will develop in 10–25% of people with diverticula at some point in their lives.[1] It is unclear why some people develop symptoms and some do not. Even after successful medical treatment of acute diverticulitis🅖 almost two thirds of people suffer recurrent pain in the lower abdomen.[8] Recurrent diverticulitis is observed in 7–35% of people with diverticular disease and once recovered from the initial attack the calculated yearly risk of suffering a further episode is 3%.[9] About half the recurrences occur within 1 year of the initial episode and 90% occur within 5 years.[10] Complications of diverticular disease (perforation, obstruction, haemorrhage, and fistula formation) are each seen in about 5% of people with colonic diverticula when followed up for between 10 and 30 years.[11] Intra-abdominal abscess formation may also occur.

Digestive system disorders

Colorectal cancer

Search date August 2001

Charles Maxwell-Armstrong and John Scholefield

What are the effects of treatments?

BENEFICIAL

Adjuvant chemotherapy

Two systematic reviews in people with colon cancer have found that adjuvant chemotherapy significantly reduces mortality after 5 years. Subsequent RCTs have found that this effect is limited to the subgroup of people with Dukes' C colon cancer●. One subsequent RCT in people with Dukes' B colon cancer found that adjuvant chemotherapy with high dose folinic acid versus low dose folinic acid had no significant effect on mortality or the number of tumour recurrences after 3 years.

TRADE OFF BETWEEN BENEFITS AND HARMS

Preoperative radiotherapy

One systematic review in people with rectal cancer has found that preoperative radiotherapy versus surgery alone significantly reduces the risk of local recurrence and mortality after 5 years. One RCT in people with Dukes' B or C rectal carcinoma comparing a short course of preoperative radiotherapy versus a longer course of postoperative radiotherapy found no significant difference in survival, but found that preoperative radiotherapy significantly reduced local tumour recurrence after 5 years (NNT 11). One systematic review has found that preoperative radiotherapy significantly increases postoperative morbidity.

UNKNOWN EFFECTIVENESS

Routine follow up

One systematic review and one subsequent RCT in people with colorectal cancer have found conflicting evidence on the effects of routine follow up.

Total mesorectal excision

We found no RCTs of total mesorectal excision in people with rectal cancer. Observational studies suggest that total mesorectal excision versus no mesorectal excision may reduce the rate of local recurrence after 1 year.

DEFINITION   Colorectal cancer is a malignant neoplasm arising from the lining (mucosa) of the large intestine (colon and rectum). Nearly two thirds of colorectal cancers occur in the rectum or sigmoid colon. Colorectal cancer may be categorised as Dukes' A, B, or C.

INCIDENCE/   Colorectal cancer is the third most common malignancy in the developed
PREVALENCE   world. It accounts for about 20 000 deaths each year in the UK and 60 000 deaths each year in the USA. Although the incidence of, and mortality from, colorectal cancer has changed little over the past 40 years, the incidence of the disease has fallen recently in both the UK and the USA.[1,2] In the UK, about a quarter of people with colorectal cancer present as emergencies with either intestinal obstruction or perforation.[3,4]

AETIOLOGY/   Colon cancer affects almost equal proportions of men and women, most
RISK FACTORS commonly between the ages of 60 and 80 years. Rectal cancer is more common in men.[1] The pathogenesis of colorectal cancer involves genetic and environmental factors. The most important environmental factor is probably diet.[5]   ▶

◀ **PROGNOSIS**   Overall 5 year survival is about 50% and has not changed over the past 40 years. Disease specific mortality in both USA and UK cancer registries is decreasing but the reasons for this are unclear.[1,2] Surgery is undertaken with curative intent in over 80% of people, but about half suffer recurrence.

Helicobacter pylori infection

Search date August 2001

Brendan Delaney, Paul Moayyedi and David Forman

What are the effects of treatments?

BENEFICIAL

H pylori eradication for healing and preventing recurrence of duodenal ulcer

Systematic reviews and one subsequent RCT have found that *H pylori* eradication increases the proportion of ulcers healed at 6 weeks and reduces 1 year recurrence. Meta-analysis of three RCTs has found that in people with a history of bleeding duodenal ulcers, eradication versus no eradication significantly reduces the risk of re-bleeding during the subsequent year (NNT 6).

H pylori eradication for healing and preventing recurrence of gastric ulcer

One systematic review has found that *H pylori* eradication heals 83% of gastric ulcers within 6 weeks of starting treatment and significantly reduces the risk of recurrence at 1 year (NNT 3).

LIKELY TO BE BENEFICIAL

H pylori eradication for non-ulcer dyspepsia

One systematic review has found that *H pylori* eradication versus placebo significantly reduces dyspeptic symptoms at 3–12 months (NNT 15).

H pylori eradication rather than endoscopy in people with uninvestigated dyspepsia not at risk of malignancy

One systematic review has found no significant difference in relief of dyspeptic symptoms with *H pylori* testing plus eradication versus endoscopy-guided management.

One week triple therapy (as good as 2 wk)

One systematic review found limited evidence from indirect comparisons of *H pylori* eradication therapy that 2 week regimens are no more effective than 1 week regimens at increasing *H pylori* eradication.

Three day quadruple therapy (as good as 1 wk triple therapy with fewer side effects)

One RCT found no significant difference in *H pylori* eradication with a 3 day quadruple regimen versus 1 week triple regimen❶, but found that people taking the 3 day quadruple regimen experienced significantly fewer days of adverse effects.

Triple therapy (versus dual therapy eradicate H pylori from more people)

We found no systematic review or RCTs about the effects of different eradication regimens on clinical outcomes. One systematic review has found that triple eradication regimens versus dual eradication regimens❶ eradicate *H pylori* from more people.

UNKNOWN EFFECTIVENESS

H pylori eradication for gastric B cell lymphoma

We found no RCTs of *H pylori* eradication in people with B cell gastric lymphoma❶. Observational studies found limited evidence that 60–93% of people with localised, low grade B cell lymphoma respond to *H pylori* eradication, and avoid the need for radical surgery, radiotherapy, or chemotherapy. ▶

◀ ### *H pylori* eradication for prevention of gastric cancer (adenocarcinoma)

We found consistent evidence from observational studies of an association between *H pylori* infection and increased risk of distal gastric adenocarcinoma of the stomach. We found no RCTs about the effects of *H pylori* eradication in preventing gastric cancer. One RCT in people with gastric atrophy or intestinal metaplasia found that *H pylori* eradication versus no eradication significantly increased the regression of high risk lesions.

H pylori eradication rather than acid suppression for uninvestigated dyspepsia

We found no RCTs of initial *H pylori* eradication versus empirical acid suppression treatment.

One triple therapy versus another

We found no systematic review or RCTs about the effects of different eradication regimens on clinical outcomes. One systematic review found that clarithromycin 500 mg twice daily versus clarithromycin 250 mg twice daily in combination with a proton pump inhibitor⬡ and amoxicillin significantly increased *H pylori* eradication (NNT 11), but found no significant difference with clarithromycin 500 mg twice daily versus clarithromycin 250 mg twice daily in combination with a proton pump inhibitor proton pump inhibitor and metronidazole. Another systematic review found that a triple regimen⬡ containing ranitidine bismuth⬡ plus clarithromycin plus metronidazole versus a triple regimen containing ranitidine bismuth plus clarithromycin plus amoxicillin significantly increased eradication at 5–7 days. Two systematic reviews found limited evidence from indirect comparisons of RCTs that triple regimens containing omeprazole and two antibiotics give consistently high eradication rates.

UNLIKELY TO BE BENEFICIAL

H pylori eradication in people with gastro-oesophageal reflux disease

One RCT in people with gastro-oesophageal reflux disease found no significant difference with *H pylori* eradication versus placebo in symptomatic relapse.

DEFINITION   *H pylori* is a Gram negative flagellated spiral organism found in the stomach, which is predominantly acquired in childhood. The organism is associated with a lifelong chronic gastritis and may cause other gastroduodenal disorders.

INCIDENCE/   Prevalence rates vary with birth cohort and social class in the developed
PREVALENCE   world. Prevalence rates of infection in most developed countries tend to be much higher (50–80%) in those born prior to 1950, in comparison to rates (< 20%) in those born more recently. In many developing countries the infection has a high prevalence (80–95%) irrespective of the period of birth.[1] Adult prevalence is believed to represent the persistence of a historically higher rate of infection acquired in childhood, rather than increasing acquisition of infection during life.

AETIOLOGY/   Overcrowded conditions associated with childhood poverty lead to increased
RISK FACTORS   transmission and higher prevalence rates. Adult re-infection rates are low — less than 1% a year.[1]

PROGNOSIS   *H pylori* infection is believed to be causally related to the development of duodenal and gastric ulceration, gastric B cell lymphoma, and distal gastric cancer. About 15% of people infected with *H pylori* will develop a peptic ulcer, and 1% of people will develop gastric cancer during their lifetime.[2] *H pylori* infection is not associated with a specific type of dyspeptic symptom.

Stomach cancer

Search date September 2001

Peter McCulloch

What are the effects of treatments?

LIKELY TO BE BENEFICIAL

Complete surgical resection

RCTs of complete surgical excision are unlikely to be conducted. Observational studies and multivariate analysis of RCTs have found a strong association between survival and complete excision of the primary tumour.

Subtotal gastrectomy (as effective as total gastrectomy) for resectable distal tumours

RCTs in people with primary tumours in the distal stomach have found no significant difference with total versus subtotal gastrectomy in 5 year survival or postoperative mortality.

UNKNOWN EFFECTIVENESS

Adjuvant chemotherapy

Systematic reviews and subsequent RCTs have found limited evidence that adjuvant chemotherapy versus surgery alone significantly increases survival. One systematic review and one subsequent RCT in people from Japan have found conflicting results on the effects of adjuvant chemotherapy versus surgery alone on survival. Two RCTs found that adjuvant chemotherapy versus surgery alone significantly increased postoperative complications. The size of any benefit remains uncertain, and many recent adjuvant chemotherapy regimens have not been evaluated fully in RCTs.

Conservative (as effective as radical) lymphadenectomy

Two RCTs comparing conservative versus radical lymphadenectomy found no significant difference in 5 year survival rates. One RCT found that radical versus conservative lymphadenectomy significantly increased perioperative mortality.

LIKELY TO BE INEFFECTIVE OR HARMFUL

Removal of adjacent organs

Retrospective analyses of observational studies and RCTs in people with stomach cancer have found that removal of additional organs (spleen and distal pancreas) versus no organ removal increased morbidity and mortality.

DEFINITION
Stomach cancer is usually an adenocarcinoma arising in the stomach and includes tumours arising at or just below the gastro-oesophageal junction (type II and III junctional tumours). Tumours are staged according to degree of invasion and spread🅣.

INCIDENCE/ PREVALENCE
The incidence of stomach cancer varies among countries and by sex (incidence per 100 000 population per year in Japanese men is about 80, Japanese women 30, British men 18, British women 10, white American men 11, white American women 7).[1] Incidence has declined dramatically in North America, Australia, and New Zealand since 1930, but the decline in Europe has been slower.[2] In the USA, stomach cancer remains relatively common among particular ethnic groups, especially Japanese Americans and some Hispanic groups. The incidence of cancer of the proximal stomach and gastro-oesophageal junction is rising rapidly in most Western countries; the reasons for this are poorly understood.[3,4]

▶

AETIOLOGY/
RISK FACTORS
Distal stomach cancer is strongly associated with lifelong infection with *Helicobacter pylori* and poor dietary intake of antioxidant vitamins (A, C, and E).[5,6] In Western Europe and North America, distal stomach cancer is associated with relative socioeconomic deprivation. Proximal stomach cancer is strongly associated with smoking (OR about 4),[7] and is probably associated with gastro-oesophageal reflux, obesity, high fat intake, and medium to high socioeconomic status.

PROGNOSIS
Invasive stomach cancer (stages T_2–T_4) is fatal without surgery. Mean survival without treatment is less than 6 months from diagnosis.[8,9] Intramucosal or submucosal cancer (stage T_1) may progress slowly to invasive cancer over several years.[10] In the USA, over 50% of people recently diagnosed with stomach cancer have regional lymph node metastasis or involvement of adjacent organs. The prognosis after macroscopically and microscopically complete resection (R0) is related strongly to disease stage❻, particularly penetration of the serosa (stage T_3) and lymph node involvement. Five year survival rates range from over 90% in intramucosal cancer to about 20% in people with stage T_3N_2 disease❶. In Japan, the 5 year survival rate for people with advanced disease is reported to be about 50%, but the explanation for the difference remains unclear. Comparisons between Japanese and Western practice are confounded by factors such as age, fitness, and disease stage, as well as by tumour location, because many Western series include gastro-oesophageal junction adenocarcinoma with a much lower survival after surgery.

Chronic suppurative otitis media

Search date November 2001

Jose Acuin

What are the effects of treatments in adults? *New*

LIKELY TO BE BENEFICIAL

Topical antibiotics
RCTs found limited evidence that topical quinolone antibiotics versus placebo improved otoscopic appearances. RCTs found no clear evidence of significant differences between topical antibiotics. Case studies have associated topical non-quinolone antibiotics with ototoxicity, affecting mainly vestibular function, although RCTs have found few adverse events associated with short term use.

UNKNOWN EFFECTIVENESS

Ear cleansing
We found no RCTs of ear cleansing (aural toilet) versus no treatment.

Oral and intravenous antibiotics
RCTs found insufficient evidence about the effects of oral and intravenous antibiotics versus placebo or no treatment. One systematic review found that oral antibiotics were significantly less effective than topical antibiotics in reducing otoscopic features of chronic suppurative otitis media. We found no evidence about long term treatment.

Topical antiseptics
We found no RCTs comparing topical antiseptics versus placebo or no treatment. One RCT compared topical antiseptics plus ear cleansing under microscopic control versus topical antibiotics alone versus oral antibiotics. It found no significant difference in the rate of persistent activity on otoscopy. However, the RCT was too small to exclude a clinically important difference.

Topical steroids
We found no RCTs comparing topical steroids versus placebo or no treatment.

Tympanoplasty with or without mastoidectomy
We found no RCTs comparing tympanoplasty❻ with or without mastoidectomy❻ versus no surgery for chronic suppurative otitis media without cholesteatoma❻.

What are the effects of treatments in children? *New*

UNKNOWN EFFECTIVENESS

Ear cleansing
One systematic review found no significant difference in persistent otorrhoea or tympanic perforations with a simple form of ear cleansing versus no ear cleansing.

Oral and intravenous antibiotics
RCTs found insufficient evidence about the effects of systemic antibiotics in children with chronic suppurative otitis media.

Topical antibiotics
We found no RCTs comparing topical antibiotics versus placebo. One small and brief RCT found no significant difference in the proportion of ears with unchanged otorrohoea on otoscopy with a topical antibiotic plus steroid mixture ▶

◄ plus ear cleansing versus ear cleansing alone. However, the confidence interval was wide and a clinically important difference cannot be excluded.

Topical antiseptics

RCTs found no significant reduction in otorrhoea with topical antiseptics versus placebo after 2 weeks. One RCT found no significant difference in otorrhoea with topical antiseptics versus topical antibiotic plus steroid. However, the RCTs were too small to exclude a clinically important effect.

Topical steroids

We found no RCTs comparing topical steroids versus placebo.

Tympanoplasty with or without mastoidectomy

We found no RCTs comparing tympanoplasty with or without mastoidectomy versus no surgery for chronic suppurative otitis media without cholesteatoma.

DEFINITION   Chronic suppurative otitis media is a persistent inflammation of the middle ear or mastoid cavity. Synonyms include "chronic otitis media (without effusion)", chronic mastoiditis, and chronic tympanomastoiditis. Chronic suppurative otitis media is characterised by recurrent or persistent ear discharge (otorrhoea) over 2–6 weeks through a perforation of the tympanic membrane. Typical findings also include thickened granular middle ear mucosa, mucosal polyps, and cholesteatoma within the middle ear. Chronic suppurative otitis media is differentiated from chronic otitis media with effusion, in which there is an intact tympanic membrane with fluid in the middle ear but no active infection. Chronic suppurative otitis media does not include chronic perforations of the eardrum, which are dry, or only occasionally discharge, and have no signs of active infection.

INCIDENCE/   The worldwide prevalence of chronic suppurative otitis media is 65–330
PREVALENCE   million people. Between 39–200 million (60%) suffer from significant hearing impairment. Otitis media has been estimated to cause 28 000 deaths and loss of over 2 million Disability Adjusted Life Years (DALYs)**G** in 2000,[1] 94% of which are in developing countries. Most of these deaths are presumably due to chronic suppurative otitis media because acute otitis media is a self limiting infection**O**.[2–33]

AETIOLOGY/   Chronic suppurative otitis media is assumed to be a complication after an
RISK FACTORS initial episode of acute otitis media, but the risk factors for development of chronic suppurative otitis media are not clear. Frequent upper respiratory tract infections and poor socioeconomic conditions (overcrowded housing,[34] hygiene, and nutrition) may be related to the development of chronic suppurative otitis media.[35,36] Improvement of housing, hygiene and nutrition in Maori children was associated with a halving of the prevalence of chronic suppurative otitis media between 1978 and 1987.[37] For risk factors (see acute otitis media, p 34).

PROGNOSIS   Most children with chronic suppurative otitis media have mild to moderate hearing impairment (about 26–60 dB increase in hearing thresholds) based on surveys among children in Africa, Brazil,[38] India,[39] and Sierra Leone,[40] and among the general population in Thailand.[41] In many developing countries chronic suppurative otitis media represents the most frequent cause of moderate hearing losses (40–60 dB).[42] Persistent hearing loss during the first 2 years of life may increase learning disabilities and poor scholastic performance.[43] Spread of infection may lead to life threatening complications such as intracranial infections and acute mastoiditis.[44] The frequency of serious complications has fallen 10-fold to about 0.24% in Thailand and 1.8% in Africa. This is believed to be associated with increased use of antibiotic treatment, tympanoplasty**G**, and mastoidectomy.[45–47] ►

Chronic suppurative otitis media

Cholesteatoma is another serious complication that has been found in a variable proportion of people with chronic suppurative otitis media (range 0–60%).[48–51] In the West, the incidence of cholesteatoma is low (in 1993 in Finland the age standardised incidence of cholesteatoma was 8 new cases per 100 000 population/year).[52]

What are the effects of treatments for acute attacks?

UNKNOWN EFFECTIVENESS

Anticholinergics; benzodiazepines; betahistine
We found no RCTs on the effects of these interventions in treating acute attacks.

What are the effects of prophylactic interventions?

UNKNOWN EFFECTIVENESS

Betahistine (for vertigo or tinnitus)
RCTs found conflicting evidence on the effects of betahistine versus placebo on the frequency and severity of attacks of vertigo, tinnitus, and on aural fullness.

Dietary modification; psychological support; systemic aminoglycosides
We found no RCTs on the effects of these interventions in preventing attacks of vertigo or tinnitus.

Diuretics
One RCT found insufficient evidence on the effects of diuretics versus placebo.

Trimetazidine
We found no RCTs comparing trimetazidine versus placebo. RCTs in people with definite or possible Menière's disease found no significant difference with trimetazidine versus betahistine in hearing or tinnitus, and found conflicting evidence on the effects of trimetazidine versus betahistine on vertigo.

UNLIKELY TO BE BENEFICIAL

Betahistine (for hearing loss)
Four RCTs found no significant difference with betahistine versus placebo in hearing as assessed by changes in pure tone audiograms.

LIKELY TO BE INEFFECTIVE OR HARMFUL

Lithium
Small crossover RCTs in people with possible Menière's disease found no difference with lithium versus placebo in vertigo, tinnitus, aural fullness, or hearing, and found that lithium was associated with tremor, thirst, and polyuria.

DEFINITION   Menière's disease is characterised by recurrent episodes of spontaneous rotational vertigo and sensorineural hearing loss with tinnitus and a feeling of fullness or pressure in the ear. It may be unilateral or bilateral. Acute episodes may occur in clusters of about 6–11 a year, although remission may last several months.[1] The diagnosis is made clinically.[2] It is important to distinguish Menière's disease from other types of vertigo that might occur independently with hearing loss and tinnitus, and respond differently to treatment (e.g. benign positional vertigo, acute labyrinthitis). Strict diagnostic criteria help. In this review we applied the classification of the American Academy of Otolaryngology–Head and Neck Surgery (AAO–HNS) to RCTs to indicate the diagnostic rigour used in RCTs❶.   ▶

INCIDENCE/ Menière's disease is most common between 40–60 years of age, although
PREVALENCE younger people can be affected.[6,7] In Europe, the incidence is about
50–200/100 000 a year. A survey of general practitioner records of
27 365 people in the UK found an incidence of 43 affected people in a
1 year period (157/100 000).[8] Diagnostic criteria were not defined in this
survey. A survey of over 8 million people in Sweden found an incidence of
46/100 000 a year with diagnosis strictly based on the triad of vertigo,
hearing loss, and tinnitus.[9] From smaller studies, the incidence appears
lower in Uganda[10] and higher in Japan (350/100 000 based on a national
survey of hospital attendances during a single wk).[7]

AETIOLOGY/ Menière's disease is associated with endolymphatic hydrops (raised endol-
RISK FACTORS ymph pressure in the membranous labyrinth of the inner ear),[11] but a causal
relationship between Menière's disease and endolymphatic hydrops
remains unproven.[12] Specific disorders associated with hydrops (such as
temporal bone fracture, syphilis, hypothyroidism, Cogan's syndrome🅖, and
Mondini dysplasia🅖 can produce similar symptoms to Menière's disease.

PROGNOSIS Menière's disease is progressive, but fluctuates unpredictably. It is difficult to
distinguish natural resolution from the effects of treatment. Significant
improvement of vertigo is usually seen in the placebo arm of RCTs.[13,14]
Acute attacks of vertigo often increase in frequency during the first few years
after presentation then decrease in frequency in association with sustained
deterioration in hearing.[6] In most people, vertiginous episodes eventually
cease completely.[15] In one 20 year cohort study in 34 people, 28 (82%)
people had at least moderate hearing loss (mean pure tone hearing loss
> 50 dB)[1] and 16 (47%) developed bilateral disease. Symptoms other than
hearing loss improve in 60–80% of people, irrespective of treatment.[16]

Middle ear pain and trauma during air travel

Search date March 2002

Simon Janvrin

What are the effects of preventive interventions?

LIKELY TO BE BENEFICIAL

Oral decongestants in adults

Two RCTs found limited evidence that oral pseudoephedrine versus placebo significantly reduced ear pain and hearing loss during air travel.

UNKNOWN EFFECTIVENESS

Oral decongestants in children

One small RCT found no significant difference with oral pseudoephedrine versus placebo in ear pain at take off or landing.

Topical nasal decongestants in adults

One small RCT found insufficient evidence about the effects of topical nasal decongestants versus placebo during air travel.

DEFINITION The effects of air travel on the middle ear can include tympanic membrane pain, vertigo, hearing loss, and perforation.

INCIDENCE/ The prevalence of symptoms depends on the altitude, type of aircraft, and
PREVALENCE characteristics of the passengers. One point prevalence study found that 20% of adult and 40% of child passengers had negative pressure in the middle ear after flight, and that 10% of adults and 22% of children had auroscopic evidence of damage to the tympanic membrane.[1] We found no data on the incidence of perforation, which seems to be extremely rare in commercial passengers.

AETIOLOGY/ During aircraft descent, the pressure in the middle ear drops relative to that
RISK FACTORS in the ear canal. A narrow, inflamed, or poorly functioning Eustachian tube impedes the necessary influx of air. As the pressure difference between the middle and outer ear increases, the tympanic membrane is pulled inward.

PROGNOSIS In most people, symptoms resolve spontaneously. Experience in military aviation shows that most ear drum perforations will heal spontaneously.[2]

Otitis media with effusion

Search date July 2001

Ian Williamson

What are the effects of preventive interventions?

UNKNOWN EFFECTIVENESS

Change in modifiable risk factors

We found no RCTs on the effects of avoiding risk factors such as passive smoking and bottle feeding in preventing otitis media with effusion.

What are the effects of treatments?

LIKELY TO BE BENEFICIAL

Autoinflation with nasal balloon (short term benefit)

One systematic review has found that autoinflation with a nasal balloon versus no treatment significantly improves effusion. Some children may find autoinflation difficult. We found insufficient evidence on the effects of other methods of autoinflation.

TRADE OFF BETWEEN BENEFITS AND HARMS

Antimicrobial drugs (short term benefit)

One systematic review has found that antimicrobial drugs versus placebo or no treatment significantly increase resolution of effusion after 1 month (NNT 7). Adverse effects (mainly nausea, vomiting, and diarrhoea) were reported in 2–32% of children.

UNKNOWN EFFECTIVENESS

Grommets with or without adenoidectomy; other autoinflation devices; tonsillectomy; topical steroids

We found insufficient evidence on the effects of these interventions.

UNLIKELY TO BE BENEFICIAL

Mucolytics

One systematic review has found no significant difference between 1–3 month courses of mucolytics versus placebo or no treatment in resolution of effusion.

LIKELY TO BE INEFFECTIVE OR HARMFUL

Antihistamines plus oral decongestants

One systematic review has found no significant difference between antihistamines plus oral decongestants versus placebo in clearance of effusion after 4 weeks.

Antimicrobials (no evidence of long term benefit)

One systematic review has found no significant difference between antimicrobial drugs versus placebo in the presence of effusion at 6 weeks to 11 months. Adverse effects were frequent (see short term benefit of antimicrobial drugs above).

Oral steroids

One systematic review has found no significant difference between oral steroids versus placebo in clearance of effusion after 2 weeks. Oral steroids may cause behavioural changes, increased appetite, and weight gain. ▶

DEFINITION Otitis media with effusion, or "glue ear", is serous or mucoid but not mucopurulent fluid in the middle ear. Children usually present with hearing loss and speech problems. In contrast to those with acute otitis media (see topic, p 34), children with otitis media with effusion do not suffer from acute ear pain, fever, or malaise. Hearing loss is usually mild and often identified when parents express concern regarding their child's behaviour, school performance, or language development.

INCIDENCE/ PREVALENCE At any time, 5% of children aged 2–4 years have persistent (at least 3 months) bilateral hearing loss associated with otitis media with effusion. The prevalence declines considerably beyond age 6 years.[1] About 80% of children aged 10 years have been affected by otitis media with effusion at some time in the past. Otitis media with effusion is the most common reason for referral for surgery in children in the UK. Middle ear effusions also occur infrequently in adults after upper respiratory tract infection or after air travel.

AETIOLOGY/ RISK FACTORS Contributory factors include upper respiratory tract infection and narrow upper respiratory airways. Prospective case control studies have identified risk factors, including age 6 years or younger at first onset, daycare centre attendance, high number of siblings, low socioeconomic group, frequent upper respiratory tract infection, bottle feeding, and household smoking.[2,3] Most factors are associated with about twice the risk of developing otitis media with effusion.[4]

PROGNOSIS In 5% of preschool children, otitis media with effusion (identified by tympanometric screening) persists for at least 1 year.[5,6] One large cohort study (534 children) found that middle ear disease increased reported hearing difficulty at age 5 years (OR 1.44, 95% CI 1.18 to 1.76) and was associated with delayed language development in children up to age 10 years.[7]

Recurrent tonsillitis

Search date December 2001

William McKerrow

What are the effects of tonsillectomy for severe tonsillitis in children and adults?

Tonsillectomy versus antibiotics

We found no RCTs evaluating tonsillectomy in adults. One RCT in children with severe tonsillitis found limited evidence that tonsillectomy versus antibiotics may reduce throat infections in the first 2 years after treatment, but found no significant difference at 3 years.

DEFINITION Tonsillitis is infection of the parenchyma of the palatine tonsils. Recurrent severe tonsillitis results in significant morbidity including time lost from school or work. The definition of severe recurrent tonsillitis is arbitrary, but criteria used recently as a measure of severity were five or more episodes of true tonsillitis per year, symptoms for at least a year, and episodes that are disabling and prevent normal functioning.[1]

INCIDENCE/ Recurrent sore throat has an incidence in general practice in the UK
PREVALENCE of 100/1000 population a year.[2] Acute tonsillitis is more common in childhood.

AETIOLOGY/ Common bacterial pathogens include β haemolytic and other streptococci.
RISK FACTORS Bacteria are cultured successfully only from a minority of people with tonsillitis. The role of viruses is uncertain.

PROGNOSIS We found no good data on the natural history of tonsillitis or recurrent sore throat in children or adults. Participants in RCTs who were randomised to medical treatment (courses of antibiotics as required) have shown a tendency towards improvement over time.[3,4]

Search date May 2001

Angus Waddell and Richard Canter

What are the effects of treatments for chronic tinnitus?

UNKNOWN EFFECTIVENESS

Acupuncture; antiepileptics; baclofen; benzodiazepines; cinnarizine; electromagnetic stimulation; hypnosis; low power laser; nicotinamide; tinnitus masking devices; zinc

We found insufficient evidence about the effects of these interventions.

Psychotherapy

We found limited evidence from two systematic reviews that psychotherapy may improve symptom scores of people with chronic tinnitus, but weakness of methods used in the reviews and in the studies they included, means that the effects of psychotherapy remain unclear.

Tricyclic antidepressants

We found no evidence about the effects of tricyclic antidepressants in people with chronic tinnitus without depressive symptoms. Systematic reviews found limited evidence in people with depression and tinnitus that tricyclic antidepressants versus placebo improved tinnitus related disability, audiometric tinnitus loudness matching, and symptoms of depression. The reviews found no significant difference in tinnitus severity.

LIKELY TO BE INEFFECTIVE OR HARMFUL

Tocainide

One RCT found no significant difference with tocainide versus placebo in improving symptoms, but found evidence that tocainide caused significantly more adverse effects over 30 days (NNH 2).

DEFINITION   In this review, tinnitus is the perception of sound that does not arise either from the external environment or from the production of a theoretically externally audible sound within the body (this excludes vascular sounds and bruits), or from auditory hallucinations caused by mental illness. Tinnitus can occur as an isolated symptom or in association with hearing loss, Meniére's disease, or with other conditions. This review concerns the management of chronic tinnitus, where tinnitus is the only, or the major, symptom in any individual.

INCIDENCE/   Up to 14% of the general population in industrialised countries are mildly
PREVALENCE   affected by chronic tinnitus, but fewer than 2% are severely affected.[1]

AETIOLOGY/   Tinnitus is associated with hearing loss in people with presbyacusis, noise-
RISK FACTORS   induced hearing loss, and Meniére's disease. In people with toxicity from aspirin or quinine, tinnitus can occur while hearing thresholds remain normal. Tinnitus is associated with depression[2] but it is unclear what proportion of people with tinnitus have depression secondary to the effects of the tinnitus, or the proportion who develop tinnitus as a manifestation of depression.   ▶

Ear, nose, and throat disorders

PROGNOSIS Tinnitus may have an insidious onset, with a long delay before clinical presentation. It may persist for many years or decades, particularly when associated with a sensorineural hearing loss. In Ménière's disease, tinnitus can fluctuate. Troublesome tinnitus may cause disruption of sleep patterns, an inability to concentrate, and depression.

What are the effects of methods to remove symptomatic ear wax?

TRADE OFF BETWEEN BENEFITS AND HARMS

Ear syringing

There is consensus that ear syringing is effective but we found no RCTs comparing ear syringing versus no treatment or versus alternative treatment. A survey found that 38% of 274 general practitioners performing ear syringing reported complications, including otitis externa, perforation of the tympanic membrane, damage to the skin of the external canal, tinnitus, pain, and vertigo.

UNKNOWN EFFECTIVENESS

Manual removal

We found no RCTs about mechanical methods of removing ear wax.

Wax softeners

One small RCT found that wax softeners were better than no treatment at completely removing ear wax without syringing (NNT 5 ears). Five RCTs found no consistent evidence that any one type of wax softener was superior to the others. RCTs found insufficient evidence to assess the effects of wax softeners prior to syringing.

DEFINITION   Ear wax is normal and becomes a problem only if it produces deafness, pain, or other aural symptoms. Ear wax may also need to be removed if it prevents inspection of the ear drum. The term "impacted"⒢ is used in different ways and can merely imply the co-existence of wax obscuring the ear drum with symptoms in that ear.[1,2]

INCIDENCE/   We found four surveys of the prevalence of impacted wax⒯.[3–6] The
PREVALENCE   prevalence was higher in men than in women, in the elderly than in the young, and in people with intellectual impairment.[7] One survey found that 289 Scottish general practitioners each saw an average of nine people a month requesting removal of ear wax.[1]

AETIOLOGY/   Factors that prevent the normal extrusion of wax from the ear canal (e.g.
RISK FACTORS   wearing a hearing aid, using cotton buds) increase the chance of ear wax accumulating.

PROGNOSIS   Most ear wax emerges from the external canal spontaneously. Without impaction or adherence to the drum, there is likely to be minimal, if any, hearing loss. One survey of 21 unselected outpatients with completely obstructing wax⒢ found that the average improvement in hearing following syringing was 5.5 dB (95% CI 0.6 to 10.5 dB).[1]

Cardiovascular disease in diabetes

Search date August 2001

Ronald Sigal, Hilary Meggison and Janine Malcolm

What are the effects of treatments?

BENEFICIAL

Antihypertensive treatment (better than placebo)

One RCT in people aged over 55 with diabetes and hypertension has found that nitrendipine or enalapril (with or without hydrochlorothiazide) versus placebo significantly reduces the risk of a first cardiovascular event within 2 years (NNT 13), but does not significantly reduce overall mortality. Another RCT in people with diabetes aged over 55 with additional cardiac risk factors, previously diagnosed coronary vascular disease, or both, has found that the angiotensin converting enzyme (ACE) inhibitor ramipril versus placebo significantly reduces major cardiovascular events (NNT 22) and overall mortality (NNT 32) within 4.5 years.

Antiplatelet therapy

One RCT has found that aspirin versus placebo significantly reduces the risk of first acute myocardial infarction🅖 within 5 years (NNT 16). Another RCT in people with diabetes and prior cardiovascular disease found no significant difference with aspirin versus placebo in the risk of acute myocardial infarction or overall mortality within 5 years. Subgroup analysis in one RCT of people presenting with unstable angina or acute myocardial infarction without ST elevation found that the addition of a glycoprotein IIb/IIIa inhibitor (tirofiban) to heparin significantly reduced the risk of death or myocardial infarction at 180 days (NNT 13).

Coronary artery bypass graft (CABG) versus percutaneous transluminal coronary angioplasty (PTCA)

One large RCT in people with diabetes and multivessel coronary artery disease has found that coronary artery bypass graft (CABG) versus percutaneous transluminal coronary angioplasty (PTCA) significantly reduces mortality or myocardial infarction within 8 years (NNT 7). Another RCT found a non-significant reduction in mortality with CABG versus PTCA at 4 years.

Lipid regulating agents (statins and fibrates)

RCTs in people with diabetes and dyslipidaemia with and without prior cardio-vascular disease have found that statins or fibrates versus placebo significantly reduce the risk of acute myocardial infarction.

Lower target blood pressures

Large RCTs in people with diabetes and hypertension have found that tighter control of blood pressure with target diastolic blood pressures of less than or equal to 80 mmHg reduces the risk of major cardiovascular events.

Stent plus glycoprotein IIb/IIIa inhibitors in people undergoing PTCA

RCTs in people with diabetes undergoing PTCA have found that the combination of stent and a glycoprotein IIb/IIIa inhibitor (abciximab) significantly reduces restenosis rates and serious morbidity.

▶

◄ LIKELY TO BE BENEFICIAL

Angiotensin converting enzyme (ACE) inhibitor versus calcium channel blocker (as initial treatment in hypertension)

One systematic review in people with type 2 diabetes has found that ACE inhibitors versus calcium channel blockers as initial treatment for hypertension significantly reduce cardiovascular events (NNT 13).

Blood glucose control

RCTs found that glucose lowering with insulin, sulphonylureas, or metformin may reduce the risk of first acute myocardial infaction. One large RCT in people with a previous myocardial infarction found that intensive versus standard insulin treatment significantly reduced mortality at 3.4 years (NNT 9).

Smoking cessation

We found no RCTs on promotion of smoking cessation. Observational evidence and extrapolation from people without diabetes suggest that promotion of smoking cessation is likely to reduce cardiovascular events.

UNKNOWN EFFECTIVENESS

ACE inhibitor versus β blockers (as initial treatment in hypertension)

One large RCT found no significant difference with the ACE inhibitor captopril versus the β blocker atenolol in the number of cardiovascular events over about 8 years.

PTCA versus thrombolysis

One RCT in people with diabetes and prior acute myocardial infarction found that PTCA versus thrombolytic therapy reduced mortality and cardiovascular events at 30 days, but the difference was not significant.

Screening for high cardiovascular risk

We found no RCTs on screening people with diabetes for cardiovascular risk.

DEFINITION   **Diabetes mellitus:** See definition under glycaemic control in diabetes, p 97. **Cardiovascular disease:** Atherosclerotic disease of the heart and/or the coronary, cerebral, or peripheral vessels leading to clinical events such as acute myocardial infarction, congestive heart failure, sudden cardiac death, stroke, gangrene, and/or need for revascularisation procedures.

INCIDENCE/   Diabetes mellitus is a major risk factor for cardiovascular disease. In the
PREVALENCE   USA, 60–75% of people with diabetes die from cardiovascular causes.[1] The annual incidence of cardiovascular disease is increased in people with diabetes (men, RR 2–3; women, RR 3–4 adjusted for age and other cardiovascular risk factors).[2] About 45% of middle aged and older white people with diabetes have evidence of coronary artery disease, compared with about 25% of people without diabetes in the same populations.[2] In a Finnish population based cohort study (1059 people with diabetes and 1373 people without diabetes, aged 45–64 years), the 7 year risk of acute myocardial infarction was as high in adults with diabetes without previous cardiac disease (20.2 per 100 person years) as it was in people without diabetes with previous cardiac disease (18.8 per 100 person years).[3]

AETIOLOGY/   Conventional risk factors for cardiovascular disease contribute to increasing
RISK FACTORS the relative risk of cardiovascular disease in people with diabetes to about the same extent as in those without diabetes (see aetiology under primary prevention, p 17). One prospective cohort study (164 women and 235 men with diabetes, mean age 65 years; 437 women and 1099 men without diabetes, mean age 61 years followed for mortality for a mean 3.7 years following acute myocardial infarction) found that more people with diabetes ▶

died compared with people without diabetes (116/399 [29%] v 204/1536 [13%]; RR 2.2, 95% CI 1.8 to 2.7).[4] It also found that the mortality risk after myocardial infarction associated with diabetes was higher for women than for men (adjusted HR 2.7, 95% CI 1.8 to 4.2 for women v 1.3, 95% CI 1 to 1.8 for men). Physical inactivity is a significant risk factor for cardiovascular events in both men and women. One cohort study of women with diabetes found that participation in little (< 1 h/wk) or no physical activity compared with physical activity for at least 7 hours a week was associated with doubling of the risk of a cardiovascular event.[5] Another cohort study (1263 men with diabetes, mean follow up 12 years) found that low baseline cardiorespiratory fitness compared with moderate or high fitness increased overall mortality (RR 2.9, 95% CI 2.1 to 3.6); and overall mortality was higher in those reporting no recreational exercise in the previous 3 months compared with those reporting any recreational physical activity in the same period (RR 1.8, 95% CI 1.3 to 2.5).[6] The absolute risk of cardiovascular disease is almost the same in women as in men with diabetes. Diabetes specific cardiovascular risk factors include the duration of diabetes during adulthood (the years of exposure to diabetes before age 20 add little to risk of cardiovascular disease); raised blood glucose concentrations (reflected in fasting blood glucose or HbA1c🔍; and any degree of microalbuminuria (albuminuria 30–299 mg/24 h).[7] People with diabetes and microalbuminuria have a higher risk of coronary morbidity and mortality than people with normal levels of urinary albumin and a similar duration of diabetes (RR 2–3).[8,9] Clinical proteinuria increases the risk of major cardiac events in type 2 diabetes (RR 3),[10] and in type 1 diabetes (RR 9),[7,11,12] compared with individuals with the same type of diabetes having normal albumin excretion. An epidemiological analysis of people with diabetes enrolled in the Heart Outcomes Prevention Evaluation (HOPE) clinical trial (3498 people with diabetes and at least 1 other cardiovascular risk factor, age > 55 years, of whom 1140 [32%] had microalbuminuria at baseline, 5 years' follow up) found higher risk for major cardiovascular events in for those with microalbuminuria (albumin:creatinine [ACR] ratio ≥ 2.0 mg/mmol) compared with those without microalbuminuria (adjusted RR 1.97, 95% CI 1.68 to 2.31); and for all cause mortality RR 2.15, 95% CI 1.78 to 2.60). It also found an association between ACR and the risk of major cardiovascular events (ACR 0.22 to 0.57 mg/mmol: RR 0.85, 95% CI 0.63 to 1.14; ACR 0.58 to 1.62 mg/mmol: RR 1.11, 95% CI 0.86 to 1.43); ACR 1.62 to 1.99 mg/mmol: RR 1.89, 95% CI 1.52 to 2.36).[13]

PROGNOSIS Diabetes mellitus increases the risk of mortality or serious morbidity after a coronary event (RR 1.5–3).[2,3,14,15] This excess risk is partly accounted for by increased prevalence of other cardiovascular risk factors in people with diabetes. A systematic review found that, in people with diabetes admitted to hospital for acute myocardial infarction, "stress hyperglycaemia" versus lower blood glucose levels was associated with increased mortality in hospital (RR 1.7, 95% CI 1.2 to 2.4).[16] One large prospective cohort study (91 285 men aged 40 to 84, 5 years' follow up) found higher all-cause and coronary heart disease (CHD) mortality in men with diabetes versus men without coronary artery disease or diabetes (age adjusted RR 3.3, 95% CI 2.6 to 4.1 in men with diabetes and without coronary artery disease v RR 2.3%, 95% CI 2.0 to 2.6 in healthy people; RR 5.6, 95% CI 4.9 to 6.3 in men with coronary artery disease but without diabetes v RR 2.2%, 95% CI 2.0 to 2.4 in healthy people; RR 12.0, 95% CI 9.9 to 14.6 in men with both risk factors v RR 4.7%, 95% CI 4.0 to 5.4 in healthy people). Multivariate analysis did not materially alter these associations. These findings support previous studies. Diabetes mellitus alone is associated with a twofold increase in risk for all cause death, a threefold increase in risk of death from CHD and, in people with pre-existing CHD, a 12-fold increase in risk of death from CHD compared with people with neither risk factor.[17]

Foot ulcers and amputations in diabetes

Search date September 2001

Hertzel Gerstein and Dereck Hunt

What are the effects of preventive interventions?

BENEFICIAL

Screening and referral to foot care clinics (reduces major amputations in those at high risk)

One RCT identified by a systemic review has found that a diabetes screening and protection programme (involving referral to a foot clinic) versus usual care significantly reduces the risk of major amputation after 2 years (NNT 91).

UNKNOWN EFFECTIVENESS

Education (ulcer recurrence and major amputation)

We found no RCTs on the effects of education on prevention of diabetic foot complications. One non-randomised trial found that specific foot care education versus routine diabetes care education significantly decreased ulcer recurrences (NNT 10) and major amputations (NNT 14) after 2 years.

Therapeutic footwear (ulcer recurrence)

We found no RCTs on therapeutic footwear. One non-randomised controlled trial identified by a systematic review found that therapeutic footwear (made according to the Towey guidelines) versus ordinary shoes significantly reduced the recurrence of ulceration after 1 year (NNT 4).

What are the effects of treatments?

BENEFICIAL

Pressure off-loading with non-removable cast (non-infected foot ulcer healing)

One RCT has found that pressure off-loading❻ with total contact casting versus traditional dressing changes significantly improves non-infected diabetic foot ulcer healing. RCTs have found that pressure off-loading with either total contact casting or non-removable fibreglass casts versus removable casts or shoes significantly improves non-infected diabetic foot ulcer healing at 12 weeks (NNT 4).

LIKELY TO BE BENEFICIAL

Cultured human dermis (non-infected foot ulcer healing)

One systematic review found a non-significant increase in ulcer healing with cultured human dermis❻ (Dermagraft, weekly for 8 wk) versus control in people with non-infected diabetic foot ulcer.

Systemic hyperbaric oxygen (infected ulcers)

One RCT in people with severe infected foot ulcers found that systemic hyperbaric oxygen plus usual care versus usual care alone significantly reduced the risk of foot amputation after 10 weeks (NNT 5). Another small and short term RCT found no significant difference in the risk of major amputation after 2 weeks.

▶

Endocrine disorders

◀ Topical growth factors (non-infected foot ulcer healing)

One systematic review found insufficient evidence about the effects of four different topical growth factors❸ versus placebo on ulcer healing rates in people with non-infected diabetic foot ulcers.

DEFINITION Diabetic foot ulceration is full thickness penetration of the dermis of the foot in a person with diabetes. Ulcer severity is often classified using the Wagner system. Grade 1 ulceration refers to superficial ulcers that involve the full skin thickness but not any underlying tissues. Grade 2 ulceration refers to deeper ulcers that penetrate down to ligaments and muscle, but do not involve bone or have any abscess formation. Grade 3 ulceration refers to deep ulcers that have evidence of cellulitis or abscess formation, and are often complicated with osteomyelitis. Ulcers with evidence of localised gangrene are classified as Grade 4, and Grade 5 ulcers have extensive gangrene involving the entire foot.

INCIDENCE/ Studies conducted in Australia, Finland, the UK, and the USA have reported
PREVALENCE the annual incidence of foot ulcers among people with diabetes as 2.5–10.7%, and the annual incidence of amputation as 0.25–1.8%.[1–8]

AETIOLOGY/ Long term risk factors for foot complications, including foot ulcers and
RISK FACTORS amputation, include duration of diabetes, poor glycaemic control, and the presence of microvascular complications (retinopathy, nephropathy, and neuropathy). However, the strongest predictors for development of foot complications are altered foot sensation and previous foot ulcer.[1–8]

PROGNOSIS People with diabetes are at risk of developing complications in the lower extremities. These include foot ulcers, infections, and vascular insufficiency. Amputation of a lower extremity is indicated if complications are severe or do not improve with appropriate treatment. As well as affecting quality of life, these complications form a large proportion of the healthcare costs of diabetes. For people with healed diabetic foot ulcers, the 5 year cumulative rate of ulcer recurrence is 66%, and of amputation is 12%.[9]

Search date September 2001

William Herman

What are the effects of intensive versus conventional glycaemic control?

BENEFICIAL

Intensive control of hyperglycaemia in people aged 13–75 years

One systematic review and large subsequent RCTs in people with type 1 or type 2 diabetes have found strong evidence that intensive versus conventional glycaemic control significantly reduces the development and progression of microvascular and neuropathic complications. A second systematic review has found that intensive versus conventional treatment is associated with a small reduction in cardiovascular risk.

RCTs have found that intensive treatment increases the incidence of hypoglycaemia and weight gain, without adverse impact on neuropsychological function or quality of life.

Large RCTs have found that diabetic complications increase with HbA1c concentrations above the non-diabetic range.

The benefit of intensive treatment is limited by the complications of advanced diabetes (such as blindness, end stage renal disease, or cardiovascular disease), major comorbidity, and reduced life expectancy.

TRADE OFF BETWEEN BENEFITS AND HARMS

Intensive control of hyperglycaemia in people with frequent severe hypoglycaemia

The benefits of intensive treatment of hyperglycaemia are described above.

It is difficult to weigh the benefit of reduced complications against the harm of increased hypoglycaemia. The risk of intensive treatment is increased by a history of severe hypoglycaemia or unawareness of hypoglycaemia, advanced autonomic neuropathy or cardiovascular disease, and impaired ability to detect or treat hypoglycaemia (such as altered mental state, immobility, or lack of social support). For people likely to have limited benefit or increased risk with intensive treatment, it may be more appropriate to negotiate less intensive goals for glycaemic management that reflect the person's self determined goals of care and willingness to make lifestyle modifications.

DEFINITION   Diabetes mellitus is a group of disorders characterised by hyperglycaemia (definitions vary slightly, one current US definition is fasting plasma glucose ≥ 7.0 mmol/L or ≥ 11.1 mmol/L 2 h after a 75 g oral glucose load, on 2 or more occasions). Intensive treatment is designed to achieve blood glucose values as close to the non-diabetic range as possible. The components of such treatment are education, counselling, monitoring, self management, and pharmacological treatment with insulin or oral antidiabetic agents to achieve specific glycaemic goals.

INCIDENCE/ PREVALENCE   Diabetes is diagnosed in around 5% of adults aged 20 years or older in the USA.[1] A further 2.7% have undiagnosed diabetes on the basis of fasting glucose. The prevalence is similar in men and women, but diabetes is more common in some ethnic groups. The prevalence in people aged 40–74 years has increased over the past decade. ▶

Glycaemic control in diabetes

AETIOLOGY/ RISK FACTORS
Diabetes results from deficient insulin secretion, decreased insulin action, or both. Many processes can be involved, from autoimmune destruction of the β cells of the pancreas to incompletely understood abnormalities that result in resistance to insulin action. Genetic factors are involved in both mechanisms. In type 1 diabetes there is an absolute deficiency of insulin. In type 2 diabetes, insulin resistance and an inability of the pancreas to compensate are involved. Hyperglycaemia without clinical symptoms but sufficient to cause tissue damage can be present for many years before diagnosis.

PROGNOSIS
Severe hyperglycaemia causes numerous symptoms, including polyuria, polydipsia, weight loss, and blurred vision. Acute, life threatening consequences of diabetes are hyperglycaemia with ketoacidosis or the non-ketotic hyperosmolar syndrome. There is increased susceptibility to certain infections. Long term complications of diabetes include retinopathy (with potential loss of vision), nephropathy (leading to renal failure), peripheral neuropathy (increased risk of foot ulcers, amputation, and Charcot joints), autonomic neuropathy (cardiovascular, gastrointestinal, and genitourinary dysfunction), and greatly increased risk of atheroma affecting large vessels (macrovascular complications of stroke, myocardial infarction, or peripheral vascular disease). The physical, emotional, and social impact of diabetes and demands of intensive treatment can also create problems for people with diabetes and their families. One systematic review (search date 1998) of observational studies in people with type 2 diabetes found a positive association between increased blood glucose concentration and mortality.[2] It found no minimum threshold level.

Endocrine disorders

What are the effects of drug treatments in adults?

TRADE OFF BETWEEN BENEFITS AND HARMS

Mazindol

One RCT found that mazindol versus placebo caused modest weight loss after 3 months in adults who were more than 15% overweight. Weight loss was not sustained after treatment stopped. We found one case report of pulmonary hypertension 1 year after stopping treatment.

Orlistat

Systematic reviews and subsequent RCTs have found that in addition to a low calorie diet, orlistat versus placebo modestly increases weight loss in adults with obesity. Adverse effects such as oily spotting from the rectum, flatulence, and faecal urgency occurred in up to 27% of people taking orlistat. We found no evidence about weight regain after stopping treatment, and no evidence on long term safety.

Phentermine

One RCT found that phentermine versus placebo caused modest weight loss after 9 months in adults who were more than 15% overweight. We found no evidence of serious adverse effects with phentermine alone, but phentermine plus fenfluramine has been associated with valvular heart disease and pulmonary hypertension. We found insufficient evidence on weight regain and long term safety.

Sibutramine

Systematic reviews and subsequent RCTs have found that sibutramine versus placebo increases modest weight loss in healthy obese adults and obese adults with controlled hypertension or diabetes (body mass index $25–40 \text{ kg/m}^2$). Weight regain occurs after stopping treatment. Adverse effects (including headache, dry mouth, anorexia, constipation, insomnia, rhinitis, and pharyngitis) occurred in up to 30% of people taking sibutramine. We found no evidence about safety beyond 2 years' treatment.

UNKNOWN EFFECTIVENESS

Diethlyproprion

Two small RCTs found conflicting evidence on the effect of diethylproprion versus placebo on weight loss.

Fluoxetine

Two small RCTs found conflicting evidence on the effect of fluoxetine versus placebo on weight loss.

Sibutramine plus orlistat *New*

One RCT found no benefit of sibutramine plus orlistat compared with sibutramine alone.

▶

Obesity

LIKELY TO BE INEFFECTIVE OR HARMFUL

Dexfenfluramine; fenfluramine; fenfluramine plus phentermine
These drugs have been associated with valvular heart disease and pulmonary hypertension and are no longer marketed.

Phenylpropanolamine
One case control study found that phenylpropanolamine significantly increased risk of haemorrhagic stroke in the first 3 days of use.

DEFINITION Obesity is a chronic condition characterised by an excess of body fat. It is most often defined by the body mass index, a mathematical formula that is highly correlated with body fat. Body mass index is weight in kilograms divided by height in metres squared (kg/m^2). In the USA and the UK, people with body mass indexes between 25–30 kg/m^2 are categorised as overweight, and those with body mass indexes above 30 kg/m^2 are categorised as obese.[1]

INCIDENCE/ PREVALENCE Obesity has increased steadily in many countries since 1900. In the UK, in 1994, it was estimated that 13% of men and 16% of women were obese.[1,2] In the past decade alone, the prevalence of obesity in the USA has increased from 12.0% in 1991 to 17.9% in 1998.[3]

AETIOLOGY/ RISK FACTORS The aetiology of obesity includes both genetic and environmental factors. Obesity may also be induced by drugs (e.g. high dose glucocorticoids), or be secondary to a variety of neuroendocrine disorders such as Cushing's syndrome and polycystic ovary syndrome.[4]

PROGNOSIS Obesity is a risk factor for several chronic diseases, including hypertension, dyslipidaemia, diabetes, cardiovascular disease, sleep apnoea, osteoarthritis, and some cancers.[1] The relation between increasing body weight and the mortality rate is curvilinear, with mortality rate increasing in people with low body weight. Whether this is caused by increased mortality risk at low body weights or by unintentional weight loss is not clear.[5] Results from five prospective cohort studies and 1991 national statistics suggest that the number of annual deaths attributable to obesity among US adults is about 280 000.[6]

Search date December 2001

Lars Kristensen and Birte Nygaard

What are the effects of treatments for clinical (overt) hypothyroidism? *New*

BENEFICIAL

Levothyroxine (L-thyroxine)

We found no RCTs on the effects of levothyroxine (L-thyroxine) versus placebo, but there is consensus that treatment is beneficial. Treating clinical (overt) hypothyroidism with thyroid hormone (levothyroxine; L-thyroxine) can induce hyperthyroidism (reduced thyroid stimulating hormone).

UNKNOWN EFFECTIVENESS

Levothyroxine (L-thyroxine) plus liothyronine

One small RCT found that levothyroxine plus liothyronine versus levothyroxine alone improved some participant measures of mood and physical symptoms. Another RCT found insufficient evidence about the effects of combination treatment with levothyroxine plus liothyronine.

What are the effects of treatments for subclinical hypothyroidism? *New*

UNKNOWN EFFECTIVENESS

Levothyroxine (L-thyroxine)

One RCT in women with biochemically defined subclinical hypothyroidism found that levothyroxine (L-thyroxine) versus placebo improved dry skin, cold intolerance, or constipation at 1 year, but the RCT was small and the difference was not significant. Two RCTs found inconclusive results about the effect of levothyroxine versus placebo on cognitive function. Treating subclinical hypothyroidism with thyroid hormone (levothyroxine; L-thyroxine) can induce hyperthyroidism (reduced thyroid stimulating hormone).

DEFINITION Hypothyroidism is characterised by low levels of blood thyroid hormone. **Clinical (overt) hypothyroidism** is diagnosed on the basis of characteristic clinical features consisting of mental slowing, depression, dementia, weight gain, constipation, dry skin, hair loss, cold intolerance, hoarse voice, irregular menstruation, infertility, muscle stiffness and pain, bradycardia, hypercholesterolaemia, combined with a raised blood level of thyroid stimulating hormone (TSH) (serum TSH levels > 12 mU/L), and a low serum thyroxine ($T_4$❻) level (serum T_4 < 60 nmol/L). **Subclinical hypothyroidism** is diagnosed when serum TSH is raised (serum TSH > 4 mU/L) but serum thyroxine (T_4) is normal and there are no symptoms or signs, or minor symptoms or signs, of thyroid dysfunction (see definition above). **Primary hypothyroidism** is seen after destruction of the thyroid gland because of autoimmune causes (the majority), or iatrogenic causes such as surgery, radioiodine, and radiation (the minority). **Secondary hypothyroidism** is because of damage of the pituitary gland or hypothalamic function resulting in insufficient production of TSH. Secondary hypothyroidism is not covered in this review. ▶

Primary hypothyroidism

INCIDENCE/ PREVALENCE Hypothyroidism is more common in women than in men (in the UK female : male ratio of 6 : 1). A study (2779 people in UK with a median age of 58 years) found that the incidence of clinical (overt) hypothyroidism was 40/10 000 women a year and 6/10 000 men a year. The prevalence was 9.3% in women and 1.3% in men.[1] In areas with high iodine intake the incidence of hypothyroidism is higher than in areas with normal to subnormal iodine intake. In Denmark, where there is moderate iodine insufficiency, the overall incidence of hypothyroidism can be 1.4/10 000 a year increasing to 8/10 000 a year in people older than 70 years of age.[2] The incidence of subclinical hypothyroidism increases with age; up to 10% of women over the age of 60 years have subclinical hypothyroidism (evaluated from data from the Netherlands and USA).[3,4]

AETIOLOGY/ RISK FACTORS Primary thyroid gland failure can occur as a result of chronic autoimmune thyroiditis, postradioactive iodine treatment, or thyroidectomy. Other causes include drug adverse effects (e.g. amiodarone and lithium), transient hypothyroidism due to silent thyroiditis, subacute thyroiditis, or postpartum thyroiditis.

PROGNOSIS Hypothyroidism results in mental slowing, depression, dementia, weight gain, constipation, dry skin, hair loss, cold intolerance, hoarse voice, irregular menstruation, infertility, muscle stiffness and pain, bradycardia, and hypercholesterolaemia. In people with subclinical hypothyroidism the risk of developing overt hypothyroidism is described in the Whickham Survey from UK (25 years' follow up, for women, OR 8, 95% CI 3 to 20; for men, OR 44, 95% CI 19 to 104; if both a raised TSH and positive antithyroid antibodies present (for women, OR 38, 95% CI 22 to 65; for men, OR 173, 95% CI 81 to 370). For women, it found an annual risk of 4.3% a year (if both raised serum TSH and antithyroid antibodies were present), 2.6% a year (if raised serum TSH was present alone); the minimum number of people with raised TSH and antithyroid antibodies who would need to be treated to prevent this progression to clinical (overt) hypothyroidism in one person over 5 years is five to eight.[1] **Cardiovascular disease:** A large cross-sectional study (25 862 participants with serum TSH between 5.1–10 mU/L) found significantly higher mean total cholesterol concentrations in hypothyroid people compared with euthyroid people (5.8 v 5.6 mmol/L).[3] Another study (124 elderly women with subclinical hypothyroidism, 931 euthyroid women) found a significantly increased risk of myocardial infarction in women with subclinical hypothyroidism (OR 2.3, 95% CI 1.3 to 4.0) and aortic atherosclerosis (OR 1.7, 95% CI 1.1 to 2.6).[4] **Mental health:** Subclinical hypothyroidism is associated with depression.[5] People with subclinical hypothyroidism may have depression that is refractory to both antidepressant drugs and thyroid hormone alone. Memory impairment, hysteria, anxiety, somatic complaint, and depressive features without depression have been described in people with subclinical hypothyroidism.[6]

Search date February 2002

André Curi, Kimble Matos and Carlos Pavesio

What are the effects of topical anti-inflammatory eye drops?

UNKNOWN EFFECTIVENESS

Non-steroidal eye drops

RCTs found no significant difference in the proportion of people judged to be clinically cured with non-steroidal versus placebo eye drops and with non-steroidal versus steroid eye drops.

Steroid eye drops

One small RCT found no significant difference in symptom severity after 14 or 21 days with steroid eye drops (betamethasone phosphate/clobetasone butyrate) versus placebo. Two RCTs found no significant difference with prednisolone versus rimexolone in the number of anterior chamber cells per examination field (a marker of disease severity in acute anterior uveitis), but two other RCTs found that prednisolone versus loteprednol significantly increased the proportion of people with less than five anterior chamber cells per examination field after 28 days. RCTs found that rimexolone and loteprednol were less likely than prednisolone to increase intraocular pressures, although differences were not significant.

DEFINITION Anterior uveitis is inflammation of the uveal tract, and includes iritis and iridocyclitis. It can be classified according to its clinical course into acute or chronic anterior uveitis, or according to its clinical appearance into granulomatous or non-granulomatous anterior uveitis. Acute anterior uveitis is characterised by an extremely painful red eye, often associated with photophobia and occasionally with decreased visual acuity. Chronic anterior uveitis is defined as inflammation lasting more than 6 weeks. It is usually asymptomatic, but many people have mild symptoms during exacerbations.

INCIDENCE/ Acute anterior uveitis is rare, with an annual incidence of 12/100 000
PREVALENCE population.[1] It is more common in Finland (annual incidence 22.6/ 100 000, prevalence 68.7/100 000), probably because of genetic factors such as the high frequency of HLA-B27 in the Finish population.[2] It has equal sex incidence, and less than 10% of cases occur before the age of 20 years.[2,3]

AETIOLOGY/ No cause is identified in 60–80% of people with acute anterior uveitis.
RISK FACTORS Systemic disorders that may be associated with acute anterior uveitis include ankylosing spondylitis; Reiter's syndrome; juvenile chronic arthritis; Kawasaki syndrome; infectious uveitis; Behçet's syndrome; inflammatory bowel disease; interstitial nephritis; sarcoidosis; multiple sclerosis; Wegener's granulomatosis; Vogt-Koyanagi-Harada syndrome; and masquerade syndromes**ⓖ**. Acute anterior uveitis also occurs in association with HLA-B27 expression not linked to any systemic disease, and it may also be the manifestation of an isolated eye disorder such as Fuchs' iridocyclitis, Posner-Schlossman syndrome, or Schwartz syndrome. Acute anterior uveitis may also occur following surgery or as an adverse drug or hypersensitivity reaction.[2,3]

▶

Acute anterior uveitis

PROGNOSIS   Acute anterior uveitis is often self limiting, but we found no evidence about how often it resolves spontaneously, in which people, or over what time period. Complications include posterior synechiae⊖, cataract, glaucoma, and chronic uveitis. In a study of 154 people (232 eyes) with acute anterior uveitis (119 people HLA-B27 positive), visual acuity was better than 20/60 in 209 of 232 (90%) eyes, 20/60 or worse in 23 of 232 (10%) eyes, and worse than 20/200 (classified as legally blind) in 11 of 232 (5%) eyes.[4]

Search date July 2001

Jennifer Arnold and Shirley Sarks

What are the effects of preventive interventions and treatments?

BENEFICIAL

Photodynamic treatment with verteporfin

Two RCTs in selected people with exudative age related macular degeneration found that photodynamic treatment🅖 with verteporfin reduced the risk of moderate and severe vision loss after 1–2 years (NNT about 7). In the first RCT, subgroup analysis suggests the benefit is greatest in people with predominantly classic lesions on fluorescein angiography. In the second RCT, a more modest benefit was seen in the second year of treatment in people with only occult (no classic) lesions on fluorescein angiography.

TRADE OFF BETWEEN BENEFITS AND HARMS

Thermal laser photocoagulation

Large RCTs in people with exudative age related macular degeneration and well demarcated lesions have found that thermal laser photocoagulation versus no treatment significantly decreases the rate of severe visual loss and preserves contrast sensitivity. Choroidal neovascularisation🅖 recurs within 2 years in about half of those treated. Photocoagulation may reduce visual acuity initially.

UNKNOWN EFFECTIVENESS

Laser to drusen (prevention)

We found insufficient evidence that drusen🅖 reduction by laser prevents late age related macular degeneration (choroidal neovascularisation or geographic atrophy). One RCT and three pilot studies for RCTs found that laser to eyes with high risk drusen significantly improved visual acuity after 2 years (NNT 9). One RCT found that visual acuity after laser treatment only improved in a subgroup of eyes with a reduction in the number of drusen of greater than 50%. One RCT found that laser to drusen significantly increased the short term incidence of choroidal neovascularisation, particularly in people with exudative age related macular degeneration in the other eye.

Proton beam and scleral plaque radiotherapy

Non-randomised pilot studies found inconclusive evidence about proton beam and scleral plaque (local) radiotherapy used in a variety of dosing and timing schedules.

Submacular surgery

We found insufficient evidence on the effects of submacular surgery🅖. Rates of recurrent choroidal neovascularisation are high, and there is a clinically important risk of ocular complications resulting in visual loss and a need for further surgical intervention.

UNLIKELY TO BE BENEFICIAL

External beam radiation

One large RCT in people with exudative age related macular degeneration comparing low dose external beam radiation versus placebo found no significant difference in the number of people with moderate visual loss after 1 year. ▶

Age related macular degeneration

Smaller RCTs comparing both low and high dose external beam radiation versus placebo or no treatment found conflicting evidence. We found insufficient evidence on long term safety, although RCTs found no evidence of toxicity to the optic nerve or retina after 12 to 24 months.

LIKELY TO BE INEFFECTIVE OR HARMFUL

Subcutaneous interferon α-2a

One large RCT found that subcutaneous interferon α-2a versus placebo increased visual loss after 1 year, although the difference was not significant, and found evidence of serious ocular and systemic adverse effects.

DEFINITION   Age related macular degeneration (AMD) is the late stage of age related maculopathy❻. AMD has two forms: atrophic (or dry) AMD, characterised by geographic atrophy;❻ and exudative (or wet) AMD, characterised by choroidal neovascularisation, which eventually causes a disciform scar.

INCIDENCE/   AMD is a common cause of blind registration in industrialised countries.
PREVALENCE   Atrophic AMD is more common than the more sight threatening exudative AMD, affecting about 85% of people with AMD.[1] End stage (blinding) AMD is found in about 2% of all people aged over 50 years, and incidence rises with age (0.7–1.4% of people aged 65–75 years; 11–19% of people aged > 85 years).[2–4]

AETIOLOGY/   Age is the strongest risk factor. Ocular risk factors for the development of
RISK FACTORS exudative AMD include the presence of soft drusen, macular pigmentary change, and choroidal neovascularisation in the other eye. Systemic risk factors include hypertension, smoking, and a family history of AMD.[5–8] Diet and exposure to ultraviolet light are suspected as aetiological agents, but this remains unproved.

PROGNOSIS   AMD impairs central vision, which is required for reading, driving, face recognition, and all fine visual tasks. **Atrophic AMD** progresses slowly over many years, and time to legal blindness❻ is highly variable (usually about 5–10 years).[9,10] **Exudative AMD** is more often threatening to vision; 90% of people with severe visual loss owing to AMD have the exudative type. This condition usually manifests with a sudden worsening and distortion of central vision. A modelling exercise (derived primarily from cohort studies) found the risk of developing exudative AMD in people with bilateral soft drusen was 1–5% at 1 year and 13–18% at 3 years.[11] The observed 5 year rate in a population survey was 7%.[12] Most eyes (estimates vary from 60–90%) with exudative AMD progress to legal blindness and develop a central defect (scotoma) in the visual field.[13–16] Peripheral vision is preserved, allowing the person to be mobile and independent. The ability to read with visual aids depends on the size and density of the central scotoma and the degree to which the person retains sensitivity to contrast. Once exudative AMD has developed in one eye, the other eye is at high risk (cumulative estimated incidence: 10% at 1 year, 28% at 3 years, and 42% at 5 years).[5]

Bacterial conjunctivitis

Search date February 2002

Christine Chung, Elisabeth Cohen and Justine Smith

What are the effects of antibiotic treatment?

BENEFICIAL

Antibiotic treatment in culture positive bacterial conjunctivitis
One systematic review has found that antibiotics (polymyxin–bacitracin, ciprofloxacin, or ofloxacin) versus placebo significantly increase rates of both clinical and microbiological cure after 3–5 days. RCTs comparing different antibiotics versus each other found conflicting results for rates of clinical and microbiological cure.

LIKELY TO BE BENEFICIAL

Empirical antibiotic treatment of suspected bacterial conjunctivitis
One systematic review found limited evidence that topical norfloxacin versus placebo significantly increased rates of clinical and microbiological improvement or cure after 5 days. RCTs comparing different topical antibiotics versus each other found no significant difference in rates of clinical or microbiological cure. One RCT found no significant difference with topical polymyxin–bacitracin ointment versus oral cefixime in the number of people who improved clinically or microbiologically.

DEFINITION   Conjunctivitis is any inflammation of the conjunctiva, generally characterised by irritation, itching, foreign body sensation, and tearing or discharge. Bacterial conjunctivitis may usually be distinguished from other types of conjunctivitis by the presence of a yellow–white mucopurulent discharge. There is also usually a papillary reaction (small bumps with fibrovascular cores on the palpebral conjunctiva, appearing grossly as a fine velvety surface). Bacterial conjunctivitis is usually bilateral. This review covers only non-gonococcal bacterial conjunctivitis.

INCIDENCE/ PREVALENCE   We found no good evidence on the incidence or prevalence of bacterial conjunctivitis.

AETIOLOGY/ RISK FACTORS   Conjunctivitis may be infectious (caused by bacteria or viruses) or allergic. In adults, bacterial conjunctivitis is less common than viral conjunctivitis, although estimates vary widely (viral conjunctivitis has been reported to account for 8–75% of acute conjunctivitis).[1–3] *Staphylococcus* species are the most common pathogens for bacterial conjunctivitis in adults, followed by *Streptococcus pneumoniae* and *Haemophilus influenzae*.[4,5] In children, bacterial conjunctivitis is more common than viral, and is mainly caused by *H influenzae*, *S pneumoniae*, and *Moraxella catarrhalis*.[6,7]

PROGNOSIS   Most bacterial conjunctivitis is self limiting. One systematic review (search date 2002) found clinical cure or significant improvement with placebo within 2–5 days in 64% of people (99% CI 54% to 73%).[8] Some organisms cause corneal or systemic complications, or both; otitis may develop in 25% of children with *H influenzae* conjunctivitis,[9] and systemic meningitis may complicate primary meningococcal conjunctivitis in 18% of people.[10]

Diabetic retinopathy

Search date January 2002

Simon Harding

What are the effects of treatments for diabetic retinopathy?

BENEFICIAL

Control of diabetes (see glycaemic control in diabetes, p 97)

Control of hypertension (see primary prevention, p 14)

Smoking cessation (see primary prevention, p 14)

Macular photocoagulation in people with clinically significant macular oedema

RCTs have found that laser photocoagulation to the macula versus no treatment significantly reduces visual loss at 3 years in eyes with clinically significant macular oedema (NNT 8 eyes), with some evidence of greater benefit in eyes with better vision.

Peripheral retinal laser photocoagulation in people with preproliferative (*moderate/severe non-proliferative**) retinopathy

RCTs have found that peripheral retinal photocoagulation versus no treatment significantly reduces the risk of severe visual loss at 5 years. The people in these RCTs had maculopathy in addition to preproliferative retinopathy; the influence of this combination is unclear.

Peripheral retinal laser photocoagulation in people with proliferative retinopathy

RCTs have found that peripheral retinal photocoagulation versus no treatment significantly reduces the risk of severe visual loss at 2–3 years.

LIKELY TO BE BENEFICIAL

Grid photocoagulation to zones of retinal thickening in people with diabetic maculopathy

One RCT found a significant improvement in visual acuity in eyes treated with grid photocoagulation versus untreated eyes at 12 months (NNT 4 eyes) and at 24 months (NNT 3 eyes). Photocoagulation versus no photocoagulation reduced the risk of moderate visual loss by 50–70%.

UNKNOWN EFFECTIVENESS

Macular photocoagulation in people with maculopathy but without clinically significant macular oedema

The role of macular photocoagulation in this population remains unclear.

What are the effects of treatments for vitreous haemorrhage? New

LIKELY TO BE BENEFICIAL

Vitrectomy in people with severe vitreous haemorrhage and proliferative retinopathy (if performed early)

One RCT found that early versus deferred (for 1 year) vitrectomy significantly reduced visual loss at 1, 2, and 3 years in eyes with severe vitreous haemorrhage and proliferative retinopathy (NNT 10 eyes).

▶

◄ **UNKNOWN EFFECTIVENESS**

Vitrectomy in people with maculopathy
The role of vitrectomy in this population remains unclear.

*Terms in italics indicate US definitions

DEFINITION	Diabetic retinopathy is characterised by varying degrees of microaneurysms, haemorrhages, exudates *(hard exudates)*, venous changes, new vessel formation, and retinal thickening. It can involve the peripheral retina or the macula, or both. The range of severity of retinopathy includes background🅖 *(mild non-proliferative)*, preproliferative🅖 *(moderate/severe non-proliferative)*, proliferative, and advanced retinopathy🅖. Involvement of the macula can be focal, diffuse, ischaemic🅖, or mixed.
INCIDENCE/ PREVALENCE	Diabetic eye disease is the most common cause of blindness in the UK, responsible for 12% of registrable blindness in people aged 16–64 years.[1]
AETIOLOGY/ RISK FACTORS	Risk factors include age, duration and control of diabetes, raised blood pressure, and raised serum lipids.[2]
PROGNOSIS	Natural history studies from the 1960s found that at least half of people with proliferative diabetic retinopathy progressed to Snellen visual acuity🅖 of less than 6/60 *(20/200)* within 3 to 5 years.[3–5] After 4 years' follow up the rate of progression to less than 6/60 *(20/200)* visual acuity in the better eye was 1.5% in people with type 1 diabetes, 2.7% in people with non-insulin requiring type 2 diabetes, and 3.2% in people with insulin requiring type 2 diabetes.[6]

Glaucoma

Search date December 2001

Rajiv Shah and Richard Wormald

What are the effects of treatments for established primary open angle glaucoma?

LIKELY TO BE BENEFICIAL

Laser trabeculoplasty (versus medical treatment)

One RCT found that combined treatment with initial laser trabeculoplasty followed by medical treatment versus medical treatment alone significantly reduced intraocular pressure and deterioration in optic disc appearance, and significantly improved visual fields after a mean of 7 years.

Topical medical treatment

One systematic review found limited evidence that topical medical treatments versus placebo significantly reduced intraocular pressure, but found no significant difference between treatments in visual field loss on long term follow up. The systematic review did not clearly define the medical treatments involved.

TRADE OFF BETWEEN BENEFITS AND HARMS

Surgical trabeculectomy

RCTs found that surgical trabeculectomy versus medical treatment significantly reduced both visual field loss and intraocular pressures, but found no significant difference between treatments in visual acuity after about 5 years. RCTs found that surgical trabeculectomy versus laser trabeculoplasty significantly reduced intraocular pressure, but found conflicting results for changes in visual acuity after 5–7 years.

UNKNOWN EFFECTIVENESS

Laser trabeculoplasty (versus surgical treatment)

RCTs found that laser trabeculoplasty reduced intraocular pressures significantly less than surgical trabeculectomy, and found conflicting results for changes in visual acuity after 5–7 years.

What are the effects of lowering intraocular pressure in normal tension glaucoma?

LIKELY TO BE BENEFICIAL

Lowering intraocular pressure

One RCT found that surgical and/or medical treatment significantly reduced progression of visual field loss (NNT 5), but found that surgery significantly increased cataract formation after 8 years.

What are the effects of treatments for acute angle closure glaucoma?

UNKNOWN EFFECTIVENESS

Medical treatments of acute angle closure glaucoma

We found no placebo controlled RCTs, but strong consensus suggests that medical treatments are effective. One RCT found no significant difference in ▶

◀ intraocular pressure after 2 hours with low dose pilocarpine versus an intensive pilocarpine regimen versus pilocarpine ocular inserts. We found no RCTs of other medical treatments.

Surgical treatments of acute angle closure glaucoma
We found no placebo controlled RCTs, but strong consensus suggests that surgical treatments are effective. One RCT found no significant difference with surgical iridectomy❻ versus laser iridotomy❻ in visual acuity or intraocular pressure after 3 years.

DEFINITION Glaucoma is a group of diseases that are characterised by progressive optic neuropathy. It is usually bilateral but asymmetric and may occur at any point within a wide range of intraocular pressures. All forms of glaucoma show optic nerve cupping with pallor associated with peripheral visual field loss. **Primary open angle glaucoma** occurs in adults with an open drainage angle and no secondary identifiable cause. **Normal tension glaucoma** occurs in people with intraocular pressures that are consistently below 21 mm Hg (a point two standard deviations above the population mean). **Acute angle closure glaucoma** is a rapid and severe rise in intraocular pressure caused by physical obstruction of the anterior chamber drainage angle.

INCIDENCE/ PREVALENCE Glaucoma occurs in 1–2% of white people aged over 40 years, rising to 5% at 70 years. Primary open angle glaucoma accounts for two thirds of those affected, and normal tension glaucoma for about a quarter.[1,2] In black people glaucoma is more prevalent, presents at a younger age with higher intraocular pressures, is more difficult to control, and is the main irreversible cause of blindness.[1,3] Glaucoma related blindness is responsible for 8% of new blind registrations in the UK.[4]

AETIOLOGY/ RISK FACTORS The major risk factor for developing primary open angle glaucoma is raised intraocular pressure. Lesser risk factors include family history and ethnic origin. The relationship between systemic blood pressure and intraocular pressure may be an important determinant of blood flow to the optic nerve head and, as a consequence, may represent a risk factor for glaucoma.[5] Systemic hypotension, vasospasm (including Raynaud's disease and migraine), and a history of major blood loss have been reported as risk factors for normal tension glaucoma in hospital based studies. Risk factors for acute angle closure glaucoma include family history, female sex, being long sighted, and cataract. A recent systematic review failed to find any evidence supporting the theory that routine pupillary dilatation with short acting mydriatics was a risk factor for acute angle closure glaucoma.[6]

PROGNOSIS Advanced visual field loss is found in about 20% of people with primary open angle glaucoma at diagnosis,[7] and is an important risk factor for glaucoma related blindness.[8] Blindness results from gross loss of visual field or loss of central vision. Once early field defects have appeared, and where the intraocular pressure is greater than 30 mm Hg, untreated people may lose the remainder of the visual field in 3 years or less.[9] As the disease progresses, people with glaucoma have difficulty moving from a bright room to a darker room, and judging steps and kerbs. Progression of visual field loss is often slower in normal tension glaucoma. Acute angle glaucoma leads to rapid loss of vision initially from corneal oedema and subsequently from ischaemic optic neuropathy.

Ocular herpes simplex

Search date August 2001

Nigel Barker

What are the effects of treatments and interventions to prevent recurrence?

BENEFICIAL

Interferon for treating epithelial disease

One systematic review has found that topical interferon versus placebo significantly increases the number of people healed after both 7 and 14 days.

Long term oral aciclovir for preventing recurrences

One large RCT in people with at least one previous episode of epithelial or stromal keratitis within the preceding year found that long term oral aciclovir versus placebo significantly reduced the risk of recurrences after 1 year.

Topical antiviral agents for treating epithelial disease

One systematic review has found that idoxuridine or vidarabine versus placebo significantly increases the number of people healed after 14 days, and that trifluridine or aciclovir versus idoxuridine significantly increases the number of people healed after 7 and 14 days.

Topical corticosteroids for treating stromal keratitis

One RCT found that topical corticosteroids versus placebo significantly reduced the progression and shortened the duration of stromal keratitis.

LIKELY TO BE BENEFICIAL

Oral aciclovir for prevention of recurrent disease in people with corneal grafts performed for herpes simplex virus infection

One small RCT found limited evidence that prophylactic use of oral aciclovir significantly reduced recurrences and improved graft survival.

UNKNOWN EFFECTIVENESS

Debridement for epithelial keratitis

One systematic review has found no significant difference with debridement versus placebo in the proportion of people healed, but has found that debridement plus antiviral treatment versus debridement alone significantly increases the number of people healed after 7 and 14 days.

UNLIKELY TO BE BENEFICIAL

Oral aciclovir for treatment of stromal keratitis

One RCT in people with stromal keratitis taking topical antiviral treatment found no significant difference with oral aciclovir versus placebo in rates of treatment failure at 16 weeks.

Short term oral aciclovir for preventing recurrences

One RCT in people with epithelial keratitis receiving topical trifluorothymidine found no significant difference between short term prophylaxis with oral aciclovir and placebo in the rate of stromal keratitis or iritis at 1 year.

▶

◀ **DEFINITION**   Ocular herpes simplex is usually caused by herpes simplex virus type 1 (HSV-1), but also occasionally by type 2 virus (HSV-2). Ocular manifestations of HSV are varied and include blepharitis, canalicular obstruction, conjunctivitis, epithelial keratitis, stromal keratitis, iritis, and retinitis. HSV infections are classified as neonatal, primary (HSV in a person with no previous viral exposure), and recurrent (previous viral exposure with humoral and cellular immunity present).

INCIDENCE/   Infections with HSV are usually acquired in early life. A US study found
PREVALENCE   antibodies against HSV-1 in about 50% of people with high socioeconomic status and 80% of people with low socioeconomic status by the age of 30 years.[1] However, only about 20–25% of people with HSV antibodies had any history of clinical manifestations of ocular or cutaneous herpetic disease.[2] Ocular HSV is the most common cause of corneal blindness in high income countries and the most common cause of unilateral corneal blindness in the world.[3] A 33 year study of the population of Rochester, Minnesota, found the annual incidence of new cases of ocular herpes simplex to be 8.4/100 000 (95% CI 6.9 to 9.9) and the annual incidence of all episodes (new and recurrent) to be 20.7/100 000 (95% CI 18.3 to 23.1).[4] The prevalence of ocular herpes was 149 cases/100 000 population (95% CI 115 to 183). Twelve per cent had bilateral disease.

AETIOLOGY/   Epithelial keratitis results from productive, lytic viral infection of the corneal
RISK FACTORS   epithelial cells. Stromal keratitis and iritis are thought to result from a combination of viral infection and compromised immune mechanisms. We found no quantified measures of risk.

PROGNOSIS   HSV epithelial keratitis tends to resolve within 1–2 weeks. In a trial of 271 people treated with topical trifluorothymidine and randomly assigned to receive either oral aciclovir or placebo, the epithelial lesion had resolved completely or was at least less than 1 mm after 1 week of treatment with placebo in 89% of people and after 2 weeks in 99% of people.[5] Stromal keratitis or iritis occurs in about 25% of people following epithelial keratitis.[6] The effects of HSV stromal keratitis include scarring, tissue destruction, neovascularisation, glaucoma, and persistent epithelial defects. Rate of recurrence of ocular herpes for people with one episode is 10% at 1 year, 23% at 2 years, and 50% at 10 years.[7] Five per cent of corneal grafts performed in Australia over a 10 year period were in people with visual disability or with actual or impending corneal perforation following stromal ocular herpes simplex. The recurrence of HSV in a corneal graft has a major effect on graft survival. The Australian Corneal Graft Registry has found that, in corneal grafts performed for HSV keratitis, there was at least one HSV recurrence in 58% of corneal grafts that failed over a follow up period of 9 years.[8]

Trachoma

Search date October 2001

Nicole Fraser-Hurt and Denise Mabey

Eye disorders

What are the effects of interventions to prevent scarring trachoma by reducing active trachoma?

LIKELY TO BE BENEFICIAL

Antibiotics (v placebo or no treatment)

One unpublished systematic review found limited evidence from low powered RCTs that antibiotics versus control significantly reduced active trachoma after 3 and 12 months. One additional RCT has found that topical tetracycline plus face washing versus no intervention significantly reduced the number of children with trachoma after 3 months.

Oral azithromycin (v topical tetracycline)

One unpublished systematic review found limited evidence from three RCTs that oral azithromycin versus topical tetracycline significantly reduced active trachoma after 3 months. These RCTs were low powered or of unusual design, and at 12 months the difference between treatments disappeared. One subsequent RCT found that oral azithromycin versus topical tetracycline significantly increased clinical resolution of trachoma at 10 weeks and 6 months.

Promotion of face washing plus topical tetracycline

One RCT identified by two systematic reviews found that promotion of face washing plus topical tetracycline versus topical tetracycline alone significantly reduced the rate of severe trachoma after 1 year, but found no significant difference in the overall rate of trachoma. However, the RCT was too small to rule out a clinically important effect. One additional large RCT has found that face washing alone versus no intervention did not significantly reduce the number of children with trachoma after 3 months, although face washing plus topical tetracycline versus no intervention significantly reduced the number of children with trachoma after 3 months.

What are the effects of surgical treatments for scarring trachoma (entropion and trichiasis)?

LIKELY TO BE BENEFICIAL

Bilamellar tarsal rotation (versus other types of eyelid surgery), when performed by an experienced operator

We found no RCTs on the effects of surgery to improve visual acuity in people with scarring trachoma. In people with major trichiasis☉, one RCT found limited evidence that tarsal rotation versus eversion splinting☉, versus tarsal advance, or tarsal grooving☉ significantly increased operative success after 2 weeks, but found no significant difference between tarsal rotation versus tarsal advance and rotation☉ in operative success after 2 weeks. A second RCT found that tarsal rotation versus tarsal advance and rotation significantly increased operative success after 25 months. In people with minor trichiasis☉, one RCT found that tarsal rotation versus cryoablation or electrolysis significantly increased operative success after 25 months.

◄ **DEFINITION** **Active trachoma** is chronic inflammation of the conjunctiva caused by infection with *Chlamydia trachomatis*. The World Health Organization classification for active trachoma defines mild trachoma (grade TF) as the presence of five or more follicles in the upper tarsal conjunctiva of at least 0.5 mm diameter. Severe trachoma (grade TI) is defined as pronounced inflammatory thickening of the upper tarsal conjunctiva that obscures more than half of the normal deep vessels. **Scarring trachoma** is caused by repeated active infection by *C trachomatis* in which the upper eyelid is shortened and distorted (entropion) and the lashes abrade the eye (trichiasis). Blindness results from corneal opacification, which is related to the degree of entropion/trichiasis.

INCIDENCE/ Trachoma is the world's leading cause of preventable blindness and is
PREVALENCE second only to cataract as an overall cause of blindness.[1] Globally, active trachoma affects an estimated 150 million people, most of them children. About 5.5 million people are blind or at risk of blindness as a consequence of trachoma. Trachoma is a disease of poverty regardless of geographical region. Scarring trachoma is prevalent in large regions of Africa, the Middle East, south-west Asia, the Indian subcontinent, and Aboriginal communities in Australia, and there are also small foci in Central and South America.[1] In areas where trachoma is constantly present at high prevalence, active disease is found in more than 50% of preschool children and may have a prevalence of 60–90%.[2] The prevalence of active trachoma decreases with increasing age, with less than 5% of adults showing signs of active disease.[2] Although similar rates of active disease are observed in male and female children, the later sequelae of trichiasis, entropion, and corneal opacification are more common in women than men.[2] As many as 75% of women and 50% of men over the age of 45 years may show signs of scarring disease.[3]

AETIOLOGY/ Active trachoma is associated with young age and with situations in which
RISK FACTORS there is close contact between people. Discharge from the eyes and nose may be a source of further reinfection.[4] Sharing a bedroom with someone who has active trachoma is a risk factor for infection.[5] Facial contact with flies is held to be associated with active trachoma, but studies reporting this relationship employed weak methods.[6]

PROGNOSIS Corneal damage from trachoma is caused by multiple processes. Scarring may cause an inadequate tear film, and a dry eye may be more susceptible to damage from inturned lashes, leading to corneal opacification. The prevalence of scarring and consequent blindness increases with age, and therefore is most commonly seen in older adults.[7]

Chickenpox

Search date July 2001

George Swingler and Jimmy Volmink

What are the effects of preventive interventions?

BENEFICIAL

High dose aciclovir (> 3200 mg/day) in people with HIV infection

One systematic review has found that high dose aciclovir (at least 3200 mg/day) versus placebo significantly reduces clinical chickenpox over 22 months (NNT 23), and reduces all cause mortality.

Live attenuated vaccine in healthy children

Two RCTs have found that live attenuated varicella vaccine versus placebo significantly reduces clinical chickenpox, with no significant increase in adverse effects.

LIKELY TO BE BENEFICIAL

Zoster immune globulin versus human serum globulin in healthy children

One small RCT in children exposed to a sibling with chickenpox found that zoster immune globulin (ZIG) versus human immune serum globulin significantly reduced the number of exposed children with clinical chickenpox at 20 days.

UNKNOWN EFFECTIVENESS

Aciclovir in people with immunocompromise other than HIV

We found no RCTs.

Live attenuated vaccine in immunocompromised people

We found no RCTs in immunocompromised people of the effects of live attenuated varicella vaccine.

Varicella zoster immune globulin versus ZIG in immunocompromised children

One RCT in immunocompromised children exposed to a sibling with chickenpox found no significant difference with varicella zoster immune globulin (VZIG) versus ZIG in clinical chickenpox at 12 weeks.

What are the effects of treatments?

BENEFICIAL

Oral aciclovir in healthy people (given < 24 h of the onset of the rash)

RCTs have found that oral aciclovir versus placebo given within 24 hours of onset of the rash significantly reduces the symptoms of chickenpox.

LIKELY TO BE BENEFICIAL

Intravenous aciclovir for treatment of chickenpox in children with malignancy

Two RCTs compared intravenous aciclovir versus placebo; one found that aciclovir significantly reduced clinical deterioration, and the other found no significant difference in clinical deterioration.

◄ **UNKNOWN EFFECTIVENESS**

Oral aciclovir in healthy people (given > 24 h after the onset of the rash)
RCTs have found no significant difference in the symptoms of chickenpox with oral aciclovir versus placebo given after 24 hours of onset of rash.

DEFINITION Chickenpox is due to primary infection with varicella zoster virus (VZV). In healthy people, it is usually a mild self limiting illness, characterised by low grade fever, malaise, and a generalised, itchy vesicular rash.

INCIDENCE/ Chickenpox is extremely contagious. Over 90% of unvaccinated people
PREVALENCE become infected, but at different ages in different parts of the world. Over 80% of people have been infected by the age of 10 years in the USA, UK, and Japan, but only by 30 years of age or older in India, Southeast Asia, and the West Indies.[1,2]

AETIOLOGY/ Chickenpox is caused by exposure to VZV.
RISK FACTORS

PROGNOSIS **Infants and children:** In healthy children, the illness is usually mild and self limited. In the USA, the death rate in children aged 1–14 years with chickenpox is about 1.4/100 000 and 7/100 000 in infants.[3] In Australia, mortality in children aged between 1 and 11 years with chickenpox is about 0.5–0.6/100 000 and 1.2/100 000 in infants.[4] Bacterial skin sepsis is the most common complication in children under 5 years, and acute cerebellar ataxia is the most common complication in older children; both cause hospital admission in 2–3/10 000 children.[5] **Adults:** Mortality in adults is higher, about 31/100 000.[3] Varicella pneumonia is the most common complication, causing 20–30 hospital admissions/10 000 adults.[5] Activation of latent VZV infection can cause shingles, also know as acute infection herpes zoster (see postherpetic neuralgia, p 143). **Cancer chemotherapy:** One case series (77 children with cancer and chickenpox) found that more children receiving chemotherapy versus those in remission developed progressive chickenpox with multiple organ involvement (19/60 [32%] v 0/17 [0%]), and more children died (4/60 [7%] v 0/17 [0%]).[6] **HIV infection:** One retrospective case series found that one in four children with HIV who acquired chickenpox in hospital developed pneumonia and 5% died.[7] In a retrospective cohort study (73 children with HIV and chickenpox), infection beyond 2 months occurred in 10 children (14%), and recurrent VZV infections occurred in 38 children (55%).[8] Half of recurrent infections involved generalised rashes and the other half had zoster. **Newborns:** We found no cohort studies of untreated children with perinatal exposure to chickenpox. One cohort study (281 neonates receiving VZIG❻ because their mothers had developed a chickenpox rash in the month before or after delivery) found that 134 (48%) developed a chickenpox rash and 19 (14%) developed severe chickenpox. Severe chickenpox occurred in neonates of mothers whose rash had started in the 7 days before delivery.[9]

Congenital toxoplasmosis

Search date July 2001

Piero Olliaro

What are the effects of treating toxoplasmosis in pregnancy?

UNKNOWN EFFECTIVENESS

Spiramycin and other antiparasitic drugs

Two systematic reviews of cohort studies in women who seroconvert during pregnancy found insufficient evidence on the effects of current antiparasitic treatment on mother or baby. We found that the quality of evidence was poor (studies included in the systematic reviews were small; groups were not directly comparable; only two studies provided information about the control group; congenital infection was common in the treatment groups; and treatment was associated with reduced transmission in only five out of nine of the included studies); therefore we are uncertain whether antiparasitic drugs are more beneficial than harmful.

DEFINITION Toxoplasmosis is caused by the parasite *Toxoplasma gondii*. Infection is asymptomatic or unremarkable in immunocompetent individuals, but leads to a lifelong antibody response. During pregnancy, toxoplasmosis can be transmitted across the placenta and cause intrauterine death, neonatal growth retardation, mental retardation, ocular defects, and blindness in later life. Congenital toxoplasmosis (confirmed infection of the fetus or newborn) can present at birth, either as subclinical disease, which may evolve with neurological or ophthalmological disease later in life, or as a disease of varying severity, ranging from mild ocular damage to severe mental retardation.

INCIDENCE/ PREVALENCE We found few prospective population surveys of toxoplasma seroprevalence. Reported rates vary across and within countries, as well as over time. The risk of primary infection is highest in young people, including young women during pregnancy. We found no cohort studies describing annual seroconversion rates in women of childbearing age nor incidence of primary infection. One systematic review (search date 1996) identified 15 studies that reported rates of seroconversion ranging from 2.4–16/1000 in Europe and from 2–6/1000 in the USA.[1] France began screening for congenital toxoplasmosis in 1978, and during the period 1980–1995 the seroconversion rate during pregnancy was 4–5/1000.[2]

AETIOLOGY/ RISK FACTORS Toxoplasma infection is usually acquired by ingesting either sporocysts (from unwashed fruit or vegetables contaminated by cat faeces) or tissue cysts (from raw or undercooked meat). The risk of contracting toxoplasma infection varies with eating habits, contact with cats and other pets, and occupational exposure. Infection can also be acquired congenitally.

PROGNOSIS One systematic review of studies conducted from 1983–1996 found no population based prospective studies of the natural history of toxoplasma infection during pregnancy.[1] One systematic review (search date 1997) reported nine controlled, non-randomised studies, and found that untreated toxoplasmosis acquired during pregnancy was associated with infection rates in children of between 10 and 100%.[3] We found two European studies that correlated gestation at time of seroconversion with risk of transmission and severity of disease at birth.[4,5] Risk of transmission increased with gestational age at maternal seroconversion, reaching 70–90% for infections acquired after 30 weeks' gestation. In contrast, the risk of the infected infant ▶

developing clinical disease was highest when infection occurred early in pregnancy. The highest risk of early signs of disease (including chorioretinitis and hydrocephaly) was about 10%, and occurred with infection between 24 and 30 weeks' gestation.[5] Infants with untreated congenital toxoplasmosis and generalised neurological abnormalities at birth develop mental retardation, growth retardation, blindness or visual defects, seizures, and spasticity. Children with untreated subclinical infection at birth may develop cognitive and motor deficits and visual defects or blindness up to the age of 20 years. One case control study (845 school children in Brazil) found mental retardation and retinochoroiditis to be significantly associated with positive toxoplasma serology (population attributable risk 6–9%).[6]

Diarrhoea

Search date May 2001

Guy de Bruyn

What are the effects of treatments?

LIKELY TO BE BENEFICIAL

Amino acid oral rehydration solution (ORS) (v standard ORS)

Small RCTs have found that amino acid ORS versus standard ORS⊙ reduces the total volume and duration of diarrhoea.

Rice based ORS (v standard ORS)

One systematic review has found that rice based ORS versus standard ORS significantly reduces the 24 hour stool volume.

TRADE OFF BETWEEN BENEFITS AND HARMS

Antimotility agents

RCTs have found that loperamide and loperamide oxide versus placebo significantly reduce the time to relief of symptoms, but frequently cause constipation. We found insufficient evidence about the effects of other antimotility agents.

Empirical antibiotic treatment in travellers' diarrhoea

One systematic review and one additional RCT have found that empirical use of antibiotics versus placebo significantly increases cure rate at 3–6 days. Adverse effects varied with each antibiotic and occurred in 2–18% of people.

Empirical antibiotic treatment in community acquired diarrhoea

RCTs have found that ciprofloxacin versus placebo reduces the duration of community acquired diarrhoea by 1–2 days. RCTs comparing empirical treatment with other antibiotics versus placebo found conflicting results. In one RCT, significantly more people taking lomefloxacin versus placebo had adverse effects (33% v 3%), and 2/44 (5%) of people taking lomefloxacin had anaphylaxis.

UNLIKELY TO BE BENEFICIAL

Bicarbonate free ORS (versus standard ORS)

One RCT found no significant difference in total stool output or duration of diarrhoea with standard ORS plus bicarbonate versus an otherwise identical ORS in which the bicarbonate was replaced with chloride. Three RCTs found no significant difference in the duration or volume of diarrhoea with standard ORS plus bicarbonate versus an otherwise identical ORS in which the bicarbonate was replaced with citrate.

LIKELY TO BE INEFFECTIVE OR HARMFUL

Reduced osmolarity ORS (versus standard ORS)

Three RCTs comparing reduced osmolarity ORS versus standard ORS found a small and inconsistent effect on total volume of stool and duration of diarrhoea.

▶

◀ **DEFINITION** Diarrhoea is watery or liquid stools, usually with an increase in stool weight above 200 g a day and an increase in daily stool frequency.

INCIDENCE/ PREVALENCE An estimated 4000 million cases of diarrhoea occurred worldwide in 1996, resulting in 2.5 million deaths.[1] In the USA, the estimated incidence for infectious intestinal disease is 0.44 episodes per person a year, or one episode per person every 2.3 years, resulting in about one consultation with a doctor per person every 28 years.[2] A recent community study in the UK reported an incidence of 19 cases per 100 person years, of which 3.3 cases per 100 person years resulted in consultation with a general practitioner.[3] The epidemiology of travellers' diarrhoea (in people who have crossed a national boundary) is not well understood. Incidence is higher in travellers visiting developing countries, but it varies widely by location and season of travel.[4]

AETIOLOGY/ RISK FACTORS The cause of diarrhoea depends on geographic location, standards of food hygiene, sanitation, water supply, and season. Commonly identified causes of sporadic diarrhoea in adults in developed countries include Campylobacter, Salmonella, Shigella, *Escherichia coli*, Yersinia, protozoa, and viruses. No pathogens are identified in more than half of people with diarrhoea. In returning travellers, about 80% of episodes are caused by bacteria such as enterotoxigenic *E coli*, Salmonella, Shigella, Campylobacter, Vibrio, enteroadherent *E coli*, Yersinia, and Aeromonas.[5]

PROGNOSIS In developing countries, diarrhoea is reported to cause more deaths in children under 5 years of age than any other condition.[1] Few studies have examined which factors predict poor outcome in adults. In developed countries, death from infectious diarrhoea is rare, although serious complications, including severe dehydration and renal failure, can occur and may necessitate admission to hospital. Elderly people and those in long term care have an increased risk of death.[6]

HIV infection

Search date July 2001

Margaret Johnson, Andrew Phillips and David Wilkinson

What are the effects of preventive interventions?

BENEFICIAL

Early diagnosis and treatment of sexually transmitted diseases

One RCT found that early diagnosis and treatment of sexually transmitted diseases significantly reduced the risk of acquiring HIV infection over 2 years.

LIKELY TO BE BENEFICIAL

Postexposure prophylaxis in healthcare workers

One case control study found limited evidence suggesting that postexposure prophylaxis with zidovudine may reduce the risk of HIV infection over 6 months. Evidence from other settings suggests that combining several antiretroviral drugs is likely to be more effective than zidovudine alone.

UNKNOWN EFFECTIVENESS

Presumptive mass treatment of sexually transmitted diseases

One RCT found no significant difference with presumptive, mass treatment for sexually transmitted diseases versus no treatment in the incidence of HIV over 20 months.

What are the effects of treatments?

BENEFICIAL

Three drug antiretroviral regimens

Two RCTs have found that using a protease inhibitor plus two nucleoside analogue drugs versus two nucleoside analogue drugs alone halves the risk of new AIDS diseases or death over about 1 year. Both RCTs found that the risk of serious adverse effects was similar with three versus two drug regimens. Triple therapy is likely to reduce the risk of drug resistance compared with double therapy.

TRADE OFF BETWEEN BENEFITS AND HARMS

Single drug regimens; two drug regimens

Large RCTs, with follow up from 1–3 years, have found that two drug regimens (zidovudine plus another nucleoside analogue or protease inhibitor drug) versus zidovudine alone significantly reduce the risk of new AIDS defining illnesses and death. Adverse events were common in all treatment groups.

UNKNOWN EFFECTIVENESS

Early versus delayed antiretroviral treatment with multidrug regimens

We found no RCTs evaluating delayed versus early treatment with two or three drug regimens. RCTs conducted when zidovudine was the only drug available found no significant difference with immediate versus delayed treatment in survival at 1 year.

▶

Infectious diseases

◄ **DEFINITION**
HIV infection refers to infection with the human immunodeficiency virus type 1 or type 2. Clinically, this is characterised by a variable period (average around 8–10 years) of asymptomatic infection, followed by repeated episodes of illness of varying and increasing severity as immune function deteriorates. The type of illness varies greatly by country, availability of specific treatment for HIV, and prophylaxis for opportunistic infections.

INCIDENCE/ PREVALENCE
Worldwide estimates suggest that, by December 1999, about 50 million people had been infected with HIV, about 16 million people had died as a result, and about 16 000 new HIV infections were occurring each day.[1] About 90% of HIV infections occur in the developing world.[1] Occupationally acquired HIV infection in healthcare workers has been documented in 95 definite and 191 possible cases, although this is likely to be an underestimate.[2]

AETIOLOGY/ RISK FACTORS
The major risk factor for transmission of HIV is unprotected heterosexual or homosexual intercourse. Other risk factors include needlestick injury, sharing drug injecting equipment, and blood transfusion. An HIV infected woman may also transmit the virus to her baby. This has been reported in 15–30% of pregnant women with HIV infection. Not everyone who is exposed to HIV will become infected, although risk increases if exposure is repeated, at high dose, or through blood. There is at least a 2–5 times greater risk of HIV infection among people with sexually transmitted diseases.[3]

PROGNOSIS
Without treatment, about half of people infected with HIV will become ill and die from AIDS over about 10 years.

Influenza

Search date July 2001

Timothy Uyeki and Andrea Winquist

What are the effects of antiviral treatment of influenza in adults?

LIKELY TO BE BENEFICIAL

Oral amantadine for early treatment of influenza A in adults (duration of symptoms reduced)

One systematic review and three additional RCTs have found that oral amantadine versus placebo reduces the duration of influenza A symptoms by about 1 day. We found insufficient evidence about adverse effects in this setting. We found no good evidence of benefit if amantadine is started more than 2 days after symptom onset.

Oral oseltamivir for early treatment of influenza A and B in adults (duration of symptoms reduced)

Two RCTs have found that oral oseltamivir versus placebo reduces the duration of influenza symptoms by about 1 day. Oral oseltamivir versus placebo increases the incidence of nausea and vomiting. We found no good evidence of benefit if oseltamivir is started more than 1.5 days after symptom onset.

Oral rimantadine for early treatment of influenza A in adults (duration of symptoms reduced)

One systematic review has found that oral rimantadine versus placebo reduces the duration of influenza A symptoms by about 1 day. We found insufficient evidence about adverse effects in this setting. We found no good evidence of benefit if rimantadine is started more than 2 days after symptom onset.

Orally inhaled zanamivir for early treatment of influenza A and B in adults (duration of symptoms reduced)

One systematic review has found that orally inhaled zanamivir versus placebo reduces the duration of influenza symptoms by about 1 day. Adverse effects were similar in people taking zanamivir and in people taking placebo. We found no good evidence of benefit if zanamivir is started more than 2 days after symptom onset.

UNKNOWN EFFECTIVENESS

All antivirals (reduction of serious influenza complications)

We found insufficient evidence about the effects of antiviral agents on reducing serious complications of influenza, but we found strong evidence that influenza immunisation reduces the risk of complications and death in people at high risk for complications from influenza, including elderly people (see influenza vaccine under community acquired pneumonia, p 259).

DEFINITION Influenza is caused by infection with influenza viruses. Uncomplicated influenza is characterised by the abrupt onset of fever, chills, non-productive cough, myalgias, headache, nasal congestion, sore throat, and fatigue.[1] Influenza is usually diagnosed clinically. Not all people infected with influenza viruses become symptomatic. People infected with other pathogens may have symptoms identical to those of influenza.[2] The percentage of infections resulting in clinical illness can vary from about 40–85%, depending on age and pre-existing immunity to the virus.[3] ▶

◀ Influenza can be confirmed by viral culture, immunofluorescence staining, enzyme immunoassay, or rapid diagnostic testing of nasopharyngeal, nasal or throat swab specimens, or by serologic testing of paired sera. Some rapid tests detect influenza A only, some detect and distinguish between influenza A and B, whereas others detect but do not distinguish between influenza A and B.

INCIDENCE/
PREVALENCE In temperate areas of the Northern Hemisphere, influenza activity typically peaks between late December and early March whereas, in temperate areas of the Southern Hemisphere, influenza activity typically peaks between May and September. In tropical areas, influenza can occur throughout the year.[2] The annual incidence of influenza varies yearly, and depends partly on the underlying level of population immunity to circulating influenza viruses.[1] One localised study in the USA found that serological conversion with or without symptoms occurred in 10–20% a year, with the highest infection rates in people aged under 20 years.[4] Attack rates are higher in institutions and in areas of overcrowding.[5]

AETIOLOGY/
RISK FACTORS Influenza viruses are transmitted primarily from person to person through respiratory droplets disseminated during sneezing, coughing, and talking.[1,6]

PROGNOSIS The incubation period of influenza is 1–4 days and infected adults are usually contagious from the day before symptom onset until 5 days after symptom onset. The signs and symptoms of uncomplicated influenza usually resolve within a week, although cough and fatigue may persist.[1] Complications include otitis media, bacterial sinusitis, secondary bacterial pneumonia, and, less commonly, viral pneumonia and respiratory failure. Complications are also caused by exacerbation of underlying disease.[1,2] In the USA each year, over 110 000 admissions to hospital and about 20 000 deaths are related to influenza.[2] The risk of hospitalisation is highest in people 65 years or older, in very young children, and in those with chronic medical conditions.[1,7,8] Over 90% of influenza related deaths during recent seasonal epidemics in the USA have been in people 65 years or older.[1] During influenza pandemics, morbidity and mortality may be high in younger age groups.[1] Severe illness is more common with influenza A infections than influenza B infections.[1]

Lyme disease

Search date September 2001

Edward Hayes

What are the effects of preventive interventions and treatments?

BENEFICIAL

Prophylactic treatment of tick bite *New*

Combined results from RCTs have found that prophylactic antibiotics versus placebo for the treatment of tick bite reduce the incidence of Lyme disease.

Three doses of recombinant Osp–A Lyme disease vaccine with adjuvant in immunocompetent people aged 15–70 years exposed to North American strains of *Borrelia burgdorferi*

One RCT has found that a vaccine (consisting of recombinant outer surface protein A [Osp–A] of *B burgdorferi* combined with adjuvant❻) versus placebo significantly reduced the incidence of Lyme disease in people at high risk of developing Lyme disease within North America.

LIKELY TO BE BENEFICIAL

Penicillin (better than placebo for Lyme arthritis)

One RCT in people with Lyme arthritis has found that penicillin versus placebo significantly increases resolution of Lyme arthritis at 3 weeks (NNT 2).

Cefotaxime (more effective than penicillin for late neurological Lyme disease)

One RCT found weak evidence from subgroup analysis of people with late Lyme disease that cefotaxime versus penicillin significantly increased the number of people with full recovery at 2 years (NNT 4).

Cefotaxime (more effective than penicillin for Lyme arthritis)

One RCT found weak evidence from subgroup analysis of people with Lyme arthritis that cefotaxime versus penicillin significantly increased the number of people with full recovery at 2 years (NNT 4).

Ceftriaxone (more effective than penicillin for Lyme arthritis)

One RCT found weak evidence from subgroup analysis of people with Lyme arthritis that ceftriaxone versus penicillin significantly improved symptoms at 3 months (NNT 2).

Doxycycline (as effective as amoxicillin and probenecid for Lyme arthritis)

One RCT in people with Lyme arthritis has found no significant difference between doxycycline versus amoxicillin plus probenecid in resolution of Lyme arthritis.

UNKNOWN EFFECTIVENESS

Ceftriaxone (in late neurological Lyme disease)

One RCT found weak evidence from subgroup analysis in people with late neurological Lyme disease found no significant difference between ceftriaxone versus cefotaxime in the proportion of people who were asymptomatic at 8 months after treatment.

◀ **Ceftriaxone plus doxycycline (in late neurological Lyme disease)** *New*
One RCT comparing ceftriaxone plus doxycycline versus placebo in people with previously treated Lyme disease and persistent neurological symptoms found no significant difference in health related quality of life at interim analysis at 180 days, and the RCT was therefore terminated.

Lyme disease vaccine in Europe or Asia
We found no evidence about the effectiveness of recombinant Osp–A vaccine in European or Asian populations. There is heterogeneity of the species that cause Lyme disease in Europe and Asia. The vaccine may not be as effective in European or Asian populations as it is in North American.

LIKELY TO BE INEFFECTIVE OR HARMFUL

Oral antibiotic treatment of people with Lyme arthritis plus neuroborreliosis
Some people have developed symptoms of neuroborreliosis◉ after oral antibiotic treatment of Lyme arthritis.

DEFINITION
Lyme disease is an inflammatory illness resulting from infection with spirochetes of the *B burgdorferi* genospecies transmitted to humans by ticks. Some infected people have no symptoms. The characteristic manifestation of early Lyme disease is erythema migrans, a circular rash at the site of the infectious tick attachment that expands over a period of days to weeks in 80–90% of people with Lyme disease. Early disseminated infection may cause secondary erythema migrans, disease of the nervous system (facial palsy or other cranial neuropathies, meningitis, and radiculoneuritis), musculoskeletal disease (arthralgia), and, rarely, cardiac disease (myocarditis or transient atrioventricular block). Untreated or inadequately treated Lyme disease can cause late disseminated manifestations weeks to months after infection. These late manifestations include arthritis, polyneuropathy, and encephalopathy. Diagnosis of Lyme disease is based primarily on clinical findings and a high likelihood of exposure to infected ticks. Serological testing may be helpful in people with endemic exposure who have clinical findings consistent with later stage disseminated Lyme disease.

**INCIDENCE/
PREVALENCE**
Lyme disease occurs in temperate regions of North America, Europe, and Asia. It is the most commonly reported vector borne disease in the USA, with over 16 000 cases reported a year.[1] Most cases occur in the northeastern and northcentral states, with a reported annual incidence in endemic states as high as 67.9/100 000 people.[1] In highly endemic communities, the incidence of Lyme disease may exceed 1000/100 000 persons a year.[2] In some countries of Europe, the incidence of Lyme disease has been estimated to be over 100/100 000 people a year.[3] Foci of Lyme disease have been described in northern forested regions of Russia, in China, and in Japan.[4] Transmission cycles of *B burgdorferi* have not been described in tropical areas or in the Southern hemisphere.[4]

**AETIOLOGY/
RISK FACTORS**
Lyme disease is caused by infection with any of the *B burgdorferi* sensu lato genospecies. Virtually all cases of Lyme disease in North America are the result of infection with *B burgdorferi*. In Europe, Lyme disease may be caused by *B burgdorferi*, *B garinii,* and *B afzelii.* The infectious spirochetes are transmitted to humans through the bite of certain *Ixodes* ticks.[4] Humans who have frequent or prolonged exposure to the habitats of infected *Ixodes* ticks are at highest risk of acquiring Lyme disease. Individual risk depends on the likelihood of being bitten by infected tick vectors, which varies with the density of vector ticks in the environment, the prevalence of infection in ticks, and the extent of a person's contact with infected ticks. The risk of Lyme ▶

disease is often concentrated in focal areas. In the USA, risk is highest in certain counties within northeastern and northcentral states during the months of April–July.[2] People become infected when they engage in activities in wooded or bushy areas that are favourable habitats for ticks, and deer and rodent hosts.

PROGNOSIS Lyme disease is rarely fatal. Untreated Lyme arthritis resolves at a rate of 10–20% a year; over 90% of facial palsies due to Lyme disease resolve spontaneously, and most cases of Lyme carditis resolve without sequelae.[5] However, untreated Lyme disease can result in arthritis (50% of untreated people), meningitis or neuropathies (15% of untreated people), carditis (5–10% of untreated people with erythema migrans), and, rarely, encephalopathy.

Search date February 2002
Aika Omari and Paul Garner

What are the effects of medical treatment for complicated falciparum malaria in non-pregnant people? New

LIKELY TO BE BENEFICIAL

Quinine
We found no RCTs comparing quinine versus placebo or no treatment, but there is consensus that treatment is likely to be beneficial.

High first dose quinine
RCTs found that an initial high dose of quinine versus the standard dose increased the speed of parasite clearance☉, but the RCTs found no significant difference in mortality. One RCT found that more participants experienced short term partial hearing loss with high versus standard dose quinine.

Artemether
Systematic reviews found no significant difference in mortality with artemether versus quinine.

Rectal artemisinin
One systematic review found no significant difference in mortality with rectal artemisinin versus quinine.

UNKNOWN EFFECTIVENESS

Initial blood transfusion
One systematic review found no significant difference in deaths in clinically stable children who received an initial blood transfusion for malaria anaemia, and found more adverse events.

Exchange blood transfusion
We found no good evidence on exchange blood transfusions.

Chloroquine
Two RCTs found no significant difference in mortality with chloroquine versus quinine in The Gambia between 1988 and 1994 when chloroquine resistance was uncommon.

Desferrioxamine mesylate
One systematic review found limited evidence that desferrioxamine mesylate versus placebo reduced the risk of persistent seizures in children with cerebral malaria, but adverse effects were more common.

Intramuscular versus intravenous quinine
One RCT found no significant difference with intramuscular versus intravenous quinine in recovery times or deaths in Kenya in 1990.

Sulfadoxine–pyrimethamine
One RCT found that sulfadoxine–pyrimethamine versus quinine cleared parasites faster in children with complicated non-cerebral malaria in 1988 in The Gambia. ▶

Infectious diseases

◄ LIKELY TO BE INEFFECTIVE OR HARMFUL

Dexamethasone

One systematic review has found no significant difference in mortality with dexamethasone versus placebo, but gastrointestinal bleeding and seizures were more common with dexamethasone.

DEFINITION Severe malaria is caused by the protozoan infection of red blood cells with *Plasmodium falciparum*. Clinically complicated malaria presents with life threatening conditions, which include coma, severe anaemia, renal failure, respiratory distress syndrome, hypoglycaemia, shock, spontaneous haemorrhage, and convulsions. Cerebral malaria is diagnosed when there is unrousable coma and no other cause of encephalopathy (e.g. hypoglycaemia, sedative drugs) in the presence of malaria parasites.[1] This review does not currently include the treatment of malaria in pregnancy.

INCIDENCE/ Malaria is a major health problem in the tropics with 300–500 million
PREVALENCE clinical cases occurring annually, and an estimated 1.1–2.7 million deaths occur each year as a result of severe malaria. Over 90% of deaths occur in children below 5 years of age, mainly from cerebral malaria and anaemia.[2] In areas where malaria transmission is stable (endemic), those most at risk of acquiring severe malaria are children under 5 years old, because adults and older children have partial immunity that offers some protection. In areas where malaria transmission is unstable (non-endemic), severe malaria affects both adults and children. Non-immune travellers and migrants are also at risk from developing severe malaria.

AETIOLOGY/ Malaria is transmitted by the bite of infected female anopheline mosquitoes.
RISK FACTORS Certain genes are associated with resistance to severe malaria. Human leukocyte antigens (HLA), namely HLA-Bw53 and HLA-DRB1*1302, protect against severe malaria. However, the associations of HLA antigens with severe malaria are limited to specific populations.[3,4] Haemoglobin S[3] and haemoglobin C[5] are also protective against severe malaria. Genes have also been associated with an increased susceptibility to severe malaria, such as the tumour necrosis factor gene (see aetiology under malaria: prevention in travellers, p 133).[6]

PROGNOSIS In children under 5 years of age with cerebral malaria, the estimated case fatality of treated malaria is 19%, although reported hospital case fatality may be as high as 10–40%.[1,7] Neurological sequelae persisting for more than 6 months occur in more than 2% of the survivors, and include ataxia, hemiplegia, speech disorders, behavioural disorders, epilepsy, and blindness. Severe malarial anaemia has a case fatality rate higher than 13%.[7] In adults, the mortality of cerebral malaria is 20%; this rises to 50% in pregnancy,[8] and neurological sequelae occur in about 3% of survivors.[9]

Search date July 2001

Ashley Croft

What are the effects of treatments?

BENEFICIAL

Insecticide treated nets

We found no RCTs in travellers. One systematic review in residents of a malaria endemic area has found that nets treated with insecticide significantly reduce the number of mild episodes of malaria and child mortality (NNT 180).

LIKELY TO BE BENEFICIAL

Doxycycline in adults

Two RCTs in soldiers have found that doxycycline versus placebo significantly reduces the risk of malaria (NNT about 1).

Insecticide treated clothing

Two RCTs in soldiers and refugee householders have found that permethrin treated fabric (clothing or sheets) significantly reduces the incidence of malaria.

Mefloquine in adults

One RCT in soldiers comparing mefloquine versus placebo has found that mefloquine has a 100% protective efficacy.

UNKNOWN EFFECTIVENESS

Aerosol insecticides

One large observational study in travellers found insufficient evidence on the effects of aerosol insecticides in preventing malaria. Two RCTs in malaria endemic areas found that indoor spraying of aerosol insecticides reduced clinical malaria.

Air conditioning and electric fans

One large observational study found that air conditioning significantly reduced the incidence of malaria.

Atovaquone plus proguanil

One RCT found no significant difference between atovaquone plus proguanil versus chloroquine plus proguanil in preventing malaria.

Chloroquine

We found no RCTs about the effects of chloroquine in travellers. One RCT in Austrian workers residing in Nigeria found no significant difference between chloroquine versus sulfadoxine plus pyrimethamine in the incidence of malaria over 22 months.

Chloroquine plus proguanil

One RCT found no significant difference between chloroquine plus proguanil versus proguanil alone or versus chloroquine plus other antimalaria drugs in incidence of in *Plasmodium falciparum* malaria. One RCT found no significant difference between chloroquine plus proguanil versus atovaquone plus proguanil in preventing malaria. ▶

Malaria: prevention in travellers

Insecticide treated nets in pregnant travellers

We found no RCTs of the effects of insecticide treated nets on pregnant travellers. One RCT of pregnant residents found inconclusive evidence on the effects of permethrin treated nets in preventing malaria.

Lifestyle change

One observational study found that wearing trousers and long sleeved shirts significantly reduced the incidence of malaria.

Mosquito coils and vaporising mats

We found no systematic review and no RCTs of the effects of coils and vaporising mats in preventing malaria in travellers. One RCT of coils and one observational study of pyrethroid vaporising mats found that these devices reduced numbers of mosquitoes in indoor spaces.

Pyrimethamine plus dapsone

We found no RCTs in travellers. One RCT in Thai soldiers comparing pyrimethamine/dapsone versus proguanil/dapsone found no significant difference in P falciparum infection rates over 40 days.

Smoke

We found no RCTs of the effects of smoke in preventing malaria. One controlled clinical trial found that smoke repelled mosquitoes during the evening.

Topical insect repellents

We found no systematic review and no RCTs on the effects of topical insect repellents in preventing malaria. One small RCT found that an insect repellent soap versus placebo soap significantly reduced the number of sandfly bites at 4 and 8 hours. One small crossover RCT found that DEET preparations protected against mosquito bites.

Vaccines

We found no RCTs in travellers. One systematic review of antimalaria vaccines in residents of malaria endemic areas has found that the SPf66 vaccine versus placebo significantly reduces first attacks of malaria.

Antimalaria drugs in airline pilots or pregnant travellers; biological control measures; insect buzzers and electrocuters; insecticides in airline pilots; mefloquine in children; insecticide treated clothing in pregnant travellers; topical insect repellents in pregnant travellers

We found no RCTs on the effects of these interventions.

LIKELY TO BE INEFFECTIVE OR HARMFUL

Amodiaquine

We found no RCTs of the effects of amodiaquine in preventing malaria in travelers. Observational evidence suggests that amodiaquine is associated with neutropenia, liver damage, and hepatitis.

Doxycycline in children

We found no RCTs in child travellers on the use of doxycycline. Case reports in young children found adverse effects with doxycycline.

Insect repellents containing DEET in children

We found no RCTs on the effects of DEET in preventing malaria in child travellers. Case reports in young children found serious adverse effects with DEET.

◄ **Sulfadoxine plus pyrimethamine**

One open label RCT comparing chloroquine plus proguanil versus chloroquine plus sulfadoxine plus pyrimethamine found no significant difference in rates of *P falciparum* malaria. One retrospective cohort study suggested that sulfadoxine plus pyrimethamine was associated with severe cutaneous reactions and a risk of mortality.

DEFINITION   Malaria is caused by a protozoan infection of red blood cells with one of four species of the genus *Plasmodium*: *P falciparum*, *P vivax*, *P ovale*, and *P malariae*.[1] Clinically, malaria may present in different ways, but is usually characterised by fever (which may be swinging), tachycardia, rigors, and sweating. Anaemia, hepatosplenomegaly, cerebral involvement, renal failure, and shock may occur.

INCIDENCE/   Each year there are 300–500 million clinical cases of malaria. About 40%
PREVALENCE   of the world's population is at risk of acquiring the disease.[2,3] Each year 25–30 million people from non-tropical countries visit malaria endemic areas, of whom 10 000–30 000 contract malaria.[4,5] Most RCTs of malaria prevention have been carried out on soldiers and travellers. The results of these trials may not be applicable to people such as refugees and migrants, who are likely to differ in their health status and their susceptibility to disease and adverse drug effects.

AETIOLOGY/   Malaria is mainly a rural disease, requiring nearby standing water. It is
RISK FACTORS transmitted by bites of infected female anopheline mosquitoes, mainly at dusk and during the night.[1,6–8] In cities, mosquito bites are usually from female culicine mosquitoes, which are not vectors of malaria.[9] Malaria is resurgent in most tropical countries and risk to travellers is increasing.[10] The sickle cell trait has been shown to convey some protection against malaria in non-immune carriers of that trait. Non-immune adults with the sickle cell trait who develop severe malaria have lower parasite densities, fewer complications (e.g. cerebral malaria), and a reduced mortality compared with adults without the trait.[11] There is little good evidence on the degree of protection afforded by the sickle cell trait.[12]

PROGNOSIS   Ninety per cent of tourists and business travellers who contract malaria do not become ill until after they return home.[5] "Imported malaria" is easily treated if diagnosed promptly, and follows a serious course in only about 12% of people.[13,14] The most severe form is cerebral malaria, with a case fatality rate in adult travellers of 2–6% mainly because of delays in diagnosis.[3,15]

Mammalian bites

Search date November 2001

Iara Marques de Medeiros and Humberto Saconato

What are the effects of interventions to prevent and treat mammalian bites? New

Antibiotics for treatment of infectious complications of mammalian bites

We found no RCTs of antibiotics versus placebo for the treatment of infectious complications of mammalian bites. However, there is consensus that antibiotics are likely to be beneficial.

Antibiotic prophylaxis

Limited evidence from one systematic review found no significant difference with antibiotics versus control in the infection rate in people bitten by a dog, cat, or human in the preceding 24 hours. Meta-analysis according to the site of the wound found that antibiotics significantly reduced infections of the hand (NNT 4). One small RCT in the review found that in people with human bites, antibiotics versus control significantly reduced the rate of infection.

Debridement, irrigation, and decontamination

We found no systematic review, RCTs, or good cohort studies assessing debridement, irrigation, decontamination measures, and serum infiltration in the wound. However, there is consensus that such measures are likely to be beneficial.

Education to prevent bites

We found no RCTs of the effect of education programmes on the incidence of mammalian bites. One RCT found that an educational programme versus no education in school children significantly increased precautionary behaviour around dogs.

Antibiotics versus other antibiotics for treatment of infectious complications of mammalian bites

One RCT in people with infected and uninfected animal and human bites comparing penicillin with or without dicloxacillin versus amoxicillin/clavulanic acid found no significant difference in failure rate (which was undefined).

Closure of cutaneous wounds

One poor quality RCT comparing primary wound closure versus no closure in people with dog bites found no significant difference in the incidence of infection, but the RCT was too small to exclude clinically important effects.

Education to prevent bites in specific occupational groups

We found no RCTs of education to prevent bites in specific occupational groups.

Tetanus toxoid after mammalian bites

We found no evidence on the effects of tetanus toxoid in preventing tetanus after human or animal bites.

▶

◀ **DEFINITION** Bite wounds are mainly caused by humans, dogs, or cats. They include superficial abrasions🄖 (30–43%), lacerations🄖 (31–45%), and puncture🄖 wounds (13–34%).[1]

INCIDENCE/ In the USA, 17–18% of people with dog bites seek medical attention and
PREVALENCE 1% require hospitalisation;[2,3] the incidence of dog bites is 3.5–4.7 million bites a year.[4] Children constitute 30–50% of all mammalian bite injuries.[5] In areas where domestic animal rabies has not been controlled, dogs account for 90% of the reported animal bites in humans. In contrast, in areas where domestic animal rabies is well controlled, dogs account for less than 5% of the reported animal bites.

AETIOLOGY/ In over 70% of cases, people are bitten by their own pets or by an animal
RISK FACTORS known to them. Males are more likely to be bitten than females, and males are most likely to be bitten by dogs whereas females are more likely to be bitten by cats.[4] One study found that children under 5 years old were significantly more likely than older children to provoke animals prior to being bitten.[6] One study of infected dog and cat bites found that the most commonly isolated bacteria was *Pasteurella*, followed by *Streptococci*, *Staphylococci*, *Moraxella*, *Corynebacterium*, and *Neisseria*.[7] Mixed aerobic and anaerobic infection was more common than anaerobic infection alone.

PROGNOSIS In the USA, dog bites cause about 20 deaths a year.[8] In children, dog bites frequently involve the face, potentially resulting in severe lacerations and scarring.[9] Rabies, a life threatening viral encephalitis, may be contracted as a consequence of being bitten or scratched by a rabid animal. More than 99% of human rabies is in developing countries where canine rabies is still endemic.[10] In people bitten by a rabid animal and not treated, the risk of contracting rabies has been estimated to be 5–80%, depending on the animal species, severity of the bite, infectivity of the animal saliva, virus inoculum, host factors, and possibly the strain of rabies virus.[11,12] One study in the USA reported that the risk of rabies in 21 people with proven rabies exposure was between 5–15%.[13]

Meningococcal disease

Search date October 2001

J Correia and C A Hart

What are the effects of treatments?

LIKELY TO BE BENEFICIAL

Prophylactic antibiotics in contacts

We found no RCTs about the effects of prophylactic antibiotics on the incidence of meningococcal disease among contacts. RCTs are unlikely to be performed because the intervention has few associated risks whereas meningitis has high associated risks. Observational evidence suggests that antibiotics reduce the risk of meningococcal disease. We found no evidence to address the question of which contacts should be treated.

UNKNOWN EFFECTIVENESS

Antibiotics for throat carriage (reduce carriage but unknown effect on risk of disease)

RCTs have found that antibiotics versus placebo significantly increases the number of people with eradication of meningococcus in the throat. We found no evidence that eradicating throat carriage reduces the risk of meningococcal disease.

Pre-admission parenteral antibiotics in suspected cases *New*

We found no RCTs on the effect of pre-admission antibiotics. It is unlikely that RCTs will be performed because of the unpredictably rapid course of meningococcal disease in some people, the intuitive risks involved in delaying treatment, and the relatively low risk of causing harm. Most of the observational studies we found show a trend toward benefit with antibiotics, but at least one found contradictory results.

DEFINITION Meningococcal disease is any clinical condition caused by *Neisseria meningitidis* (the meningococcus) groups A, B, C, or other serogroups. These conditions include purulent conjunctivitis, septic arthritis, meningitis, and septicaemia with or without meningitis.

INCIDENCE/ PREVALENCE Meningococcal disease is sporadic in temperate countries, and is most commonly caused by group B or C meningococci. The incidence in the UK varies from 2–8 cases/100 000 people a year,[1] and in the USA from 0.6–1.5/100 000 people.[2] Occasional outbreaks occur among close family contacts, secondary school pupils, and students living in halls of residence. Sub-Saharan Africa has regular epidemics because of serogroup A, particularly in countries lying between Gambia in the west and Ethiopia in the east (the "meningitis belt"), where incidence during epidemics reaches 500/100 000 people.[3]

AETIOLOGY/ RISK FACTORS The meningococcus infects healthy people and is transmitted by close contact, probably by exchange of upper respiratory tract secretions❶.[4–12] Risk of transmission is greatest during the first week of contact.[7] Risk factors include crowding and exposure to cigarette smoke.[13] Children younger than 2 years have the highest incidence, with a second peak between ages 15–24 years. There is currently an increased incidence of meningococcal disease among university students, especially among those in their first term and living in catered accommodation,[14] although we found no accurate numerical estimate of risk from close contact in, for example, halls of residence. Close contacts of an index case have a much higher risk of ▶

◀ infection than do people in the general population.[7,10,11] The risk of epidemic spread is higher with groups A and C meningococci than with group B meningococci.[4–6,8] It is not known what makes a meningococcus virulent, but certain clones tend to predominate at different times and in different groups. Carriage of meningococcus in the throat has been reported in 10–15% of people; recent acquisition of a virulent meningococcus is more likely to be associated with invasive disease.

PROGNOSIS   Mortality is highest in infants and adolescents, and is related to disease presentation: case fatality rates are 19–25% in septicaemia, 10–12% in meningitis plus septicaemia, and less than 1% in meningitis alone.[15–17]

Infectious diseases

Mother to child transmission of HIV

Search date May 2001

Jimmy Volmink

What are the effects of measures to reduce mother to child transmission of human immunodeficiency virus (HIV)?

BENEFICIAL

Antiretroviral drugs

One systematic review has found that, in mothers with human immuno-deficiency virus (HIV), zidovudine versus placebo given to mothers significantly reduces the incidence of HIV in infants at follow up of about 3–18 months. One RCT has found that nevirapine versus zidovudine given to mothers with HIV and to their newborns significantly reduces the incidence of HIV in infants. One RCT has found that a longer versus a shorter course of zidovudine given to mother and infant significantly reduces the incidence of HIV in infants.

LIKELY TO BE BENEFICIAL

Elective caesarean section

One RCT found limited evidence that elective caesarean section versus vaginal delivery in women with HIV reduced the incidence of HIV in infants at 18 months (NNT 11).

TRADE OFF BETWEEN BENEFITS AND HARMS

Avoiding breast feeding

One RCT, in women with HIV who had access to clean water and health education, has found that formula feeding versus breast feeding significantly reduces the incidence of HIV in infants after 24 months (NNT 6), without increasing infant mortality. However, in countries with high infant mortality, avoiding breast feeding may further increase infant morbidity and mortality.

UNKNOWN EFFECTIVENESS

Vaginal microbicides

We found insufficient evidence about the effects of vaginal microbicides on the transmission of HIV to infants.

UNLIKELY TO BE BENEFICIAL

Immunotherapy

One RCT found no significant difference in the incidence of HIV in infants of mothers taking hyperimmune globulin versus immunoglobulin without HIV antibody, in addition to a standard zidovudine regimen.

LIKELY TO BE INEFFECTIVE OR HARMFUL

Vitamin supplements

RCTs found no significant difference in the incidence of HIV in the infants of pregnant women given vitamin A or multivitamins versus placebo.

DEFINITION   Mother to child transmission of HIV type 1🅖 infection can occur during pregnancy, in the intrapartum period, or postnatally through breast feeding.[1] In contrast, HIV type 2🅖 is rarely transmitted from mother to child.[2] Infected children usually have no symptoms and signs of HIV at birth, but develop them over subsequent months or years.[3]

▶

INCIDENCE/ PREVALENCE A review of 13 cohorts found that the risk of mother to child transmission of HIV is about 15–20% in Europe, 15–30% in the USA, and 25–35% in Africa.[4] One global report estimated that 620 000 children below the age of 15 years were infected with HIV during 1999, bringing the total number of children with HIV/AIDS to 1.3 million worldwide.[5] Most of these children were infected from their mother and 90% live in sub-Saharan Africa.

AETIOLOGY/ RISK FACTORS Transmission of HIV to children is more likely if the mother has a high viral load.[1,6,7] Women with detectable viraemia (by p24 antigen or culture) have double the risk of transmitting HIV-1 to their infants than those who do not.[1] Breast feeding has also been shown in prospective studies to be a risk factor.[8,9] Other risk factors include sexually transmitted diseases, chorio-amnionitis, prolonged rupture of membranes, and vaginal mode of delivery.[5,10–13]

PROGNOSIS About 25% of infants infected with HIV progress rapidly to AIDS or death in the first year. Some survive beyond 12 years of age.[3] One European study found a mortality of 15% in the first year of life, and a mortality of 28% by the age of 5 years.[14]

Opportunistic infections and HIV

Search date January 2002

John Ioannidis and David Wilkinson

What are the effects of drug prophylaxis?

BENEFICIAL

Atovaquone (no difference from dapsone or aerosolised pentamidine for *Pneumocystis carinii* pneumonia [PCP] in people intolerant of trimethoprim/sulfamethoxazole [TMP/SMX; co-trimoxazole])

We found no RCTs of atovaquone versus placebo. RCTs found no significant difference in the incidence of PCP with atovaquone versus dapsone or versus aerosolised pentamidine.

TMP/SMX (for PCP and toxoplasmosis)

Systematic reviews have found that TMP/SMX versus placebo or pentamidine significantly reduces the incidence of PCP or toxoplasmosis. Systematic reviews have found that TMP/SMX versus dapsone (with or without pyrimethamine) reduces the incidence of PCP, but found no difference in the incidence of toxoplasmosis. One systematic review and one subsequent RCT found no significant difference between high and low dose TMP/SMX for PCP prophylaxis, although adverse effects were more common with the higher dose.

Aciclovir (for herpes simplex virus and varicella zoster virus)

One systematic review has found that aciclovir versus placebo significantly reduces herpes simplex virus and varicella zoster virus infection and overall mortality in people at different clinical stages of HIV infection. It found no reduction in cytomegalovirus.

Tuberculosis prophylaxis (versus placebo)

Systematic reviews have found that in people who are HIV and tuberculin skin test positive, antituberculosis prophylaxis versus placebo significantly reduces the frequency of tuberculosis over 2–3 years. The reviews have found no evidence of benefit in people who are HIV positive but tuberculin skin test negative. One RCT found that the benefit of prophylaxis diminished with time after treatment was stopped.

LIKELY TO BE BENEFICIAL

Azithromycin (for *Mycobacterium avium* complex [MAC])

One RCT has found that azithromycin versus placebo significantly reduces the incidence of MAC.

Azithromycin (for PCP)

One RCT has found that azithromycin, either alone or in combination with rifabutin versus rifabutin alone, reduces the risk of PCP in people receiving standard PCP prophylaxis.

Clarithromycin (for MAC)

One RCT has found that clarithromycin versus placebo significantly reduces the incidence of MAC.

Clarithromycin plus ethambutol (for MAC in people with previous MAC)

RCTs have found that clarithromycin plus ethambutol, with or without rifabutin, significantly reduces the incidence of MAC.

◀ **Discontinuing prophylaxis for MAC in people with CD4 > 100/mm³ on highly active antiretroviral treatment (HAART)**

Two RCTs in people taking HAART found that discontinuation of prophylaxis for MAC disease did not increase the incidence of MAC disease.

Discontinuing prophylaxis for PCP and toxoplasmosis in people with CD4 > 200/mm³ on HAART

One systematic review of two unblinded RCTs in people taking HAART found that discontinuation of prophylaxis did not increase the incidence of PCP. Two unblinded RCTs found that discontinuation of prophylaxis did not increase the incidence of toxoplasmosis.

Itraconazole (for *Penicillium marneffei* and cryptococcal meningitis)

Two RCTs have found that itraconazole versus placebo significantly reduces the incidence of relapse of *P marneffei*Ⓖ infection and candidiasis. One RCT has found that itraconazole versus fluconazole significantly reduces the relapse of cryptococcal meningitis.

TRADE OFF BETWEEN BENEFITS AND HARMS

Fluconazole or itraconazole (invasive fungal disease)

RCTs in people with advanced HIV disease have found that both fluconazole and itraconazole versus placebo significantly reduce the incidence of invasive fungal infections. One RCT found that fluconazole versus clotrimazole reduced the incidence of invasive fungal disease and mucocutaneous candidiasis. One RCT found no difference between high and low dose fluconazole.

Oral ganciclovir (in people with severe CD4 depletion)

One RCT has found that oral ganciclovir versus placebo significantly reduces the incidence of cytomegalovirus in people with severe CD4 depletion. It found that 25% of people who did not develop cytomegalovirus developed severe neutropenia. A second RCT found no significant differences.

Isoniazid tuberculosis prophylaxis for 6–12 months (*v* combination treatment for 2 months — similar benefits, fewer harms)

RCTs found no evidence of a difference in effectiveness between regimens using combinations of tuberculosis drugs for 2–3 months and those using isoniazid alone for 6–12 months. One RCT found that multidrug regimens increased the number of people with adverse reactions resulting in cessation of treatment.

Rifabutin plus either clarithromycin or azithromycin (for MAC)

One RCT has found that rifabutin plus clarithromycin versus rifabutin alone significantly reduces the incidence of MAC. Another RCT has found that rifabutin plus azithromycin versus azithromycin alone or rifabutin alone significantly reduces the incidence of MAC at 1 year.

UNKNOWN EFFECTIVENESS

Famciclovir (for recurrent herpes simplex virus)

One small RCT found that famciclovir versus placebo reduced the rate of viral shedding, but provided insufficient evidence on the effect of famciclovir on herpes simplex virus recurrence.

Itraconazole (for histoplasmosis)

We found no RCTs. One open label uncontrolled study found that itraconazole may be effective in preventing the relapse of histoplasmosis.

▶

Opportunistic infections and HIV

◄ **Stopping prophylaxis for cytomegalovirus in people with CD4 > 100/mm³ on HAART**

We found insufficient evidence on the effects of discontinuation of maintenance treatment for cytomegalovirus retinitis or other end organ disease in people taking HAART.

LIKELY TO BE INEFFECTIVE OR HARMFUL

Clofazimine or high dose clarithromycin (for MAC in people with previous MAC)

RCTs have found that clofazimine or high dose clarithromycin versus other combination treatment are associated with increased mortality.

Valaciclovir (for cytomegalovirus)

One RCT has found that valaciclovir versus aciclovir reduces the incidence of cytomegalovirus, but is associated with increased mortality.

DEFINITION Opportunistic infections are intercurrent infections that occur in people infected with HIV. Prophylaxis aims to avoid either the first occurrence of these infections (primary prophylaxis) or their recurrence (secondary prophylaxis, maintenance treatment). This review includes PCP, *Toxoplasma gondii* encephalitis, *Mycobacterium tuberculosis*, MAC disease, cytomegalovirus disease (most often retinitis), infections from other herpes viruses (herpes simplex virus and varicella zoster virus), and invasive fungal disease (*Cryptococcus neoformans*, *Histoplasma capsulatum*, and *P marneffei*.

INCIDENCE/ The incidence of opportunistic infections is high in people with immune
PREVALENCE impairment. Data available before the introduction of HAART suggest that, with a CD4 < 250/mm³, the 2 year probability of developing an opportunistic infection is 40% for PCP, 22% for cytomegalovirus, 18% for MAC, 6% for toxoplasmosis, and 5% for cryptococcal meningitis.[1] The introduction of HAART has reduced the rate of opportunistic infections. A recent cohort study found that the introduction of HAART decreased the incidence of PCP by 94%, cytomegalovirus by 82%, and MAC by 64%, as presenting AIDS events. HAART decreased the incidence of events subsequent to the diagnosis of AIDS by 84% for PCP, 82% for cytomegalovirus, and 97% for MAC.[2]

AETIOLOGY/ Opportunistic infections are caused by a wide array of pathogens and result
RISK FACTORS from immune defects induced by HIV. The risk of developing opportunistic infections increases dramatically with progressive impairment of the immune system. Each opportunistic infection has a different threshold of immune impairment, beyond which the risk increases substantially.[1] Opportunistic pathogens may infect the immunocompromised host *de novo*, but usually they are simply reactivations of latent pathogens in such hosts.

PROGNOSIS Prognosis depends on the type of opportunistic infection. Even with treatment they may cause serious morbidity and mortality. Most deaths owing to HIV infection are caused by opportunistic infections.

Search date January 2002

Tim Lancaster, David Wareham and John Yaphe

What are the effects of interventions to prevent postherpetic neuralgia?

BENEFICIAL

Oral antiviral agents (aciclovir, famciclovir, valaciclovir, netivudine)

Systematic reviews have found that daily aciclovir versus placebo reduces the prevalence of postherpetic pain at 6 months by about 50% (NNT 7). One RCT found that famciclovir versus placebo significantly reduced pain duration after acute herpes zoster. One systematic review of one RCT found that valaciclovir versus aciclovir significantly reduced the prevalence of postherpetic neuralgia at 6 months (NNT 16). One RCT found no significant difference in outcomes between netivudine and aciclovir. One RCT found no significant difference in postherpetic neuralgia between valaciclovir and famciclovir.

LIKELY TO BE BENEFICIAL

Amitriptyline

One small RCT found that amitriptyline versus placebo started during the acute episode reduced the prevalence of postherpetic neuralgia at 6 months, but the reduction did not quite reach significance.

UNKNOWN EFFECTIVENESS

Adenosine monophosphate, amantadine; cimetidine; isoprinosine; levodopa

We found insufficient evidence on the effects of these interventions.

UNLIKELY TO BE BENEFICIAL

Topical antiviral agents (idoxuridine)

One systematic review has found that idoxuridine versus placebo or versus oral aciclovir increases short term pain relief in acute herpes zoster, but has found no significant difference in pain at 6 months.

LIKELY TO BE INEFFECTIVE OR HARMFUL

Corticosteroids

Systematic reviews have found conflicting evidence about the effects of corticosteroids alone on postherpetic neuralgia. One RCT found limited evidence that high dose steroids added to antiviral agents may be of short term benefit in acute herpes zoster, but found no significant effect on pain at 6 months. There is concern that corticosteroids may cause dissemination of herpes zoster.

What are the effects of treatments in established postherpetic neuralgia?

BENEFICIAL

Gabapentin

One systematic review and one additional RCT have found that gabapentin versus placebo significantly relieves pain.

▶

Postherpetic neuralgia

◄ **Tricyclic antidepressants**
One systematic review has found that tricyclic antidepressants (amitryptyline or desipramine) versus placebo significantly increase pain relief at 6 weeks.

UNKNOWN EFFECTIVENESS

Oxycodone (oral opioid)
One crossover RCT found that oral oxycodone versus placebo significantly reduced pain after 4–8 weeks, but was associated with more adverse effects.

Topical anaesthesia
One small RCT found that lidocaine patches versus placebo increased pain relief over 12 hours.

Topical counterirritants
RCTs found that capsaicin versus placebo significantly improved pain relief, but also caused painful skin reactions.

LIKELY TO BE INEFFECTIVE OR HARMFUL

Dextromethorphan
One RCT found no significant difference with dextromethorphan versus placebo in pain at 6 weeks.

Epidural morphine
One small RCT found that epidural morphine versus placebo reduced pain by more than 50% but the reduction was not maintained beyond 36 hours. Epidural morphine caused intolerable opioid effects in 75% of people.

DEFINITION Postherpetic neuralgia is pain that sometimes follows resolution of acute herpes zoster and healing of the zoster rash. It can be severe, accompanied by itching, and follows the distribution of the original infection. Herpes zoster is an acute infection caused by activation of latent varicella zoster virus (human herpes virus 3) in people who have been rendered partially immune by a previous attack of chickenpox. Herpes zoster infects the sensory ganglia and their areas of innervation. It is characterised by pain along the distribution of the affected nerve and crops of clustered vesicles over the area.

INCIDENCE/ PREVALENCE In a UK general practice survey of 321 cases, the annual incidence of herpes zoster was 3.4/1000.[1] Incidence varied with age. Herpes zoster was relatively uncommon in people under the age of 50 years (< 2/1000 a year), but rose to 5–7/1000 a year in people aged 50–79 years, and 11/1000 in people aged 80 years or older. In a population based study of 590 cases in Rochester, Minnesota, USA, the overall incidence was lower (1.5/1000) but with similar increases in incidence with age.[2] Prevalence of postherpetic neuralgia depends on when it is measured after acute infection, and there is no agreed time point.

AETIOLOGY/ RISK FACTORS The main risk factor for postherpetic neuralgia is increasing age. In a UK general practice study (involving 3600–3800 people, 321 cases of acute herpes zoster) there was little risk in those under the age of 50 years, but postherpetic neuralgia developed in over 20% of people who had had acute herpes zoster aged 60–65 years and in 34% aged over 80 years.[1] No other risk factor has been found to predict consistently which people with herpes zoster will experience continued pain. In a general practice study in Iceland (421 people followed for up to 7 years after an initial episode of herpes zoster), the risk of postherpetic neuralgia was 1.8% (95% CI 0.6% to 4.2%) for people under 60 years of age and the pain was mild in all cases.[2] The risk of severe pain after 3 months in people aged over 60 years was 1.7% (95% CI 0% to 6.2%).

►

◀ **PROGNOSIS**   About 2% of people with acute herpes zoster in the UK general practice survey had pain for more than 5 years.[1] Prevalence of pain falls as time elapses after the initial episode. Among 183 people aged over 60 years in the placebo arm of a UK trial, the prevalence of pain was 61% at 1 month, 24% at 3 months, and 13% at 6 months after acute infection.[3] In a more recent RCT, the prevalence of postherpetic pain in the placebo arm at 6 months was 35% in 72 people over 60 years of age.[4]

Tuberculosis

Search date August 2001

Paul Garner and Alison Holmes

What are the effects of interventions in newly diagnosed pulmonary tuberculosis and multidrug resistant tuberculosis?

BENEFICIAL

Short course chemotherapy (as good as longer courses)

RCTs in people with newly diagnosed tuberculosis found no evidence of a difference in relapse rates with standard short course (6 months) versus longer term (8–9 months) chemotherapy.

LIKELY TO BE BENEFICIAL

Intermittent short course chemotherapy (as good as daily treatment)

Limited evidence from two RCTs in people with newly diagnosed tuberculosis found no significant difference in cure rates with daily versus twice or three times weekly short course chemotherapy regimens.

Pyrazinamide

RCTs found that, in people with newly diagnosed tuberculosis, regimens containing pyrazinamide versus other regimens speed up sputum clearance in the first 2 months, but have found conflicting evidence about effects on relapse rates.

UNKNOWN EFFECTIVENESS

Comparative benefits of different regimens in multidrug resistant tuberculosis

We found no RCTs in people with newly diagnosed tuberculosis comparing different drug regimens for multidrug resistant tuberculosis.

Regimens containing quinolones

We found insufficient evidence in people with newly diagnosed tuberculosis comparing regimens containing quinolones versus existing regimens.

LIKELY TO BE INEFFECTIVE OR HARMFUL

Chemotherapy for less than 6 months

One systematic review in people with newly diagnosed tuberculosis found limited evidence that reducing the duration of chemotherapy to less than 6 months significantly increased relapse rates.

What are the effects of interventions to improve adherence and screening attendance?

LIKELY TO BE BENEFICIAL

Cash incentives

One systematic review has found that cash incentives versus usual care significantly improve attendance among people living in deprived circumstances. Two subsequent RCTs found conflicting results on the effect of cash incentives on treatment completion.

▶

◀ **Community health advisors**

One RCT found that health advisors recruited from the community versus usual care significantly increased attendance for treatment.

Defaulter actions⊙

RCTs have found that intensive action (repeated home visits and reminder letters) versus routine action (single reminder letter and home visit) for defaulters significantly improves completion of treatment.

Health education by a nurse

One RCT found that health education by a nurse versus an educational leaflet significantly improved treatment completion.

UNKNOWN EFFECTIVENESS

Directly observed treatment

RCTs found conflicting evidence about the effects of direct observation.

Health education by a doctor; prompts to adhere to treatment; sanctions for non-adherence; staff training

We found insufficient evidence on the effects of these interventions.

Prompts and contracts to improve reattendance for Mantoux test reading

One RCT in healthy people found that telephone prompts to return for Mantoux test reading versus no prompts slightly increased the number of people who reattended, but the difference was not significant. Another RCT in healthy people found that a verbal commitment versus no commitment significantly increased reattendance for Mantoux reading.

DEFINITION   Tuberculosis is caused by *Mycobacterium tuberculosis* and can affect many organs. Specific symptoms relate to site of infection and are generally accompanied by fever, sweats, and weight loss.

INCIDENCE/   About a third of the world's population is infected with *M tuberculosis*. The
PREVALENCE   organism kills more people than any other infectious agent. The World Health Organization estimates that 95% of cases are in developing countries, and that 25% of avoidable deaths in developing countries are caused by tuberculosis.[1]

AETIOLOGY/   Social factors include poverty, overcrowding, homelessness, and inadequate
RISK FACTORS health services. Medical factors include HIV and immunosuppression.

PROGNOSIS   Prognosis varies widely and depends on treatment.[2]

Acute renal failure

Search date August 2001

John A Kellum, Martine Leblanc and Ramesh Venkataraman

What are the effects of interventions to prevent acute renal failure in people at high risk?

BENEFICIAL

Low osmolality contrast media (better than standard)
One systematic review comparing low osmolality with standard contrast media⊙ has found that the development of acute renal failure or need for dialysis are rare events. However, nephrotoxicity⊙ (assessed by serum creatinine) was less likely with low osmolality contrast media, especially in people with underlying renal impairments.

LIKELY TO BE BENEFICIAL

Fluids
We found no RCTs of fluids to prevent acute renal failure. However, dehydration is an important risk factor for acute renal failure and recommended volumes of fluid have little potential for harm.

Single (better than multiple doses of aminoglycosides)
One RCT found that single daily dosing versus standard dosing of aminoglycosides significantly reduced nephrotoxicity (NNT 5).

UNKNOWN EFFECTIVENESS

Acetylcysteine
One small RCT found limited evidence that acetylcysteine versus placebo significantly reduced the incidence of acute renal failure induced by contrast media (NNT 6).

Lipid formulations of amphotericin (better than standard formulations)
One RCT found limited evidence that lipid versus standard formulations of amphotericin may cause less nephrotoxicity. We found no evidence about the long term safety of lipid formulations of amphotericin⊙.

UNLIKELY TO BE BENEFICIAL

Theophylline in acute renal failure induced by contrast media
RCTs found that theophylline versus placebo did not prevent acute renal failure induced by contrast media when people are adequately hydrated.

Mannitol
Small RCTs in people with traumatic rhabdomyolysis, or undergoing coronary artery bypass, vascular, or biliary tract surgery found that mannitol versus hydration alone did not reduce acute renal failure. One RCT found that mannitol versus saline increased the risk of acute renal failure, but the difference was not significant.

LIKELY TO BE INEFFECTIVE OR HARMFUL

Calcium channel blockers for early allograft dysfunction
One large RCT found no significant difference with calcium channel blockers versus placebo in reducing graft dysfunction in renal transplantation. We found no RCTs about the effects of calcium channel blockers in other forms of acute renal failure.

▶

◀ **Dopamine**

One systematic review and one subsequent RCT found that dopamine did not prevent the onset of acute renal failure, the need for dialysis, or mortality.

Loop diuretics

One systematic review has found that loop diuretics versus fluids alone do not prevent acute renal failure. One RCT in people with acute tubular necrosis induced by contrast media found that diuretics versus saline significantly increased acute renal failure (NNH 4). Another RCT found that diuretics versus saline significantly increased acute renal failure following cardiac surgery (NNH 6).

Natriuretic peptides

One large RCT found no significant difference with natriuretic peptides versus placebo in the prevention of acute renal failure induced by contrast media. Subgroup analysis in another RCT found that atrial natriuretic peptide versus placebo reduced dialysis-free survival in non-oliguric people (NNH 8).

What are the effects of treatments in critically ill people with acute renal failure?

LIKELY TO BE BENEFICIAL

Biocompatible dialysis membranes (better than non-biocompatible membranes)

Limited evidence from RCTs suggests that biocompatible🅖 membranes versus non-biocompatible membranes reduce mortality.

High dose continuous replacement renal therapy (better than low dose)

One RCT found good evidence that high dose versus low dose continuous renal replacement therapy (haemofiltration) significantly reduces mortality (NNT 7).

UNKNOWN EFFECTIVENESS

Continuous versus intermittent renal replacement therapy

One systematic review of observational studies found insufficient evidence of the effects of continuous versus intermittent renal replacement therapy🅖. One poor quality subsequent RCT found limited evidence that continuous versus intermittent renal replacement therapy increased mortality in intensive care units and in hospital.

Combined diuretics and albumin; continuous versus bolus diuretics; dopamine; loop diuretics

We found insufficient evidence on the effects of these interventions.

LIKELY TO BE INEFFECTIVE OR HARMFUL

Natriuretic peptides

RCTs have found no significant difference with atrial natriuretic peptide or ularitide (urodilantin) versus placebo in dialysis-free survival in oliguric🅖 and non-oliguric people. One of the RCTs found that atrial natriuretic peptide may reduce survival in non-oliguric people. ▶

DEFINITION Acute renal failure is characterised by abrupt and sustained decline in glomerular filtration rate**ⓖ**,[1] which leads to accumulation of urea and other chemicals in the blood. There is no clear consensus on a biochemical definition,[2] but most studies define it as a serum creatinine of 2–3 mg/dL (200–250 µmol/L), an elevation of more than 0.5 mg/dL (45 µmol/L) over a baseline creatinine below 2 mg/dL (170 µmol/L) or a twofold increase of baseline creatinine. "Severe" acute renal failure has been defined as a serum concentration of creatinine above 5.5 mg/dL (500 µmol/L) or as requiring renal replacement therapy. Acute renal failure is usually classified according to the location of the predominant primary pathology (prerenal, intrarenal, and postrenal failure). People who are critically ill are those who are unstable and at imminent risk of death, which usually implies that they are people who need to be in, or have been admitted to, the intensive care unit.

INCIDENCE/ PREVALENCE Two prospective observational studies (2576 people) have found that established acute renal failure affects nearly 5% of people in hospital and as many as 15% of critically ill people depending on the definitions used.[3,4]

AETIOLOGY/ RISK FACTORS **For acute renal failure prevention:** Risk factors for acute renal failure that are consistent across multiple aetiologies include hypovolemia, hypotension, sepsis, pre-existing renal, hepatic, or cardiac dysfunction, diabetes mellitus, and exposure to nephrotoxins (e.g. aminoglycosides, amphotericin, immuno-suppressive agents, non-steroidal anti-inflammatory drugs, angiotensin converting enzyme inhibitors, intravenous contrast media)**ⓣ**. Isolated episodes of acute renal failure are rarely seen in critically ill people, but are usually part of multiple organ dysfunction syndromes**ⓖ**. Acute renal failure requiring dialysis is rarely seen in isolation (> 5% of people). The kidneys are often the first organs to fail.[5] In the perioperative setting, acute renal failure risk factors include prolonged aortic clamping, emergency rather than elective surgery, and use of higher volumes (> 100 mL) of intravenous contrast media. One study (3695 people) using multiple logistic regression identified these independent risk factors: baseline creatinine clearance below 47 mL/minute (OR 1.20, 95% CI 1.12 to 1.30), diabetes (OR 5.5, 95% CI 1.4 to 21), and identified a marginal effect for doses of contrast media above 100 mL (OR 1.01, 95% CI 1.00 to 1.01). The mortality rate of people with acute renal failure requiring dialysis was 36% during hospitalisation.[6] **For acute renal failure in critically ill people:** Prerenal acute renal failure**ⓖ** is caused by reduced blood flow to the kidney from renal artery disease, systematic hypotension, or maldistribution of blood flow. Intrarenal acute renal failure**ⓖ** is caused by parenchymal injury (acute tubular necrosis, interstitial nephritis, embolic disease, glomerulonephritis, vasculitis, or small vessel disease). Postrenal acute renal failure**ⓖ** is caused by urinary tract obstruction. Observational studies (in several hundred people from Europe, North America, and West Africa with acute renal failure) found a prerenal cause in 40–80%, an intrarenal cause in 10–50%, and a postrenal cause in the remaining 10%.[7–11] Prerenal acute renal failure**ⓖ** is the commonest type of acute renal failure in people who are critically ill,[7,12] but acute renal failure in this context is usually part of multisystem failure, and most frequently due to acute tubular necrosis resulting from ischaemic or nephrotoxic injury, or both.[13,14]

PROGNOSIS One retrospective study (1347 people with acute renal failure) found that mortality was less than 15% in people with isolated acute renal failure.[15] One recent prospective study (over 700 people) found that, in people with acute renal failure, overall mortality and the need for dialysis was higher in an intensive care unit than in a non-intensive care unit setting, despite no significant difference between the groups in mean maximal serum creatinine (need for dialysis 71% in intensive care unit v 18%; P < 0.001; mortality 72% in intensive care unit v 32%; P = 0.001).[16]

What are the effects of treatments?

BENEFICIAL

α Blockers

Two systematic reviews and one subsequent RCT have found that α blockers are more effective than placebo for improving lower urinary tract symptoms. One systematic review and subsequent RCTs found no significant differences between different α blockers. Two RCTs found limited evidence that α blockers were more effective in improving symptoms than 5α reductase inhibitors. We found no direct comparison of α blockers with surgical treatment.

5α reductase inhibitors

One systematic review and one subsequent RCT have found that 5α reductase inhibitors are more effective than placebo for improving lower urinary tract symptoms and reducing complications in men with benign prostatic hyperplasia, especially in men with larger prostates. Two RCTs found limited evidence that 5α reductase inhibitors were less effective at improving symptoms than α blockers. We found no direct comparison of 5α reductase inhibitors with surgical treatment.

Transurethral microwave thermotherapy

RCTs have found that transurethral microwave thermotherapy versus sham treatment significantly reduces symptoms. One systematic review and one RCT found limited evidence that transurethral resection relieved short term symptoms more than transurethral microwave thermotherapy. One RCT found limited evidence that transurethral microwave thermotherapy improved symptoms more than α blockers over 18 months.

Transurethral resection

We found limited evidence from two RCTs that transurethral resection was more effective than watchful waiting for improving symptoms and reducing complications, and did not increase the risk of erectile dysfunction or incontinence. One systematic review found greater symptom improvement with transurethral resection versus visual laser ablation, but transurethral resection was associated with a higher risk of blood transfusion.

LIKELY TO BE BENEFICIAL

β–sitosterol plant extract

One systematic review found that β–sitosterol plant extract versus placebo significantly improved lower urinary tract symptoms in the short term.

Rye grass pollen extract

One systematic review found limited evidence that rye grass pollen extract versus placebo increased self rated improvement and reduced nocturia in the short term.

Saw palmetto plant extracts

One systematic review has found that self rated improvement is better in men taking saw palmetto compared with placebo. It found no significant difference in symptom scores between saw palmetto and finasteride. ▶

Benign prostatic hyperplasia

◄ **UNKNOWN EFFECTIVENESS**

Transurethral resection versus less invasive surgical techniques
Three systematic reviews of transurethral resection versus less invasive techniques found few clear differences in outcomes. One of the reviews found greater symptom improvement with transurethral resection versus visual laser ablation, but transurethral resection was associated with a higher risk of blood transfusion.

Transurethral resection versus transurethral needle ablation
We found limited evidence from one RCT that transurethral resection versus transurethral needle ablation reduced symptoms of benign prostatic hyperplasia, although transurethral needle ablation caused fewer adverse effects.

DEFINITION
Benign prostatic hyperplasia is defined histologically. Clinically, it is characterised by lower urinary tract symptoms (urinary frequency, urgency, a weak and intermittent stream, needing to strain, a sense of incomplete emptying, and nocturia), and can lead to complications, including acute urinary retention.

INCIDENCE/ PREVALENCE
Estimates of the prevalence of symptomatic benign prostatic hyperplasia range from 10–30% for men in their early 70s, depending on how benign prostatic hyperplasia is defined.[1]

AETIOLOGY/ RISK FACTORS
The mechanisms by which benign prostatic hyperplasia causes symptoms and complications are unclear, although bladder outlet obstruction is an important factor.[2] The best documented risk factors are increasing age and functioning testes.[3]

PROGNOSIS
Community and practice based studies suggest that men with lower urinary tract symptoms can expect slow progression of the symptoms.[4,5] However, symptoms can wax and wane without treatment. In men with symptoms of benign prostatic hyperplasia, rates of acute urinary retention range from 1–2% a year.[5–7]

Search date October 2001

Anthony Schaeffer and Jeffrey Stern

What are the effects of treatments for chronic bacterial prostatitis?

LIKELY TO BE BENEFICIAL

α Blockers (when added to antimicrobials)

We found limited evidence from one RCT suggesting that adding α blockers to antimicrobials versus antimicrobials alone may significantly improve symptoms and reduce recurrence.

UNKNOWN EFFECTIVENESS

Oral antimicrobial drugs

We found no RCTs of the effects of oral antimicrobial drugs. Retrospective cohort studies report cure rates of 0–90% depending on the drug used and the duration of treatment.

Local injection of antimicrobials; radical prostatectomy; transurethral resection

We found no RCTs on the effects of these interventions.

What are the effects of treatments for chronic abacterial prostatitis?

UNKNOWN EFFECTIVENESS

Allopurinol

One systematic review found limited evidence from one small RCT that allopurinol versus placebo significantly improved symptoms over about 8 months.

α Blockers

One systematic review found limited evidence suggesting that α blockers versus placebo may significantly improve maximal flow time and pain.

5α-Reductase inhibitors *New*

One systematic review of one poor quality RCT found insufficient evidence on the effects of 5α reductase inhibitors.

Anti-inflammatory medications (pentosan polysulfate) *New*

One RCT found no significant with pentosan polysulfate versus placebo in symptoms, but the RCT may have been too small to rule out a clinically important difference.

Biofeedback; prostatic massage; Sitz bath

We found no good evidence on these interventions.

Transurethral microwave thermotherapy

One systematic review found limited evidence from one RCT suggesting that transurethral microwave thermotherapy versus sham treatment may significantly improve quality of life at 3 months and symptoms over 21 months.

▶

Chronic prostatitis

◄ **DEFINITION** **Chronic bacterial prostatitis** is characterised by a positive culture of expressed prostatic secretions. It can be symptomatic (recurrent urinary tract infection, or suprapubic, lower back, or perineal pain), asymptomatic, or associated with minimal urgency, frequency, and dysuria. **Chronic abacterial prostatitis** is characterised by pelvic or perineal pain, often associated with urinary urgency, nocturia, weak urinary stream, frequency, dysuria, hesitancy, dribbling after micturition, interrupted flow, and inflammation (white cells) in prostatic secretions. Symptoms can also include suprapubic, scrotal, testicular, penile, or lower back pain or discomfort, known as prostodynia in the absence of inflammation in prostatic secretions.

INCIDENCE/ One US community based study (58 955 visits by men ≥ 18 years of age
PREVALENCE to office based physicians) estimated that 9% of men have a diagnosis of chronic prostatitis at any one time.[1] Another study found that, of men with genitourinary symptoms, 8% presenting to urologists and 1% presenting to primary care physicians are diagnosed with chronic prostatitis.[2] Most cases of chronic prostatitis are abacterial. Acute bacterial prostatitis, although easy to diagnose and treat, is rare.

AETIOLOGY/ Organisms commonly implicated in bacterial prostatitis include *Escherichia*
RISK FACTORS *coli*, other Gram negative *Enterobacteriaceae*, occasionally *Pseudomonas* species, and rarely Gram positive enterococci. The cause of abacterial prostatitis is unclear, but autoimmunity could be involved.[3]

PROGNOSIS One recent study found that chronic abacterial prostatitis had an impact on quality of life similar to that from angina, Crohn's disease, or a previous myocardial infarction.[4]

Search date August 2001

Michael O'Leary

What are the effects of treatments?

BENEFICIAL

Intracavernosal alprostadil
One large RCT found that intracavernosal alprostadil versus placebo significantly increased the chances of a satisfactory erection.

Intraurethral alprostadil
One large RCT found limited evidence (in men who had previously had erections when taking alprostadil) that intraurethral alprostadil versus placebo significantly increased the number of men who had successful sexual intercourse and at least one orgasm over 3 months.

Sildenafil
RCTs have found that sildenafil versus placebo significantly increases the number of men reporting successful intercourse and significantly increases erections. We found no RCTs directly comparing sildenfil versus other treatments. Transient adverse effects are reported in up to a fifth of men, and deaths have been reported in men on concomitant treatment with oral nitrates.

Yohimbine
One systematic review has found that yohimbine versus placebo significantly improves self reported sexual function and penile rigidity at 2–10 weeks. We found no RCTs directly comparing yohimbine versus other treatments. Transient adverse effects are reported in up to a third of men.

UNKNOWN EFFECTIVENESS

Topical alprostadil
Two quasi randomised trials found limited evidence that topical alprostadil versus placebo increased the number of men with erections sufficient for intercourse (NNT about 3).

L-arginine
One small RCT found no significant difference in sexual function with L-arginine versus placebo, but the RCT may have been too small to exclude a clinically important difference.

Penile prostheses; vacuum devices
We found insufficient evidence on the effects of these interventions.

Trazodone
One small RCT found no significant difference in erections or libido with trazodone versus placebo, but the RCT may have been too small to exclude a clinically important difference.

DEFINITION Erectile dysfunction has largely replaced the term "impotence". It is defined as the persistent inability to obtain or maintain sufficient rigidity of the penis to allow satisfactory sexual performance.

INCIDENCE/ PREVALENCE We found little good epidemiological information, but current normative data suggest that age is the variable most strongly associated with erectile dysfunction, and that up to 30 million men in the USA may be affected.[1] ▶

Erectile dysfunction

Even among men in their 40s, nearly 40% report at least occasional difficulty obtaining or maintaining erection, whereas this approaches 70% in 70 year olds.

AETIOLOGY/ It is now believed that about 80% of cases of erectile dysfunction have an
RISK FACTORS organic cause, the rest being psychogenic in origin. Risk factors include increasing age, smoking, and obesity. Erectile problems fall into three categories: failure to initiate; failure to fill, caused by insufficient arterial inflow into the penis to allow engorgement and tumescence because of vascular insufficiency; and failure to store because of veno-occlusive dysfunction.

PROGNOSIS We found no good evidence on prognosis in untreated organic erectile dysfunction.

Search date May 2001

Dror Michaelson, James Talcott and Matthew Smith

What are the effects of treatment in men with metastatic prostate cancer?

LIKELY TO BE BENEFICIAL

Androgen deprivation

We found limited evidence from RCTs suggesting that androgen deprivation versus no initial treatment reduced mortality. One non-systematic review of RCTs found that orchiectomy, diethylstilbestrol, and luteinising hormone releasing hormone agonists initially improved symptoms and objective signs of disease in most men, but found no evidence of a difference between different types of androgen deprivation.

Combined androgen blockade (androgen deprivation and non-steroidal antiandrogen) compared with androgen deprivation alone

Inconclusive evidence from four systematic reviews suggests that there could be a 2–5% improvement in 5 year survival associated with combined androgen blockade (androgen deprivation plus a non-steroidal antiandrogen) versus androgen deprivation alone.

UNKNOWN EFFECTIVENESS

Intermittent androgen deprivation

We found no RCTs evaluating the long term effects of intermittent versus continuous androgen deprivation on mortality, morbidity, or quality of life.

LIKELY TO BE INEFFECTIVE OR HARMFUL

Deferred androgen deprivation without surveillance

One small RCT has found that immediate androgen deprivation versus deferring androgen deprivation until disease progression becomes apparent in men with stage D1 prostate cancer significantly increases overall survival after a median of 7 years. Subgroup analysis from a larger RCT found that immediate versus deferred androgen deprivation significantly increased survival in men with stage C prostate cancer after about 10 years. This RCT also found that, without surveillance, deferred androgen deprivation resulted in higher rates of complications.

What are the effects of treatment in men with symptomatic androgen independent metastatic disease?

LIKELY TO BE BENEFICIAL

Chemotherapy (palliation but no evidence of an effect on survival)

RCTs have found that chemotherapy plus corticosteroids versus corticosteroids alone reduces pain, lengthens palliation, and improves quality of life, but found no improvement in overall survival.

Radiation therapy (palliation but no evidence of an effect on survival)

One systematic review comparing different radiation schedules has found that external beam radiation provides effective pain relief in some men. A systematic review in men with symptomatic bone metastases found no difference in survival between external beam radiation, strontium-89, or the combination; ▶

Prostate cancer: metastatic

however, strontium-89 may reduce the number of new sites of pain. Two small RCTs suggest a benefit of radionuclide therapy versus other palliative treatments.

UNKNOWN EFFECTIVENESS

Bisphosphonates

One systematic review of two poor quality RCTs found insufficient evidence about the effects of bisphosphonates.

DEFINITION	See non-metastatic prostate cancer, p 159. Androgen independent metastatic disease is defined as disease that progresses despite androgen deprivation.
INCIDENCE/ PREVALENCE	See non-metastatic prostate cancer, p 159.
AETIOLOGY/ RISK FACTORS	See non-metastatic prostate cancer, p 159.
PROGNOSIS	Prostate cancer metastasises predominantly to bone. Metastatic prostate cancer can result in pain, weakness, paralysis, and death.

What are the effects of treating clinically localised prostate cancer?

UNKNOWN EFFECTIVENESS

Androgen suppression

We found some evidence from one RCT that androgen suppression🅖 with bicalutamide reduced disease progression, but interpreting the results was difficult because men with prostate cancer of different stages were included in the trial.

Androgen suppression in asymptomatic men with raised prostate specific antigen concentrations after early treatment; brachytherapy; cryosurgery

We found no RCTs on the effects of these interventions.

External beam radiation

We found no RCTs comparing external beam radiation versus watchful waiting. Limited evidence from one small RCT suggests that external beam radiation versus radical prostatectomy🅖 may increase the risk of metastases.

Radical prostatectomy

One small RCT found no evidence that radical prostatectomy improved survival compared with watchful waiting. Limited evidence from one RCT in men with clinically localised prostate cancer suggests that radical prostatectomy versus radiation treatment may reduce the risk of metastases (NNT 5).

Watchful waiting

One small RCT found no significant difference in survival between radical prostatectomy versus watchful waiting in men with clinically localised prostate cancer. We found no information from RCTs on quality of life.

What are the effects of treating locally advanced prostate cancer?

BENEFICIAL

Androgen suppression in addition to early external beam radiation (improves survival compared with radiation and deferred androgen suppression alone)

One systematic review has found that immediate versus deferred androgen suppression in men with locally advanced disease treated with radiotherapy significantly increases survival at 5 years (NNT 12). One RCT found no difference in overall survival or local disease control after orchiectomy, whether or not it was combined with radiotherapy, but the results are difficult to interpret.

LIKELY TO BE BENEFICIAL

Androgen suppression initiated at diagnosis

RCTs found limited evidence that, in men with locally advanced disease, androgen suppression initiated at diagnosis versus deferred androgen suppression reduces complications and may improve survival. ▶

Prostate cancer: non-metastatic

Immediate androgen suppression after radical prostatectomy and pelvic lymphadenectomy in men with node-positive prostate cancer (compared with radical prostatectomy and deferred androgen suppression)

One RCT has found that immediate androgen suppression versus deferred androgen suppression after radical prostatectomy and pelvic lymphadenectomy significantly reduces mortality at 7 years (NNT 4).

DEFINITION Prostatic cancer is staged according to two systems: the tumour, node, metastasis (TNM) classification system, and the American Urologic Staging system❶. Non-metastatic prostate cancer can be divided into clinically localised and advanced disease. Clinically localised disease is prostate cancer thought to be confined to the prostate gland by clinical examination. Locally advanced disease is disease that has spread outside the capsule of the prostate gland but has not yet spread to other organs. Metastatic disease is prostate cancer that has spread outside the prostate gland to either local, regional, or systemic lymph nodes, seminal vesicles, or to other body organs (e.g. bone, liver, brain) and is not connected to the prostate gland. We consider clinically localised and locally advanced disease in a separate chapter from metastatic disease. See prostate cancer: metastatic, p 157.

INCIDENCE/ PREVALENCE Prostate cancer is the most common non-dermatological malignancy worldwide and is the second most common cause of cancer death in men in the USA.[1] There were an estimated 180 400 new cases and 31 900 deaths in the USA in 2000.[2] For a 50 year old man with a life expectancy of 25 years, the lifetime risk of microscopic prostate cancer is about 42%, the risk of clinically evident prostate cancer is 10%, and that of fatal prostate cancer is 3%.[3]

AETIOLOGY/ RISK FACTORS Risk factors include age, family history of prostate cancer, black race, and possibly higher dietary fat and calcium intake. In the USA, black men have about a 60% higher incidence rate than white men.[4] The prostate cancer incidence rate for black men living in the USA is about 90/100 000 (ages < 65 years) and about 1300/100 000 (ages 65–74 years). For white men, incidence rates are about 44/100 000 (ages < 65 years) and 900/100 000 (ages 65–74 years).

PROGNOSIS The chance that men with well to moderately differentiated, palpable, clinically localised prostate cancer will remain free of symptomatic progression is 70% at 5 years and 40% at 10 years.[5] The risk of symptomatic disease progression is higher in men with poorly differentiated prostate cancer.[6] One retrospective analysis of a large surgical series in men with clinically localised prostate cancer found that the median time from the increase in prostate specific antigen (PSA) concentration to the development of metastatic disease was 8 years. Time to PSA progression, PSA doubling time, and Gleason score❻ were predictive of the probability and time to development of metastatic disease. Once men developed metastatic disease, the median actuarial time to death was 5 years.[7] Morbidity from local or regional disease progression includes haematuria, bladder obstruction, and lower extremity oedema. In the USA, population based studies found that death rates from prostate cancer have declined by only about 1/100 000 men since 1992, despite widespread testing for PSA and increased rates of radical prostatectomy and radiotherapy.[8,9] Regions of the USA with the greatest decreases in mortality are those with the lowest rates of testing for PSA and treatment with radical prostatectomy or radiation.[9] Countries with low rates of testing and treatment do not have consistently higher age adjusted rates of death from prostate cancer than countries with high rates of testing and treatment such as the USA.

Search date April 2001

Janet Treasure and Ulrike Schmidt

What are the effects of treatments?

UNKNOWN EFFECTIVENESS

Different specialised psychological treatments

One small RCT found limited evidence that focal analytical therapy or family therapy❻ versus treatment as usual significantly increased the number of people recovered or improved as assessed by the Morgan and Russell❻ scale at 1 year. One small RCT found no significant difference in outcomes with psychotherapy❻ and dietary advice❻ at 1 year. A second RCT comparing cognitive therapy versus dietary advice had a 100% withdrawal rate with dietary advice. Seven small RCTs found no significant difference between different psychotherapies. However, all the RCTs were small and were unlikely to have been powered to detect a clinically important difference between treatments.

Fluoxetine

One small RCT found no significant difference with fluoxetine versus placebo in weight gain, eating symptoms, or depressive symptoms after 36 days of treatment.

Inpatient versus outpatient treatment setting (in people not so severely ill as to warrant emergency intervention)

Limited evidence from one small RCT found that outpatient treatment was as effective as inpatient treatment❻ in increasing weight and improving Morgan and Russell scale global scores at 1, 2, and 5 years in those individuals who do not warrant emergency intervention.

Oestrogen treatment (for prevention of fractures)

We found no good evidence about the effects of hormonal treatment on fracture rates. One small RCT found no effect of oestrogen on bone mineral density.

Zinc

One small RCT in people admitted to an eating disorder unit found no significant difference with zinc versus placebo in average daily weight gain.

LIKELY TO BE INEFFECTIVE OR HARMFUL

Cisapride

One small RCT found no significant difference with cisapride versus placebo in weight gain at 8 weeks. The QT interval in anorexia nervosa is prolonged even in the absence of medication; therefore, cisapride is not recommended in anorexia nervosa. Cisapride has now been withdrawn in many countries because of an increased risk of cardiac irregularities, including ventricular tachycardia, torsades de pointes, and sudden death.

Cyproheptadine

Three small RCTs found no significant difference with cyproheptadine versus placebo in weight gain.

Neuroleptics that increase the QT interval

We found no RCTs. The QT interval may be prolonged in people with anorexia nervosa, and many neuroleptics (haloperidol, pimozide, sertindole, thioridazine, chlorpromazine, and others) also increase the QT interval. Prolongation of the QT interval may be associated with increased risk of ventricular tachycardia, torsades de pointes, and sudden death.

▶

◀ **Tricyclic antidepressants**

Small RCTs found no significant difference in outcomes with amitriptyline versus placebo. The QT interval may be prolonged in people with anorexia nervosa, and tricyclic antidepressants (amitriptyline, protriptyline, nortriptyline, doxepin, maprotiline) also increase the QT interval. Prolongation of the QT interval may be associated with increased risk of ventricular tachycardia, torsades de pointes, and sudden death.

DEFINITION
Anorexia nervosa is characterised by a refusal to maintain weight at or above a minimally normal weight (< 85% of expected weight for age and height, or body mass index [BMI]🅖 < 17.5 kg/m^2), or a failure to show the expected weight gain during growth. In association with this, there is often an intense fear of gaining weight, preoccupation with weight, denial of the current low weight and its adverse impact on health, and amenorrhoea. Two subtypes of anorexia nervosa, binge–purge and restricting, have been defined.[1]

INCIDENCE/ PREVALENCE
A mean incidence in the general population of 19/100 000 a year in females and 2/100 000 a year in males has been estimated from 12 cumulative studies.[2] The highest rate was in female teenagers (age 13–19 years), where there were 50.8 cases/100 000 a year. A large cohort study of Swedish school children (4291 people, age 16 years) were screened by weighing and subsequent interview, and the prevalence of anorexia nervosa cases (defined using DSM-III and DSM-III-R criteria) was found to be 7/1000 for girls and 1/1000 for boys.[3] Little is known of the incidence or prevalence in Asia, South America, or Africa.

AETIOLOGY/ RISK FACTORS
The aetiology of anorexia nervosa has been related to family, biological, social, and cultural factors.[4] Studies have found that anorexia nervosa is associated with a family history of anorexia nervosa (HR 11.4, 95% CI 1.1 to 89), of bulimia nervosa (adjusted HR 3.5, 955 CI 1.1 to 14),[5] depression, generalised anxiety disorder, obsessive compulsive disorder, or obsessive compulsive personality disorder (adjusted RR 3.6, 95% CI 1.6 to 8).[6] A twin study estimated the heritability to be 58% (95% CI 33% to 77%), with the remaining variance apparently because of a non-shared environment. However, the study was unable to completely rule out a contribution of a non-shared environment. Specific aspects of childhood temperament thought to be related include perfectionism, negative self evaluation, and extreme compliance.[7] Perinatal factors include prematurity (OR 3.2, 95% CI 1.6 to 6.2), particularly if the baby was small for gestational age (OR 5.7, 95% CI 1.4 to 4.1).

PROGNOSIS
We found no good evidence on the prognosis of people with anorexia nervosa who do not access formal medical care. A summary of treatment studies (68 studies published between 1953 and 1989, 3104 people, length of follow up 1–33 years) found that 43% of people recover completely (range 7–86%), 36% improve (range 1–69%), 20% develop a chronic eating disorder (range 0–43%), and 5% die from anorexia nervosa (range 0–21%).[8] Favourable prognostic factors include an early age at onset and a short interval between onset of symptoms and the beginning of treatment. Unfavourable prognostic factors include vomiting, bulimia, profound weightloss, chronicity, and a history of premorbid developmental or clinical abnormalities. The all cause standardised mortality ratio of eating disorders (anorexia nervosa and bulimia nervosa) has been estimated at 538, about three times higher than other psychiatric illness.[9] The average annual risk of mortality was 0.59% a year in females in 10 eating disorder populations (1322 people) with a minimum follow up of 6 years.[10] The mortality risk was higher for people with lower weight and with older age at presentation. Young women with anorexia nervosa are at an increased risk of fractures later in life.[11]

What are the effects of treatments?

LIKELY TO BE BENEFICIAL

Antidepressant medication
Systematic reviews have found that antidepressants versus placebo significantly reduce bulimic symptoms in the short term (NNT about 9).

Cognitive behavioural therapy
Systematic reviews have found that cognitive behavioural therapy⊙ versus remaining on a waiting list significantly reduces specific symptoms of bulimia nervosa⊙ (binge eating, purging, disturbed eating patterns), and improves non-specific symptoms such as depression.

Combination treatment with an antidepressant and psychotherapy
One systematic review has found that combination treatment (antidepressants plus psychotherapy) versus antidepressants alone reduces binge frequency and depressive symptoms but not binge eating⊙ remission rates. It has also found that combination treatment versus psychotherapy alone reduces short term remission from binge eating and depressive symptoms but has no significant effect on binge eating frequency.

Other psychotherapies
One systematic review and one subsequent RCT have found that non-cognitive psychotherapy versus being on a waiting list significantly improves the symptoms of bulimia nervosa.

UNKNOWN EFFECTIVENESS

Antidepressants as maintenance
RCTs found insufficient evidence about the role of antidepressants in maintenance treatment.

New antidepressants (venlafaxine, mirtazapine, and reboxetine)
We found no RCTs on the effects of venlafaxine, mirtazapine, and reboxetine.

Selective serotonin reuptake inhibitors (other than fluoxetine)
We found insufficient evidence about the effects of selective serotonin reuptake inhibitors other than fluoxetine. RCTs found that fluoxetine versus placebo significantly increased abstinence from binge eating in the short term.

DEFINITION Bulimia nervosa is an intense preoccupation with body weight and shape, with regular episodes of uncontrolled overeating of large amounts of food (binge eating) associated with use of extreme methods to counteract the feared effects of overeating. If a person also meets the diagnostic criteria for anorexia nervosa, then the diagnosis of anorexia nervosa takes precedence.[1] Bulimia nervosa can be difficult to identify because of extreme secrecy about binge eating and purgative behaviour. Weight may be normal but there is often a history of anorexia nervosa or restrictive dieting. Some people alternate between anorexia nervosa and bulimia nervosa.

INCIDENCE/ PREVALENCE In community based studies, the prevalence of bulimia nervosa is between 0.5% and 1.0% in young women, with an even social class distribution.[2–4] About 90% of people diagnosed with bulimia nervosa are women. The ▶

numbers presenting with bulimia nervosa in industrialised countries increased during the decade that followed its recognition in the late 1970s and "a cohort effect" is reported in community surveys,[2,5,6] implying an increase in incidence. The prevalence of eating disorders such as bulimia nervosa is lower in non-industrialised populations[7] and varies across ethnic groups. African-American women have a lower rate of restrictive dieting than white American women, but have a similar rate of recurrent binge eating.[8]

AETIOLOGY/ RISK FACTORS
Young women from the developed world who restrict their dietary intake are at greatest risk of developing bulimia nervosa and other eating disorders. One community based case control study compared 102 people with bulimia nervosa with 204 healthy controls and found higher rates of the following in people with the eating disorder: obesity, mood disorder, sexual and physical abuse, parental obesity, substance misuse, low self esteem, perfectionism, disturbed family dynamics, parental weight/shape concern, and early menarche.[9] Compared with a control group of 102 women who had other psychiatric disorders, women with bulimia nervosa had higher rates of parental problems and obesity.

PROGNOSIS
A 10 year follow up study (50 people with bulimia nervosa from a former trial of mianserin treatment) found that 52% had fully recovered, and only 9% continued to experience symptoms of bulimia nervosa.[10] A larger study (222 people from a trial of antidepressants and structured intensive group psychotherapy) found that, after a mean follow up of 11.5 years, 11% still met criteria for bulimia nervosa, whereas 70% were in full or partial remission.[11] Short term studies found similar results: about 50% of people made a full recovery, 30% made a partial recovery, and 20% continued to be symptomatic.[12] There are few consistent predictors of longer term outcome. Good prognosis has been associated with shorter illness duration, a younger age of onset, higher social class, and a family history of alcoholism.[10] Poor prognosis has been associated with a history of substance misuse,[11] premorbid and paternal obesity,[13] and, in some studies, personality disorder.[14–17] One study (102 people) of the natural course of bulimia nervosa found that 31% still had the disorder at 15 months, and 15% at 5 years.[18] Only 28% received treatment during the follow up period. In an evaluation of response to cognitive behavioural therapy, early progress (by session 6) best predicted outcome.[19] A subsequent systematic review of the outcome literature found no consistent evidence to support early intervention and a better prognosis.[20]

What are the effects of treatments?

BENEFICIAL

Donepezil (cognitive benefit, Alzheimer's disease)

One systematic review has found that donepezil versus placebo significantly improves cognitive function at 12–24 weeks.

Galantamine (cognitive benefit, Alzheimer's disease)

One systematic review has found that galantamine versus placebo significantly improves functioning and cognition (NNT 7 for 4 point change in Alzheimer's Disease Assessment Scale cognitive subscale score) at 6 months.

LIKELY TO BE BENEFICIAL

Carbamazepine (for behavioural symptoms) *New*

One RCT found that carbamazepine versus placebo significantly reduced agitation and aggression in people with unspecified dementia.

Ginkgo biloba (cognitive benefit, Alzheimer's disease)

One systematic review has found that Ginkgo biloba versus placebo significantly improves cognitive function and is well tolerated.

Oestrogen (cognitive benefit, Alzheimer's disease)

One systematic review in women with established Alzheimer's disease found that hormone replacement therapy versus no hormone replacement therapy significantly improved cognition.

Olanzapine (improved agitation, hallucinations, and delusions)

One RCT found that olanzapine (5–10 mg daily) versus placebo significantly improved agitation, hallucinations, and delusions.

Reality orientation (cognitive and behavioural symptoms)

One systematic review in people with unspecified dementia found that reality orientation❻ versus no treatment significantly improved cognitive function and behaviour.

Risperidone (reduced psychotic symptoms and aggression)

One RCT has found that risperidone versus placebo significantly improves behavioural symptoms after 6 weeks (risperidone 2 mg, NNT 6).

Selegiline (cognitive benefit, Alzheimer's disease)

One systematic review has found that in people with Alzheimer's disease, selegiline versus placebo significantly improves cognitive function, behavioural disturbance, and mood after about 3 months, but found no evidence of improved clinical global state.

Sodium valproate (for behavioural symptoms) *New*

One RCT found that sodium valproate versus placebo significantly reduced agitation in unspecified dementia.

▶

Clin Evid Concise 2002;7:165–168.

Physostigmine (for cognitive outcomes, Alzheimer's disease) *New*

One systematic review found limited evidence that slow release physostigmine versus placebo improved cognition, but adverse effects, including nausea, vomiting, diarrhoea, dizziness, and stomach pain, were common.

Rivastigmine (for cognitive outcomes, Alzheimer's disease)

One systematic review has found that rivastigmine versus placebo significantly improves cognitive function, but increases the frequency of nausea, vomiting, anorexia, diarrhoea, and discontinuation of treatment.

Behaviour management (for behavioural outcomes) *New*

RCTs in people with unspecified dementia or Alzheimer's disease have found conflicting evidence on the effects of behavioural management.

Donepezil (for vascular and Lewy body dementia); galantamine (for vascular and Lewy body dementia); oestrogen (for vascular and Lewy body dementia); physostigmine (for vascular and Lewy body dementia) *New;* **selegiline (for vascular and Lewy body dementia)**

We found no RCTs on the effects of these interventions in vascular dementia or Lewy body dementia.

Ginkgo biloba (for vascular and Lewy body dementia)

One systematic review and one subsequent RCT found no clear evidence of benefit with ginkgo biloba versus placebo in people with vascular dementia. We found no RCTs in people with Lewy body dementia.

Haloperidol (for behavioural outcomes)

RCTs found no significant improvement with haloperidol versus placebo.

Lecithin *New*

One systematic review in people with Alzheimer's disease found no significant difference between lecithin versus placebo in cognition, functional performance, quality of life, or global impression. We found insufficient evidence about lecithin versus placebo in people with vascular and Lewy body dementia.

Music therapy (for behavioural outcomes)

One systematic review of studies with weak methods found insufficient evidence about music therapy.

Nicotine *New*

One systematic review found no RCTs of adequate quality on the effects of nicotine.

Non-steroidal anti-inflammatory drugs

Two RCTs found conflicting evidence about non-steroidal anti-inflammatory drugs versus placebo in people with Alzheimer's disease. We found no evidence about non-steroidal anti-inflammatory drugs in people with vascular or Lewy body dementia.

Reminiscence therapy (for behavioural outcomes)

We found insufficient evidence on the effects of reminiscence therapy🅖.

◀ ### Rivastigmine (for vascular and Lewy body dementia)

One RCT in people with Lewy body dementia found that rivastigmine versus placebo significantly improved cognitive function and behaviour after 20 weeks (NNT 3 for at least 30% improvement on Neuropsychiatric Inventory score). Discontinuation of treatment and adverse effects including nausea, vomiting, anorexia, and diarrhoea are common. We found insufficient evidence about the effects of rivastigmine in people with vascular dementia.

Tacrine

Systematic reviews found limited evidence that tacrine versus placebo significantly improved cognitive function and global state in Alzheimer's disease, but adverse effects, including nausea and vomiting, diarrhoea, anorexia, and abdominal pain, were common. We found no RCTs in people with vascular or Lewy body dementia.

Trazodone (for behavioural outcomes) *New*

One RCT in people with Alzheimer's disease found no significant difference between trazodone versus placebo in reducing agitation. Another RCT in people with dementia plus agitated behaviour found no significant difference in agitation between trazodone versus haloperidol, but it may have been too small to exclude a clinically important difference.

Vitamin E

One RCT of vitamin E versus placebo in people with Alzheimer's disease found no clear evidence of benefit. We found no RCTs about vitamin E in vascular or Lewy body dementia.

DEFINITION   **Dementia** is characterised by chronic, global, non-reversible impairment of cerebral function. It usually results in loss of memory (initially of recent events), loss of executive function (such as the ability to make decisions or sequence complex tasks), and changes in personality. **Alzheimer's disease** is a type of dementia characterised by an insidious onset and slow deterioration, and involves speech, motor, personality, and executive function impairment. It should be diagnosed after other systemic, psychiatric, and neurological causes of dementia have been excluded clinically and by laboratory investigation. **Vascular dementia** (multi-infarct dementia) is a stepwise deterioration of executive function with or without language and motor dysfunction occurring as a result of cerebral arterial occlusion. It usually occurs in the presence of vascular risk factors (diabetes, hypertension, and smoking). Characteristically, it has a more sudden onset and stepwise progression than Alzheimer's disease. **Lewy body dementia** is an insidious impairment of executive functions with (1) Parkinsonism; (2) visual hallucinations; and (3) fluctuating cognitive abilities and increased risk of falls or autonomic failure.[1,2] Careful clinical examination of people with mild to moderate dementia, and the use of established diagnostic criteria, has an antemortem positive predictive value of 70–90% compared with the gold standard of postmortem diagnosis.[3,4]

INCIDENCE/ About 6% of people aged over 65 years and 30% of people aged over 90
PREVALENCE years have some form of dementia.[5] Dementia is rare before the age of 60 years. The most common types of dementia are Alzheimer's disease, vascular dementia, mixed vascular and Alzheimer's disease, and Lewy body dementia. Alzheimer's disease and vascular dementia (including mixed dementia) are each estimated to account for 35–50% of dementia, and Lewy body dementia is estimated to account for up to 20% of dementia in the elderly, varying with geographical, cultural, and racial factors.[1,5–10] ▶

Dementia

◀ **AETIOLOGY/** The cause of Alzheimer's disease is unclear. A key pathological process is
RISK FACTORS deposition of abnormal amyloid in the central nervous system.[11] Most
people with the relatively rare condition of early onset Alzheimer's disease
(before age 60 years) show an autosomal dominant inheritance due to
mutations on presenelin or amyloid precursor protein genes. Several genes
(*APP*, *PS-1*, and *PS-2*) have been identified. Later onset dementia is
sometimes clustered in families, but specific gene mutations have not been
identified. Head injury, Down's syndrome, and lower premorbid intellect may
be risk factors for Alzheimer's disease. Vascular dementia is related to
cardiovascular risk factors, such as smoking, hypertension, and diabetes.
The aetiology of Lewy body dementia is unknown. Brain acetylcholine activity
is reduced in many forms of dementia, and the level of reduction correlates
with cognitive impairment. Many treatments for Alzheimer's disease
enhance cholinergic activity.[1,6]

PROGNOSIS Alzheimer's disease usually has an insidious onset with progressive reduction in cerebral function. Diagnosis is difficult in the early stages. Average life
expectancy after diagnosis is 7–10 years.[10] People with Lewy body dementia
have an average life expectancy of around 6 years after diagnosis.[5] Behavioural problems, depression, and psychotic symptoms are common in all
types of dementia.[12,13] Eventually, most people with dementia find it difficult
to perform simple tasks without help.

Search date May 2001

John Geddes and Rob Butler

Mental health

What are the effects of treatments?

BENEFICIAL

Cognitive therapy (in mild to moderate depression)
One systematic review has found that cognitive therapy℗ versus placebo significantly improves the symptoms of depression.

Continuation drug treatment℗ (reduces risk of relapse)
One systematic review and subsequent RCTs have found that continuing antidepressant drug treatment for 4–6 months after recovery significantly reduces the risk of relapse.

Electroconvulsive therapy
Two systematic reviews have found that electroconvulsive therapy versus sham electroconvulsive therapy is effective in treating depression.

Interpersonal therapy (in mild to moderate depression)
One large RCT has found that interpersonal therapy℗ significantly improves rates of recovery from depression after 16 weeks (NNT 5).

Monoamine oxidase inhibitors
Systematic reviews have found that antidepressant drugs versus placebo are effective in acute treatment of all grades of depressive disorders, in all common treatment settings, and in people with or without co-existent physical illness. One systematic review found that monoamine oxidase inhibitors were less effective than tricyclic antidepressants in people with severe depressive disorders, but may be more effective in atypical depressive disorders, for example, increased sleep, increased appetite, mood reactivity, and rejection sensitivity.

Selective serotonin reuptake inhibitors and related drugs
Systematic reviews have found that antidepressant drugs versus placebo are effective in acute treatment of all grades of depressive disorders, in all common treatment settings, and in people with or without co-existent physical illness. Systematic reviews found no significant difference in improvement of symptoms or incidence of adverse effects with selective serotonin reuptake inhibitors versus tricyclic antidepressants, but found that significantly fewer people taking selective serotonin reuptake inhibitors withdrew from RCTs. We found no strong evidence that fluoxetine increased the risk of suicide.

Tricyclic and heterocyclic antidepressants
Systematic reviews have found that antidepressant drugs versus placebo are effective in acute treatment of all grades of depressive disorders, in all common treatment settings, and in people with or without co-existent physical illness. Systematic reviews found no significant difference in improvement of symptoms with tricyclic antidepressants versus selective serotonin reuptake inhibitors.

LIKELY TO BE BENEFICIAL

Combining drug and psychological treatment (in severe depression)
RCTs have found limited evidence that the addition of drug treatment to psychological treatment may have significant benefits in severe depression.

Problem solving therapy (in mild to moderate depression)
Small RCTs have found no difference between problem solving therapy℗ versus drug treatment in improving symptoms.

▶

Depressive disorders

◀ **St John's Wort (in mild to moderate depression)**
One systematic review of mixed quality RCTs in people with mild to moderate depression has found that St John's Wort *(Hypericum perforatum)* versus placebo significantly improves symptoms.

UNKNOWN EFFECTIVENESS

Befriending⊕; bibliotherapy⊕; exercise
RCTs found limited evidence that these interventions may improve the symptoms of mild to moderate depression.

Care pathways
Five RCTs found limited evidence that collaborative working between primary care physicians and psychiatrists, case management, telephone support, and patient education versus standard care each significantly improved mild to moderate depressive symptoms.

Non-directive counselling
One systematic review in people with moderate depression found limited evidence that non-directive counselling⊕ is no more effective than routine physician care in improving symptoms, but found that counselling increased patient satisfaction.

Psychological treatments in severe depression
We found limited evidence about the effects of psychological treatments in severe depression.

DEFINITION **Depressive disorders** are characterised by persistent low mood, loss of interest and enjoyment, and reduced energy. They often impair function. **Older adults:** Older adults are generally defined as people aged 65 years or older. The presentation of depression in older adults may be atypical: low mood may be masked and anxiety or memory impairment may be the principal presenting symptoms. Dementia should be considered in the differential diagnosis of depression in older adults.[1]

INCIDENCE/ **Younger adults:** Depressive disorders are common, with a prevalence of
PREVALENCE major depression between 5% and 10% of people seen in primary care settings.[2] Two to three times as many people may have depressive symptoms but do not meet criteria for major depression. Women are affected twice as often as men. Depressive disorders are the fourth most important cause of disability worldwide and they are expected to become the second most important cause by the year 2020.[3,4] **Older adults:** Between 10% and 15% of older people have significant depressive symptomatology, although major depression is relatively rare in older adults.[5]

AETIOLOGY/ The causes are uncertain but include both childhood events and current
RISK FACTORS psychosocial adversity.

PROGNOSIS About half of people suffering a first episode of major depressive disorder experience further symptoms in the next 10 years.[6] Different levels of severity[7,8] indicate different prognosis and treatment. **Mild to moderate depression** is characterised by depressive symptoms and some functional impairment. Many people recover in the short term but about half experience recurrent symptoms. **Severe depression** is characterised by additional agitation or psychomotor retardation with marked somatic symptoms. In this review, treatments are considered to have been evaluated in severe depression if the RCTs included inpatients. **Psychotic depression** is characterised by additional hallucinations, delusions, or both. **Older adults:** The prognosis may be especially poor in elderly people with a chronic or relapsing course.[9]

Search date June 2001

Christopher Gale and Mark Oakley-Browne

What are the effects of treatments?

BENEFICIAL

Cognitive therapy

Systematic reviews have found that cognitive therapy (using a combination of behavioural interventions such as exposure, relaxation, and cognitive restructuring) improves anxiety and depression more than remaining on a waiting list (no treatment), anxiety management training alone, or non-directive treatment.

LIKELY TO BE BENEFICIAL

Buspirone

RCTs have found that buspirone versus placebo increases physician rated improvement. Limited evidence from RCTs found no significant difference with buspirone versus benzodiazepines or antidepressants.

Certain antidepressants (paroxetine, imipramine, trazodone, opipramol, venlafaxine)

RCTs have found that paroxetine, imipramine, trazodone, opipramol, and venlafaxine versus placebo significantly improve symptoms. One RCT found that paroxetine improved symptoms more than a benzodiazepine.

TRADE OFF BETWEEN BENEFITS AND HARMS

Benzodiazepines

One systematic review has found that benzodiazepines versus placebo improve symptoms. However, RCTs and case control studies have found that benzodiazepines increase dependence, sedation, and road traffic accidents and are associated with neonatal and infant morbidity when used late in pregnancy or while breast feeding.

UNKNOWN EFFECTIVENESS

Abecarnil

RCTs found conflicting evidence of the effects of abecarnil versus placebo in improving scores on the Hamilton Anxiety Scale. One RCT found that abercarnil versus placebo significantly increased drowsiness (NNH 4), fatigue (NNH 9), and equilibrium loss (NNH 20).

Antipsychotic drugs

One RCT found that trifluoperazine versus placebo significantly reduced anxiety after 4 weeks, but caused more drowsiness, extrapyramidal reactions, and other movement disorders.

Applied relaxation☉; β Blockers

We found insufficient evidence about the effects of these interventions.

UNLIKELY TO BE BENEFICIAL

Hydroxyzine

One non-systematic review found no clear evidence of benefit with hydroxyzine. ▶

Generalised anxiety disorder

DEFINITION Generalised anxiety disorder (GAD) is defined as excessive worry and tension, on most days, for at least 6 months, together with the following symptoms and signs: increased motor tension (fatigability, trembling, restlessness, muscle tension); autonomic hyperactivity (shortness of breath, rapid heart rate, dry mouth, cold hands, and dizziness) but not panic attacks; and increased vigilance and scanning (feeling keyed up, increased startling, impaired concentration). One non-systematic review of epidemiological and clinical studies found marked reduction of quality of life and psychosocial functioning in people with anxiety disorder (including GAD).[1] It also found that (using the Composite Diagnostic International Instrument) people with GAD have low overall life satisfaction and some impairment in ability to fulfil roles and/or social tasks.[1]

INCIDENCE/ PREVALENCE Assessment of the incidence and prevalence is difficult. There is a high rate of comorbidity with other anxiety and depressive disorders.[2] The reliability of the measures used in epidemiological studies is unsatisfactory.[3] One US study, with explicit diagnostic criteria (DSM-III-R), estimated that 5% of people will develop GAD at some time during their lives.[4] The reliability of measures used in cross sectional studies to diagnose GAD are unsatisfactory.[2] A recent cohort study that followed people with depressive and anxiety disorders over 2 years found the diagnosis was consistently maintained in 49% of those initially diagnosed with GAD.[5] One recent non-systematic review found that the incidence of GAD in men is only half the incidence in women.[6] One non-systematic review of seven studies found reduced prevalence of anxiety disorders in older people.[7]

AETIOLOGY/ RISK FACTORS One community study and a clinical study have found GAD is associated with an increase in the number of minor stressors, independent of demographic factors,[8] but this finding was common in people with other diagnoses in the clinical population.[5] One non-systematic review (5 case control studies) of psychological sequelae to civilian trauma found rates of GAD reported in four of the five studies were increased significantly compared with a control population (rate ratio 3.3, 95% CI 2.0 to 5.5).[9] A systematic review of bullying (or peer victimisation) found that bullying was associated with GAD (effect size 0.21).[10]

PROGNOSIS GAD is a long term condition. It often begins before or during young adulthood and can be a lifelong problem. Spontaneous remission is rare.[4]

Search date September 2001

G Mustafa Soomro

What are the effects of initial treatments in adults?

BENEFICIAL

Behavioural therapy

One systematic review has found that behavioural therapy improves symptoms compared with relaxation. Two observational studies found that improvement was maintained for up to two years. Another systematic review found no significant difference in symptoms between behavioural therapy versus cognitive therapy. One additional RCT found limited evidence that group behaviour therapy versus group cognitive therapy improved symptoms after 3 months (NNT 3).

Drug treatment (fluvoxamine) plus behavioural therapy

Systematic reviews have found that monotherapy with drug therapy (serotonin reuptake inhibitors) or behavioural therapy improve symptoms. However, RCTs have found only limited evidence that behavioural therapy plus fluvoxamine reduces symptoms more than behavioural therapy alone.

Selective and non-selective serotonin reuptake inhibitors

Systematic reviews and subsequent RCTs have found that serotonin reuptake inhibitors versus placebo significantly improve symptoms after 12 weeks.

LIKELY TO BE BENEFICIAL

Cognitive therapy

One systematic review has found no significant difference in symptoms between cognitive therapy versus behavioural therapy. One subsequent RCT found limited evidence that group cognitive therapy improved symptoms less than group behavioural therapy after 12 weeks.

What are the effects of treatments in adults who have not responded to initial serotonin reuptake inhibitors?

LIKELY TO BE BENEFICIAL

Addition of antipsychotics to serotonin reuptake inhibitors

Two small RCTs in people unresponsive to serotonin reuptake inhibitors have found that the addition of antipsychotics significantly improves symptoms (NNT 2).

DEFINITION Obsessive compulsive disorder (OCD) involves obsessions or compulsions (or both) that are not caused by drugs or a physical disorder, and which cause significant personal distress or social dysfunction. **Obsessions** are recurrent and persistent ideas, images, or impulses that cause pronounced anxiety and that the person perceives to be self produced. **Compulsions** are intentional repetitive behaviours or mental acts performed in response to obsessions or according to certain rules, and are aimed at reducing distress or preventing certain imagined dreaded events. Obsessions and compulsions are usually recognised as pointless and are resisted by the person. (There are minor differences in the criteria for OCD between the third, revised third, and fourth editions of the *Diagnostic and Statistical Manual*: DSM–III, DSM–III–R, and DSM–IV[1].) ▶

Obsessive compulsive disorder

INCIDENCE/ One national, community based survey of OCD in the UK (1993, 10 000
PREVALENCE people) found a prevalence of 1% in men and 1.5% in women.[2] A survey in
the USA (18 500 people) found a lifetime prevalence of OCD of between
1.9 and 3.3% in 1984.[3] An international study found a lifetime prevalence
of 3% in Canada, 3.1% in Puerto Rico, 0.3–0.9% in Taiwan, and 2.2% in
New Zealand.[2]

AETIOLOGY/ Behavioural, cognitive, genetic, and neurobiological factors are implicated in
RISK FACTORS OCD.[4–10]

PROGNOSIS One study (144 people followed for a mean of 47 years) found that an
episodic❸ course was more common during the initial years (about 1–9
years), but a chronic❸ course was more common afterwards.[11] Over time,
the study found that 39–48% of people had symptomatic improvement. A
1 year prospective cohort study found 46% of people had an episodic course
and 54% had a chronic course.[12]

Search date September 2001
Shailesh Kumar and Mark Oakley-Browne

What are the effects of drug treatments?

BENEFICIAL

Selective serotonin reuptake inhibitors
One systematic review and one subsequent RCT have found that selective serotonin reuptake inhibitors versus placebo significantly improve symptoms.

Tricyclic antidepressants (imipramine)
One systematic review and subsequent RCTs have found that imipramine versus placebo significantly improves symptoms. One RCT found that imipramine significantly reduced relapse rates over 12 months (NNT 5).

TRADE OFF BETWEEN BENEFITS AND HARMS

Benzodiazepines
One systematic review and one additional RCT have found that alprazolam versus placebo significantly reduces the number of panic attacks and improves symptoms. However, benzodiazepines are associated with a wide range of adverse effects both during and after treatment.

UNKNOWN EFFECTIVENESS

Buspirone
RCTs found insufficient evidence on the effects of buspirone versus placebo.

Monoamine oxidase inhibitors
We found no RCTs on the effects of monoamine oxidase inhibitors.

DEFINITION   A panic attack is a period in which there is sudden onset of intense apprehension, fearfulness, or terror often associated with feelings of impending doom. Panic disorder occurs when there are recurrent, unpredictable attacks followed by at least 1 month of persistent concern about having another panic attack, worry about the possible implications or consequences of the panic attacks, or a significant behavioural change related to the attacks.[1] The term panic disorder excludes panic attacks attributable to the direct physiological effects of a general medical condition, substance, or another mental disorder. Panic disorder is sometimes categorised as with or without agoraphobia.[1] Alternative categorisations focus on phobic anxiety disorders and specify agoraphobia with or without panic disorder.[2]

INCIDENCE/   Panic disorder often starts around 20 years of age (between late adoles-
PREVALENCE   cence and the mid 30s).[3] Lifetime prevalence is between 1–3%, and panic disorder is more common in women than in men.[4] An Australian community study found 1 month prevalence rates for panic disorder (with or without agoraphobia) of 0.4% using ICD-10 diagnostic criteria and of 0.5% using DSM-IV diagnostic criteria.[5]

AETIOLOGY/   Stressful life events tend to precede the onset of panic disorder,[6,7] although
RISK FACTORS   a negative interpretation of these events in addition to their occurrence has been suggested as an important aetiological factor.[8] Panic disorder is associated with major depression,[9] social phobia, generalised anxiety disorder, obsessive compulsive disorder,[10] and a substantial risk of drug and alcohol abuse.[11] It is also associated with avoidant, histrionic, and dependent personality disorders.[10]

▶

Panic disorder

◀ **PROGNOSIS**   The severity of symptoms in people with panic disorder fluctuates considerably, with periods of no attacks, or only mild attacks with few symptoms,
being common. There is often a long delay between the initial onset of
symptoms and presentation for treatment. Recurrent attacks may continue
for a number of years, especially if associated with agoraphobia. Reduced
social or occupational functioning varies among people with panic disorder
and is worse in people with associated agoraphobia. Panic disorder is also
associated with an increased rate of attempted but unsuccessful suicide.[12]

Search date May 2001

Jonathan Bisson

What are the effects of preventive psychological interventions?

LIKELY TO BE BENEFICIAL

Multiple episode cognitive behavioural therapy or prolonged exposure therapy versus supportive counselling

Two small RCTs in people with acute stress disorder after a traumatic event (accident or non-sexual assault) found that five sessions of either cognitive behavioural therapy🟢 or prolonged exposure therapy🟢 versus supportive counselling🟢 significantly reduced the number of people with post-traumatic stress disorder (PTSD) after 6 months.

UNKNOWN EFFECTIVENESS

Multiple episode cognitive behavioural therapy versus no treatment or versus standard care

One RCT in people who were involved in a road traffic accident in the previous month found no significant difference between three to six sessions of educational and cognitive behavioural techniques versus no psychological intervention in the number of people with PTSD after 6 months. One RCT found that one to six sessions of cognitive behavioural therapy versus standard care significantly reduced anxiety and intrusive symptoms after 6 months but found no significant difference in depression or avoidance symptoms.

UNLIKELY TO BE BENEFICIAL

Single episode psychological interventions (debriefing)

One systematic review in people who had been exposed to a traumatic event in the previous month found no significant difference between debriefing🟢 versus no debriefing in the incidence of PTSD at 3–5 months. One of the RCTs identified by the systematic review found that debriefing versus no debriefing significantly increased the risk of PTSD at 1 year.

What are the effects of treatments?

BENEFICIAL

Cognitive behavioural therapies

RCTs have found that cognitive behavioural therapies versus no treatment or versus supportive counselling significantly improve PTSD symptoms, anxiety, and depression.

LIKELY TO BE BENEFICIAL

Eye movement desensitisation and reprocessing

RCTs have found that eye movement desensitisation and reprocessing versus waiting list control or versus relaxation therapy improves symptoms. Two RCTs found no significant difference between eye movement desensitisation and reprocessing versus exposure therapy in improving symptoms. ▶

Post-traumatic stress disorder

◄ **Sertraline**

One systematic review found limited evidence that sertraline versus placebo significantly reduced symptoms.

UNKNOWN EFFECTIVENESS

Affect management⊕; drama therapy⊕; hypnotherapy⊕; inpatient programmes; other drug treatments (fluoxetine, brofaromine, amitriptyline, lamotrigine, benzodiazepines, antipsychotics, carbamazepine, imipramine, or phenelzine); psychodynamic psychotherapy⊕; supportive counselling

We found insufficient evidence of the effects of these interventions in improving symptoms.

DEFINITION   PTSD occurs after a major traumatic event. Symptoms include upsetting thoughts and nightmares about the traumatic event, avoidance behaviour, numbing of general responsiveness, increased irritability, and hypervigilance.[1]

INCIDENCE/   One large cross sectional study in the USA found that 10% women and 5%
PREVALENCE   men experience PTSD at some stage in their lives.[2]

AETIOLOGY/   Risk factors include major trauma such as rape, a history of psychiatric
RISK FACTORS disorders, acute distress and depression after the trauma, lack of social support, and personality factors (such as neuroticism).[3]

PROGNOSIS   One large cross sectional study in the USA found that over a third of sufferers continued to satisfy the criteria for a diagnosis of PTSD 6 years after diagnosis.[2] Cross sectional studies provide weak evidence about prognosis.

Mental health

What are the effects of treatments?

BENEFICIAL

Clozapine in people resistant to standard treatment

One systematic review in people resistant to standard treatment has found that clozapine versus standard treatment improves symptoms after 12 weeks (NNT 5) and after 2 years.

Continuation of medication for 6–9 months after an acute episode

Systematic reviews have found that continuing antipsychotic medication for at least 6 months after an acute episode significantly reduces relapse rates over 6–10 months (NNT 3), and that some benefit of continuing treatment is apparent for up to 2 years (NNT 5). We found no evidence of a difference in relapse rates among standard antipsychotic drugs, but one systematic review has found that clozapine versus standard antipsychotic drugs reduces relapse rates over 12 weeks (NNT 20).

Family interventions to reduce relapse rates

One systematic review has found that family intervention versus usual care significantly reduces relapse rates at 12 and 24 months. Seven families would have to be treated to avoid one additional relapse in the family member with schizophrenia.

Psychoeducational interventions to reduce relapse rates

One systematic review has found that psychoeducation versus control intervention significantly reduces relapse rates at 9–18 months (NNT 9).

LIKELY TO BE BENEFICIAL

Behavioural therapy for improving adherence

One RCT found that behavioural interventions versus usual treatment improved adherence to antipsychotic medication over 3 months. One RCT found that behavioural interventions improved adherence compared with psychoeducational therapy.

Cognitive behavioural therapy to reduce relapse rates

Limited evidence from RCTs suggests that the addition of cognitive behavioural therapy to standard care reduced relapse rates (NNT 6 at 18 months).

"Compliance" therapy

Three RCTs found limited evidence that compliance therapy🅖 versus non-specific counselling may increase adherence to antipsychotic medication.

Psychoeducational therapy for improving adherence

One systematic review found limited evidence that psychoeducation improved adherence to antipsychotic medication.

TRADE OFF BETWEEN BENEFITS AND HARMS

Amisulpride *New;* loxapine; molindone; olanzapine; pimozide; quetiapine; risperidone; sulpiride; thioridazine; ziprasidone; zotepine

Systematic reviews have found that these antipsychotic drugs are as effective as standard antipsychotics, and have different profiles of adverse effects. ▶

Chlorpromazine

One systematic review has found that chlorpromazine versus placebo significantly reduces the proportion of people who at 6 months had no improvement (NNT 7), or had marked/worse severity of illness (NNT 5) on a psychiatrist rated scale. Adverse effects make it unacceptable to many people.

Clozapine

Systematic reviews have found some evidence that clozapine may be more effective than standard antipsychotic drugs. However, clozapine was associated with potentially fatal blood dyscrasias. Systematic reviews found no strong evidence about the effectiveness or safety of clozapine compared with new antipsychotic drugs.

Depot haloperidol decanoate

One RCT found that depot haloperidol decanoate versus placebo reduced the need for additional medication at 4 months (NNT 2 with 4 months' treatment). Haloperidol is associated with acute dystonia, akathisia, and parkinsonism.

Depot pipotiazine palmitate

RCTs found no significant difference in psychotic symptoms at 18 months with depot pipotiazine (pipothiazine) palmitate versus standard oral antipsychotic drugs. There was no significant difference in the number of people requiring anticholinergic drugs.

Haloperidol *New*

One systematic review has found that haloperidol versus placebo produces global improvement for up to 2 years (NNT 3), but is associated with acute dystonia (NNH 5), akathisia (NNH 6), and parkinsonism (NNH 3).

UNKNOWN EFFECTIVENESS

Polyunsaturated fatty acids

One systematic review found limited evidence that polyunsaturated fatty acids versus placebo significantly reduced the use of antipsychotic medication within 12 weeks.

Social skills training to reduce relapse rates

Limited evidence from RCTs suggests that social skills training versus usual care may reduce relapse rates.

UNLIKELY TO BE BENEFICIAL

Family therapy for improving adherence

One systematic review has found that family therapy versus usual care is unlikely to improve adherence to antipsychotic medication.

DEFINITION   Schizophrenia is characterised by the "positive symptoms"Ⓖ of auditory hallucinations, delusions, and thought disorder, and the "negative symptoms"Ⓖ of demotivation, self neglect, and reduced emotion.[1]

INCIDENCE/ PREVALENCE   Onset of symptoms typically occurs in early adult life (average age 25 years) and is earlier in men than women. Prevalence worldwide is 2–4/1000. One in 100 people will develop schizophrenia in their lifetime.[2,3]

AETIOLOGY/ RISK FACTORS   Risk factors include a family history (although no major genes have been identified); obstetric complications; developmental difficulties; central nervous system infections in childhood; cannabis use; and acute life events.[2] The precise contributions of these factors and ways in which they may interact are unclear.

◀ **PROGNOSIS** About three quarters of people suffer recurrent relapse and continued disability, although outcomes were worse in the pretreatment era.[4] Outcome may be worse in people with insidious onset and delayed initial treatment, social isolation, or a strong family history; in people living in industrialised countries; in men; and in people who misuse drugs.[3] Drug treatment is generally successful in treating positive symptoms, but up to a third of people derive little benefit and negative symptoms are notoriously difficult to treat. About half of people with schizophrenia do not adhere to treatment in the short term. The figure is even higher in the longer term.[5]

Ankle sprain

Search date July 2001

Peter Struijs and Gino Kerkhoffs

What are the effects of treatments for acute ankle ligament ruptures?

LIKELY TO BE BENEFICIAL

Functional treatment

One systematic review and one subsequent RCT found limited evidence that functional treatment versus minimal treatment significantly reduced the risk of the ankle giving way. Systematic reviews comparing surgery versus functional treatment found conflicting evidence. We found insufficient evidence comparing different functional treatments.

Immobilisation

One systematic review and one subsequent RCT have found no clear difference with functional treatment versus immobilisation in pain or persistent subjective instability. One systematic review has found no significant difference with immobilisation versus surgery in pain.

Surgery

One systematic review has found no significant difference with surgery versus immobilisation in pain. Systematic reviews comparing surgery versus functional treatment found conflicting evidence.

UNKNOWN EFFECTIVENESS

Diathermy

One systematic review has found conflicting evidence on the effects of diathermy versus placebo in walking ability and reduction in swelling.

Homeopathy

One systematic review of one RCT found that homeopathic ointment versus placebo treatment significantly improved pain scores after 10 days.

UNLIKELY TO BE BENEFICIAL

Cold pack compression

One systematic review has found no significant difference in symptoms with cold pack placement versus no treatment, heat, or contrast baths.

Ultrasound

RCTs have found no significant difference with ultrasound versus sham ultrasound in improvement in symptoms, overall clinical score, or ability to walk without a limp. Two RCTs found no significant difference with ultrasound versus electrotherapy or immobilisation in ability to walk.

DEFINITION	Ankle sprain is an injury of the lateral ligament complex of the ankle joint. Such injury can range from mild to severe and is graded according to the following scale on the basis of severity.[1–5] Grade I is a mild stretching of the ligament complex without joint instability. Grade II is a partial rupture of the ligament complex with mild instability of the joint (such as isolated rupture of the anterior talofibular ligament). Grade III involves complete rupture of the ligament complex with instability of the joint.

◀ **INCIDENCE/**
PREVALENCE

Ankle sprain is a common problem in acute medical care occurring at a rate of about one injury/10 000 population a day.[6] Injuries of the lateral ligament complex of the ankle form a quarter of all sports injuries.[6]

AETIOLOGY/
RISK FACTORS

The usual mechanism of injury is inversion and adduction (usually referred to as supination) of the plantar flexed foot. Predisposing factors are a history of ankle sprains and specific malalignment, like crus varum and pes cavo-varus.

PROGNOSIS

Some sports (e.g. basketball, soccer, and volleyball) have a particularly high incidence of ankle injuries. Pain is the most frequent residual problem, often localised on the medial side of the ankle.[4] Other residual complaints include mechanical instability, intermittent swelling, and stiffness. People with more extensive cartilage damage have a higher incidence of residual complaints.[4] Long term cartilage damage can lead to degenerative changes and this is especially true if there is persistent or recurrent instability; every sprain has the potential to add new damage.

Musculoskeletal disorders

Carpal tunnel syndrome

Search date May 2001

Shawn Marshall

What are the effects of treatments?

BENEFICIAL

Local corticosteroid injection (short term)

One systematic review has found that local corticosteroid injections versus placebo injection significantly improve symptoms after 1 month (NNT 3). One subsequent RCT has found that hydrocortisone injections versus no injections significantly improve symptoms after 6 weeks (NNT 2).

Oral corticosteroids (short term)

Two RCTs have found that oral corticosteroids (prednisone or prednisolone) versus placebo significantly improve symptoms after 2 weeks.

TRADE OFF BETWEEN BENEFITS AND HARMS

Endoscopic carpal tunnel release versus open carpal tunnel release

One non-systematic review and additional RCTs found no significant difference with endoscopic versus open carpal tunnel release surgery in reduction of symptoms and improvement in postoperative grip strength. Harms resulting from endoscopic and open carpal tunnel release vary between RCTs.

UNKNOWN EFFECTIVENESS

Local corticosteroid injection (long term); nerve and tendon gliding exercises⑤; oral corticosteroids (long term); surgery versus no surgery

We found no RCTs about the effects of these interventions.

Pyridoxine; therapeutic ultrasound

RCTs found conflicting results on the effects of these interventions.

Wrist splints

We found no RCTs comparing wrist splints versus no treatment. RCTs found no significant difference in symptom severity with neutral angle versus 20° extension wrist splinting, or with full time versus night time only neutral angle wrist splinting.

UNLIKELY TO BE BENEFICIAL

Diuretics

One RCT found no significant difference with diuretics versus placebo in mean global symptom score⑤ after 6 weeks.

Internal neurolysis in conjunction with open carpal tunnel release

Three RCTs found no significant difference with open carpal tunnel release alone versus open release plus internal neurolysis⑤ in symptomatic improvement after 6–12 months.

Non-steroidal anti-inflammatory drugs

One RCT found no significant difference with non-steroidal anti-inflammatory drugs versus placebo in mean global symptom score after 6 weeks.

▶

◀ **LIKELY TO BE INEFFECTIVE OR HARMFUL**

Wrist splinting after carpal tunnel release surgery

Two RCTs in people after carpal tunnel release surgery found no significant difference with wrist splinting versus no splinting in median grip strength or in the number of people who considered themselves "cured". Another RCT found that splinting versus no splinting significantly increased pain and the number of days taken to return to work.

DEFINITION Carpal tunnel syndrome is a neuropathy caused by compression of the median nerve within the carpal tunnel.[1] Classical symptoms of carpal tunnel syndrome include numbness, tingling, burning, or pain in at least two of the three digits supplied by the median nerve (i.e. the thumb, index, and middle fingers).[2] The American Academy of Neurology 🄖 has described diagnostic criteria that rely on a combination of symptoms and physical examination findings.[3] Other diagnostic criteria include results from electrophysiological studies.[2]

INCIDENCE/ PREVALENCE A general population survey in Rochester, Minnesota, found the age adjusted incidence of carpal tunnel syndrome to be 105 (95% CI 99 to 112) cases per 100 000 person years.[4,5] Age adjusted incidence rates were 52 (95% CI 45 to 59) cases for men and 149 (95% CI 138 to 159) cases for women per 100 000 person years. The study found incidence rates increased from 88 (95% CI 75 to 101) cases per 100 000 person years in 1961–1965 to 125 (95% CI 112 to 138) cases per 100 000 person years in 1976–1980. Incidence rates of carpal tunnel syndrome increased with age for men, whereas for women they peaked between the ages of 45–54 years. A general population survey in the Netherlands found prevalence to be 1% for men and 7% for women.[6] A more comprehensive study in southern Sweden found the general population prevalence for carpal tunnel syndrome was 3% (95% CI 2 to 3%).[7] As in other studies, the overall prevalence in women was higher than in men (male : female ratio 1 : 1.4); however, among older people the prevalence in women was almost four times that in men (age group 65–74 years: men 1%, 95% CI 0 to 4%; women 5%, 95% CI 3 to 8%).

AETIOLOGY/ RISK FACTORS Most cases of carpal tunnel syndrome have no easily identifiable cause (idiopathic). Non-specific tenosynovitis is believed to contribute to compression of the median nerve within the carpal tunnel.[4] Secondary causes of carpal tunnel syndrome include the following: space occupying lesions (tumours, hypertrophic synovial tissue, fracture callus, and osteophytes); metabolic and physiological (pregnancy, hypothyroidism, rheumatoid arthritis); infections; neuropathies (associated with diabetes mellitus or alcoholism); and familial disorders. One case control study found that risk factors in the general population included repetitive activities requiring wrist extension or flexion, obesity, very rapid dieting, shorter height, hysterectomy without oophorectomy, and recent menopause.[8]

PROGNOSIS We found little good evidence. One observational study (carpal tunnel syndrome defined by symptoms and electrophysiological study results) found that 34% of people with idiopathic carpal tunnel syndrome without treatment had complete resolution of symptoms (remission) within 6 months of diagnosis.[9] Remission rates were higher for younger age groups, for women versus men, and for pregnant versus non-pregnant women.

Chronic fatigue syndrome

Search date November 2001

Steven Reid, Trudie Chalder, Anthony Cleare Matthew Hotopf and Simon Wessely

---

What are the effects of treatments?

BENEFICIAL

Cognitive behavioural therapy

One systematic review has found that cognitive behavioural therapy administered by highly skilled therapists in specialist centres improves quality of life and physical functioning. One additional multicentre RCT has found that cognitive behavioural therapy may also be effective when administered by less experienced therapists.

Graded aerobic exercise

RCTs have found that a graded aerobic exercise programme versus flexibility and relaxation training or general advice significantly improves measures of fatigue and physical functioning at 12 weeks (NNT 9). One RCT has found a significant improvement in measures of physical functioning, fatigue, mood, and sleep at 1 year with an educational package to encourage graded exercise versus written information only.

UNKNOWN EFFECTIVENESS

Antidepressants; corticosteroids; oral nicotinamide adenine dinucleotide

RCTs found insufficient evidence on the effects of these interventions.

Evening primrose oil

One small RCT found no significant difference with evening primrose oil versus placebo in depression scores at 3 months.

Magnesium (intramuscular)

One small RCT found that magnesium injections versus placebo significantly improved symptoms at 6 weeks (NNT 2).

UNLIKELY TO BE BENEFICIAL

Immunotherapy

Small RCTs found that immunoglobulin G versus placebo modestly improved physical functioning and fatigue at 3–6 months, but was associated with considerable adverse effects. Small RCTs found insufficient evidence on the effects of interferon alfa versus placebo.

Prolonged rest

We found no RCTs on the effects of prolonged rest. Indirect observational evidence in healthy volunteers and in people recovering from a viral illness suggests that prolonged rest may perpetuate or worsen fatigue and symptoms.

◀ **DEFINITION** Chronic fatigue syndrome is characterised by severe, disabling fatigue and other symptoms, including musculoskeletal pain, sleep disturbance, impaired concentration, and headaches. Two widely used definitions of chronic fatigue syndrome, from the US Centers for Disease Control and Prevention[1] and from Oxford, UK,[2] were developed as operational criteria for research❶. There are two important differences between these definitions. The UK criteria insist upon the presence of mental fatigue, whereas the US criteria include a requirement for several physical symptoms, reflecting the belief that chronic fatigue syndrome has an underlying immunological or infective pathology.

INCIDENCE/ Community and primary care based studies have reported the prevalence
PREVALENCE of chronic fatigue syndrome to be 0–3%, depending on the criteria used.[3,4] Systematic population surveys have found similar prevalence of chronic fatigue syndrome in people of different socioeconomic status and in all ethnic groups.[4,5]

AETIOLOGY/ The cause of chronic fatigue syndrome is poorly understood. Women are at
RISK FACTORS higher risk than men (RR 1.3 to 1.7 depending on diagnostic criteria used).[6]

PROGNOSIS Studies have focused on people attending specialist clinics. A systematic review of studies of prognosis (search date 1996) found that children with chronic fatigue syndrome had better outcomes than adults: 54–94% of children showed definite improvement (after up to 6 years' follow up), whereas 20–50% of adults showed some improvement in the medium term and only 6% returned to premorbid levels of functioning.[7] Despite the considerable burden of morbidity associated with chronic fatigue syndrome, we found no evidence of increased mortality. The systematic review found that outcome was influenced by the presence of psychiatric disorders (depression and anxiety), and beliefs about causation and treatment.[7]

Fracture prevention in postmenopausal women

Search date May 2001

Olivier Bruyere and Jean-Yves Reginster

What are the effects of treatments to prevent fractures in postmenopausal women?

UNKNOWN EFFECTIVENESS

Hormone replacement therapy (HRT) to reduce risk of vertebral fracture

Three RCTs found no significant difference in the number of women with vertebral fractures with HRT versus placebo.

HRT to reduce risk of non-vertebral fracture

RCTs found conflicting evidence on the effects of HRT versus placebo in reducing the risk of non-vertebral fractures.

DEFINITION A fracture is a break or disruption of bone or cartilage. Symptoms and signs may include immobility, pain, tenderness, numbness, bruising, joint deformity, joint swelling, limb deformity, and limb shortening. Diagnosis is usually based on a typical clinical picture combined with results from an appropriate imaging technique.

INCIDENCE/ PREVALENCE The lifetime risk of fracture in white women is 20% for the spine, 15% for the wrist, and 18% for the hip.[1]

AETIOLOGY/ RISK FACTORS Fractures usually arise from trauma. Risk factors include those associated with an increased tendency to fall (such as ataxia, drug and alcohol intake, loose carpets), age, osteoporosis, bony metastases, and other disorders of bone.

PROGNOSIS Fractures may result in pain, short or long term disability, haemorrhage, thromboembolic disease (see thromboembolism, p 27), shock, and death. Vertebral fractures are associated with pain, physical impairment, muscular atrophy, changes in body shape, loss of physical function, and lower quality of life. About 20% of women die in the first year after a hip fracture, representing an increase in mortality of 12–20% compared with women of similar age and no hip fracture. Half of elderly women who had been independent become partly dependent after hip fracture. A third become totally dependent.

Hallux valgus (bunions)

Search date September 2001

Jill Ferrari

What are the effects of interventions?

LIKELY TO BE BENEFICIAL

Absorbable pin fixation (similar to standard bone fixation)
Two RCTs comparing standard fixation using sutures or Kirschner wire⊕ versus absorbable pins following Mitchell's osteotomy⊕ found no significant difference in clinical or radiological outcomes after a mean of 1 year.

Chevron-Akin osteotomy
One RCT found that the chevron osteotomy⊕ plus Akin osteotomy⊕ versus distal soft tissue reconstruction plus Akin osteotomy significantly improved hallux valgus and intermetatarsal angles.

Chevron osteotomy (compared with no treatment or with orthoses)
One RCT has found that chevron osteotomy versus no treatment or versus orthoses significantly reduces pain and global assessment of satisfaction at 12 months (NNT 2).

Crepe postoperative bandage
One RCT of crepe bandage versus plaster cast slippers after Wilson osteotomy⊕ found no significant difference in any outcome, but was too small to rule out a clinically important effect.

Early weightbearing
One systematic review has found that the incidence of non-union at the site of arthrodesis is similar after early compared with late weightbearing after surgery.

UNKNOWN EFFECTIVENESS

Chevron osteotomy (compared with proximal osteotomy)
RCTs found limited evidence that chevron osteotomy was more likely to produce poor outcomes than proximal osteotomy⊕.

Chevron osteotomy with additional tenotomy
One RCT found no signficant difference in hallux abductus angle, pain, or mobility between chevron osteotomy plus additional tenotomy versus chevron osteotomy alone.

Continuous passive motion
One systematic review found no significant difference between continuous passive motion versus routine rehabilitation on joint range of motion or return to normal footwear, but was too small to rule out a clinically important effect.

Keller's arthroplasty (compared with proximal osteotomy or arthrodesis)
One systematic review found little good evidence on the effects of Keller's arthroplasty⊕ versus other types of operation.

Orthoses to treat hallux valgus in adults
One RCT found that orthoses versus no treatment significantly improved pain intensity at 6 months, but found no significant difference in pain at 12 months. ▶

Hallux valgus (bunions)

UNLIKELY TO BE BENEFICIAL

Night splints

One RCT found no significant difference between night splints versus no treatment in deformity or pain at 6 months.

Orthoses to prevent hallux valgus in high risk adults

One RCT in men with rheumatoid arthritis found no significant difference in development of hallux valgus with orthoses versus no treatment.

LIKELY TO BE INEFFECTIVE OR HARMFUL

Antipronatory orthoses in children

One RCT found no significant difference in hallux abductus angle after 3 years between antipronatory orthoses🅖 versus no treatment in children with bilateral deformity. In children with unilateral deformity, orthoses were associated with greater deterioration in joint position.

DEFINITION   **Hallux valgus** is a deformity of the great toe characterised by a lateral deviation (abduction) and valgus rotation of the toe with adduction and varus rotation of the first metatarsal.[1] Radiological criteria for hallux valgus vary, but a commonly accepted criterion is a metatarsal joint angle greater than 14.5°.[2] **Bunion** is the lay term used to describe a prominent and often inflamed metatarsal head and overlying bursa. Symptoms include pain, limitation in walking, and problems with wearing normal shoes.

INCIDENCE/   The prevalence of hallux valgus varies in different populations. In a recent
PREVALENCE   study of 6000 UK school children aged 9–10 years, 2.5% had clinical evidence of hallux valgus, and 2% met both clinical and radiological criteria for hallux valgus. An earlier study found hallux valgus in 48% of adults.[2] Differences in prevalence may result from different methods of measurement, varying age groups, or different diagnostic criteria (e.g. metatarsal joint angle > 10° or > 15°).[3]

AETIOLOGY/   Nearly all population studies have found that hallux valgus is more common
RISK FACTORS   in women. Footwear may contribute to the deformity, but studies comparing people who wear shoes with those who do not have been contradictory. Hypermobility of the first ray🅖 and excessive foot pronation are associated with hallux valgus.[4]

PROGNOSIS   We found no studies that looked at progression of hallux valgus. Progression of deformity and symptoms is rapid in some people, others remain asymptomatic. One study found that hallux valgus is often unilateral initially, but usually progresses to bilateral deformity.[2]

What are the effects of treatments?

BENEFICIAL

High specification versus standard hospital mattress on operating tables to prevent pressure sores

One systematic review has found that high specification foam mattresses and pressure relieving mattresses on operating tables versus standard hospital mattresses significantly reduce the number of pressure sores.

Perioperative antibiotic prophylaxis

One systematic review has found that multidose perioperative and single dose preoperative antibiotic prophylaxis regimens versus control or no antibiotics significantly reduce infection after hip surgery.

Sliding hip screw device for internal fixation of extracapsular fracture

One systematic review found no significant difference with sliding hip screws⑤ versus fixed nail plates⑥ in mortality, pain at follow up, or impairment of mobility, but found that sliding hip screws significantly reduced the risk of fixation failure. It found limited evidence that a sliding hip screw versus the RAB fixed nail plate⑥ significantly increased the risk of leg shortening.

LIKELY TO BE BENEFICIAL

Cyclical compression of the foot or calf to reduce venous thromboembolism

One systematic review has found that cyclical compression devices (foot or calf pumps) significantly reduce deep venous thrombosis, but are associated with non-compliance and skin abrasion.

Geriatric hip fracture programmes in acute orthopaedic units

One systematic review of RCTs and observational studies, and one subsequent RCT in elderly people who have suffered hip fracture, found that geriatric hip fracture programmes versus control programmes significantly increased the number of people able to return to their previous residence, and significantly reduced morbidity whilst in hospital, but had no significant effect on mortality. The systematic review found that geriatric hip fracture programmes also reduced the length of stay in hospital. Two additional RCTs found that a geriatrician led geriatric hip fracture programme versus control significantly reduced the incidence of severe delirium.

Nutritional supplementation after fracture

One systematic review in people who had undergone surgery for hip fracture found limited evidence that nutritional supplementation (oral protein and energy feeds) versus control significantly reduced postoperative complications.

Perioperative prophylaxis with antiplatelet agents

One systematic review has found that perioperative antiplatelet prophylaxis versus placebo or no prophylaxis significantly reduces the incidence of pulmonary embolism (NNT 25), but has no significant effect on the incidence of deep venous thrombosis. One subsequent RCT has found that aspirin versus placebo ▶

significantly reduces the incidence of both deep venous thrombosis and pulmonary embolism. The systematic review and subsequent RCT both found that antiplatelet treatment versus control significantly increases the risk of bleeding complications.

Perioperative prophylaxis with heparin to reduce venous thromboembolism

One systematic review has found that perioperative prophylaxis with either unfractionated heparin or low molecular weight heparin versus placebo or no treatment significantly reduces the incidence of deep venous thrombosis confirmed by imaging (NNT 7). The systematic review has also found that low molecular weight heparin versus unfractionated heparin significantly reduces deep venous thrombosis confirmed by imaging (NNT 11).

Regional (versus general) anaesthesia for surgery

One systematic review of people after hip fracture surgery found limited evidence that regional versus general anaesthesia significantly reduced the risk of deep venous thrombosis (NNT 6), but had no significant effect on short term mortality.

TRADE OFF BETWEEN BENEFITS AND HARMS

Arthroplasty for intracapsular fracture

One systematic review of randomised and observational studies, and five subsequent RCTs in people with displaced intracapsular fractures, found limited evidence that arthroplasty❶ versus internal fixation❶ significantly reduced the need for re-operation at 12–15 or 24 months after surgery, but significantly increased the number of deep infections and operative blood loss. Two of the subsequent RCTs found that arthroplasty versus internal fixation increased mortality.

Early supported discharge programmes

One systematic review of RCTs and observational studies has found that early supported discharge versus control significantly increases the number of people returning to their previous residence and reduces length of hospital stay, but significantly increases the frequency of readmission to hospital.

Intramedullary fixation with condylocephalic nail for extracapsular fracture

One systematic review has found that condylocephalic nails versus extramedullary fixation significantly reduce length of surgery, the incidence of deep wound sepsis, and operative blood loss. The review has also found that condylocephalic nails significantly increase reoperation rates and the incidence of leg shortening and of external rotation deformity.

UNKNOWN EFFECTIVENESS

Arthroplasty for extracapsular fracture

One systematic review in people with unstable extracapsular hip fractures found limited evidence that arthroplasty versus internal fixation using a sliding hip screw did not significantly affect operating times, local wound complications, mortality, or mobility. Arthroplasty significantly increased the number of people who received a blood transfusion (NNH 4).

Different types of implant for intracapsular fracture

One systematic review found insufficient evidence to determine the best implant for internal fixation of intracapsular fractures.

◀ Nerve blocks for pain control before and after hip fracture

One systematic review of small RCTs and quasi-randomised trials found that nerve blocks versus control significantly reduced total analgesic intake.

Specialised orthopaedic rehabilitation units for elderly people

One systematic review and one subsequent RCT found that rehabilitation in a geriatric outpatient rehabilitation unit versus control significantly increased the number of people able to return to their previous residence, although they found conflicting results on length of hospital stay. The systematic review found that geriatric outpatient rehabilitation units significantly reduced rates of readmission for acute care, but did not significantly reduce mortality or increase quality of life scores.

Systematic home based rehabilitation

One RCT comparing a systematic home based rehabilitation programme versus existing services found no significant difference in recovery to prefracture levels of self care, home management, social activity, balance, or lower extremity strength after 12 months.

Use of graduated elastic compression to prevent venous thromboembolism

We found no RCTs in elderly people with hip fracture involving thromboembolism stockings for prevention of thrombotic complications. One systematic review in people undergoing elective total hip replacement has found that graduated elastic compression versus placebo significantly reduces the risk of deep venous thrombosis (NNT 4).

UNLIKELY TO BE BENEFICIAL

Conservative (non-surgical) treatment of extracapsular fractures

One systematic review of people with extracapsular hip fractures comparing conservative versus operative treatment found limited evidence that operative treatment significantly reduced the number of people remaining in hospital after 12 weeks. The review found that conservative treatment significantly increased both leg shortening and varus deformity❸ (NNH 2), but found insufficient evidence to determine whether any significant difference exists between treatments in medical complications, mortality, or long term pain.

Intramedullary fixation with cephalocondylic nail for extracapsular fracture (less effective/more harmful than sliding hip screw)

One systematic review and one subsequent RCT found no significant difference with cephalocondylic❸ intramedullary fixation versus extramedullary fixation in pain at follow up, ability to return to a previous residence, and ability to walk after 3–12 months. The review also found no significant difference between treatments in mortality, wound infection, or blood loss, but found that cephalocondylic intramedullary fixation significantly increased intraoperative femoral fractures and re-operation rates.

Preoperative bed traction to the injured limb

One systematic review found no significant difference in analgesic use or ease of fracture reduction with routine preoperative traction versus control. One RCT identified by the review found that skeletal versus skin traction significantly reduced analgesic use.

Hip fracture

◀ **DEFINITION** Hip fracture is a fracture of the femur above a point 5 cm below the distal part of the lesser trochanter.[1] **Intracapsular fractures** occur proximal to the point at which the hip joint capsule attaches to the femur, and can be subdivided into displaced and undisplaced fractures. Undisplaced fractures include impacted or adduction fractures. Displaced intracapsular fractures may be associated with disruption of the blood supply to the head of the femur. Numerous subdivisions and classification methods exist for these fractures. In the most distal part of the proximal femoral segment (below the lesser trochanter), the term "subtrochanteric" is used. **Extracapsular fractures** occur distal to the hip joint capsule.

INCIDENCE/ Hip fractures may occur at any age but are most common in elderly people.
PREVALENCE In industrialised societies, the lifetime risk of hip fracture is about 18% in women and 6% in men.[2] A recent study reported that prevalence increases from about 3/100 women aged 65–74 years to 12.6/100 women aged 85 years and above.[3] The age stratified incidence has also increased in some societies during the past 25 years; not only are people living longer, but the incidence of fracture in each age group may have increased.[4]

AETIOLOGY/ Hip fractures are usually sustained through a fall from standing height or
RISK FACTORS less. The pattern of incidence is consistent with two main risk factors: increased risk of falling and loss of skeletal strength from osteoporosis. Both are associated with aging.

PROGNOSIS One in five people die in the first year after a hip fracture,[5] and one in four elderly people require a higher level of long term care after a fracture.[5,6] Those who do return to live in the community after a hip fracture have greater difficulty with activities of daily living than age and sex matched controls.[3]

Search date June 2001

Gavin Young

What are the effects of treatments for idiopathic leg cramps?

BENEFICIAL

Quinine
One systematic review has found that quinine versus placebo significantly reduces the frequency of nocturnal leg cramp attacks over 4 weeks.

UNKNOWN EFFECTIVENESS

Analgesics; antiepileptic drugs; compression hosiery
We found no RCTs on the effects of these interventions on idiopathic leg cramps❿.

Quinine plus theophylline
One RCT with weak methods found that quinine plus theophylline versus quinine alone significantly reduced the number of nights affected by leg cramp over 2 weeks.

Vitamin E
One small RCT comparing vitamin E versus placebo found no significant difference in the number of nights disturbed by leg cramps.

DEFINITION	Leg cramps are involuntary, localised, and usually painful skeletal muscle contractions, which commonly affect calf muscles. Leg cramps typically occur at night and usually last only seconds to minutes. Leg cramps may be idiopathic or related to a definable process or disease such as renal dialysis, pregnancy, or venous insufficiency.
INCIDENCE/ PREVALENCE	Leg cramps are common and their incidence increases with age. About half of the people attending a general medicine clinic have had leg cramps within 1 month of their visit, and over two thirds of people over 50 years of age have experienced leg cramps.[1]
AETIOLOGY/ RISK FACTORS	Very little is known about the causes of leg cramps. Risk factors include exercise, pregnancy, salt depletion, renal dialysis, electrolyte imbalances, peripheral vascular disease (both venous and arterial), peripheral nerve injury, polyneuropathies, motor neuron disease, muscle diseases, and the use of certain drugs. Other causes of calf pain include trauma, deep venous thrombosis (see thromboembolism, p 27), and ruptured Baker's cyst❿.
PROGNOSIS	Leg cramps may cause severe pain and sleep disturbance, both of which are distressing.

Low back pain and sciatica: acute

Search date October 2001

Maurits van Tulder and Bart Koes

What are the effects of treatments?

Advice to stay active

Two systematic reviews and one subsequent RCT have found that advice to stay active versus no advice significantly increases the rate of recovery and reduces pain, disability, and time spent off work.

Non-steroidal anti-inflammatory drugs

Systematic reviews and one additional RCT have found that non-steroidal anti-inflammatory drugs versus placebo significantly increase the number of people with overall improvement after 1 week and significantly reduce the number of people requiring additional analgesics. Systematic reviews and additional RCTs have found no significant difference in pain relief with non-steroidal anti-inflammatory drugs versus each other or versus other treatments (paracetamol, opioids, muscle relaxants, and non-drug treatments).

Behavioural therapy

Two RCTs have found that behavioural therapy versus traditional care or electromyographic biofeedback reduces acute low back pain and disability.

Multidisciplinary treatment programmes

One systematic review in people with subacute low back pain found limited evidence that multidisciplinary treatment⊙, including a workplace visit, versus usual care reduced sick leave.

Muscle relaxants

Systematic reviews have found that muscle relaxants versus placebo reduce pain and muscle tension and increase mobility, but have found no significant difference in outcomes with muscle relaxants versus each other. Adverse effects in people using muscle relaxants were common and included dependency, drowsiness, and dizziness.

Acupuncture

We found no systematic review and no RCTs of acupuncture⊙ specifically in people with acute low back pain.

Analgesics (paracatemol, opioids)

Systematic reviews have found no consistent difference with analgesics versus non-steroidal anti-inflammatory drugs in reducing pain, but have found that electroacupuncture⊙ or ultrasound versus analgesics significantly improves pain relief at 4–6 months.

◀ **Back schools**

One systematic review found limited evidence that back schools versus placebo increased rates of recovery and reduced sick leave in the short term. The review found no significant difference in outcomes with back school versus physiotherapy, and found that back school versus McKenzie exercises❸ increased pain and sick leave.

Colchicine; electromyographic biofeedback❸; temperature treatments (short wave diathermy, ultrasound, ice, heat); transcutaneous electrical nerve stimulation (TENS)

We found insufficient evidence on the effects of these interventions.

Epidural steroid injections

One RCT found that epidural steroids versus subcutaneous lidocaine injections increased the proportion of people who were pain free after 3 months. A second RCT found no significant difference in the number of people cured or improved with epidural steroids versus epidural saline versus epidural bupivacaine and versus dry needling.

Lumbar supports

We found no evidence on the effects of lumbar supports.

Massage

Systematic reviews have found no significant difference in pain, functional status, or mobility with massage❸ versus spinal manipulation or electrical stimulation.

Spinal manipulation

Systematic reviews found conflicting evidence on the effects of spinal manipulation.

Traction

RCTs found conflicting evidence on the effects of traction.

UNLIKELY TO BE BENEFICIAL

Back exercises

Systematic reviews and additional RCTs have found either no significant difference with back exercises versus conservative or inactive treatments in pain or disability, or found that back exercises increase pain or disability.

LIKELY TO BE INEFFECTIVE OR HARMFUL

Bed rest

Systematic reviews have found no evidence that bed rest is better, but have found evidence that it could be worse than no treatment, advice to stay active, back exercises, physiotherapy, spinal manipulation, or non-steroidal anti-inflammatory drugs. One systematic review has found that adverse effects of bed rest include joint stiffness, muscle wasting, loss of bone mineral density, pressure sores, and venous thromboembolism.

DEFINITION   Low back pain is pain, muscle tension, or stiffness localised below the costal margin and above the inferior gluteal folds, with or without leg pain (sciatica❸),[1] and is designated as acute when it persists for less than 12 weeks (see definition of chronic low back pain, p 201).[2] Non-specific low back pain is low back pain not attributed to a recognisable pathology (such as infection, tumour, osteoporosis, rheumatoid arthritis, fracture, or inflammation).[1] This review excludes low back pain or sciatica with symptoms or signs at presentation that suggest a specific underlying condition.   ▶

Low back pain and sciatica: acute

INCIDENCE/ PREVALENCE	Over 70% of people in developed countries will experience low back pain at some time in their lives.[3] Each year, 15–45% of adults suffer low back pain, and 1/20 people present to hospital with a new episode. Low back pain is most common between the ages of 35–55 years.[3]
AETIOLOGY/ RISK FACTORS	Symptoms, pathology, and radiological appearances are poorly correlated. Pain is non-specific in about 85% of people. About 4% of people with low back pain in primary care have compression fractures and about 1% have a tumour. The prevalence of prolapsed intervertebral disc is about 1–3%.[3] Ankylosing spondylitis and spinal infections are less common.[4] Risk factors for the development of back pain include heavy physical work, frequent bending, twisting, lifting, and prolonged static postures. Psychosocial risk factors include anxiety, depression, and mental stress at work.[3,5]
PROGNOSIS	Acute low back pain is usually self limiting (90% of people recover within 6 wk), although 2–7% develop chronic pain. One study found recurrent pain accounted for 75–85% of absenteeism from work.[6]

Search date October 2001

Maurits van Tulder and Bart Koes

What are the effects of treatments?

BENEFICIAL

Exercise (v other treatments)

Systematic reviews and additional RCTs have found that exercise versus other treatments (including usual care) improves pain and functional status. Systematic reviews and additional RCTs have found conflicting evidence on the effects of exercise versus inactive treatments.

Multidisciplinary treatment programmes (v non-multidisciplinary treatments)

Systematic reviews have found that intensive multidisciplinary biopsychosocial rehabilitation⊙ with functional restoration versus inpatient or outpatient non-multidisciplinary treatments or versus usual care reduces pain and improves function. The reviews found no significant difference in pain or function with less intensive multidisciplinary treatments versus non-multidisciplinary treatments or usual care.

LIKELY TO BE BENEFICIAL

Analgesics

One RCT found that tramadol versus placebo decreased pain and increased functional status. A second RCT found that paracetamol versus diflunisal increased the number of people who rated the treatment as good or excellent.

Back schools in occupational settings (v no treatment)

One systematic review has found that in occupational settings, back schools versus no treatment improve pain and reduce disability. Systematic reviews and one subsequent RCT found conflicting evidence on the effects of back schools.

Behavioural therapy

Systematic reviews have found that behavioural therapy versus no treatment, placebo, or waiting list control reduces pain and improves functional status and behavioural outcomes. Systematic reviews have found no significant difference with different types of behavioural therapy versus each other in functional status, pain, or behavioural outcomes, and found conflicting results with behavioural therapy versus other treatments in pain, behavioural outcomes, or functional status.

Massage (v other treatments)

Systematic reviews and subsequent RCTs have found that massage⊙ versus other treatments reduces pain and improves functioning.

Non-steroidal anti-inflammatory drugs

One RCT found that naproxen versus placebo increased pain relief. Systematic reviews and additional RCTs have found no significant difference with non-steroidal anti-inflammatory drugs versus each other in outcomes. Two RCTs found conflicting evidence on the effects of non-steroidal anti-inflammatory drugs versus analgesics. ▶

Low back pain and sciatica: chronic

◄ **Trigger point and ligamentous injections**

One systematic review found limited evidence that steroid plus local anaesthetic injection of trigger points versus local anaesthetic injection alone increased pain relief after 3 months, and that phenol versus saline injection of the lumbar interspinal ligament increased pain relief after 6 months.

UNKNOWN EFFECTIVENESS

Acupuncture

Two systematic reviews have found no significant difference in outcomes with acupuncture⊙ versus placebo or no treatment. One systematic review and one subsequent RCT have found that acupuncture versus transcutaneous electrical nerve stimulation significantly reduces pain intensity and significantly increases overall improvement.

Antidepressants

Systematic reviews and additional RCTs have found that antidepressants versus placebo significantly increase pain relief, but have found no significant difference in functioning or depression. Additional RCTs have found conflicting results on pain relief with antidepressants versus each other or versus analgesics.

Electromyographic biofeedback

One systematic review found no significant difference in pain relief or functional status with electromyographic biofeedback⊙ versus placebo or waiting list control, but found conflicting results on the effects of electromyographic biofeedback versus other treatments.

Epidural steroid injections

Systematic reviews comparing epidural steroids versus placebo, local anaesthetic, local anaesthetic plus an opioid, or benzodiazepines (midazolam) found insufficient evidence on outcomes. One systematic review has found no difference with epidural steroid injections versus placebo in pain relief after 6 weeks or 6 months. One systematic review has found that epidural steroids versus other treatments significantly increase pain relief in the short term.

Lumbar supports

We found insufficient evidence on the effects of lumbar supports.

Muscle relaxants

We found insufficient evidence on the benefits of muscle relaxants. Systematic reviews have found that adverse effects, including dependency, drowsiness, and dizziness, occur in up to 70% of people.

Spinal manipulation

One systematic review has found that spinal manipulation versus placebo improves outcomes. Three other systematic reviews have found conflicting results on the effects of spinal manipulation versus placebo or conservative treatments.

Transcutaneous electrical nerve stimulation

One systematic review has found no significant difference with transcutaneous electrical nerve stimulation versus control in pain relief. Two systematic reviews found conflicting evidence on the effects of transcutaneous electrical nerve stimulation.

▶

◄ **LIKELY TO BE INEFFECTIVE OR HARMFUL**

Facet joint injections

Two systematic reviews found no significant difference in pain relief with facet joint injections versus placebo or facet joint nerve blocks.

Traction

One systematic review and two additional RCTs have found no significant difference in pain relief or functional status with traction versus placebo or with traction plus massage versus interferential treatment (electrotherapy).

DEFINITION	Low back pain is pain, muscle tension, or stiffness localised below the costal margin and above the inferior gluteal folds, with or without leg pain (sciatica **G**),[1] and is defined as chronic when it persists for 12 weeks or more (see definition of acute low back pain, p 198).[2] Non-specific low back pain is low back pain not attributed to a recognisable pathology (such as infection, tumour, osteoporosis, rheumatoid arthritis, fracture, or inflammation).[1] This review excludes low back pain or sciatica with symptoms or signs at presentation that suggest a specific underlying condition.
INCIDENCE/ PREVALENCE	See incidence of acute low back pain, p 198.
AETIOLOGY/ RISK FACTORS	See aetiology of acute low back pain, p 198.
PROGNOSIS	See prognosis of acute low back pain, p 198.

Neck pain

Search date September 2001

Allan Binder

What are the effects of treatments for uncomplicated neck pain without severe neurological deficit?

LIKELY TO BE BENEFICIAL

Manual treatments (mobilisation and manipulation)

Systematic reviews have found that manipulation or mobilisation versus other treatments improve symptoms. One additional and one subsequent RCT have found no significant difference with mobilisation versus manipulation in pain. Rare but serious adverse effects have been reported following manipulation of the cervical spine.

Physical treatments (physiotherapy, pulsed electromagnetic field therapy, exercise therapy)

Systematic reviews and subsequent RCTs have found that pulsed electromagnetic field therapy versus sham treatment, exercise versus stress management, and active physiotherapy versus passive treatment all significantly reduce pain.

UNKNOWN EFFECTIVENESS

Drug treatments (analgesics, non-steroidal anti-inflammatory drugs, antidepressants, or muscle relaxants)

We found insufficient evidence on the effects of analgesics, non-steroidal anti-inflammatory drugs, antidepressants, or muscle relaxants for neck pain, although they are widely used as a first line intervention. Some are associated with well documented adverse effects.

Multidisciplinary (multimodal) treatment *New*

One systematic review and two subsequent RCTs have found no consistent differences in pain or time off work over 18 months with multimodal cognitive behavioural therapy versus other treatments.

Patient education *New*

Two systematic reviews and one subsequent RCT found insufficient evidence about the effects of patient education (advice or group instruction).

Physical treatments (acupuncture, biofeedback, cold or heat, laser, spray and stretch, traction)

Systematic reviews found insufficient evidence about the effects of these physical treatments.

Soft collars or special pillows *New*

We found no evidence of the effects of soft collars. One RCT found limited evidence that water based pillows versus standard and roll pillows significantly reduced morning pain and improved quality of sleep. ▶

◄ *What are the effects of treatments for acute whiplash injury?*

LIKELY TO BE BENEFICIAL

Early mobilisation

Systematic reviews and subsequent RCTs found limited evidence that early mobilisation versus immobilisation or versus rest plus a collar significantly reduced pain.

Early return to normal activity

Systematic reviews and subsequent RCTs found limited evidence that advice to act as usual plus anti-inflammatory drugs versus immobilisation plus 14 days sick leave improved mild subjective symptoms.

Electrotherapy

One RCT found limited evidence that electromagnetic field therapy versus placebo significantly reduced pain after 4 weeks but not after 3 months.

Multimodal treatment *New*

One RCT found that multimodal treatment versus physical therapy significantly reduced pain at the end of treatment and after 6 months.

What are the effects of treatments for chronic whiplash injury?

LIKELY TO BE BENEFICIAL

Percutaneous radiofrequency neurotomy for zygapophyseal joint pain in people with chronic whiplash

One RCT found limited evidence that percutaneous radiofrequency neurotomy versus a sham procedure significantly increased the number of people who were pain free after 27 weeks (NNT 2).

What are the effects of treatments for neck pain with radiculopathy?

UNKNOWN EFFECTIVENESS

Drug treatments (epidural steroid injections, analgesics, non-steroidal anti-inflammatory drugs, or muscle relaxants)

We found no RCTs about the effects of epidural steroid injections, analgesics, non-steroidal anti-inflammatory drugs, or muscle relaxants.

Surgery versus conservative treatment

One RCT found no significant difference with surgery versus conservative treatment in symptoms after 1 year.

DEFINITION   Neck pain can be divided into uncomplicated pain, whiplash, and pain with radiculopathy. Neck pain often occurs in combination with limitation of movement and poorly defined neurological symptoms affecting the upper limbs. The pain can be severe and intractable, and can occur with radiculopathy or myelopathy.

►

Neck pain

INCIDENCE/ PREVALENCE
About two thirds of people will experience neck pain at some time in their lives.[1,2] Prevalence is highest in middle age. In the UK about 15% of hospital based physiotherapy, and in Canada 30% of chiropractic referrals, are for neck pain.[3,4] In the Netherlands neck pain contributes up to 2% of general practitioner consultations.[5]

AETIOLOGY/ RISK FACTORS
Most uncomplicated neck pain is associated with poor posture, anxiety and depression, neck strain, occupational injuries, or sporting injuries. With chronic pain, mechanical and degenerative factors (often referred to as cervical spondylosis) become more evident. Some neck pain results from soft tissue trauma, most typically seen in whiplash injuries. Rarely, disc prolapse and inflammatory, infective, or malignant conditions affect the cervical spine and present with neck pain with or without neurological features.

PROGNOSIS
Neck pain usually resolves within days or weeks but can recur or become chronic. In some industries, neck related disorders account for as much time off work as low back pain (see low back pain and sciatica, p 196).[6] The percentage of people in whom neck pain becomes chronic depends on the cause but is thought to be about 10%:[1] similar to low back pain. Neck pain causes severe disability in 5% of affected people.[2] One systematic review of the clinical course and prognostic factors of non-specific neck pain identified six observational studies and 17 RCTs.[7] In people who had had pain for at least 6 months, a median of 46% (22–79%) improved with treatment. Whiplash injuries were more likely to cause disability; up to 40% of sufferers reported symptoms even after 15 years of follow up.[8] Factors associated with a poorer outcome after whiplash are not well defined.[9] The incidence of chronic disability following whiplash varies among countries, although reasons for this variation are unclear.[10]

Non-steroidal anti-inflammatory drugs

Search date May 2001

Peter Gøtzsche

Are there any important differences between available non-steroidal anti-inflammatory drugs (NSAIDs)?

BENEFICIAL

NSAIDs in rheumatoid arthritis

Systematic reviews have found no important differences in benefits among different non-steroidal anti-inflammatory drugs or doses, but found differences in harms related to increased doses and to the nature of the NSAID.

TRADE OFF BETWEEN BENEFITS AND HARMS

NSAIDs in osteoarthritis

Systematic reviews have found no important differences in benefits among different NSAIDs or doses, but found differences in harms related to increased doses and to the nature of the NSAID.

UNKNOWN EFFECTIVENESS

NSAIDs versus simple analgesics in acute musculoskeletal syndromes

We found no RCTs in people with acute musculoskeletal syndromes comparing NSAIDs versus simple analgesics such as paracetamol.

Switch between different NSAIDs

Observational evidence suggests that if the response to one NSAID is unsatisfactory, there is no benefit in switching to another NSAID.

UNLIKELY TO BE BENEFICIAL

NSAIDs in increased doses

Systematic reviews have found that benefits of NSAIDs increase towards a maximum value at high doses. Recommended doses are close to creating the maximum benefit. In contrast, three systematic reviews found no ceiling for adverse effects, which increased in an approximately linear fashion with dose.

What are the effects of co-treatments to reduce the risk of gastrointestinal adverse effects of NSAIDs?

BENEFICIAL

Misoprostol in people at high risk who cannot avoid NSAIDs

One systematic review in people who had taken NSAIDs for at least 3 months has found that misoprostol versus placebo significantly reduces the development of gastric or duodenal ulcers. One additional RCT in people with rheumatoid arthritis taking NSAIDs found that misoprostol versus placebo significantly reduced the incidence over 6 months of serious upper gastrointestinal complications such as perforation, gastric outlet obstruction, or bleeding (NNT 263). However, RCTs have found that misoprostol versus placebo significantly increases minor gastrointestinal adverse effects such as diarrhoea and abdominal pain.

▶

◄ LIKELY TO BE BENEFICIAL

H$_2$ blockers in people at high risk who cannot avoid NSAIDs
One systematic review in people who had taken NSAIDs for 3 months has found that H$_2$ blockers versus placebo significantly reduce the development of gastric and duodenal ulcers.

Omeprazole in people at high risk who cannot avoid NSAIDs
One systematic review in people who had taken NSAIDs for at least 3 months has found that omeprazole versus placebo significantly reduces the incidence of endoscopically diagnosed gastric and duodenal ulcers.

What are the effects of topical NSAIDs?

BENEFICIAL

Topical NSAIDs in acute and chronic pain conditions
One systematic review in people with acute and chronic pain conditions has found that topical NSAIDs versus placebo significantly reduce pain (NNT 5 in acute pain conditions; NNT 3 in chronic pain conditions, no time frame stated).

UNKNOWN EFFECTIVENESS

Topical versus systemic NSAIDs or versus alternative analgesics
One systematic review found no high quality RCTs of topical NSAIDs versus oral forms of the same drug, or versus paracetamol.

DEFINITION NSAIDs have anti-inflammatory, analgesic, and antipyretic effects, and inhibit platelet aggregation. The drugs have no documented effect on the course of musculoskeletal diseases.

INCIDENCE/ NSAIDs are widely used. Almost 10% of people in the Netherlands used a
PREVALENCE non-aspirin NSAID in 1987, and the overall use was 11 defined daily doses ⓖ per 1000 people a day.[1] In Australia in 1994, overall use was 35 defined daily doses per 1000 people a day, with 36% of the people receiving NSAIDs for osteoarthritis, 42% for sprain and strain or low back pain, and 4% for rheumatoid arthritis; 35% were aged over 60 years.[2]

Search date June 2001

Paul Dieppe, Jiri Chard, Stefan Lohmander and Claire Smith

What are the effects of treatments?

BENEFICIAL

Hip replacement

One systematic review of observational studies has found that hip replacement is effective for at least 10 years.

Knee replacement

Systematic reviews have found that knee replacement is effective in relieving pain and improving function. One RCT found limited evidence that unicompartmental knee operations are more effective than tricompartmental replacement. We found limited evidence that unicompartmental knee operations are more effective than bicompartmental operations.

Systemic analgesics (short term pain relief and improved function)

Systematic reviews in people with osteoarthritis of the hip or knee found limited evidence that simple analgesics, such as paracetamol (acetaminophen), versus placebo reduced pain.

Systemic non-steroidal anti-inflammatory drugs (short term pain relief)

Systematic reviews in people with osteoarthritis of the hip have found that non-steroidal anti-inflammatory drugs (NSAIDs) reduce pain. We found no good evidence that NSAIDs are superior to simple analgesics, such as paracetamol (acetaminophen), or that there are differences between NSAIDs in relieving pain.

Topical agents (short term pain relief)

One systematic review and one additional RCT have found that topical agents containing NSAIDs versus placebo significantly reduce pain. RCTs found that capsaicin versus placebo significantly improved pain.

LIKELY TO BE BENEFICIAL

Exercise (pain relief and improved function)

RCTs have found that exercise and physical therapy reduce pain and disability in people with hip or knee osteoarthritis, although many of the trials were limited by methodological and reporting issues.

Hip replacement in older people (worse outcomes than for age 45–75 years)

One systematic review of observational studies found that people over 75 years may have worse outcomes in terms of pain relief and function.

Intra-articular glucocorticoid injections of the knee (short term pain relief)

One systematic review found limited evidence that intra-articular glucocorticoids versus placebo reduced pain for 1–4 weeks.

Intra-articular hyaluronan injections of the knee

One systematic review, and subsequent non-systematic reviews and RCTs, found limited evidence that hyaluronan versus placebo reduced pain for 1–6 months.

▶

◀ **Knee replacement in older people**

We found limited evidence from observational studies suggesting that knee replacement is effective in older people.

Physical aids

RCTs in people with knee osteoarthritis found limited evidence that physical aids (joint braces or taping of the joint) may improve disease specific quality of life.

TRADE OFF BETWEEN BENEFITS AND HARMS

Hip replacement in obese people (greater risk of revision)

One systematic review of observational studies suggested that people who weigh over 70 kg may have worse outcomes in terms of pain relief and function after hip replacement. One study found lower rates of long term survival of implant in obese people.

Hip replacement in younger people (greater risk of revision)

One systematic review of observational studies suggested that people under 45 years old may have worse outcomes in terms of pain relief and function after hip replacement. One cohort study found that younger people were at greater risk of revision.

UNKNOWN EFFECTIVENESS

Analgesic versus non-steroidal anti-inflammatory drugs

RCTs found no good evidence that simple analgesics, such as paracetamol (acetaminophen), are significantly different to NSAIDs in terms of relieving pain.

Chondroitin *New*

One systematic review found no clear evidence that chondroitin versus placebo improved symptoms.

Education, dietary advice, empowerment, and support

We found insufficient evidence to assess the effects of education and behavioural change in people with hip or knee osteoarthritis.

Glucosamine *New*

Systematic reviews and subsequent RCTs found limited evidence that glucosamine versus placebo improved symptoms.

Glucosamine plus chondroitin *New*

We found no RCTs on glucosamine plus chondroitin alone. We found limited evidence in people with mild or moderate osteoarthritis that glucosamine plus chondroitin plus manganese ascorbate versus placebo significantly improved disease severity scores.

Knee replacement in obese people

We found limited and conflicting evidence from observational studies on the effects of obesity on outcomes after knee replacement.

Other intra-articular injections of the knee

We found limited evidence on other intra-articular treatments such as radioactive isotopes, glycosaminoglycan poly sulfuric acid, orgotein and morphine.

LIKELY TO BE INEFFECTIVE OR HARMFUL

Systemic analgesics in people with existing liver damage

Observational evidence suggests that lower doses of paracetemol (acetaminophen) may cause liver damage in people with liver disease.

▶

◀ **Systemic non-steroidal anti-inflammatory drugs in older people and people at risk of renal disease or peptic ulceration**

One RCT found that NSAIDs increased the risk of renal or gastrointestinal damage in older people with osteoarthritis, particularly those with intercurrent disease. Case control studies suggest that the odds ratio of gastrointestinal haemorrhage when taking any NSAID is about 4–5.

DEFINITION   Osteoarthritis is a heterogeneous condition for which the prevalence, risk factors, clinical manifestations, and prognosis vary according to the joints affected. It most commonly affects hands, knees, hips, and spinal apophyseal joints. It is usually defined by pathological or radiological criteria rather than clinical features, and is characterised by focal areas of damage to the cartilage surfaces of synovial joints, associated with remodelling of the underlying bone and mild synovitis. When severe, there is characteristic joint space narrowing and osteophyte formation, with visible subchondral bone changes on radiography.

INCIDENCE/   Osteoarthritis is common and an important cause of pain and disability in
PREVALENCE   older adults.[1,2] Radiographic features are practically universal in at least some joints in people aged over 60 years, but significant clinical disease probably affects 10–20% of people. Knee disease is about twice as prevalent as hip disease in people aged over 60 years (about 10% v 5%).[3,4]

AETIOLOGY/   The main initiating factors are abnormalities in joint shape or injury. Genetic
RISK FACTORS factors are probably implicated.

PROGNOSIS   The natural history of osteoarthritis is poorly understood. Only a minority of people with clinical disease of the hip or knee joint progress to requiring surgery.

Plantar heel pain (including plantar fasciitis)

Search date September 2001

Fay Crawford

What are the effects of treatments?

TRADE OFF BETWEEN BENEFITS AND HARMS

Corticosteroid plus local anaesthetic injection versus local anaesthetic injections alone (short term)

One RCT found limited evidence that prednisolone plus lidocaine injection versus lidocaine injection alone significantly improved pain at 1 month. Observational studies have found a high rate of plantar fascia rupture and other complications associated with corticosteroid injections, which may lead to chronic disability in some people.

UNKNOWN EFFECTIVENESS

Casted orthoses (custom made insoles⊕)

We found no RCTs about the effects of casted orthoses versus placebo or no treatment. One systematic review and subsequent RCTs found limited and conflicting evidence about the effects of orthoses versus heel pads or other physical supports.

Corticosteroid injections alone or plus local anaesthetic injection versus placebo (short term)

One small RCT found no significant difference in pain relief with corticosteroid injections versus placebo. One systematic review identified no RCTs comparing corticosteroids plus local anaesthetic injection versus placebo.

Extracorporeal shock wave therapy

One systematic review and one subsequent large RCT found limited evidence that extracorporeal shock wave therapy⊕ versus placebo may improve pain for up to 12 weeks.

Heel pads

We found no RCTs about the effects of heel pads⊕ versus placebo or no treatment. One systematic review and subsequent RCTs found limited and conflicting evidence about the effects of heel pads versus corticosteroids, corticosteroids plus local anaesthesia, or other physical supports.

Lasers

One small RCT identified by a systematic review found no significant difference in pain with laser treatment versus placebo.

Local anaesthetic injection

One RCT found that local anaesthesia alone reduced pain at 1 month significantly less than local anasthesia plus corticosteroids, but found no significant difference in pain at 3 months.

Night splints

One poor quality RCT found no significant difference in pain at 3 months with splinting versus no splinting.

Surgery

One systematic review identified no RCTs of surgery.

▶

◄ **Ultrasound**

One small RCT found no significant difference in pain with ultrasound and sham ultrasound.

LIKELY TO BE INEFFECTIVE OR HARMFUL

Corticosteroid injections alone or plus local anaesthetic injection versus placebo (medium to long term)

We found no evidence from systematic reviews or RCTs of medium to long term benefit for corticosteroid injections with or without local anaesthetics versus placebo or other treatments. Observational studies have reported plantar fascia rupture (in 10–33% of people) and other complications associated with corticosteroid injections, which may lead to chronic disability in some people.

Corticosteroid plus local anaesthetic injection versus local anaesthetic alone (medium to long term)

One RCT found no significant difference in pain at 3 months with prednisolone injections plus lidocaine versus lidocaine injections alone. Observational studies have reported plantar fascia rupture (in 10–33% of people) and other complications associated with corticosteroid injections, which may lead to chronic disability in some people.

Corticosteroid plus local anaesthetic injection versus pads (medium to long term)

One RCT found no significant difference in pain at 6 months with corticosteroid plus lidocaine injections versus pads. A second RCT found no significant difference at 3 months.

DEFINITION   Plantar heel pain is soreness or tenderness of the heel. It often radiates from the central part of the heel pad or the medial tubercle of the calcaneum, but may extend along the plantar fascia into the medial longitudinal arch of the foot. Severity may range from an irritation at the origin of the plantar fascia, noticeable on rising after rest, to an incapacitating pain. This review excludes clinically evident underlying disorders, for example, infection, calcaneal fracture, and calcaneal nerve entrapment, which can be distinguished by their characteristic history and signs. (A calcaneal fracture may present after trauma, whereas calcaneal nerve entrapment gives rise to shooting pains and feelings of "pins and needles" on the medial aspect of the heel.)

INCIDENCE/   The incidence and prevalence of plantar heel pain is uncertain. Plantar heel
PREVALENCE   pain primarily affects those in mid to late life.[1]

AETIOLOGY/   Unknown.
RISK FACTORS

PROGNOSIS   One systematic review (search date 1998) found that almost all the included trials reported an improvement in discomfort regardless of the intervention received (including placebo), suggesting that the condition is at least partially self limiting.[1] A telephone survey of 100 people treated conservatively (average follow up 47 months) found that 82 people had resolution of symptoms, 15 had continued symptoms but no limitations of activity or work, and three had continued symptoms that limited activity or changed work status.[2] Thirty one people said that they would have seriously considered surgical treatment at the time medical attention was sought. The three people still with limitation had bilateral symptoms but no other clear risk factors.

Rheumatoid arthritis

Search date November 2001

Paul Emery, Wednesday Foster and Maria Suarez-Almazor

What are the effects of treatments?

BENEFICIAL

Antimalarials

One systematic review has found that hydroxychloroquine versus placebo for 6–12 months significantly reduces disease activity and joint inflammation. Two RCTs found no evidence of improved functional status or reduced radiological progression. One systematic review found no consistent differences between antimalarials and other disease modifying antirheumatic drugs. Another systematic review of observational studies and RCTs has found that over 2 years people are less likely to continue treatment with antimalarials than with methotrexate but more likely than with parenteral gold or sulfasalazine. One RCT found significantly fewer people were still taking hydoxychloroquine versus pencillamine at 5 years, but found similar numbers versus parenteral gold and auranofin.

Early intervention with disease modifying antirheumatic drugs (DMARDs)

RCTs found limited evidence that early treatment with DMARDs versus delayed treatment or placebo may reduce pain, joint inflammation, disease activity, and disability. We found insufficient evidence about the effects of early DMARD treatment on radiological progression.

Methotrexate

One systematic review has found that methotrexate versus placebo for 12–18 weeks significantly reduces joint inflammation and radiological progression, and improves functional status. One systematic review has found no consistent differences between methotrexate and other DMARDs, but another systematic review of observational studies and RCTs has found that people are more likely to continue treatment with methotrexate than with other DMARDs.

Minocycline

RCTs have found that minocycline versus placebo improves control of disease activity. We found no RCTs comparing minocycline versus other DMARDs.

Short term low dose oral corticosteroids

One systematic review has found that low dose oral corticosteroids versus placebo for several weeks significantly reduces disease activity and joint inflammation.

Sulfasalazine

Systematic reviews have found that sulfasalazine versus placebo for 6 months significantly reduces disease activity and joint inflammation. We found inadequate evidence on radiological progression and functional status. One systematic review found no consistent differences between sulfasalazine and other DMARDs, but another systematic review of observational studies and RCTs found that over 5 years people were less likely to continue sulfasalazine than methotrexate.

LIKELY TO BE BENEFICIAL

Auranofin (less effective than other DMARDs)

One systematic review has found that auranofin (oral gold) versus placebo reduces disease activity and joint inflammation, but found no evidence on radiological progression or long term functional status. Limited evidence from RCTs suggests that auranofin is less effective than DMARDs.

▶

◀ **Leflunomide (long term safety unclear)**
One systematic review has found that leflunomide versus placebo reduces disease activity and joint inflammation, improves functional status and health related quality of life, and decreases radiological progression. We found no good evidence on long term adverse effects.

Prolonged treatment with DMARDs
One RCT found a significant increase in flare among people in remission who discontinued DMARDs.

Treatment with several DMARDs combined
One systematic review and subsequent RCTs have found that combining certain DMARDs is more effective than using individual drugs alone. However, the balance between benefit and harm varies between combinations.

Tumour necrosis factor antagonists (long term safety unclear)
RCTs have found that tumour necrosis factor antibodies (etanercept and infliximab) versus placebo significantly improve symptoms, and reduce long term disease activity and joint inflammation. Short term toxicity is relatively low, but long term safety is less clear. Case reports of reactivation of demyelinating disease and tuberculosis have been published.

TRADE OFF BETWEEN BENEFITS AND HARMS

Azathioprine
One systematic review has found that azathioprine versus placebo reduces disease activity in the short term. We found no evidence on radiological progression or long term functional status. A high level of toxicity limits its usefulness.

Ciclosporin
One systematic review has found that ciclosporin (cyclosporin) versus methotrexate for a minimum of 4 months significantly reduces disease activity and joint inflammation, improves functional status, and may decrease the rate of radiological progression. A very high frequency of toxicity limits its usefulness.

Cyclophosphamide
One systematic review has found that cyclophosphamide versus placebo significantly reduces disease activity and joint inflammation at 6 months. It may also reduce the rate of radiological progression, but the evidence we found was limited. We found no evidence of its effect on long term functional status. Severe toxicity limits its usefulness.

Longer term low dose oral corticosteroids
One systematic review has found that low dose oral corticosteroids versus placebo for at least 3 months significantly reduces pain, joint inflammation, and functional status. One RCT found that prednisolone versus placebo for 2 years may reduce radiological progression. However, long term use is associated with considerable adverse effects.

Parenteral gold
One systematic review has found that parenteral gold versus placebo significantly reduces disease activity and joint inflammation, and slows radiological progression over 6 months. We found no evidence on long term functional status. One systematic review and a subsequent RCT found increased withdrawals because of toxicity.

▶

Rheumatoid arthritis

◀ **Penicillamine**

One systematic review has found that penicillamine versus placebo reduces disease activity and joint inflammation. We found no evidence of its effect on radiological progression or long term functional status. Common and potentially serious adverse effects limit its usefulness.

DEFINITION   Rheumatoid arthritis is a chronic inflammatory disorder. It is characterised by a chronic polyarthritis that primarily affects the peripheral joints and related periarticular tissues. It usually starts as an insidious symmetric polyarthritis, often with non-specific systemic symptoms. Diagnostic criteria include arthritis lasting longer than 6 weeks (although evidence suggests that 12 wks is more specific), positive rheumatoid factor, and radiological damage.[1]

INCIDENCE/   Prevalence ranges from 0.5–1.5% of the population in industrialised
PREVALENCE   countries.[2,3] Rheumatoid arthritis occurs more frequently in women than men (ratio 2.5 : 1).[2,3] The annual incidence in women was recently estimated at 36/100 000 and in men at 14/100 000.[3]

AETIOLOGY/   The evidence suggests that the cause is multifactorial in people with genetic
RISK FACTORS susceptibility.[4]

PROGNOSIS   The course of rheumatoid arthritis is variable and unpredictable. Some people experience flares and remissions, and others a progressive course. Over the years structural damage occurs, leading to articular deformities and functional impairment. About half of people will be unable to work within 10 years.[5] Rheumatoid arthritis shortens life expectancy.[6]

Musculoskeletal disorders

What are the effects of treatments?

LIKELY TO BE BENEFICIAL

Extracorporeal shock wave therapy (calcifying tendinitis)

One RCT found limited evidence that extracorporeal shock wave therapy versus placebo significantly improved pain in calcifying tendinitis after two sessions 1 week apart (NNT 2).

Hydrodistension and intra-articular corticosteroid injection (frozen shoulder)

One small RCT in people with frozen shoulder found limited evidence that distending the glenohumeral joint in addition to intra-articular steroid injection versus steroid injection alone significantly reduced severity of symptoms (NNT 2) and increased range of movement at 12 weeks.

UNKNOWN EFFECTIVENESS

Arthroscopic laser subacromial decompression *New*

One systematic review found no RCTs on arthroscopic laser treatment.

Electrical stimulation

One RCT found no evidence of a significant effect on pain with electrical stimulation versus dummy electrical stimulation. In people with shoulder pain after stroke, one systematic review found no clear evidence of reduced pain with electrical stimulation versus no stimulation, but found limited evidence that electrical stimulation may increase the range of passive external rotation of the shoulder.

Ice; simple analgesics (paracetamol and opiates); topical non-steroidal anti-inflammatory drugs

We found no RCTs about these interventions.

Intra-articular corticosteroid injection

Systematic reviews found no clear evidence of benefit from intra-articular corticosteroid injection versus control treatment.

Intra-articular guanethidine

One small RCT found that intra-articular guanethidine versus placebo significantly reduced pain 8 weeks after treatment, but found no evidence of an altered range of abduction.

Intra-articular non-steroidal anti-inflammatory drugs

One RCT found insufficient evidence about intra-articular injection of non-steroidal anti-inflammatory drugs versus placebo.

Laser treatment

We found conflicting evidence from four small RCTs about laser treatment versus placebo for shoulder pain.

Multidisciplinary biopsychosocial rehabilitation

One systematic review of poor quality RCTs found no significant difference in outcomes with multidisciplinary biopsychosocial rehabilitation❿ versus usual care.

▶

Shoulder pain

Oral non-steroidal anti-inflammatory drugs

RCTs found weak evidence that oral non-steroidal anti-inflammatory drugs versus placebo may reduce pain after 2–4 weeks.

Phonophoresis

One small RCT found no evidence of a benefit after 5–10 days from phonophoresis◉ using topical dexamethasone, lignocaine, and aqueous gel versus placebo phonophoresis using only aqueous gel.

Physiotherapy (exercises and manual therapies)

Systematic reviews of one small RCT found no significant difference in pain with manual therapy plus exercises versus no treatment.

Subacromial corticosteroid injection

One systematic review found that subacromial bursa corticosteroid injection versus injection without corticosteroid significantly improved abduction but did not reduce pain at 4 weeks. One additional RCT found no significant pain reduction or improved abduction after 12 weeks with subacromial corticosteroid injection plus local anaesthestic versus local anaesthetic alone.

Surgery

We found no RCTs on most surgical interventions. One small RCT in people with frozen shoulder found that forced manipulation versus intra-articular injection of corticosteroid significantly increased the number of people who completely recovered at 3 months.

Transdermal glyceryl trinitrate

One small RCT in people with supraspinatus tendinitis found insufficient evidence about pain relief with transdermal glyceryl trinitrate versus placebo.

UNLIKELY TO BE BENEFICIAL

Oral corticosteroids

Two small RCTs found no evidence of reduced pain or improved abduction with oral corticosteroids versus placebo or versus no treatment at 4–8 months. Adverse effect of corticosteroids are well documented (see rheumatoid arthritis, p 212 and asthma, p 253).

Ultrasound

One systematic review and two subsequent RCTs have found no significant difference in pain or abduction with ultrasound versus no treatment.

DEFINITION Shoulder pain arises in or around the shoulder from the glenohumeral, acromioclavicular, sternoclavicular, "subacromial", and scapulothoracic articulations, and surrounding soft tissues. Regardless of the disorder, pain is the reason for most consultations. In adhesive capsulitis (frozen shoulder), pain is associated with pronounced restriction of movement. For most shoulder disorders, diagnosis is based on clinical features, with imaging studies playing a role in some people.

INCIDENCE/ PREVALENCE Each year in primary care in the UK, about 1% of adults aged over 45 years present with a new episode of shoulder pain.[1] Prevalence is uncertain, with estimates from 4–20%.[2–6] One community survey (392 people) found a 1 month prevalence of shoulder pain of 34%.[7] A second community survey (644 people aged over 70 years) reported a point prevalence of 21%, with a higher frequency in women than men (25% v 17%).[8] Seventy per cent of cases involved the rotator cuff. One survey of 134 people in a community based rheumatology clinic found that 65% of cases were rotator cuff lesions; 11% were caused by localised tenderness in the pericapsular ▶

musculature; 10% acromioclavicular joint pain; 3% glenohumeral joint arthritis; and 5% were referred pain from the neck.[9] One survey found that in adults the annual incidence of frozen shoulder was about 2%, with those aged 40–70 years most commonly affected.[10] The age distribution of specific shoulder disorders in the community is unknown.

AETIOLOGY/ RISK FACTORS Rotator cuff disorders are associated with excessive overloading, instability of the glenohumeral and acromioclavicular joints, muscle imbalance, adverse anatomical features (narrow coracoacromial arch and a hooked acromion), cuff degeneration with aging, ischaemia, and musculoskeletal diseases that result in wasting of the cuff muscles.[11–14] Risk factors for frozen shoulder include female sex, older age, shoulder trauma, surgery, diabetes, cardiorespiratory disorders, cerebrovascular events, thyroid disease, and hemiplegia.[10,15,16] Arthritis of the glenohumeral joint can occur in numerous forms, including primary and secondary osteoarthritis, rheumatoid arthritis, and crystal arthritides.[11]

PROGNOSIS One survey in an elderly community found that most people with shoulder pain were still affected 3 years after the initial survey.[17] One prospective cohort study of 122 people in primary care found that 25% of people with shoulder pain reported previous episodes and 49% reported full recovery at 18 months' follow up.[18]

Bell's palsy

Search date July 2001

Rodrigo Salinas

What are the effects of treatments?

UNKNOWN EFFECTIVENESS

Antiviral treatment

Systematic reviews found no clear evidence about the long term effects of aciclovir versus placebo. One RCT found limited evidence that aciclovir plus prednisone versus prednisone alone improved recovery after 1 year.

Corticosteroids

RCTs found no clear evidence that corticosteroids versus placebo improve the recovery of facial motor function.

Surgery

One systematic review identified no RCTs of facial nerve decompression.

DEFINITION	Bell's palsy is an acute, unilateral paresis or paralysis of the face in a pattern consistent with peripheral nerve dysfunction, without detectable causes.[1] Additional symptoms may include pain in or behind the ear, numbness in the affected side of the face, hyperacusis, and disturbed taste on the ipsilateral anterior part of the tongue.[2-5]
INCIDENCE/ PREVALENCE	The incidence is about 23/100 000 people a year, or about 1/60–70 people in a lifetime.[6] Bell's palsy affects men and women more or less equally, with a peak incidence between the ages of 10 and 40 years. It occurs with equal frequency on the right and left sides of the face.[7]
AETIOLOGY/ RISK FACTORS	The cause is unclear. Viral infection, vascular ischaemia, autoimmune inflammatory disorders, and heredity have been proposed as underlying causes.[2,8,9] A viral cause has gained popularity since the isolation of the herpes simplex virus 1 genome from facial nerve endoneurial fluid in people with Bell's palsy.[10]
PROGNOSIS	More than two thirds of people with Bell's palsy achieve full spontaneous recovery. The largest series of people with Bell's palsy who received no specific treatment (1011 people) found the first signs of improvement within 3 weeks of onset in 85% of people.[11] For the other 15%, some improvement occurred 3–6 months later. The same series found that 71% of people recovered normal function of the face, 13% had insignificant sequelae, and the remaining 16% had permanently diminished function, with contracture and synkinesis Ⓖ. These figures are roughly similar to those of other series of people receiving no specific treatment for Bell's palsy.[7,8,12]

Neurological disorders

What are the effects of treatments?

BENEFICIAL

Amitriptyline (only short term evidence)

Systematic reviews of small, brief RCTs have found that amitriptyline versus placebo improves duration and frequency of chronic tension-type headache (CTTH).

UNKNOWN EFFECTIVENESS

Acupuncture *New*; botulinum toxin; cognitive behavioural therapy; relaxation and electromyographic biofeedback therapy☺; serotonin reuptake inhibitors; tricyclic antidepressants other than amitriptyline

We found insufficient evidence about the effects of these interventions.

LIKELY TO BE INEFFECTIVE OR HARMFUL

Benzodiazepines

RCTs found insufficient evidence about any benefits of benzodiazepines to outweigh the harms associated with their regular use.

Regular acute relief medication

One systematic review of observational studies has suggested that regular analgesic medication may lead to a daily headache and reduce the effectiveness of prophylactic medication.

DEFINITION The 1988 International Headache Society criteria for CTTH are headaches on 15 or more days a month (180 days/year) for at least 6 months; pain that is bilateral, pressing, or tightening in quality, of mild or moderate intensity, that does not prohibit activities, and that is not aggravated by routine physical activity; presence of no more than one additional clinical feature (nausea, photophobia, or phonophobia); and no vomiting.[1] CTTH is distinguished from chronic daily headache, which is simply a descriptive term for any headache type occurring for 15 days or more a month that may be because of CTTH as well as migraine or analgesic associated headache.[2] In contrast to CTTH, episodic tension-type headache can last for 30 minutes to 7 days and occurs for fewer than 180 days a year. Terms based on assumed mechanisms (muscle contraction headache, tension headache) are not operationally defined, and old studies that used these terms may have included people with many different types of headache. The greatest obstacle to the study of tension-type headache is the lack of any single proven specific or reliable, clinical, or biological defining characteristic of the disorder.

INCIDENCE/ The prevalence of chronic daily headache from a survey of the general
PREVALENCE population in the USA was 4.1%. Half of sufferers met the criteria for CTTH.[3] In a survey of 2500 undergraduate students in the USA, the prevalence of CTTH was 2%.[4] The prevalence of CTTH was 2.5% in a Danish population based survey of 975 individuals.[5] ▶

Chronic tension-type headache

AETIOLOGY/ RISK FACTORS   Tension-type headache is more prevalent in women (65% of cases in one survey).[6] Symptoms begin before the age of 10 years in 15% of people with CTTH. Prevalence declines with age.[7] There is a family history of some form of headache in 40% of people with CTTH.[8]

PROGNOSIS   The prevalence of CTTH declines with age.[7]

Search date December 2001

Anthony Marson and Sridharan Ramaratnam

What are the effects of treatments?

BENEFICIAL

Antiepileptic monotherapy in generalised epilepsy

We found no placebo controlled trials of the main antiepileptic drugs (carbamazepine, phenobarbital [phenobarbitone], phenytoin, sodium valproate), but widespread consensus holds that these drugs are effective. Systematic reviews have found no good evidence on which to base a choice among these drugs in terms of seizure control.

Antiepileptic monotherapy in partial epilepsy

We found no placebo controlled trials of the main antiepileptic drugs (carbamazepine, phenobarbital [phenobarbitone], phenytoin, sodium valproate), but widespread consensus holds that these drugs are effective. Systematic reviews have found no good evidence on which to base a choice among these drugs in terms of seizure control. A systematic review has found that phenobarbital is more likely to be withdrawn, presumably because of side effects.

Addition of second line drugs for drug resistant partial epilepsy

Systematic reviews have found that the addition of second line drugs significantly reduces the seizure frequency in people with partial epilepsy who have not responded to usual treatment. Each additional drug increases the frequency of adverse effects, the need for withdrawal of additional treatment, or both. RCTs found no good evidence on which to base a choice among drugs.

TRADE OFF BETWEEN BENEFITS AND HARMS

Antiepileptic drugs after a single seizure

RCTs have found that immediate treatment of single seizures with antiepileptic drugs versus no treatment reduces the risk of further seizures within 2 years by about half, but found no evidence that treatment alters long term prognosis. Long term antiepileptic drug treatment is potentially harmful.

UNKNOWN EFFECTIVENESS

Antiepileptic drug withdrawal for people in remission

Long term antiepileptic drug treatment is potentially harmful. One systematic review of observational studies and one RCT have found that antiepileptic drug withdrawal for people in remission is associated with a higher risk of seizure recurrence than continued treatment. Clinical predictors of relapse after drug withdrawal include age, seizure type, number of antiepileptic drugs being taken, whether seizures have occurred since antiepileptic drugs were started, and the period of remission before drug withdrawal.

Biofeedback *New;* relaxation therapy☉ *New;* yoga *New*

Systematic reviews have found insufficient evidence on the effects of these interventions.

▶

Epilepsy

Cognitive behavioural therapy New

Two small RCTs found no significant difference with cognitive behavioural therapy⑤ versus control in seizure frequency or psychosocial function. Another small RCT found that cognitive behavioural treatment versus control treatment significantly improved a depression score in people with epilepsy plus depressed mood.

Educational interventions New

RCTs found improvement in knowledge and understanding of epilepsy, adjustment to epilepsy, and improved psychosocial functioning with educational interventions versus control. No information was available regarding reduction in seizure frequency.

Family counselling New

One small RCT with weak methods found that family counselling versus no treatment significantly improved perceived acceptance by the family, emotional adjustment, interpersonal adjustment, adjustment to seizures, and overall psychosocial function. The RCT gave no information on seizure reduction.

Relaxation plus behavioural modification therapy New

RCTs found insufficient evidence about the effects of combined relaxation and behavioural modification on seizures. One RCT found that relaxation plus behavioural therapy versus control significantly improved anxiety and adjustment.

DEFINITION Epilepsy is a group of disorders rather than a single disease. Seizures can be classified by type as partial (categorised as simple partial⑤, complex partial⑤, and secondary generalised tonic clonic seizures), or generalised (categorised as generalised tonic clonic, absence, myoclonic, tonic, and atonic seizures⑤).[1]

INCIDENCE/ PREVALENCE Epilepsy is common, with an estimated prevalence in the developed world of 5–10/1000, and an annual incidence of 50/100 000 people.[2] About 3% of people will be given a diagnosis of epilepsy at some time in their lives.[3]

AETIOLOGY/ RISK FACTORS Epilepsy can also be classified by cause.[1] Idiopathic generalised epilepsies (such as juvenile myoclonic epilepsy or childhood absence epilepsy) are largely genetic. Symptomatic epilepsies result from a known cerebral abnormality — for example, temporal lobe epilepsy may result from a congenital defect, mesial temporal sclerosis, or a tumour. Cryptogenic epilepsies are those that cannot be classified as idiopathic or symptomatic and in which no causative factor has been identified, but is suspected.

PROGNOSIS For most people with epilepsy the prognosis is good. About 70% go into remission, defined as being seizure free for 5 years on or off treatment. This leaves 20–30% who develop chronic epilepsy, often treated with multiple antiepileptic drugs.[4] About 60% of untreated people suffer no further seizures in the 2 years after their first seizure.[5]

What are the effects of drug treatments in people with essential tremor of the hand?

LIKELY TO BE BENEFICIAL

Propranolol (evidence only for short term)

Small RCTs have found that propranolol versus placebo significantly improves short term clinical scores, tremor amplitude, and self evaluation of severity for up to 6 weeks (NNT about 2).

TRADE OFF BETWEEN BENEFITS AND HARMS

Botulinum A toxin-haemagglutinin complex (evidence only for short term)

RCTs comparing botulinum A toxin-haemagglutinin complex versus placebo found short term improvement of clinical rating scales, but no consistent improvement of motor task performance or functional disability. Hand weakness, which is dose dependent and transient, is a frequent adverse effect.

Phenobarbital ([phenobarbitone] evidence only for short term)

One small RCT found limited evidence that phenobarbital versus placebo significantly improved clinical scores at 5 weeks. Phenobarbital (phenobarbitone) is associated with depression and cognitive and behavioural effects.

Primidone (evidence only for short term)

Small RCTs found limited evidence that primidone versus placebo significantly improved clinical scores and self evaluation of tremor at 2–5 weeks. Withdrawal due to adverse effects (including first dose acute toxic reaction, sedation, and depression) was frequent.

UNKNOWN EFFECTIVENESS

All treatment options (long term)

We found no RCTs that reported the long term effects of drug treatments for essential tremor.

β Blockers other than propranolol (atenolol, metoprolol, nadolol, pindolol, sotalol)

Small RCTs found weak evidence that sotalol or atenolol versus placebo significantly improved symptoms and self evaluated measures of tremor at 5 days to 4 weeks.

Calcium channel blockers (nicardipine, nimodipine)

Poor quality RCTs found conflicting evidence about the effects of dihydropyridine calcium channel blockers versus placebo.

Flunarizine

One small RCT found weak evidence that flunarizine versus placebo may improve symptoms after 1 month of treatment.

Gabapentin

Small crossover RCTs found conflicting evidence about the effects of gabapentin versus placebo. ▶

Neurological disorders

Methazolamide

One small RCT found no significant difference with methazolamide versus placebo in clinical score, functional tasks, or self evaluation.

UNLIKELY TO BE BENEFICIAL

Clonidine

One RCT found no significant difference with clonidine versus placebo in the number of people who improved.

Isoniazid

One RCT found no significant difference with isoniazid versus placebo in clinical score.

LIKELY TO BE INEFFECTIVE OR HARMFUL

Benzodiazepines

Two brief RCTs found weak evidence that benzodiazepines versus placebo have no significant benefit in people with essential tremor. Adverse effects with benzodiazepines, including sedation and cognitive and behavioural effects, have been well described for other conditions (see panic disorder, p 175).

DEFINITION   Tremor is a rhythmic, mechanical oscillation of at least one body region. The term essential tremor is used when there is either a persistent bilateral tremor of hands and forearms, or an isolated tremor of the head without abnormal posturing, and when there is no evidence that the tremor arises from another identifiable or separately named cause. The diagnosis is not made if there are abnormal neurological signs, known causes of enhanced physiological tremor, a history or signs of psychogenic tremor, sudden change in severity, primary orthostatic tremor, isolated voice tremor, isolated position specific or task specific tremors, and isolated tongue, chin, or leg tremor.[1]

INCIDENCE/   Essential tremor is one of the most common movement disorders through-
PREVALENCE   out the world, with a prevalence of 0.4–3.9% in the general population.[2]

AETIOLOGY/   Essential tremor is sometimes inherited with an autosomal dominant
RISK FACTORS   pattern. About 40% of people with essential tremor have no family history. Alcohol ingestion provides symptomatic benefit in 50–70% of people.[3]

PROGNOSIS   Essential tremor is a persistent and progressive condition. It usually begins during young adulthood and the severity of the tremor increases slowly. Only a small proportion of people with essential tremor seek medical advice, but the proportion in different surveys varies from 0.5–11%.[2] Most people with essential tremor are only mildly affected. However, most of the people who seek medical care are disabled to some extent, and most are socially handicapped by the tremor.[4] A quarter of people receiving medical care for the tremor change jobs or retire because of essential tremor induced disability.[3,5]

What are the effects of drug treatment?

BENEFICIAL

Eletriptan

One systematic review and one subsequent RCT have found that eletriptan versus placebo significantly increases headache relief⦿. One subsequent RCT found that eletriptan versus sumitriptan significantly increased headache relief.

Naratriptan

Three RCTs have found that naratriptan versus placebo significantly increases headache relief at 4 hours. One RCT comparing naratriptan versus sumatriptan found no significant difference in headache recurrence⦿.

Rizatriptan

One systematic review has found that rizatriptan versus placebo significantly improves headache relief.

Salicylates (L-acetylsalicylate [L-ASA] alone or in combination with metoclopramide; effervescent aspirin in combination with metoclopramide; aspirin in combination with paracetamol and caffeine)

Five RCTs have found that lysine acetylsalicylate (L-ASA) (alone or in combination with metoclopramide) versus placebo significantly increases the proportion of people with headache relief. Two RCTs found that effervescent aspirin (alone or plus metoclopramide) versus placebo significantly increased headache relief. One RCT found that aspirin plus paracetamol plus caffeine versus placebo significantly increased headache relief. One RCT found no significant difference between aspirin versus paracetamol plus codeine in headache relief.

Sumatriptan

RCTs have found that subcutaneous, oral, or intranasal sumatriptan versus placebo significantly increases headache relief.

Zolmitriptan

Large RCTs have found that oral zolmitriptan versus placebo significantly increases headache relief. One RCT found no significant difference between zolmitriptan versus sumatriptan in headache relief.

LIKELY TO BE BENEFICIAL

Diclofenac

Three RCTs found that diclofenac versus placebo significantly improved headache relief. One RCT found that intramuscular diclofenac versus intramuscular paracetamol significantly increased the number of people with partial relief of symptoms.

Ergotamine derivatives

One systematic review has found that ergotamine derivatives versus placebo significantly increase headache relief. One additional RCT found that ergotamine plus caffeine versus sumatriptan was significantly less effective for headache relief or reducing the need for rescue medication⦿. Another additional RCT found no difference between ergotamine alone versus ergotamine plus metoclopramide in headache intensity⦿. One overview of harms suggests that ergotamine versus placebo increases nausea and vomiting. ▶

Migraine headache

◄ **Ibuprofen**

Four RCTs found that ibuprofen versus placebo significantly improved headache relief.

Naproxen

One crossover RCT found limited evidence that naproxen versus placebo significantly reduced headache intensity. Three RCTs comparing naproxen versus ergotamine found that naproxen significantly reduced migraine intensity.

Tolfenamic acid

One RCT found limited evidence that tolfenamic acid versus placebo significantly increased the number of people with pain relief, and found no significant difference between tolfenamic acid versus sumatriptan. One RCT found no significant difference between tolfenamic acid versus paracetamol in migraine symptoms. One crossover RCT found that tolfenamic acid (alone or in combination with either metoclopramide or caffeine) versus placebo significantly reduced headache intensity.

DEFINITION Migraine is a primary headache disorder manifesting as recurring attacks, usually lasting for 4–72 hours, and involving pain of moderate to severe intensity, often with nausea, and sometimes vomiting, and/or sensitivity to light, sound, and other sensory stimuli. The 1988 International Headache Society◉ criteria include separate criteria for migraine with and without aura.[1]

INCIDENCE/ Migraine is common worldwide. Prevalence has been reported to be
PREVALENCE between 5% and 25% in women and 2% and 10% in men. Overall, the highest incidence for migraine without aura has been reported between the ages of 10 and 11 years at 10/1000 person years. The peak incidence of migraine without aura in males is between ages 10 and 11 years (10/1000 person years) and in females between ages 14 and 17 years (19/1000 person years). The incidence of migraine with aura peaks in males around age 5 years (7/1000 person years) and in females around age 12–13 years (14/1000 person years).[2]

AETIOLOGY/ Data arising from independent representative samples from Canada,[3,4] the
RISK FACTORS USA,[5,6] several countries in Latin America,[7] several countries in Europe,[8–11] Hong Kong,[12] and Japan[13] demonstrate a female to male predominance and a peak in middle aged women. Migraine risk has been reported to be 50% more likely in people with a family history of migraine.[14]

PROGNOSIS Acute migraine is self limited and only rarely results in permanent neurological complications. Chronic recurrent migraine may cause disability through pain, and may affect daily functioning and quality of life. Female prevalence of migraine with or without aura has a declining trend after age 45–50 years.

Search date November 2001
Mike Boggild and Helen Ford

Neurological disorders

What are the effects of treatments?

LIKELY TO BE BENEFICIAL

Interferon beta-1a/b

RCTs in people with a first clinical episode of demyelination have found that interferon beta-1a versus placebo significantly delays a second clinical event. One systematic review in people with active relapsing and remitting multiple sclerosis has found that interferon beta-1a/b versus placebo significantly reduces relapse rates over 2 years, and may delay development of neurological disability. We found conflicting evidence from two RCTs about effects of interferon beta on disease progression in people with secondary progressive multiple sclerosis.

Intravenous or oral methylprednisolone or corticotrophin (for acute relapses)

One systematic review in people with multiple sclerosis requiring treatment for acute exacerbations has found that corticosteroids (methylprednisolone or corticotrophin) versus placebo significantly reduce the risk of deterioration during the first 5 weeks. The optimal dose, route, and duration of treatment are unclear.

UNKNOWN EFFECTIVENESS

Azathioprine

One systematic review in people with relapsing and remitting or progressive multiple sclerosis has found that azathioprine versus placebo has a modest but significant effect on relapse rates over 2 years, but found no significant effect on disability.

Botulinum toxin (for focal hip adductor spasticity) *New*

One brief RCT found limited evidence that botulinum toxin versus placebo improved adductor spasticity.

Glatiramer acetate

One RCT in people with relapsing and remitting multiple sclerosis found that glatiramer acetate versus placebo significantly reduced relapse rates over 2 years, but found no evidence of an effect on disability. We found no good RCTs in people with secondary progressive multiple sclerosis.

Intravenous immunoglobulin

One RCT in people with relapsing and remitting multiple sclerosis found limited evidence from baseline comparisons that intravenous immunoglobulin versus placebo may reduce disability over 2 years. We found no good RCTs in people with secondary progressive multiple sclerosis.

Methotrexate

One small RCT in people with secondary progressive multiple sclerosis found weak evidence suggesting that low dose, weekly methotrexate versus placebo may significantly delay disease progression. ▶

Mitoxantrone

Limited evidence from small RCTs found that pulsed intravenous mitoxantrone (mitozantrone) improved outcome in people with very active multiple sclerosis, in whom the risk of severe neurological disability may outweigh the risks of cytotoxic treatment.

Multidisciplinary care (rehabilitation)

Two RCTs found limited evidence that 3–4 weeks of inpatient rehabilitation versus remaining on the waiting list or exercises at home improved disability in the short term, despite no reduction in neurological impairment. The duration of this effect is uncertain. One small RCT found that prolonged outpatient rehabilitation versus remaining on the waiting list reduced multiple sclerosis symptom frequency and fatigue.

Plasma exchange

We found insufficient evidence about the effects of plasma exchange on neurological disability in people with acute demyelinating episodes who had previously failed to respond to intravenous steroids.

Treatments for fatigue (amantadine, behaviour modification, exercise)

One systematic review has found that amantadine versus placebo modestly reduces fatigue in multiple sclerosis. We found insufficient evidence on the effects of behavioural modification treatment or exercise.

Treatments for spasticity (oral drug treatments, physiotherapy, intrathecal baclofen)

RCTs found limited evidence that tizanidine versus placebo reduced spasticity, but did not improve mobility. We found insufficient evidence on the effects of other oral drug treatments. One small RCT found that physiotherapy for 8 weeks briefly improved mobility and subjective wellbeing. One small RCT in non-ambulant people with symptomatic spasticity resistant to oral baclofen found that intrathecal baclofen versus intrathecal saline significantly reduced spasticity and spasm frequency.

UNLIKELY TO BE BENEFICIAL

Pemoline

One systematic review found no significant difference in self reporting of fatigue with pemoline versus placebo.

DEFINITION Multiple sclerosis is a chronic inflammatory disease of the central nervous system. Diagnosis requires evidence of lesions that are separated in both time and space, and the exclusion of other inflammatory, structural, or hereditary conditions that might give a similar clinical picture. The disease takes three main forms: relapsing and remitting multiple sclerosis, characterised by episodes of neurological dysfunction interspersed with periods of stability; primary progressive multiple sclerosis, where progressive neurological disability occurs from the outset; and secondary progressive multiple sclerosis, where progressive neurological disability occurs later in the course of the disease.

INCIDENCE/ PREVALENCE Prevalence varies with geography and racial group; it is highest in white populations in temperate regions.[1] In Europe and North America, prevalence is 1/800 people, with an annual incidence of 2–10/100 000, making multiple sclerosis the most common cause of neurological disability in young adults. Age of onset is broad, peaking between 20 and 40 years.[2] ▶

AETIOLOGY/ The cause remains unclear, although current evidence suggests that multiple
RISK FACTORS sclerosis is an autoimmune disorder of the central nervous system resulting
from an environmental stimulus in genetically susceptible individuals. Multiple sclerosis is currently regarded as a single disorder with clinical variants,
but there is some evidence that it may comprise several related disorders
with distinct immunological, pathological, and genetic features.[1,3]

PROGNOSIS In 90% of people, early disease is relapsing and remitting. Although some
people follow a relatively benign course over many years, most develop
secondary progressive disease, usually 6–10 years after onset. In 10% of
people, initial disease is primary progressive. Apart from a minority of people
with "aggressive" multiple sclerosis, life expectancy is not greatly affected
and the disease course is often of more than 30 years' duration.

Parkinson's disease

Search date August 2001

Carl Clarke and A Peter Moore

What are the effects of treatments?

LIKELY TO BE BENEFICIAL

Dopamine agonists versus levodopa* in younger people with early disease

One systematic review and one subsequent RCT have found that dopamine agonist monotherapy versus levodopa monotherapy reduces the incidence of dyskinesias☺ and fluctuations in motor response☺.

TRADE OFF BETWEEN BENEFITS AND HARMS

Dopamine agonists plus levodopa* in people with a fluctuating response to levodopa*

Systematic reviews in people with later stage disease taking levodopa have found that adjuvant dopamine agonists reduce "off" time☺, improve motor impairments and activities of daily living, and reduce levodopa dose, but increase dopaminergic adverse effects☺ and dyskinesia.

Levodopa* in early disease

Levodopa plus dopa decarboxylase in either immediate or modified release preparation improves motor function (evidence not presented in *Clinical Evidence*) but increases nausea, and is also associated with other adverse effects.

UNKNOWN EFFECTIVENESS

Occupational therapy *New*; physiotherapy *New*; speech and language therapy for speech disturbance *New*; swallowing therapy for dysphagia *New*

Systematic reviews of poor quality RCTs found insufficient evidence of the effects of these interventions in later Parkinson's disease.

Pallidotomy

One systematic review found limited evidence that unilateral posteroventral pallidotomy☺ versus medical treatment reduced contralateral tremor and rigidity during "off" time, and dyskinesia during "on" time☺, but with significant risk of morbidity and mortality. Bilateral pallidotomy is associated with a variety of axial effects☺, including mutism. One RCT found insufficient evidence to assess the effects of pallidotomy versus deep brain stimulation☺.

Selegiline

RCTs have found that selegiline versus placebo significantly improves the symptoms of Parkinson's disease, but one of the RCTs found increased mortality in people treated with selegiline. One large RCT in people with early Parkinson's disease found that selegiline versus placebo delayed the need for levodopa for 9 months.

▶

◀ **UNLIKELY TO BE BENEFICIAL**

Modified release levodopa* (versus immediate release levodopa*)

RCTs in people with early Parkinson's disease found no significant difference with modified versus immediate release levodopa in motor complications or disease control after 5 years.

*We have used the term "levodopa" to refer to a combination of levadopa and a peripheral decarboxylase inhibitor.

DEFINITION Idiopathic Parkinson's disease is an age related neurodegenerative disorder and the most common cause of the parkinsonian syndrome: a combination of asymmetric bradykinesia, hypokinesia, and rigidity, sometimes combined with rest tremor and postural changes. Clinical diagnostic criteria have a sensitivity of 80% and specificity of 30% compared with the gold standard of diagnosis at autopsy.[1] The primary pathology is progressive loss of cells producing the neurotransmitter dopamine from the substantia nigra in the brainstem. Treatment aims to replace or compensate for the lost dopamine. A good response to treatment supports, but does not confirm, the diagnosis. Several other catecholaminergic neurotransmitter systems are also affected in Parkinson's disease.

INCIDENCE/ PREVALENCE Parkinson's disease occurs worldwide with equal incidence in both sexes. In 5–10% of people who develop Parkinson's disease it appears before the age of 40 years (young onset), with a mean age of onset of about 65 years. Overall age adjusted prevalence is 1% worldwide and 1.6% in Europe, rising from 0.6% at age 60–64 years to 3.5% at age 85–89 years.[2,3]

AETIOLOGY/ RISK FACTORS The cause is unknown. Parkinson's disease may represent different conditions with a final common pathway. People may be affected differently by a combination of genetic and environmental factors (viruses, toxins, 1-methyl-4-phenyl-1,2,3,6-tetrahydropyridine, well water, vitamin E, and smoking).[7–10] First degree relatives of affected people may have twice the risk of developing Parkinson's disease (17% chance of developing the condition in their lifetime) compared with people in the general population.[4–6] However, purely genetic varieties probably comprise a small minority of people with Parkinson's disease.[11,12] The parkin gene on chromosome 6 may be associated with Parkinson's disease in families with at least one member with young onset Parkinson's disease, and multiple genetic factors, including the tau gene on chromosome 17q21, may be involved in idiopathic late onset disease.[13,14]

PROGNOSIS Parkinson's disease is currently incurable. Disability is progressive and associated with increased mortality (RR of death compared with matched control populations ranges from 1.6 to 3).[15] Treatment can reduce symptoms and slow progression but rarely achieves complete control. The question of whether treatment reduces mortality remains controversial.[16] Levodopa seemed to reduce mortality in the UK for 5 years after its introduction, before a "catch up" effect was noted and overall mortality rose towards previous levels. This suggested a limited prolongation of life.[17] An Australian cohort study followed 130 people treated for 10 years.[18] The standardised mortality ratio was 1.58 (P < 0.001). At 10 years, 25% had been admitted to a nursing home and only four were still employed. The mean duration of disease until death was 9.1 years. In a similar Italian cohort study over 8 years, the relative risk of death for affected people versus healthy controls was 2.3 (95% CI 1.60 to 3.39).[19] Age at initial census date was the main predictor of outcome (for people aged < 75 years, the RR of death was 1.80, 95% CI 1.04 to 3.11; for people aged > 75 years: the RR of death was 5.61, 95% CI 2.13 to 14.8).

Trigeminal neuralgia

Search date November 2001

Joanna M Zakrzewska

Neurological disorders

What are the effects of treatments?

LIKELY TO BE BENEFICIAL

Carbamazepine

One systematic review of three crossover RCTs has found that carbamazepine versus placebo increases the number of people who have pain relief at 5–14 days (NNT 3), but increases drowsiness, dizziness, constipation, and ataxia (NNH 3). A second systematic review found similar results.

TRADE OFF BETWEEN BENEFITS AND HARMS

Pimozide

One RCT found that pimozide versus carbamazepine significantly reduced pain over 8 weeks (NNT 3), but increased adverse effects including hand tremors, memory impairment, and involuntary movements (NNH 3). The use of pimozide is limited by cardiac toxicity and reports of sudden death.

UNKNOWN EFFECTIVENESS

Baclofen

We found insufficient evidence from two small crossover trials on the effects of baclofen versus placebo or versus other active drugs.

Combined streptomycin and lidocaine nerve block *New*

Small poor quality RCTs found insufficient evidence about the effects of nerve block with streptomycin plus lidocaine versus nerve block with lidocaine alone.

Cryotherapy© of peripheral nerves *New;* **peripheral acupuncture** *New;* **peripheral alcohol injection** *New;* **peripheral injection of phenol** *New;* **peripheral neurectomy** *New;* **peripheral radiofrequency thermocoagulation** *New;* **peripheral laser treatment©** *New*

We found no RCTs about the effects of these interventions.

Lamotrigine

One small crossover trial found limited evidence that lamotrigine versus placebo (added to either carbamazepine or phenytoin) improved pain after 2 weeks (NNT 2).

Other drugs (phenytoin, clonazepam, sodium valproate, gabapentin, mexiletine, oxcarbazepine)

We found no RCTs about the effects of other antiepileptic drugs.

Tizanidine

One small RCT found insufficient evidence about the effects of tizanidine.

UNLIKELY TO BE BENEFICIAL

Proparacaine

One RCT found no significant difference in pain at 30 days with single application of proparacaine hydrochloride versus placebo eye drops to the eye on the same side as the pain.

◄ **LIKELY TO BE INEFFECTIVE OR HARMFUL**

Tocainide

One crossover RCT found weak evidence of benefit with tocainide versus carbamazepine. The use of tocainide is limited by considerable harms. A postscript to the RCT reported a death attributed to haematological effects of tocainide.

DEFINITION   Trigeminal neuralgia is a characteristic pain in the distribution of one or more branches of the fifth cranial nerve. The diagnosis is made on the history alone, based on characteristic features of the pain. It occurs in paroxysms that last a few seconds to 2 minutes. The frequency of paroxysms is highly variable: from hundreds of attacks a day to long periods of remission that can last years. The pain is severe and described as intense, sharp, superficial, stabbing, burning, or like an electric shock. In any individual, the pain has the same character in different attacks. It is often triggered by touch in a specific area or by eating, talking, washing the face, or cleaning the teeth. Between paroxysms the person is asymptomatic. Other causes of facial pain may need to be excluded.[1] In trigeminal neuralgia the neurological examination is usually normal.[2,3]

INCIDENCE/   Most evidence about the incidence and prevalence of trigeminal neuralgia
PREVALENCE   is from the USA.[4] The annual incidence (when age adjusted to 1980 age distribution of the USA) is 5.9/100 000 women and 3.4/100 000 men. The incidence tends to be slightly higher in women at all ages. The incidence increases with age. In men aged over 80 years the incidence is 45.2/100 000.[5] Other published surveys are small. One questionnaire survey of neurological disease in a single French village found one person with trigeminal neuralgia among 993 people.[6]

AETIOLOGY/   The cause of trigeminal neuralgia remains unclear.[7] It is more common in
RISK FACTORS people with multiple sclerosis (RR 20, 95% CI 4.1 to 59).[5] Hypertension is a risk factor in women (RR 2.1, 95% CI 1.2 to 3.4) but the evidence is less clear for men (RR 1.53, 95% CI 0.3 to 4.5).[5] A study in the USA found that people with trigeminal neuralgia smoked less, consumed less alcohol, had fewer tonsillectomies, and were less likely than matched controls to be Jewish or an immigrant.[8]

PROGNOSIS   One study found no reduction of 10 year survival with trigeminal neuralgia.[9] We found no evidence about the natural history of trigeminal neuralgia. The illness is characterised by recurrences and remissions. Many people have periods of remission with no pain for months or years.[3] Anecdotal reports suggest that in many people it becomes more severe and less responsive to treatment with time.[10] Most people with trigeminal neuralgia are initially managed medically, and a proportion eventually have a surgical procedure.[5] We found no good evidence about the proportion of people who require surgical treatment for pain control.

Aphthous ulcers: recurrent

Search date August 2001

Stephen Porter and Crispian Scully

What are the effects of treatments?

LIKELY TO BE BENEFICIAL

Chlorhexidine (but no effect on recurrence rates)

RCTs found that chlorhexidine gluconate mouth rinses versus control preparations may reduce the duration and severity of each episode of ulceration, but do not affect the incidence of recurrent ulceration.

UNKNOWN EFFECTIVENESS

Topical corticosteroids

Small RCTs found no consistent difference in the incidence of new ulcers with topical corticosteroids versus control preparations. They found weak evidence that topical corticosteroids may reduce the duration of ulcers and hasten pain relief.

UNLIKELY TO BE BENEFICIAL

Hexidine

RCTs found no significant difference in the incidence or duration of ulceration with hexidine mouthwash or a proprietary antiseptic mouthwash versus control mouthwashes.

DEFINITION   Recurrent aphthous ulcers are superficial and rounded, with painful mouth ulcers usually occurring in recurrent bouts at intervals of a few days to a few months.[1]

INCIDENCE/ PREVALENCE   The point prevalence of recurrent aphthous ulcers in Swedish adults has been reported as 2%.[1] Prevalence may be 5–10% in some groups of children. Up to 66% of young adults give a history consistent with recurrent aphthous ulceration.[1]

AETIOLOGY/ RISK FACTORS   The causes of aphthous ulcers remain unknown. Associations with haematinic deficiency, infections, gluten sensitive enteropathy, food sensitivities, and psychological stress have rarely been confirmed. Similar ulcers are seen in Behçet's syndrome.

PROGNOSIS   About 80% of people with recurrent aphthous ulcers develop a few ulcers smaller than 1 cm in diameter that heal within 5–14 days without scarring (the pattern known as minor aphthous ulceration). The episodes recur typically after an interval of 1–4 months. One in 10 sufferers has a more severe form (major aphthous ulceration) with lesions larger than 1 cm that may recur after a shorter interval and can cause scarring. Likewise, 1/10 people with such recurrent ulceration may have multiple minute ulcers (herpetiform ulceration).

Search date February 2002
John Buchanan and Joanna Zakrzewska

What are the effects of treatments?

LIKELY TO BE BENEFICIAL

Cognitive behavioural therapy
One small RCT found that cognitive behavioural therapy versus no cognitive behavioural therapy significantly reduced symptom intensity after 6 months.

UNKNOWN EFFECTIVENESS

Antidepressants; benzydamine hypochloride; dietary supplementation; hormone replacement therapy in postmenopausal women
We found insufficient evidence on the effects of these interventions.

DEFINITION　Burning mouth syndrome is a psychogenic or idiopathic burning discomfort or pain affecting people with clinically normal oral mucosa in whom a medical or dental cause has been excluded.[1–3] Terms previously used to describe what is now called burning mouth syndrome include glossodynia, glossopyrosis, stomatodynia, stomatopyrosis, sore tongue, and oral dysaesthesia.[4] A survey of 669 men and 758 women randomly selected from 48 500 people aged between 20 and 69 years found that people with burning mouth also have subjective dryness (66%), take some form of medication (64%), report other systemic illnesses (57%), and have altered taste (11%).[5] Many studies of people with symptoms of burning mouth do not distinguish those with burning mouth syndrome (i.e. idiopathic disease) from those with other conditions (such as vitamin B deficiency) making results unreliable.

INCIDENCE/ PREVALENCE　Burning mouth syndrome mainly affects women,[6–8] particularly after the menopause when its prevalence may be 18–33%.[9] One recent study in Sweden found a prevalence of 4% for the symptom of burning mouth without clinical abnormality of the oral mucosa (11/669 [2%] men, mean age 59 years; 42/758 [6%] women, mean age 57 years), with the highest prevalence (12%) in women aged 60–69 years.[5] Reported prevalence in general populations varies from 1%[10] to 15%.[6] Incidence and prevalence vary according to diagnostic criteria,[4] and many studies included people with the symptom of burning mouth rather than with burning mouth syndrome as defined above.

AETIOLOGY/ RISK FACTORS　The cause is unknown, and we found no good aetiological studies. Hormonal disturbances associated with the menopause[7–9] and psychogenic factors (including anxiety, depression, stress, life events, personality disorders, and phobia of cancer) are possible causal factors.[11–13] Local and systemic factors (such as infections, allergies, ill fitting dentures,[12] hypersensitivity reactions,[14] and hormone and vitamin deficiencies[15–17]) may cause the symptom of burning mouth and should be excluded before diagnosing burning mouth syndrome.

PROGNOSIS　We found no prospective cohort studies or other reliable evidence describing the natural history of burning mouth syndrome.[18] We found anecdotal reports of at least partial spontaneous remission in about half of people with burning mouth syndrome within 6–7 years.[12]

Impacted wisdom teeth

Search date October 2001

Stephen Worrall

What are the effects of prophylactic removal of impacted wisdom teeth?

LIKELY TO BE INEFFECTIVE OR HARMFUL

Extraction of asymptomatic impacted wisdom teeth

We found limited evidence that the harms of removing asymptomatic impacted wisdom teeth outweigh the benefits.

DEFINITION   Wisdom teeth are third molars that develop in almost all adults by about the age of 20 years. In some people, the teeth become partially or completely impacted below the gumline because of lack of space, obstruction, or abnormal position. Impacted wisdom teeth may be diagnosed because of pain and swelling or incidentally by routine dental radiography.

INCIDENCE/ PREVALENCE   Third molar impaction is common. Over 72% of Swedish people aged 20–30 years have at least one impacted lower third molar.[1] The surgical removal of impacted third molars (symptomatic and asymptomatic) is the most common procedure performed by oral and maxillofacial surgeons. It is performed on about 4/1000 people per year in England and Wales, making it one of the top 10 inpatient and day case procedures.[2–4] Up to 90% of people on oral and maxillofacial surgery hospital waiting lists are awaiting removal of wisdom teeth.[3]

AETIOLOGY/ RISK FACTORS   Impacted wisdom teeth are partly a by-product of improved oral hygiene and changes in diet. Less gum disease and dental caries, and less wear and tear on teeth because of a more refined diet, have increased the likelihood of retaining teeth into adult life, leaving less room for wisdom teeth.

PROGNOSIS   Impacted wisdom teeth can cause pain, swelling, and infection, as well as destroying adjacent teeth and bone. The removal of diseased and symptomatic wisdom teeth alleviates pain and suffering and improves oral health and function. We found no good evidence on what happens without treatment in people with asymptomatic impacted wisdom teeth.

What are the effects of preventive interventions?

BENEFICIAL

Antifungal prophylaxis in advanced HIV disease
RCTs have found that daily or weekly antifungal prophylaxis with fluconazole, itraconazole, or nystatin significantly reduces the incidence of oropharyngeal candidiasis.

Antifungal prophylaxis in people with cancer and neutropenia
Systematic reviews have found that systemic or topical antifungals versus placebo or no treatment significantly reduce the number of episodes of oral candiasis (NNT about 4).

LIKELY TO BE BENEFICIAL

Antifungal prophylaxis in immunocompromised infants and children
One RCT has found that fluconazole versus oral polyenes significantly reduces the incidence of oropharyngeal candidiasis.

UNKNOWN EFFECTIVENESS

Chlorhexidine oral rinse in neutropenic adults undergoing treatment for cancer
Two RCTs found conflicting evidence about chlorhexidine oral rinse versus placebo or nystatin.

Continuous prophylaxis versus intermittent treatment in people with HIV infection and acute episodes of oropharyngeal candidiasis (in terms of preventing antifungal resistance)
One RCT found no significant difference in the emergence of antifungal resistance with continuous antifungal prophylaxis versus intermittent treatment.

Preventive interventions in people with diabetes
We found no systematic review or RCTs.

What are the effects of treatments?

BENEFICIAL

Antifungal treatment in immunocompetent and immunocompromised infants and children
In immunocompetent infants, RCTs have found that miconazole gel versus nystatin suspension significantly increases the rate of clinical cure. In immunocompromised infants and children, one RCT has found that fluconazole versus oral polyenes (oral nystatin or oral amphotericin B) significantly increases clinical cure after 2 weeks (NNT 2).

Oral suspension of systemic azoles in people with HIV infection
RCTs have found that topical preparations (suspensions or pastilles) of itraconazole, fluconazole, or clotrimazole effectively treat oropharyngeal candidiasis in people with HIV infection. One RCT found that fluconazole versus topical nystatin significantly reduced symptoms and signs of oropharyngeal candidiasis after 14 days (NNT 3).

▶

Oropharyngeal candidiasis

◄ UNKNOWN EFFECTIVENESS

Antifungal treatment for denture stomatitis

RCTs found conflicting evidence about the effects of antifungal agents versus placebo in clinical improvement or cure of denture stomatitis. Trial methods included professional cleaning of the dentures at the start of the study, combined with advice on denture hygiene and advice not to wear the dentures while asleep at night, which may explain the high clinical cure rate in the placebo groups.

Denture hygiene *New*

Two RCTs found insufficient evidence about the effects of mouth rinses or disinfectants versus placebo in preventing or treating denture stomatitis.

Fluconazole versus amphotericin B in adults undergoing treatment for cancer

One small RCT found limited evidence that fluconazole versus amphotericin B lozenges significantly increased clinical cure.

Treatments in people with diabetes mellitus

We found no RCTs assessing treatments for oral candidiasis in people with diabetes mellitus.

DEFINITION Oropharyngeal candidiasis is an opportunistic mucosal infection, caused in over 85% of cases by *Candida albicans*. The four main types of oropharyngeal candidiasis are: (1) pseudomembranous (thrush), comprising white discrete plaques on an erythematous background, located on the buccal mucosa, throat, tongue, or gingivae; (2) erythematous, comprising smooth red patches on the hard or soft palate, dorsum of tongue, or buccal mucosa; (3) hyperplastic, comprising white, firmly adherent patches or plaques, usually bilateral on the buccal mucosa; (4) denture induced stomatitis, presenting as either a smooth or granular erythema confined to the denture-bearing area of the hard palate. Symptoms vary, ranging from none to a sore, painful mouth with a burning tongue and altered taste, which can impair speech, nutritional intake, and quality of life.

INCIDENCE/ PREVALENCE Candida species are commensals in the gastrointestinal tract. Transmission occurs directly between infected people or on fomites (objects that can harbour pathogenic organisims). Candida is found in the mouth of 31–60% of healthy people.[1] Denture stomatitis associated with candida is prevalent in 65% of denture wearers.[1] Oropharyngeal candidiasis affects 15–60% of people with haematological or oncological malignancies during periods of immunosuppression.[2] Oropharyngeal candidiasis occurs in 7–48% of people with HIV infection and in over 90% of those with advanced disease. In severely immunosuppressed people, relapse rates are high (30–50%) and usually occur within 14 days of treatment cessation.[3]

AETIOLOGY/ RISK FACTORS Risk factors associated with symptomatic oropharyngeal candidiasis include local or systemic immunosuppression, haematological disorders, broad spectrum antibiotic use, inhaled or systemic steroids, xerostomia, diabetes, and wearing dentures, obturators, or orthodontic appliances. The same strain may persist for months or years in the absence of infection. In people with HIV infection, there is no direct correlation between the number of organisms and the presence of clinical disease. Symptomatic oropharyngeal candidiasis associated with *in vitro* resistance to fluconazole occurs in 5% of ►

◄ people with advanced HIV disease.[4] Resistance to azole antifungals is associated with severe immunosuppression (≤ 50 CD4 cells/mm^3), more episodes treated with antifungal drugs, and longer median duration of systemic azole treatment.[5]

PROGNOSIS   Untreated candidiasis persists for months or years unless associated risk factors are treated or eliminated. In neonates, spontaneous cure of oropharyngeal candidiasis usually occurs after 3–8 weeks.

Paracetamol (acetaminophen) poisoning

Search date July 2001

Nick Buckley and Michael Eddleston

What are the effects of treatments?

BENEFICIAL

Acetylcysteine

One small RCT in people with established paracetamol induced liver failure found that acetylcysteine versus placebo significantly reduced mortality. One observational study found that people given early treatment with acetylcysteine were less likely to develop liver damage than untreated historical controls.

LIKELY TO BE BENEFICIAL

Methionine

One small RCT found that methionine versus supportive care significantly reduced the risk of hepatotoxicity.

UNKNOWN EFFECTIVENESS

Activated charcoal (single or multiple dose); gastric lavage; ipecacuanha

We found no evidence on the effects of these interventions on mortality, liver failure, or hepatoxicity.

DEFINITION Paracetamol poisoning occurs as a result of either accidental or intentional overdose with paracetamol (acetaminophen).

INCIDENCE/ PREVALENCE Paracetamol is the most common drug used for self poisoning in the UK.[1] It is also a common means of self poisoning in the rest of Europe, North America, and Australasia. An estimated 41 200 cases of poisoning with products containing paracetamol occurred in 1989–1990 in England and Wales, with a mortality of 0.40% (95% CI 0.38% to 0.46%). Overdoses owing to paracetamol alone result in an estimated 150–200 deaths and 15–20 liver transplants each year in England and Wales.

AETIOLOGY/ RISK FACTORS Most cases in the UK are impulsive acts of self harm in young people.[1,2] In one study of 80 people who had overdosed with paracetamol, 42 had obtained the tablets for the specific purpose of taking an overdose and 33 had obtained them less than 1 hour before the act.[2]

PROGNOSIS People with blood paracetamol concentrations above the standard treatment line (defined in the UK as a line joining 200 mg/L at 4 h and 30 mg/L at 15 h on a semilogarithmic plot) have a poor prognosis without treatment🔎.[4,5] In one study of 57 untreated people with blood concentrations above this line, 33 developed severe liver damage and three died.[4] People with a history of chronic alcohol misuse, use of enzyme inducing drugs, eating disorders, or multiple paracetamol overdoses may be at risk of liver damage with blood concentrations below this line.[6] In the USA, a lower line is used as an indication for treatment but we found no data relating this line to prognostic outcomes.[7] **Dose effect:** The dose ingested also indicates the risk of hepatotoxicity. People ingesting less than 125 mg/kg had no significant hepatotoxicity with a sharp dose dependent rise for higher doses.[8] The threshold for toxicity after acute ingestion may be higher in children, where a single dose of less than 200 mg/kg has not been reported to lead to death and rarely causes hepatotoxicity.[9]

Search date July 2001

Andrew Smith

What are the effects of interventions to reduce postoperative pulmonary infections?

BENEFICIAL

Chest physiotherapy (deep breathing exercises and incentive spirometry)

One systematic review and one subsequent RCT have found that deep breathing exercises⊙ significantly reduce postoperative pulmonary infections. The review also found that incentive spirometry⊙ versus control significantly reduces pulmonary complications.

Epidural anaesthesia

Two systematic reviews have found that epidural anaesthesia versus general anaesthesia followed by systemic opioid analgesia significantly reduces postoperative pulmonary infection. Neither review provided information on adverse effects. Two subsequent and one additional RCT found inconsistent results.

LIKELY TO BE BENEFICIAL

Chest physiotherapy (intermittent positive pressure breathing)

One RCT has found that intermittent positive pressure breathing⊙ versus control significantly reduces postoperative pulmonary complications.

UNKNOWN EFFECTIVENESS

Advice to stop smoking preoperatively

We found no RCTs of the effects of preoperative advice to stop cigarette smoking on postoperative pulmonary infection. Two observational studies have found that stopping smoking reduces the risk of postoperative pulmonary complications.

DEFINITION   A working diagnosis of postoperative pulmonary infection may be based on three or more new findings from cough, phlegm, shortness of breath, chest pain, temperature above 38°C, and pulse rate above 100/min[-1.1] In this topic, the diagnosis of pneumonia implies consolidation observed on a chest x ray.[2]

INCIDENCE/   Reported morbidity for chest complications depends on how carefully they are
PREVALENCE   investigated. One study found blood gas and chest radiograph abnormalities in about 50% of people after open cholecystectomy.[3] However, less than 20% of these had abnormal clinical signs and only 10% had a clinically significant chest infection. Another study estimated the incidence of pneumonia as 20%.[4] Another used a similarly strict definition and found 23%.[5]

AETIOLOGY/   Risk factors include increasing age (> 50 years), cigarette smoking, obesity,
RISK FACTORS   thoracic or upper abdominal operations, and pre-existing lung disease.[6] One multivariate analysis did not confirm the association with cigarette smoking but suggested that longer preoperative hospital stay and higher grading on the American Society of Anesthesiologists' physical status scale (> 2) increased the risk of postoperative pulmonary complications.[5] Depression of the immune system may also contribute.[7]

Postoperative pulmonary infections

◄ **PROGNOSIS**   In one large systematic review (search date 1997, 141 RCTs, 9559 people), 10% of people with postoperative pneumonia died.[8] If systemic sepsis ensues, mortality is likely to be substantial.[9] Pneumonia delays recovery from surgery and poor tissue oxygenation may contribute to delayed wound healing.

Search date October 2001

David Jewell

What are the effects of treatment for nausea and vomiting in early pregnancy?

BENEFICIAL

Antihistamines (H1 antagonists)
One systematic review has found that antihistamines versus placebo significantly reduce the number of women with nausea and vomiting, but increase drowsiness (NNH 7).

LIKELY TO BE BENEFICIAL

Cyanocobalamin (vitamin B$_{12}$)
One systematic review has found that cyanocobalamin⊕ versus placebo significantly reduces vomiting episodes.

Dietary ginger
One RCT found that ginger reduced nausea and vomiting after 4 and 7 days (NNT 2 at 7 days).

UNKNOWN EFFECTIVENESS

Dietary interventions (excluding ginger)
We found no RCTs on the effects of other dietary interventions.

P6 acupressure
One systematic review including small RCTs found limited evidence that P6 acupressure⊕ versus sham acupressure⊕ or no intervention significantly reduced self reported morning sickness. One subsequent RCT found that P6 acupressure reduced duration, but not intensity, of nausea and vomiting.

Phenothiazines
One systematic review found limited evidence that phenothiazines versus placebo reduced nausea and vomiting.

Pyridoxine (vitamin B$_6$)
One systematic review found limited evidence that pyridoxine versus placebo has no significant effect on vomiting, but may reduce the severity of nausea.

What are the effects of treatments for hyperemesis gravidarum?

UNKNOWN EFFECTIVENESS

Corticosteroids
One systematic review found no significant difference in the frequency of hospital admission with corticosteroids versus placebo or antihistamine. The rate of spontaneous resolution of symptoms in control groups was high.

Diazepam
One RCT found no significant difference in vomiting with diazepam versus placebo after 2 days, but found that diazepam reduced readmission to hospital. ▶

Pregnancy and childbirth

◀ **Dietary interventions (including ginger)**

One crossover RCT found no significant difference in nausea, vomiting, and weight loss with ginger versus placebo. We found no RCTs on the effects of other dietary interventions.

Ondansetron

We found no RCTs of ondansetron versus placebo. One RCT comparing ondansetron versus promethazine found no significant difference in persistence of vomiting.

DEFINITION The severity of nausea and vomiting in early pregnancy varies greatly among women. Hyperemesis gravidarum is persistent vomiting that is severe enough to cause fluid and electrolyte disturbance. It usually requires hospital admission.

INCIDENCE/ Nausea and vomiting are the most common symptoms experienced in the
PREVALENCE first trimester of pregnancy, affecting 70–85% of women.[1-3] Only 17% of women report that nausea and vomiting are confined to the morning and 13% are affected beyond 20 weeks' gestation.[2] Hyperemesis is much less common, with an incidence of 3.5/1000 deliveries.[4]

AETIOLOGY/ The causes of nausea and vomiting in pregnancy are unknown. One theory,
RISK FACTORS that they are caused by the rise in human chorionic gonadotrophin concentration, is compatible with the natural history of the condition, its severity in pregnancies affected by hydatidiform mole🅖 and its good prognosis (see below).[4] The aetiology of hyperemesis gravidarum is also uncertain. Again, endocrine and psychological factors are suspected, but evidence is inconclusive.[4]

PROGNOSIS One systematic review (search date 1988, 11 studies) found that nausea and vomiting were associated with a reduced risk of miscarriage (OR 0.36, 95% CI 0.32 to 0.42), but found no relationship with perinatal mortality.[5] Nausea and vomiting and hyperemesis usually improve over the course of pregnancy, but one study found that 13% of women reported nausea and vomiting to persist beyond 20 weeks' gestation.[2]

Pregnancy and childbirth

What are the effects of intrapartum interventions on rates of perineal trauma and of different methods and materials used for primary repair of perineal trauma?

BENEFICIAL

Absorbable synthetic material for perineal repair of first and second degree tears and episiotomies (reduces short term pain)

One systematic review has found that absorbable synthetic suture materials versus catgut sutures significantly reduce analgesia use within 10 days of birth (NNT 18). There was no significant difference between absorbable synthetic suture materials versus catgut sutures in perineal pain or dyspareunia 3 months after birth. One large RCT included in the systematic review found that absorbable synthetic sutures versus catgut sutures significantly reduced dyspareunia at 12 months (NNT 20).

Continuous subcutaneous technique of perineal skin closure of first and second degree tears and episiotomies (reduces short term pain)

One systematic review has found that continuous subcutaneous suture versus interrupted, transcutaneous suture of perineal skin significantly reduces pain in the 10 days after birth (NNT 14).

Restrictive use of episiotomy (reduces risk of posterior trauma)

One systematic review has found that restricting episiotomy to specific fetal and maternal indications significantly reduces rates of posterior perineal trauma (NNT 10), need for suturing (NNT 4), and healing complications (NNT 11), but increases the rates of anterior vaginal and labial trauma (NNH 11).

LIKELY TO BE BENEFICIAL

Continuous support during labour (reduces instrumental delivery)

One systematic review has found that providing continuous support for women during childbirth versus usual care significantly reduces the rate of instrumental delivery (NNT 41), but found no significant difference in the risk of perineal trauma.

Non-suturing of perineal skin in first and second degree tears and episiotomies (reduces dyspareunia)

One large RCT has found no significant difference between leaving the perineal skin unsutured versus conventional suturing in pain 10 days after birth, but found that non-suturing significantly reduces dyspareunia 3 months after birth.

TRADE OFF BETWEEN BENEFITS AND HARMS

"Hands poised" versus "hands on" method of delivery (increases pain, no significant difference in rate of perineal trauma and reduces episiotomy rate)

One RCT found that the "hands poised" method (not touching the baby's head or supporting the mother's perineum) versus the conventional "hands on" method (applying pressure to the baby's head during delivery and supporting the mother's perineum) significantly increased perineal pain at day 10 (NNH 33) but reduced episiotomy rates (NNT 38). However, it found no evidence of an effect on the overall risk of perineal trauma or third/fourth degree tears. ▶

◄ **Upright versus recumbent position during delivery**

One systematic review comparing any upright position versus supine or lateral positions for delivery found that an upright position significantly reduced episiotomies (NNT 17), but this was offset by a significant increase in second degree tears (NNH 40).

Vacuum extractor (less perineal trauma than with forceps but newborns have increased risk of cephalhaematoma)

One systematic review has found that the use of the vacuum extractor versus forceps delivery significantly reduces the rate of perineal trauma (NNT 10), but increases the incidence of neonatal cephalhaematoma and retinal haemorrhage (NNH 7).

UNKNOWN EFFECTIVENESS

Different methods and materials for repair of third and fourth degree tears

We found no RCTs on the best method or material for repairing third and fourth degree tears and major vaginal lacerations.

Non-suturing of perineal muscle in second degree tears and episiotomies

One small RCT found no significant difference with non-suturing versus suturing of first and second degree tears in burning sensation or soreness 2–3 days after birth or in healing 2–3 days or 8 weeks after birth.

Sustained breath holding (Valsalva) method of pushing

One systematic review of two poor quality controlled trials found no significant difference in the extent or rate of perineal trauma when sustained breath holding (Valsalva) versus spontaneous exhalatory methods of pushing are used during the second stage of labour.

UNLIKELY TO BE BENEFICIAL

Midline episiotomy incision (associated with higher risk of third/fourth degree tears compared with mediolateral incision)

We found no evidence that midline episiotomy incision versus mediolateral incision improved perineal pain or wound dehiscence. Limited evidence from one quasi randomised trial suggests that midline incision versus mediolateral incision may increase the risk of third and fourth degree tears (NNH 6).

LIKELY TO BE INEFFECTIVE OR HARMFUL

Epidural anaesthesia (increases instrumental delivery, which is associated with increased rates of perineal trauma)

One systematic review found no direct evidence about the effect of epidural versus other forms of anaesthesia on rates of perineal trauma. However, RCTs found that epidural anaesthesia maintained beyond the first stage of labour versus epidural restricted to the first stage of labour significantly increased risk of instrumental delivery (NNH 10), which in turn is associated with an increased risk of perineal trauma.

DEFINITION Perineal trauma is any damage to the genitalia during childbirth that occurs spontaneously or intentionally by surgical incision (episiotomy). Anterior perineal trauma is injury to the labia, anterior vagina, urethra, or clitoris, and is usually associated with little morbidity. Posterior perineal trauma is any injury to the posterior vaginal wall, perineal muscles, or anal sphincter. ▶

Depending on severity, posterior perineal trauma is associated with increased morbidity. First degree spontaneous tears involve only skin; second degree involve perineal muscles; third degree partially or completely disrupt the anal sphincter; and fourth degree tears completely disrupt the external and internal anal sphincter and epithelium.[1]

INCIDENCE/ PREVALENCE

Over 85% of women having a vaginal birth sustain some form of perineal trauma,[2] and 60–70% receive stitches — equivalent to 400 000 women per year in the UK in 1997.[2,3] There are wide variations in rates of episiotomy: 8% in the Netherlands, 26–67% in the UK, 50% in the USA, and 99% in east European countries.[4–8] Sutured spontaneous tears are reported in about a third of women in the USA[4] and the UK,[6] but this is probably an underestimate because of inconsistency of reporting and classification of perineal trauma. The incidence of anal sphincter tears varies between 0.5% in the UK, 2.5% in Denmark, and 7% in Canada.[9]

AETIOLOGY/ RISK FACTORS

Perineal trauma occurs during spontaneous or assisted vaginal delivery and is usually more extensive after the first vaginal delivery.[1] Associated risk factors include parity, size of baby, mode of delivery, malpresentation, and malposition of the fetus. Other maternal factors that may contribute to the extent and degree of trauma are ethnicity, age, tissue type, and nutritional state.[10] Clinicians' practices or preferences in terms of intrapartum interventions may influence the severity and rate of perineal trauma.

PROGNOSIS

Perineal trauma affects women's physical, psychological, and social wellbeing in the immediate postnatal period as well as the long term. It can also disrupt breast feeding, family life, and sexual relations. In the UK, about 23–42% of women will continue to have pain and discomfort for 10–12 days after birth, and 7–10% of women will continue to have long term pain (3–18 months after delivery);[2,3,11] 23% of women will experience superficial dyspareunia at 3 months; 3–10% will report faecal incontinence;[12,13] and up to 24% will have urinary problems.[2,3] Complications depend on severity of perineal trauma and on effectiveness of treatment.

Pre-eclampsia and hypertension

Search date December 2001

Lelia Duley

Pregnancy and childbirth

What are the effects of preventive interventions?

BENEFICIAL

Antiplatelet drugs

One systematic review has found that, in women considered at risk of pre-eclampsia, antiplatelet drugs (mainly aspirin) versus placebo or no treatment significantly reduces the risk of pre-eclampsia (NNT 59), death of the baby (NNT 250), and prematurity (NNT 72), with no significant difference in other important outcomes. Two large RCTs of aspirin found no adverse effects in children at 12–18 months old.

Calcium supplementation (in high risk women or those with low intake)

One systematic review has found that calcium supplementation (≥ 1 g daily) versus placebo reduces the risk of pre-eclampsia and hypertension (NNT 40), and reduces the risk of having a baby with birthweight under 2500 g (NNT 67). There was no significant effect on the risk of caesarean delivery, preterm delivery, or death of the baby.

UNKNOWN EFFECTIVENESS

Evening primrose oil; fish oil

We found six RCTs of evening primrose plus fish oil, which were too small to draw reliable conclusions.

Other pharmacological interventions

Two small RCTs comparing atenolol or glyceryl trinitrate patches versus placebo were too small to draw reliable conclusions.

Magnesium supplementation

One systematic review found insufficient evidence about the effects of magnesium supplements on the risk of pre-eclampsia or its complications.

Salt restriction

Limited evidence from one systematic review found no significant difference in the risk of pre-eclampsia with a low salt diet versus a normal diet.

Vitamin C and E

One RCT found limited evidence that vitamins C and E versus placebo reduced the risk of pre-eclampsia.

What are the effects of treatments?

BENEFICIAL

Magnesium sulphate for eclampsia (better than other anticonvulsants)

Systematic reviews have found that magnesium sulphate versus phenytoin, diazepam, or lytic cocktail significantly reduces further fits in women with eclampsia. All reviews found trends towards reduced maternal mortality with magnesium sulphate, although the benefit was not significant.

▶

◀ **LIKELY TO BE BENEFICIAL**

Antihypertensive drugs for very high blood pressure (although insufficient evidence on best choice of agent)

One systematic review in women with blood pressures high enough to merit immediate treatment found no evidence of a difference in the control of blood pressure by various antihypertensive drugs, with the possible exceptions of diazoxide and ketanserin, which seem less effective. The studies were too small to draw any further conclusions about the relative effects of different agents.

UNKNOWN EFFECTIVENESS

Aggressive versus expectant management for severe early onset pre-eclampsia

Two RCTs found that a policy of expectant versus agressive management for severe early onset pre-eclampsia reduced the risk of respiratory distress syndrome in the baby. They found insufficient evidence to assess maternal effects.

Antihypertensive drugs for mild to moderate hypertension

Two systematic reviews have found that antihypertensive agents versus placebo significantly reduce the chance of developing severe hypertension (NNT 12), but found no clear effect on pre-eclampsia and perinatal death. Systematic reviews found that angiotensin converting enzyme inhibitors used in pregnancy were associated with fetal renal failure, and that β blockers increased the risk of the baby being small for its gestational age.

Antioxidants in severe pre-eclampsia

One RCT found insufficient evidence about the effects of a combination of vitamin E, vitamin C, and allopurinol versus placebo.

Bed rest/hospital admission

We found insufficient evidence about hospital admission, bed rest, or day care versus outpatient care or normal activities in hospital.

Bed rest for proteinuric hypertension

One systematic review found insufficient evidence about the effects of bed rest in hospital versus normal ambulation in hospital.

Choice of analgesia during labour with severe pre-eclampsia

One RCT found that epidural analgesia during labour versus intravenous patient controlled analgesia significantly reduced mean pain scores, but the clinical importance of the difference was unclear.

Hospital admission for non-proteinuric hypertension

One systematic review found no significant difference in any major outcome with hospital admission versus outpatient clinic assessment.

Plasma volume expansion in severe pre-eclampsia

One systematic review found insufficient evidence about the effects of plasma volume expansion versus no expansion.

Prophylactic anticonvulsants in severe pre-eclampsia

One systematic review found that prophylactic anticonvulsants may reduce the risk of eclampsia, but found little evidence about the effects on other important outcomes. Limited evidence from case control studies suggests that *in utero* exposure to magnesium sulphate may reduce the risk of cerebral palsy, but it is possible that such exposure may increase infant mortality.

▶

Pre-eclampsia and hypertension

DEFINITION
Hypertension during pregnancy may be associated with one of several conditions. **Pregnancy induced hypertension** is a rise in blood pressure, without proteinuria, during the second half of pregnancy. **Pre-eclampsia** is a multisystem disorder, unique to pregnancy, which is usually associated with raised blood pressure and proteinuria. It rarely presents before 20 weeks' gestation. **Eclampsia** is one or more convulsions in association with the syndrome of pre-eclampsia. **Pre-existing hypertension** is known hypertension before pregnancy or raised blood pressure before 20 weeks' gestation. It may be essential hypertension or, less commonly, secondary to underlying disease.[1]

INCIDENCE/ PREVALENCE
Pregnancy induced hypertension affects 10% of pregnancies and pre-eclampsia complicates 2–8%.[2] Eclampsia occurs in about 1/2000 deliveries in developed countries.[3] In developing countries, estimates of the incidence of eclampsia vary from 1/100 to 1/1700.[4,5]

AETIOLOGY/ RISK FACTORS
The cause of pre-eclampsia is unknown. It is likely to be multifactorial and may result from deficient placental implantation during the first half of pregnancy.[6] Pre-eclampsia is more common among women likely to have a large placenta, such as those with multiple pregnancy, and among women with medical conditions associated with microvascular disease, such as diabetes, hypertension, and collagen vascular disease.[7,8] Other risk factors include genetic susceptibility, increased parity, and older maternal age.[9] Cigarette smoking seems to be associated with a lower risk of pre-eclampsia, but this potential benefit is outweighed by an increase in adverse outcomes such as low birth weight, placental abruption, and perinatal death.[10]

PROGNOSIS
The outcome of pregnancy in women with pregnancy induced hypertension alone is at least as good as that for normotensive pregnancies.[7,11] However, once pre-eclampsia develops, morbidity and mortality rise for both mother and child. For example, perinatal mortality for women with severe pre-eclampsia is double that for normotensive women.[7] Perinatal outcome is worse with early gestational hypertension.[7,9,11] Perinatal mortality also increases in women with severe essential hypertension.[12]

Search date September 2001

Bridgette Byrne and John J Morrison

Pregnancy and childbirth

What are the effects of treatments?

BENEFICIAL

Antenatal corticosteroids

One systematic review in women with anticipated preterm delivery has found that antenatal treatment with corticosteroids versus placebo or no treatment significantly reduces the risk of respiratory distress syndrome, neonatal mortality, and intraventricular haemorrhage in preterm infants.

LIKELY TO BE BENEFICIAL

Antibiotic treatment for premature rupture of the membranes (prolongs gestation and may reduce infection, but unknown effect on perinatal mortality)

One systematic review and one subsequent RCT in women with preterm premature rupture of membranes❶ have found that antibiotics versus placebo significantly prolong pregnancy and reduce the risk of neonatal infection, but do not significantly reduce perinatal❶ mortality.

Prophylactic cervical cerclage for women at risk of cervical incompetence

One large RCT has found that, in women presumed to have cervical incompetence, prophylactic cervical cerclage❶ versus no cerclage significantly reduces preterm birth (< 33 weeks' gestation) (NNT 24), but doubles the risk of puerperal pyrexia (NNH 33).

TRADE OFF BETWEEN BENEFITS AND HARMS

Tocolytic treatment in threatened preterm labour

One systematic review has found that atosiban, β mimetics, indomethacin, and ethanol versus placebo or no tocolytic significantly prolong pregnancy for women in threatened preterm labour❶, but do not significantly reduce perinatal mortality or neonatal morbidity. One subsequent RCT found that atobisan versus placebo significantly prolonged pregnancy for up to 7 days (NNT 6). The systematic review found no significant difference with magnesium sulphate versus placebo or no tocolytic in prolongation of pregnancy or reduction of perinatal mortality or neonatal morbidity. Tocolytics significantly increase maternal adverse effects, such as chest pain, nausea and vomiting, and breathlessness.

UNKNOWN EFFECTIVENESS

Amnioinfusion for preterm rupture of the membranes

One systematic review found insufficient evidence about the effects of amnioinfusion❶.

UNLIKELY TO BE BENEFICIAL

Enhanced antenatal care programmes for socially deprived population groups/high risk groups

RCTs carried out in a range of countries have found no significant difference with enhanced antenatal care❶ versus usual care in reducing the risk of preterm delivery.

▶

◄ **LIKELY TO BE INEFFECTIVE OR HARMFUL**

Antibiotic treatment for preterm labour with intact membranes

One systematic review in women in preterm labour with intact membranes has found that antibiotics versus placebo or no antibiotics significantly prolong pregnancy, and reduce the incidence of maternal infection and necrotising enterocolitis. One large subsequent RCT has found no significant difference in length of pregnancy or neonatal outcomes. The review found that antibiotics versus placebo or no treatment significantly increased perinatal mortality, but the subsequent RCT found no significant difference in perinatal mortality.

Thyrotropin releasing hormone before preterm delivery

One systematic review in women at risk of preterm birth has found no significant difference with thyrotropin releasing hormone plus corticosteroids versus corticosteroids alone in improving neonatal outcomes. Thyrotropin releasing hormone plus corticosteroids versus corticosteroids alone significantly increased maternal and fetal adverse events.

DEFINITION Preterm or premature birth is defined by the World Health Organization as delivery of an infant before 37 completed weeks of gestation.[1] There is no set lower limit to this definition, but 23–24 weeks' gestation is widely accepted,[1] which approximates to an average fetal weight of 500 g.

INCIDENCE/ PREVALENCE Preterm birth occurs in about 5–10% of all births in developed countries,[2–4] but in recent years the incidence seems to have increased in some countries, particularly the USA.[5] We found little reliable evidence for less developed countries that used the exact definition of premature birth. The rate in northwestern Ethiopia has been reported to vary between 11–22% depending on the age group studied, being highest in teenagers.[6]

AETIOLOGY/ RISK FACTORS About 30% of preterm births are unexplained and spontaneous.[4,7,8] The two strongest risk factors for idiopathic preterm labour are low socioeconomic status and previous preterm delivery. Multiple pregnancy accounts for about another 30% of cases.[4,7] Other known risk factors include genital tract infection, preterm premature rupture of the membranes, antepartum haemorrhage, cervical incompetence, and congenital uterine abnormalities, which collectively account for about 20–25% of cases. The remaining cases (15–20%) are attributed to elective preterm delivery secondary to hypertensive disorders of pregnancy, intrauterine fetal growth restriction, congenital abnormalities, and medical disorders of pregnancy.[4,5,7,8]

PROGNOSIS Preterm labour usually results in preterm birth. One systematic review (search date not stated) of tocolysis versus placebo found that about 27% of preterm labours spontaneously resolved, and about 70% progressed to preterm delivery.[9] Observational studies have found that one preterm birth significantly raises the risk of another in a subsequent pregnancy.[10]

Christopher Cates and J Mark FitzGerald

Respiratory disorders

What are the effects of treatments for chronic and acute asthma?

BENEFICIAL

Adding inhaled long acting β_2 agonists to inhaled corticosteroids in poorly controlled asthma (for symptom control)

One systematic review and one additional RCT have found that adding long acting, inhaled β_2 agonists versus placebo significantly improves symptoms and lung function. We found no evidence that regular use of long acting β_2 agonists causes deterioration in asthma control.

Inhaled short acting β_2 agonists as needed for symptom relief in mild or moderate persistent asthma

One systematic review and one subsequent RCT found no significant difference in clinical benefits with "as needed" versus "regular" use of inhaled short acting β_2 agonists.

Ipratropium bromide added to β_2 agonists for acute exacerbations

One systematic review and one subsequent RCT have found that short acting β_2 agonists plus ipratropium bromide versus β_2 agonists alone significantly reduce hospital admissions (NNT 18) and improve lung function.

Low dose, inhaled corticosteroids in mild, persistent asthma

Two systematic reviews and eight RCTs have found that low dose inhaled corticosteroids versus placebo or regular β_2 agonists significantly improve symptoms and lung function.

Short courses of oral corticosteroids for acute exacerbations

One systematic review has found that oral corticosteroids versus placebo taken at the start of an acute exacerbation significantly reduce the number of relapses requiring additional care within the first week (NNT 10) and significantly reduce hospital admissions. A second systematic review has also found that oral corticosteroids versus placebo significantly reduce hospital admissions and relapse.

Spacer devices for delivering inhaled medications from pressurised metered dose inhalers in acute asthma (as good as nebulisers)

One systematic review in people with acute but not life threatening exacerbations of asthma found no significant difference between β_2 agonists delivered by spacer device/holding chamber versus nebulisers in rates of hospital admission, time spent in the emergency department, peak expiratory flow rate🅖, or forced expiratory volume in 1 second🅖.

LIKELY TO BE BENEFICIAL

Asthma education for people with acute asthma

One systematic review has found that education to facilitate asthma self management versus usual care significantly reduces hospital admission, unscheduled visits to physicians, and days off work. ▶

Asthma

◀ **Continuous nebulised delivery of bronchodilators for acute asthma (better than intermittent treatment)**

One large RCT found limited evidence that continuous treatment with short acting β_2 agonists versus as needed treatment in people with severe asthma significantly improved peak expiratory flow rate at 2 hours and reduced hospital admissions.

Leukotriene antagonists for people with mild to moderate, persistent asthma

Three RCTs in people taking short acting β_2 agonists have found that the addition of leukotriene antagonists versus placebo significantly reduces asthma symptoms. One systematic review found no significant difference with leukotriene antagonists versus inhaled corticosteroids in the rate of asthma exacerbations, but found that inhaled corticosteroids significantly increased quality of life, lung function, and symptom control.

Magnesium sulphate for people with more severe acute asthma

Subgroup analysis from one systematic review suggests that intravenous magnesium sulphate versus placebo may reduce rates of hospital admission. One small subsequent RCT in people with acute exacerbations of asthma found that nebulised magnesium sulphate versus saline significantly improved peak expiratory flow rate.

Mechanical ventilation for people with near fatal asthma

We found no RCTs of mechanical ventilation, but clinical experience, retrospective cohort studies, and case series suggest that it is likely to reduce death rates.

Oxygen supplementation for acute asthma

There is a strong consensus that oxygen should be a key component of acute treatment. We found no RCTs in people with acute exacerbations of asthma of oxygen treatment. Clinical monitoring and case control studies have found that people with near fatal asthma suffer from significant hypoxaemia.

Specialist versus generalist care for acute exacerbations

One non-systematic review of non-randomised trials found that specialist care versus generalist care improved outcomes.

UNKNOWN EFFECTIVENESS

Inhaled corticosteroids as add on treatment for acute asthma

One systematic review has found that inhaled corticosteroids plus oral corticosteroids versus oral corticosteroids alone significantly reduce hospital admission (NNT 6). A second systematic review in people with acute exacerbations of asthma discharged from the emergency department found no significant difference with inhaled corticosteroids plus oral corticosteroids versus oral corticosteroids alone in relapse rates.

Intravenous versus nebulised delivery of short acting β_2 agonists for acute asthma

Three RCTs found conflicting evidence about the effects of intravenous short acting β_2 agonists versus nebulised short acting β_2 agonists. Intravenous administration was associated with more adverse effects.

▶

◀ **LIKELY TO BE INEFFECTIVE OR HARMFUL**

Regular use of short acting inhaled β$_2$ agonists in mild, intermittent asthma

One systematic review and one subsequent RCT found that regular use of inhaled short acting β$_2$ agonists versus as needed use provided no important clinical benefits.

DEFINITION Asthma is characterised by variable airflow obstruction and airway hyper-responsiveness. Symptoms include dyspnoea, cough, chest tightness, and wheezing. The normal diurnal variation🕒 of peak expiratory flow rate is increased in people with asthma🛈. **Chronic asthma** is defined here as asthma requiring maintenance treatment. Asthma is classified differently in the USA and UK🛈: where necessary, the text specifies the system of classification used.[1,2] **Acute asthma** is defined here as an exacerbation of underlying asthma requiring urgent or emergency treatment.

INCIDENCE/ Reported prevalence of asthma is increasing worldwide. About 10% of
PREVALENCE people have suffered an attack of asthma.[3–5]

AETIOLOGY/ Most people with asthma are atopic. Exposure to certain stimuli initiates
RISK FACTORS inflammation and structural changes in airways causing airway hyperrespon-siveness and variable airflow obstruction, which in turn cause most asthma symptoms. There are a large number of such stimuli; the more important include environmental allergens, occupational sensitising agents, and respiratory viral infections.[6,7]

PROGNOSIS **Chronic asthma:** In people with mild asthma, prognosis is good and progression to severe disease is rare. However, as a group, people with asthma lose lung function faster than those without asthma, although less quickly than people without asthma who smoke.[8] People with chronic asthma can improve with treatment. However, for reasons not clearly understood, some people (possibly up to 5%) have severe disease that responds poorly to treatment. These people are most at risk of morbidity and death from asthma. **Acute asthma:** About 10–20% of people presenting to the emergency department with asthma are admitted to hospital. Of these, fewer than 10% receive mechanical ventilation,[9,10] although previous ven-tilation is associated with a 19-fold increased risk of ventilation for a subsequent episode.[11] It is unusual for people to die unless they have suffered respiratory arrest before reaching hospital.[12] One prospective study of 939 people discharged from emergency care found that 17% (95% CI 14% to 20%) relapsed by 2 weeks.[13]

Chronic obstructive pulmonary disease

Search date June 2001

Huib Kerstjens and Dirkje Postma

What are the short term effects of maintenance drug treatment?

BENEFICIAL

Inhaled anticholinergic drugs
RCTs have found that anticholinergic drugs versus placebo significantly improve forced expiratory volume in 1 second (FEV_1) in the short term (up to 3 months).

Inhaled β_2 agonists
Short term RCTs have found that short and long acting inhaled β_2 agonists versus placebo significantly improve FEV_1.

Inhaled anticholinergics plus β_2 agonists
RCTs have found that combining a β_2 agonist with an anticholinergic drug versus either drug alone significantly improves FEV_1.

Oral corticosteroids
One systematic review has found that oral corticosteroids versus placebo significantly improve lung function over 2–4 weeks. Systemic corticosteroids are associated with adverse effects including osteoporosis and induction of diabetes.

TRADE OFF BETWEEN BENEFITS AND HARMS

Theophyllines
Small, short term RCTs of theophyllines found limited evidence of a small bronchodilatory effect, but the usefulness of these drugs is limited by adverse effects and the need for frequent monitoring of blood concentrations.

UNLIKELY TO BE BENEFICIAL

Inhaled corticosteroids
Short term RCTs (10 days to 10 wk) found no significant difference in lung function with inhaled corticosteroids versus placebo.

What are the long term effects of maintenance drug treatment?

BENEFICIAL

Mucolytics
Systematic reviews have found that mucolytics versus placebo significantly reduce the frequency and duration of exacerbations.

LIKELY TO BE BENEFICIAL

Domiciliary oxygen (in people with hypoxaemia)
One systematic review in people with chronic obstructive pulmonary disorder and hypoxaemia found limited evidence that domiciliary oxygen treatment versus control treatment improved survival at 3–5 years. One RCT found that continuous treatment versus nocturnal treatment significantly reduced mortality over 2 years.

◀ **UNKNOWN EFFECTIVENESS**

Antibiotics; inhaled β_2 agonists; deoxyribonuclease *New;* oral corticosteroids; theophyllines

We found no RCTs about the long term effects of these interventions.

α_1 Antitrypsin augmentation *New*

One RCT in people with α_1 antitrypsin deficiency and moderate emphysema found no significant difference with α_1 antitrypsin versus placebo in the decline in FEV_1 after 1 year.

UNLIKELY TO BE BENEFICIAL

Inhaled anticholinergic drugs

One large RCT found that a long term anticholinergic drug plus a smoking cessation programme versus a smoking cessation programme alone had no significant impact on the decline in FEV_1 at 5 years.

Inhaled corticosteroids

Large RCTs lasting at least 6 months have found that inhaled steroids versus placebo increase FEV_1 during the first 3–6 months of use, but found no subsequent effect on decline in lung function.

DEFINITION	Chronic obstructive pulmonary disorder is airflow obstruction caused by chronic bronchitis or emphysema. Emphysema is abnormal permanent enlargement of the air spaces distal to the terminal bronchioles, accompanied by destruction of their walls and without obvious fibrosis. Chronic bronchitis is chronic cough or mucus production for at least 3 months in at least 2 successive years when other causes of chronic cough have been excluded.[1]
INCIDENCE/ PREVALENCE	Chronic obstructive pulmonary disorder mainly affects middle aged and elderly people. It is one of the leading causes of morbidity and mortality worldwide. In the USA, it affects about 14 million people and is the fourth leading cause of death. Both morbidity and mortality are rising. Estimated prevalence in the USA has risen by 41% since 1982, and age adjusted death rates rose by 71% between 1966 and 1985. All cause age adjusted mortality declined over the same period by 22% and mortality from cardiovascular diseases by 45%.[1] In the UK, physician diagnosed prevalence was 2% in men and 1% in women between 1990 and 1997.[2]
AETIOLOGY/ RISK FACTORS	Chronic obstructive pulmonary disorder is largely preventable. The main cause is exposure to cigarette smoke. Chronic obstructive pulmonary disorder is rare in lifetime non-smokers (estimated incidence 5% in 3 large representative US surveys from 1971–1984), in whom exposure to environmental tobacco smoke will explain at least some diseases.[3,4] Other proposed causes include airway hyperresponsiveness, air pollution, and allergy.[5–7]
PROGNOSIS	Airway obstruction is usually progressive in those who continue to smoke, resulting in early disability and shortened survival. Smoking cessation reverts the rate of decline in lung function to that of non-smokers.[8] Many people will need medication for the rest of their lives, with increased doses and additional drugs during exacerbations.

Community acquired pneumonia

Search date August 2001

Mark Loeb

What are the effects of treatments?

LIKELY TO BE BENEFICIAL

Prompt administration of antibiotics in people severely ill with community acquired pneumonia

Retrospective studies found that prompt administration of antibiotics significantly improved survival. It would probably be unethical to perform an RCT of delayed antibiotic treatment.

UNKNOWN EFFECTIVENESS

Bottle blowing

One unblinded RCT found limited evidence that bottle blowing physiotherapy plus early mobilisation plus encouragement to regularly sit up and take deep breaths versus early mobilisation alone significantly reduced hospital stay.

Guidelines for treating pneumonia (for clinical outcomes)

One systematic review found no significant difference between the use of guidelines incorporating early switch from intravenous to oral antibiotics and/or early discharge strategies and usual care alone in improving clinical outcomes in community acquired pneumonia.

Specific combinations of antibiotics in intensive care settings

We found no RCTs comparing one combination of antibiotics versus another in intensive care units.

UNLIKELY TO BE BENEFICIAL

Intravenous antibiotics versus oral antibiotics in immunocompetent people in hospital without life threatening illness

RCTs in immunocompetent people in hospital found no significant difference with intravenous versus oral antibiotics in cure of community acquired pneumonia. Intravenous antibiotics increased the duration of hospital stay.

New antibiotics versus older antibiotics in hospital, unless microbes are resistant to older drugs

RCTs have found no significant difference between new and older antibiotics in cure of people with community acquired pneumonia admitted to hospital. However, most trials were small and not designed to detect differences between treatments.

New antibiotics versus older antibiotics in outpatient settings, unless microbes are resistant to older drugs

One systematic review comparing different oral antibiotics in outpatient settings has found cure or improvement in over 90% of people. ▶

◀ *What are the effects of preventive interventions?*

BENEFICIAL

Pneumococcal vaccine in immunocompetent adults

One systematic review in immunocompetent people has found that, over one winter season, pneumococcal vaccination versus no vaccination significantly reduces pneumococcal pneumonia.

LIKELY TO BE BENEFICIAL

Influenza vaccine in elderly people

One RCT in people aged 60 years or over found that influenza vaccine versus placebo significantly reduced the incidence of influenza at 5 months (NNT 64).

UNKNOWN EFFECTIVENESS

Pneumococcal vaccine in chronically ill, immunosuppressed, or elderly people

One systematic review has found no significant difference in pneumococcal pneumonia with pneumococcal vaccination versus no vaccination in elderly people or people likely to have an impaired immune system.

DEFINITION Community acquired pneumonia is pneumonia contracted in the community rather than in hospital.

INCIDENCE/ PREVALENCE In the northern hemisphere, community acquired pneumonia affects about 12/1000 people a year, particularly during winter and at the extremes of age (incidence: < 1 year old 30–50/1000 people a year; 15–45 years 1–5/1000 people a year; 60–70 years 10–20/1000 people a year; 71–85 years 50/1000 people a year).[1–6]

AETIOLOGY/ RISK FACTORS Over 100 microorganisms have been implicated in community acquired pneumonia, but most cases are caused by *Streptococcus pneumoniae* 🛈.[4–7] Smoking is probably an important risk factor.[8]

PROGNOSIS Severity varies from mild to life threatening illness within days of the onset of symptoms. One systematic review (search date 1995, 33 148 people) of prognosis studies for community acquired pneumonia found overall mortality to be 13.7%, ranging from 5.1% for ambulant people to 36.5% for people requiring intensive care.[9] The following prognostic factors were significantly associated with mortality: male sex (OR 1.3, 95% CI 1.2 to 1.4); pleuritic chest pain (OR 0.5, 95% CI 0.3 to 0.8, i.e. lower mortality); hypothermia (OR 5, 95% CI 2.4 to 10.4); systolic hypotension (OR 4.8, 95% CI 2.8 to 8.3); tachypnoea (OR 2.9, 95% CI 1.7 to 4.9); diabetes mellitus (OR 1.3, 95% CI 1.1 to 1.5); neoplastic disease (OR 2.8, 95% CI 2.4 to 3.1); neurological disease (OR 4.6, 95% CI 2.3 to 8.9); bacteraemia (OR 2.8, 95% CI 2.3 to 3.6); leucopenia (OR 2.5, 95% CI 1.6 to 3.7); and multilobar radiographic pulmonary infiltrates (OR 3.1, 95% CI 1.9 to 5.1).

Lung cancer

Search date September 2001

Alan Neville

What are the effects of treatments for non-small cell lung cancer?

BENEFICIAL

Palliative chemotherapy with cisplatin or docetaxel containing regimens in stage 4 non-small cell lung cancer

Systematic reviews in people with stage 4 non-small cell lung cancer have found that chemotherapy regimens containing cisplatin plus best supportive care versus supportive care alone significantly increase survival at 1 year. Limited evidence from RCTs suggests that chemotherapy plus best supportive care versus best supportive care alone may improve quality of life.

Thoracic irradiation plus chemotherapy versus irradiation alone in unresected stage 3 non-small cell lung cancer

Systematic reviews and one subsequent RCT in people with unresectable stage 3 non-small cell lung cancer have found that adding chemotherapy to thoracic irradiation significantly improves survival at 2–5 years. Another subsequent RCT has found no significant difference in median survival between radical radiotherapy plus chemotherapy versus radiotherapy alone.

UNKNOWN EFFECTIVENESS

Hyperfractionated radiation treatment versus conventional radiotherapy in unresectable stage 3 non-small cell lung cancer

One systematic review in people with stage 3 non-small cell lung cancer has found no significant difference between standard hyperfractionation versus conventional radiotherapy in survival at 2 years. One RCT in people with stage 3 non-small cell lung cancer found that continuous, hyperfractionated, accelerated radiotherapy**G** versus conventional radiotherapy significantly increased survival at 2 years.

Newer single drug or combined drug regimens in stage 4 non-small cell lung cancer (not clearly better than cisplatin or docetaxel based regimens)

One systematic review and subsequent RCTs in people with stage 3 and 4 non-small cell lung cancer found conflicting evidence on the effects of single versus combined chemotherapy. One RCT in people with stage 3 and 4 non-small cell lung cancer found no significant difference in survival at 1 year between first line platinum based versus non-platinum based chemotherapy.

Preoperative chemotherapy in people with resectable stage 3 non-small cell lung cancer

One systematic review of two small RCTs in people with technically resectable stage 3A non-small cell lung cancer has found that preoperative chemotherapy versus no chemotherapy significantly improves survival at 2 years (NNT 4). ▶

◀ **UNLIKELY TO BE BENEFICIAL**

Postoperative chemotherapy in people with resected stage 1–3 non-small cell lung cancer

Systematic reviews and one subsequent RCT in people with completely resected stage 2 and 3 non-small cell lung cancer have found no significant difference in survival at 5 years between postoperative cisplatin based chemotherapy versus surgery alone.

What are the effects of treatments for small cell lung cancer?

BENEFICIAL

Chemotherapy plus thoracic irradiation versus chemotherapy alone in limited stage small cell lung cancer

Two systematic reviews in people with limited stage small cell lung cancer have found that adding thoracic irradiation to chemotherapy significantly improves survival at 3 years. However, one of these reviews has found that chemotherapy plus thoracic irradiation significantly increased deaths related to treatment.

LIKELY TO BE BENEFICIAL

Prophylactic cranial irradiation for people in complete remission with limited or extensive stage small cell lung cancer

One systematic review in people in with small cell lung cancer in complete remission has found that prophylactic cranial irradiation versus no irradiation significantly improves survival at 3 years and reduces the risk of developing brain metastases. Long term cognitive dysfunction following cranial irradiation has been described, but longer follow up studies are needed to assess its significance and importance.

LIKELY TO BE INEFFECTIVE OR HARMFUL

Dose intensive chemotherapy versus standard chemotherapy

Two RCTs in people with limited or extensive stage small cell lung cancer have found no significant difference in progression free survival with dose intensive treatment versus standard chemotherapy, but have found that the dose intensive treatment significantly increases deaths related to toxicity (NNH 14).

Oral etoposide in extensive stage small cell lung cancer

RCTs in people with extensive stage small cell lung cancer have found that oral etoposide improves survival at 1 year significantly less than combination chemotherapy. One RCT found that etoposide versus combination chemotherapy caused less nausea and vomiting in the short term, but found no evidence that etoposide offers significantly better quality of life overall.

DEFINITION   Lung cancer (bronchogenic carcinoma) is an epithelial cancer arising from the bronchial surface epithelium or bronchial mucous glands❶.

INCIDENCE/   Lung cancer is the leading cause of cancer death in both men and women,
PREVALENCE   affecting about 100 000 men and 80 000 women annually in the USA, and about 40 000 men and women in the UK. Small cell lung cancer constitutes about 20–25% of all lung cancers, the remainder being non-small cell lung cancers, of which adenocarcinoma is now the most prevalent form.[1]

▶

Lung cancer

AETIOLOGY/ RISK FACTORS Smoking remains the major preventable risk factor, accounting for about 80–90% of all cases.

PROGNOSIS Lung cancer has an overall 5 year survival rate of 10–12%.[2] At the time of diagnosis, 10–15% of people with lung cancer have localised disease. Of these, half will have died at 5 years despite potentially curative surgery. Over half of people have metastatic disease at the time of diagnosis. People with non-small cell cancer who undergo surgery have a 5 year survival of 60–80% for stage 1 disease and 25–50% for stage 2 disease.[2] In people with small cell cancer, those with limited stage disease who undergo combined chemotherapy and mediastinal irradiation have a median survival of 18–24 months, whereas those with extensive stage disease who are given palliative chemotherapy have a median survival of 10–12 months.[2] About 5–10% of people with small cell lung cancer present with central nervous system involvement, and half develop symptomatic brain metastases by 2 years. Of these, only half respond to palliative radiation, and their median survival is less than 3 months.[2]

Search date August 2001

John Cunnington

What are the effects of treatments?

UNKNOWN EFFECTIVENESS

Chest tube drainage

We found no sufficiently large RCTs comparing chest tube drainage versus observation. Two small RCTs found that resolution is faster with chest tube drainage that with needle aspiration, but found no difference in recurrence rate. One of the RCTs found that chest tube drainage significantly increased pain and increased the time spent in hospital by an average of 2 days.

Chest tube drainage plus suction

One small RCT found no difference in the rate of resolution whether chest tube drainage bottles were connected to suction or not, but the trial was too small to exclude a clinically important difference.

Needle aspiration

One small RCT found no good evidence of an improved rate of resolution with needle aspiration versus observation alone. Two small RCTs found that resolution is slower with needle aspiration than with chest tube drainage, but found no difference in recurrence rate. One of the RCTs found that people treated with needle aspiration experienced significantly less pain and spent an average of two fewer days in hospital.

One way valves on chest tubes versus bottles with underwater seal

One small RCT found no significant difference in the rate of resolution with one way valves versus drainage bottles with an underwater seal, but people treated with one way valves required less analgesia and spent less time in hospital.

Small versus standard sized chest tubes

One non-randomised trial found no significant difference in duration of tube drainage between small and standard sized chest tubes, but for people with larger pneumothoraces, successful resolution was more likely with larger tubes.

What are the effects of interventions to prevent recurrence?

TRADE OFF BETWEEN BENEFITS AND HARMS

Chemical pleurodesis

Two RCTs found that chemical pleurodesis versus no chemical pleurodesis significantly reduced the rate of recurrence within 2.5–5 years, but one of the RCTs found that chemical pleurodesis caused severe chest pain. One RCT and one non-randomised study found conflicting evidence about the effects of chemical pleurodesis versus no chemical pleurodesis on length of hospital stay.

Surgical pleurodesis

One non-randomised prospective study found no significant difference in recurrence rate with surgical versus chemical pleurodesis. One small RCT found that video-assisted thorascopic surgery versus thoracotomy significantly reduced hospital stay. The rate of recurrence was not significantly different, but the limited evidence cannot exclude a clinically important difference. ▶

◄ **UNKNOWN EFFECTIVENESS**

Optimal timing of pleurodesis (after first, second, or third spontaneous pneumothorax)

> We found insufficient evidence on whether pleurodesis should take place after the first, second, or subsequent episodes of spontaneous pneumothorax.

DEFINITION A pneumothorax is air in the pleural space. A spontaneous pneumothorax occurs when there is no provoking factor, such as trauma, surgery, or diagnostic intervention. It implies a leak of air from the lung parenchyma through the visceral pleura into the pleural space.

INCIDENCE/ PREVALENCE In a survey in Minnesota, USA, the incidence of spontaneous pneumothorax was 7/100 000 men and 1/100 000 for women.[1] Smoking increases the likelihood of spontaneous pneumothorax by 22 times for men and eight times for women. A dose–response relationship has been observed.[2]

AETIOLOGY/ RISK FACTORS Spontaneous pneumothorax can be primary (typically in young fit people and thought to be because of a congenital abnormality of the pleura) or secondary (caused by underlying lung disease, typically occurring in older people with emphysema or pulmonary fibrosis).

PROGNOSIS Death from spontaneous pneumothorax is rare and in some cases a consequence of tension pneumothorax. Morbidity with pain and shortness of breath is common. Published recurrence rates vary; one cohort study in Denmark found that, after a first episode of primary spontaneous pneumothorax, 23% of people suffered a recurrence within 5 years, most within a year.[3] Recurrence rates had been thought to increase substantially after the first recurrence, but one case control study of military personnel found that 28% of men with a first spontaneous pneumothorax had a recurrence; 23% of the 28% had a second recurrence; and only 14% of that 23% had a third recurrence, giving a total recurrence rate of 35%.[4]

Search date October 2001

Chris Del Mar and Paul Glasziou

What are the effects of treatments?

BENEFICIAL

Analgesia/anti-inflammatories for symptom relief

One systematic review has found that analgesics and anti-inflammatory drugs versus placebo significantly reduce sore throat at 1–5 days. One RCT in people with acute sinusitis taking antibiotics found that steroid spray versus placebo significantly improved symptoms over 21 days.

Antibiotics for preventing (rare) complications of β haemolytic streptococcal pharyngitis

One systematic review has found that antibiotics versus no antibiotics can prevent non-suppurative complications of β haemolytic streptococcal pharyngitis, but in industrialised countries such complications are rare.

LIKELY TO BE BENEFICIAL

Antibiotics for decreasing time to recovery in people with proven infection with *Haemophilus influenzae*, *Moraxella catarrhalis*, or *Streptococcus pneumoniae*

In a minority of people, the upper respiratory tract infection is found to be caused by *H influenzae*, *M catarrhalis*, or *S pneumoniae*. One RCT found that in these people antibiotics versus placebo significantly increased recovery at 5 days (NNT 4 for people with a positive nasopharyngeal culture at first consultation). However, we have no methods currently of easily identifying this subgroup within the majority of people with negative nasopharyngeal cultures.

Antihistamines for runny nose and sneezing

One systematic review has found that antihistamines versus placebo reduce runny nose and sneezing after 2 days, but the clinical benefit is small.

Agonists for reducing duration of cough

Two RCTs in people with acute bronchitis have found that salbutamol versus erythromycin significantly increases the number of people who are cough free at 7 days (NNT about 4), although a third RCT found that this benefit may be limited to people with bronchial hyperresponsiveness, wheeze, or airflow limitation.

Decongestants for short term relief of congestive symptoms

One systematic review has found limited evidence that a single dose of decongestant versus placebo may reduce congestion in the short term.

Vitamin C

One systematic review has found that vitamin C versus placebo slightly but significantly reduces the duration of cold symptoms, but the benefit was small and may be explained by publication bias.

Zinc intranasal gel for reducing the duration of cold symptoms

Two RCTs have found conflicting evidence about the effects of intranasal zinc versus placebo on the duration of cold symptoms. ▶

Respiratory disorders

Upper respiratory tract infection

TRADE OFF BETWEEN BENEFITS AND HARMS

Antibiotics for reducing time to recovery in people with acute bronchitis, pharyngitis, and sinusitis

Systematic reviews have found that antibiotics versus placebo slightly but significantly improve symptoms. Adverse effects (nausea, vomiting, headache, rash, vaginitis) were more common with antibiotics.

UNKNOWN EFFECTIVENESS

Echinacea for prevention

One systematic review found limited evidence that echinachea versus no treatment significantly reduced the number of people who had one infection episode, but found insufficient evidence of the effects of echinachea versus placebo.

Echinacea for treatment

Systematic reviews found limited evidence that some preparations of echinacea versus placebo may improve symptoms, but we found insufficient evidence about the effects of any specific product.

Steam inhalation

One systematic review found conflicting evidence about the effects of steam inhalation.

Zinc lozenges

Two systematic reviews found inconsistent evidence on the effects of zinc gluconate or acetate lozenges versus placebo on duration of symptoms.

LIKELY TO BE INEFFECTIVE OR HARMFUL

Antibiotics in people with colds, coughs, and sore throat

Systematic reviews found no significant difference between antibiotics versus placebo in cure or general improvement.

Decongestants for long term relief of congestive symptoms

One systematic review found no good evidence on the effects of repeated use of decongestants over several days.

DEFINITION Upper respiratory tract infection involves inflammation of the respiratory mucosa from the nose to the lower respiratory tree, but not including the alveoli. In addition to malaise, it causes localised symptoms that constitute several overlapping syndromes: sore throat (pharyngitis), rhinorrhoea (common cold), facial fullness and pain (sinusitis), and cough (bronchitis).

INCIDENCE/ PREVALENCE Upper respiratory tract infections, nasal congestion, throat complaints, and cough are responsible for 11% of general practice consultations in Australia.[1] Each year, children suffer about five such infections and adults two to three infections.[1]

AETIOLOGY/ RISK FACTORS Infective agents include over 200 viruses (with 100 rhinoviruses) and several bacteria. Transmission is mostly through hand to hand contact with subsequent passage to the nostrils or eyes rather than, as commonly perceived, through droplets in the air.[2]

▶

PROGNOSIS Upper respiratory tract infections are usually self limiting. Although they cause little mortality or serious morbidity, upper respiratory tract infections are responsible for considerable discomfort, lost work, and medical costs. Clinical patterns vary and overlap between infective agents. In addition to nasal symptoms, half of sufferers experience sore throat and 40% experience cough. Symptoms peak within 1–3 days and generally clear by 1 week, although cough often persists.[2]

Bacterial vaginosis

Search date July 2001

M Joesoef and George Schmid

What are the effects of antianaerobic treatments?

BENEFICIAL

Antianaerobic treatment in symptomatic non-pregnant women

One systematic review has found no significant difference between oral and intravaginal antianaerobic drugs in cure rates after 5–10 days or at 4 weeks. Another systematic review has found that a 7 day course of twice daily oral metronidazole versus a single 2 g dose significantly increases cure rates at 3–4 weeks. Limited evidence from RCTs found no significant difference in cure rates with oral clindamycin versus oral metronidazole twice daily for 7 days, and no difference between once and twice daily dosing with intravaginal metronidazole gel. One RCT found no difference in cure rates at 35 days with intravaginal clindamycin ovules for 3 days versus intravaginal clindamycin cream for 7 days.

LIKELY TO BE BENEFICIAL

Antianaerobic treatment before surgical abortion

RCTs found that oral antianaerobic treatment in women with bacterial vaginosis about to undergo surgical abortion reduced the risk of pelvic inflammatory disease.

Antianaerobic treatment (except clindamycin) in pregnant women who have had a previous preterm birth

Limited evidence from a subgroup analysis in pregnant women with bacterial vaginosis who had a previous preterm birth found that oral antianaerobic treatment versus placebo significantly reduced the risk of premature delivery (NNT 4).

UNKNOWN EFFECTIVENESS

Antianaerobic treatment before gynaecological procedures (other than abortion)

We found no evidence on the effects of antianerobic treatment in women with bacterial vaginosis about to undergo gynaecological procedures other than abortion.

Antianaerobic treatment (except clindamycin) in low risk pregnancy

One systematic review and subsequent RCTs in pregnant women who have not had a previous preterm delivery have found no significant difference in the risk of preterm birth with antianaerobic treatment for bacterial vaginosis versus placebo.

LIKELY TO BE INEFFECTIVE OR HARMFUL

Treating pregnant women with intravaginal clindamycin

Four RCTs found that intravaginal clindamycin cream increased the risk of preterm delivery and low birth weight, but the increase was not significant.

Treating pregnant women without bacterial vaginosis

Subgroup analysis in two RCTs of pregnant women without bacterial vaginosis found that intravaginal clindamycin cream or oral metronidazole plus erythromycin increased the risk of preterm delivery before 34 weeks' gestation, although the difference was significant in only one of the RCTs (NNH 12).

◄ *What are the effects of interventions to prevent recurrence?*

LIKELY TO BE INEFFECTIVE OR HARMFUL

Treating a woman's one steady male sexual partner
One systematic review has found that, in women with one steady male sexual partner, treating the partner with an oral antianaerobic agent does not reduce the woman's risk of recurrence.

DEFINITION Bacterial vaginosis is a microbial disease characterised by an alteration in the bacterial flora of the vagina from a predominance of *Lactobacillus* species to high concentrations of anaerobic bacteria. Diagnosis requires three out of four features: the presence of clue cells; a homogenous discharge adherent to the vaginal walls; pH of vaginal fluid greater than 4.5; and a "fishy" amine odour of the vaginal discharge before or after addition of 10% potassium hydroxide. The condition is asymptomatic in 50% of infected women. Women with symptoms have an excessive white to grey, or malodorous vaginal discharge, or both; the odour may be particularly noticeable during sexual intercourse.

INCIDENCE/ PREVALENCE Bacterial vaginosis is the most common infectious cause of vaginitis, being about twice as common as candidiasis.[1] Prevalences of 10–61% have been reported among unselected women from a range of settings.[2] Data on incidence are limited but one study found that, over a 2 year period, 50% of women using an intrauterine contraceptive device had at least one episode, as did 20% of women using oral contraceptives.[3] Bacterial vaginosis is particularly prevalent in lesbians.[4]

AETIOLOGY/ RISK FACTORS The cause is not understood fully. Risk factors include new or multiple sexual partners[1,3,5] and early age of sexual debut,[6] but no causative microorganism has been shown to be transmitted between partners. Use of an intrauterine contraceptive device[3] and douching[5] have also been reported as risk factors. Infection seems to be most common around the time of menstruation.[7]

PROGNOSIS The course of bacterial vaginosis varies and is poorly understood. Without treatment, symptoms may persist or resolve in both pregnant and non-pregnant women. Recurrence after treatment occurs in about a third of women. The condition is associated with complications of pregnancy: low birth weight; preterm birth (pooled OR from 10 cohort studies: 1.8, 95% CI 1.5 to 2.6);[8] preterm labour; premature rupture of membranes; late miscarriage; chorioamnionitis (48% v 22%, OR 2.6, 95% CI 1.0 to 6.6);[9] endometritis after normal delivery (8.2% v 1.5%, OR 5.6, 95% CI 1.8 to 17.2);[10] endometritis after caesarean section (55% v 17%, OR 5.8, 95% CI 3.0 to 10.9);[11] and surgery to the genital tract. Women who have had a previous premature delivery are especially at risk of complications in pregnancy, with a sevenfold increased risk of preterm birth (AR 24/428 [6%] in all women v 10/24 [42%] in women with a previous preterm birth).[12] Bacterial vaginosis can also enhance HIV acquisition and transmission.[13]

Genital chlamydial infection

Search date May 2001

Nicola Low and Frances Cowan

What are the effects of antibiotic treatment for men and non-pregnant women with uncomplicated genital chlamydial infection?

BENEFICIAL

Multiple dose regimens of doxycycline, teracycline, rosaramicin

Small RCTs with short term follow up and high withdrawal rates comparing different antibiotic regimens have found that multiple dose regimens of tetracyclines (doxycycline, tetracycline) and macrolides (rosaramicin) achieve microbiological cure in at least 95% of people with genital chlamydia. We found no differences in microbiological cure rates between men and women or between those with proven or presumed infection.

LIKELY TO BE BENEFICIAL

Multiple dose regimens of erythromycin

Three small RCTs found that erythromycin achieved microbiological cure in 75–100% of people, with the highest cure rate with a 2 g versus a 1 g daily dose.

Single dose azithromycin

One systematic review of short term RCTs has found no significant difference in cure rate between a single dose of azithromycin versus a 7 day course of doxycycline.

UNKNOWN EFFECTIVENESS

Multiple dose regimens of ofloxacin, trovafloxacin, minocycline, lymecycline, clarithromycin, ampicillin, rifampicin

We found limited evidence on the effects of these regimens.

UNLIKELY TO BE BENEFICIAL

Multiple dose regimens of ciprofloxacin

Two RCTs found that ciprofloxacin cured 63–92% of people. One meta-analysis found that ciprofloxacin versus doxycycline significantly increased microbiological failure.

What are the effects of antibiotic treatment for pregnant women with uncomplicated genital chlamydial infection?

LIKELY TO BE BENEFICIAL

Multiple dose regimens of erythromycin, amoxicillin

Two systematic reviews have found that both amoxicillin and erythromycin versus placebo significantly increase microbiological cure.

Single dose azithromycin

One systematic review has found that a single dose of azithromycin versus a 7 day course of erythromycin significantly increases microbiological cure.

◀ **UNKNOWN EFFECTIVENESS**

Clindamycin

One small RCT has found no significant difference in cure between clindamycin versus erythromycin.

DEFINITION Uncomplicated genital chlamydia is a sexually transmitted infection of the urethra in men and of the endocervix, urethra, or both, in women that has not ascended to the upper genital tract. Infection is asymptomatic in up to 80% of women, but may cause non-specific symptoms, including vaginal discharge and intermenstrual bleeding. Infection in men causes urethral discharge and urethral irritation or dysuria, but may also be asymptomatic in up to half of cases.[1]

INCIDENCE/ PREVALENCE Genital chlamydia is the commonest bacterial sexually transmitted infection in developed countries. In the USA, over 642 000 cases of chlamydia were reported in the year 2000.[2] The prevalence of uncomplicated genital chlamydia in women attending general practice surgeries in the UK is reported to be 3–5%.[3] Prevalence is highest in young adults. Reported rates in 15–19 year old women are about 800/100 000 in the UK,[4] 1000/100 000 in Sweden,[1] and 2500/100 000 in the USA.[5]

AETIOLOGY/ RISK FACTORS Infection is caused by the bacterium *Chlamydia trachomatis* serotypes D–K. It is transmitted primarily through sexual intercourse.

PROGNOSIS Untreated chlamydial infection may persist asymptomatically in women for at least 15 months[6] and for an unknown period in men. In women, untreated chlamydial infection that ascends to the upper genital tract causes pelvic inflammatory disease in an estimated 30–40% of women (see pelvic inflammatory disease, p 280).[7] Tubal infertility has been found to occur in about 11% of women after a single episode of pelvic inflammatory disease, and the risk of ectopic pregnancy is increased six to sevenfold.[8] Ascending infection in men causes epididymitis, but evidence that this causes male infertility is limited.[9] Maternal to infant transmission can lead to neonatal conjunctivitis and pneumonitis in 30–40% of cases.[1] Chlamydia may co-exist with other genital infections and may facilitate transmission and acquisition of HIV infection.[1]

Genital herpes

Search date July 2001

Anna Wald

What are the effects of treatments?

BENEFICIAL

Daily oral antiviral treatment in people with high rates of recurrence
RCTs have found that daily maintenance treatment with oral antiviral agents versus placebo reduces the frequency of recurrences and viral shedding.

Oral antiviral treatment in first episodes
RCTs in people with first episode genital herpes have found that oral antiviral treatment versus placebo reduces the duration of symptoms, lesions, and viral shedding but found no significant difference in the time to recurrence or frequency of subsequent recurrences.

Oral antiviral treatment taken at the start of a recurrence
RCTs have found that oral antiviral treatment versus placebo taken at the start of a recurrence reduces the duration of lesions, symptoms, and viral shedding in people with recurrent genital herpes.

LIKELY TO BE BENEFICIAL

Daily oral antiviral treatment in late pregnancy (36 or more wks of gestation) in women with a history of genital herpes
Limited evidence from RCTs in pregnant women near term with genital herpes suggests that antiviral treatment may reduce the number of women with genital lesions at term. Because women with genital lesions at term are usually offered abdominal deliveries, antiviral treatment may reduce the rate of abdominal delivery.

Male condom use to prevent sexual transmission to women
Limited evidence from a prospective cohort study suggested that male condom use versus no condom use significantly reduced the risk of sexual aquisition of herpes simplex virus type 2 in women who had sexual partners with genital herpes.

UNKNOWN EFFECTIVENESS

Male condom use to prevent sexual transmission to men
One prospective cohort study found no significant difference between male condom use versus no condom use in preventing aquisition of herpes simplex virus type 2 in men who had sexual partners with genital herpes.

Oral antiviral treatment in people with HIV infection
RCTs found insufficient evidence on the effects of antiviral treatment in people with HIV infection.

Psychotherapy to reduce recurrence
One systematic review found insufficient evidence on the effects of psychotherapy on genital herpes recurrence.

Serological screening and counselling in late pregnancy
The highest risk of mother to baby transmission is in women newly infected with genital herpes in late pregnancy. We found insufficient evidence of the effects of interventions to prevent infection in late pregnancy (such as serological screening and counselling).

◀ **UNLIKELY TO BE BENEFICIAL**

Recombinant glycoprotein vaccine (gB2 and gD2)

One RCT comparing recombinant glycoprotein vaccine (gB2 and gD2) versus placebo in people who were seronegative for HSV-2 and HIV found no significant difference in the rate of aquisition of genital herpes or HSV-2 infection.

LIKELY TO BE INEFFECTIVE OR HARMFUL

Abdominal delivery in women with genital lesions at term

We found insufficient evidence of the effects of abdominal delivery on mother to baby transmission of genital herpes. The procedure carries the risk of increased maternal morbidity and mortality.

DEFINITION Genital herpes is an infection with herpes simplex virus type 1 or type 2, causing ulceration in the genital area. Herpes simplex virus infections can be defined on the basis of virological and serological findings. Types of infection include first episode primary infection, which is herpes simplex virus in a person without prior herpes simplex virus type 1 or type 2 antibodies; first episode non-primary infection, which is herpes simplex virus type 2 in a person with prior herpes simplex virus type 1 antibodies or vice versa; first recognised recurrence, which is herpes simplex virus type 2 (or type 1) in a person with prior herpes simplex virus type 2 (or type 1) antibodies; and recurrent genital herpes, which is caused by reactivation of latent herpes simplex virus.

INCIDENCE/ Genital herpes infections are among the most common sexually transmit-
PREVALENCE ted diseases. Seroprevalence studies show that 22% of adults in the USA have herpes simplex virus type 2 antibodies.[1] A UK study found that 23% of adults attending sexual medicine clinics and 7.6% of blood donors in London had antibodies to herpes simplex virus type 2.[2]

AETIOLOGY/ Both herpes simplex virus type 1 and 2 can cause a first episode of genital
RISK FACTORS infection, but herpes simplex virus type 2 is more likely to cause recurrent disease.[3] Most people with herpes simplex virus type 2 infection are not aware that they have genital herpes, as their symptoms are mild. However, these people can pass on the infection to sexual partners and newborns.[4,5]

PROGNOSIS Sequelae of herpes simplex virus infection include neonatal herpes simplex virus infection, opportunistic infections in immunocompromised people, recurrent genital ulceration, and psychosocial morbidity. Herpes simplex virus type 2 infection is associated with an increased risk of HIV transmission and acquisition. The most common neurological complications are aseptic meningitis (reported in about a quarter of women during primary infection) and urinary retention. The absolute risk of neonatal infection is high (41%, 95% CI 26% to 56%) in babies born to women who acquire infection near the time of labour[6,7] and low (< 3%) in women with established infection, even in those who have a recurrence at term. About 15% of neonatal infections result from postnatal transmission from oral lesions.

Genital warts

Search date May 2001

DJ Wiley

What are the effects of treatments?

BENEFICIAL

Cryotherapy (as effective as podophyllin, trichloroacetic acid, and electrosurgery)

We found no RCTs comparing cryotherapy versus placebo. RCTs found no significant difference in clearance after 3 months with cryotherapy versus podophyllin, trichloroacetic acid, or electrosurgery.

Electrosurgery (better than intramuscular or subcutaneous interferon)

We found no RCTs comparing electrosurgery versus no treatment. One RCT found that electrosurgery versus intramuscular or subcutaneous interferon significantly increased wart clearance.

Imiquimod

RCTs have found that imiquimod versus placebo significantly increases wart clearance after 3 months.

Interferon, intralesional injection

RCTs have found that intralesional injection of interferon versus placebo significantly increases partial or total wart clearance.

Interferon, topical

RCTs have found that topical interferon versus placebo significantly increases wart clearance at 4 weeks (NNT 2–33).

Laser surgery (as effective as surgical excision)

We found no RCTs comparing laser surgery versus placebo or no treatment. One RCT found no significant difference with laser versus conventional surgery in wart clearance at 36 months.

Podophyllin

We found no RCTs comparing podophyllin versus placebo. RCTs have found that podophyllin resin is as effective in clearing warts as most other treatments, but is significantly less effective than surgical excision.

Podophyllotoxin

RCTs have found that podophyllotoxin versus placebo significantly increases wart clearance within 16 weeks.

Surgical excision (as effective as laser surgery)

We found no RCTs comparing surgical excision versus placebo or no treatment. One RCT found no significant difference with surgical excision versus laser surgery in wart clearance.

UNKNOWN EFFECTIVENESS

5-Fluorouracil cream; condoms in preventing human papillomavirus transmission; treatment of warts in preventing human papillomavirus transmission

We found no RCTs on the effects of these interventions.

▶

◀ **Bi- and trichloroacetic acid; interferon, topical as adjuvant treatment to laser surgery**

RCTs found insufficient evidence on the effects of these interventions.

UNLIKELY TO BE BENEFICIAL

Systemic interferon

RCTs found no significant difference with systemic interferon versus placebo in wart clearance after 3 months and found that it is associated with a range of adverse effects.

DEFINITION   External genital warts are benign epidermal growths on the external perianal and perigenital region. There are four morphological types: condylomatous, keratotic, papular, and flat warts.

INCIDENCE/   In 1996, external and internal genital warts accounted for over 180 000
PREVALENCE   initial visits to private physicians' offices in the USA: about 60 000 fewer than were reported for 1995.[1] In the USA, 1% of sexually active men and women aged 18–49 years are estimated to have external genital warts.[2]

AETIOLOGY/   External genital warts are caused by the human papillomavirus (HPV).
RISK FACTORS Although more than 70 types of HPV have been identified, most external genital warts in immunocompetent people are caused by HPV types 6 and 11.[3,4] HPV infections and, more specifically, external genital warts are sexually transmissible.

PROGNOSIS   Clinical trials have found that recurrences are frequent and may necessitate repeated treatment. Without treatment, external genital warts may remain unchanged, may increase in size or number, or may completely resolve. They rarely, if ever, progress to cancer.[5] Juvenile laryngeal papillomatosis, a rare and sometimes life threatening condition, occurs in children of women with a history of genital warts. Its rarity makes it hard to design studies that can evaluate whether treatment in pregnant women alters the risk.[6,7]

Gonorrhoea

Search date August 2001

John Moran

What are the effects of treatments?

BENEFICIAL

Single dose regimens using selected fluoroquinolones, selected cephalosporins, or spectinomycin in uncomplicated infection in men and non-pregnant women

One systematic review found limited evidence by combining cure rates across different arms of RCTs. It found that single dose regimens based on an antimicrobial agent other than a penicillin or a tetracycline achieve cure rates of 95% or higher in urogenital or rectal infection. Cure rates were lower ($\leq$80%) for pharyngeal infection. Resistance is now widespread to penicillins, tetracyclines, and sulphonamides.

Single dose regimens using selected cephalosporins or spectinomycin in uncomplicated infection in pregnant women

RCTs comparing different antimicrobial agents have found that ceftriaxone and spectinomycin cure 89–97% of rectal, cervical, and pharyngeal infections.

LIKELY TO BE BENEFICIAL

Selected injectable fluoroquinolones or selected injectable cephalosporins in disseminated infection

We found no RCTs assessing treatments for disseminated gonococcal infection published in the last 20 years, but there is strong consensus that multidose regimens using injectable cephalosporins or quinolones are the most effective treatment. We found no reports of treatment failures with these regimens.

UNKNOWN EFFECTIVENESS

Dual treatment for gonorrhoea and chlamydia infections in all people diagnosed with gonorrhoea

Dual treatment for gonorrhoea and chlamydia infections is based on theory and expert opinion rather than on evidence from RCTs. The balance between benefits and harms will vary with the prevalence of co-infection in each population.

DEFINITION Gonorrhoea is caused by infection with *Neisseria gonorrhoeae*. In men, uncomplicated urethritis is the most common manifestation, with dysuria and urethral discharge. Less typically, signs and symptoms are mild and indistinguishable from chlamydial urethritis. In women the most common manifestation is cervicitis, which produces symptoms (e.g. vaginal discharge, lower abdominal discomfort, and dyspareunia) in only half of the women. Co-infection with chlamydia is reported in 20–40% of people.[1]

INCIDENCE/ PREVALENCE Between 1975 and 1996, the incidence of reported gonorrhoea in the USA fell by 74%, reaching a level in 1996 of 122/100 000 people. Since 1996, between 123 and 133 cases have been reported per 100 000 people each year.[2] In the UK, diagnoses of gonorrhoea have increased since 1994, reaching 39/100 000 males and 17/100 000 females in 1999.[3] In poor communities, rates may be higher: the estimated incidence in people aged 15–59 years living in three inner London boroughs in 1994–1995 ▶

was 138/100 000 women and 292/100 000 men.[4] Rates are highest in younger people. In the USA in 1999, incidence was highest in women aged 15–19 years (716/100 000) and men aged 20–24 years (590/100 000).[2]

AETIOLOGY/ RISK FACTORS Most infections result from penile-vaginal, penile-rectal, or penile-pharyngeal contact. An important minority of infections are transmitted from mother to child during birth, which can cause ophthalmia neonatorum. Less common are ocular infections in older children and adults as a result of sexual exposure, poor hygiene, or the medicinal use of urine.

PROGNOSIS The natural history of untreated gonococcal infection is spontaneous resolution after weeks or months of unpleasant symptoms. During this time, there is a substantial likelihood of transmission to others and of complications developing in the infected individual.[5] Symptoms in most men are severe enough to cause them to seek treatment, but an estimated 1–3% of infected men remain asymptomatic. These men, and men who are infectious but not yet symptomatic, are largely responsible for the spread of the disease. In many women, the lack of readily discernible signs or symptoms of cervicitis means that infections go unrecognised and untreated. An unknown proportion of untreated infections causes local complications, including lymphangitis, periurethral abscess, bartholinitis, and urethral stricture; epididymitis in men; and in women involvement of the uterus, fallopian tubes, or ovaries causing pelvic inflammatory disease (see pelvic inflammatory disease, p 280). It is the association of gonorrhoea with pelvic inflammatory disease — a major cause of secondary infertility, ectopic pregnancy, and chronic pelvic pain — that makes gonorrhoea an important public health issue. Manifestations of disseminated infection are petechial or pustular skin lesions; asymmetrical arthropathies, tenosynovitis, or septic arthritis; and, rarely, meningitis or endocarditis.

Partner notification

Search date July 2001

Catherine Mathews, Nicol Coetzee, Merrick Zwarenstein and Sally Guttmacher

Sexual health

What are the effects of different partner notification strategies in different groups of people and what are the effects of interventions to improve patient referral?

LIKELY TO BE BENEFICIAL

Contract referral (as effective as provider referral in people with syphilis)

One systematic review of one RCT comparing different partner notification strategies in people with syphilis found no significant difference in the proportion of partners notified between provider🅖 and contract referral🅖, when people receiving the contract referral option were given only 2 days to notify their partners.

Provider referral, contract referral, or offering a choice between provider and patient referral (versus patient referral alone) in people with HIV, gonorrhoea, or chlamydia

One systematic review comparing different partner notification strategies found that in people with HIV, offering a choice between provider referral (where the identity of the index patient was not revealed) and patient referral🅖 was more effective than offering patient referral alone. It found that in people with gonorrhoea infections, contract referral versus patient referral significantly increased the number of partners presenting for treatment. In chlamydia infections, provider referral versus patient referral significantly increased the proportion of partners assessed per patient (NNT 2) and of positive partners detected per patient (NNT 17). The systematic review found no good evidence on the effects of these strategies on relationships between patients and partners and, in particular, on the rate of violence, abuse, and abandonment of patient or partner.

UNKNOWN EFFECTIVENESS

Adding telephone reminders and contact cards to patient referral; patient referral with educational videos; patient referral by different types of healthcare professionals

We found insufficient evidence about the effects of these interventions in improving partner notification.

DEFINITION Partner notification is a process whereby the sexual partners of people with a diagnosis of sexually transmitted infection are informed of their exposure to infection. The main methods are patient referral, provider referral, contract referral, and outreach assistance.

INCIDENCE/ PREVALENCE A large proportion of people with sexually transmitted infections will have neither symptoms nor signs of infection. For example, 22–68% of men with gonorrhoea who were identified through partner notification were asymptomatic.[1] Partner notification is one of the two strategies to reach such individuals, the other strategy being screening. Managing infection in people with more than one current sexual partner is likely to have the greatest impact on the spread of sexually transmitted infections.[2]

◀ PROGNOSIS Studies showing that partner notification results in a health benefit, either to the partner or to future partners of infected partners, are not available. Obtaining such evidence would be technically and ethically difficult. One RCT in asymptomatic women compared identifying, testing, and treating women at increased risk for cervical chlamydial infection versus usual care. It found testing reduced incidence of pelvic inflammatory disease (RR 0.44, 95% CI 0.2 to 0.9).[3] This evidence suggests that partner notification, which also aims to identify and treat people who are largely unaware of infection, would provide a direct health benefit to partners who are infected.

Pelvic inflammatory disease

Search date August 2001

Jonathan Ross

What are the effects of treatments?

LIKELY TO BE BENEFICIAL

Antibiotics (symptoms improved and microbiological clearance in women with confirmed pelvic inflammatory disease)

One systematic review of observational studies and RCTs has found that several regimens of antibiotic treatment are effective in relieving the symptoms of pelvic inflammatory disease and achieving high rates of microbiological cure.

UNKNOWN EFFECTIVENESS

Different durations of antibiotic treatment

Systematic reviews found no good evidence on the optimal duration of treatment.

Empirical antibiotic treatment

We found no RCTs comparing empirical treatment with antibiotics (before receiving results of microbiological tests) versus delaying treatment until test results are available.

Oral versus parenteral antibiotics

Two RCTs found no significant difference between different oral and parenteral regimens.

Routine antibiotic prophylaxis prior to intrauterine device insertion *New*

One systematic review found no significant difference with routine prophylaxis with doxycycline versus placebo prior to intrauterine contraceptive device insertion in pelvic inflammatory disease. The absolute risk of pelvic inflammatory disease following intrauterine contraceptive device insertion was low. However, the systematic review may have insufficient power to rule out a clinically important difference.

DEFINITION   Pelvic inflammatory disease is inflammation and infection of the upper genital tract in women, typically involving the fallopian tubes, ovaries, and surrounding structures.

INCIDENCE/   The exact incidence of pelvic inflammatory disease is unknown because
PREVALENCE   the disease cannot be diagnosed reliably from clinical symptoms and signs.[1–3] Direct visualisation of the fallopian tubes by laparoscopy is the best single diagnostic test, but it is invasive and not used routinely in clinical practice. Pelvic inflammatory disease is the most common gynaecological reason for admission to hospital in the USA, accounting for 49/10 000 recorded hospital discharges. However, because most pelvic inflammatory diseases are asymptomatic, this figure underestimates the true prevalence.[1,4] A crude marker of pelvic inflammatory disease in developing countries can be obtained from reported hospital admission rates, where it accounts for 17–40% of gynaecological admissions in sub-Saharan Africa, 15–37% in Southeast Asia, and 3–10% in India.[5]

AETIOLOGY/   Factors associated with pelvic inflammatory disease mirror those for sexually
RISK FACTORS transmitted infections: young age, reduced socioeconomic circumstances, African/Afro-Caribbean ethnicity, lower educational attainment, and recent new sexual partner.[2,6,7] Most cases seem to result from ascending infection from the cervix. Initial epithelial damage caused by bacteria (especially ▶

Chlamydia trachomatis and *Neisseria gonorrhoeae*) allows the opportunistic entry of other organisms. Isolates from the upper genital tract are polymicrobial, including *Mycoplasma hominis* and anaerobes.[8] The spread of infection to the upper genital tract may be increased by vaginal douching and instrumentation of the cervix, but reduced by the barrier method and oral contraceptives compared with other forms of contraception.[9–12]

PROGNOSIS   Pelvic inflammatory disease has high morbidity; about 20% of affected women become infertile, 20% develop chronic pelvic pain, and 10% of those who conceive have an ectopic pregnancy.[2] We found no placebo controlled trials of antibiotic treatment. Uncontrolled observations suggest that clinical symptoms and signs resolve in a significant number of untreated women.[13] Repeated episodes of pelvic inflammatory disease are associated with a four to six times increase in the risk of permanent tubal damage.[14]

Athlete's foot and fungally infected toe nails

Search date October 2001

Fay Crawford

What are the effects of treatments?

BENEFICIAL

Oral allylamines* for athlete's foot *New*

One RCT identified by a systematic review found limited evidence that oral terbinafine versus placebo for 6 weeks significantly improved cure rates at 8 weeks (NNT 2). One RCT found that oral terbinafine versus oral itraconazole for 2 weeks significantly increased cure rates, but found no significant difference in cure rates with 2 weeks of oral terbinafine versus 4 weeks of oral itraconazole.

Topical allylamines* for athlete's foot

One systematic review and two subsequent RCTs have found that allylamines versus placebo significantly increase the proportion of people cured at 6–16 weeks (NNT about 2). One systematic review and two additional RCTs have found that allylamines produce a faster response than azoles, but the cure rates are similar.

Oral azoles* for athlete's foot *New*

One RCT identified by a systematic review found that oral itraconazole versus placebo for 1 week significantly increased cure rates at 8 weeks. The review found no significant difference in cure rates between individual azoles and oral allylamines, or between oral azoles and oral griseofulvin.

Topical azoles* for athlete's foot

One systematic review has found that azole creams versus placebo administered for 4–6 weeks significantly increase cure rates at 6–10 weeks (NNT 2). One systematic review and two additional RCTs have found that azoles produce a slower response than allylamines, but the cure rates are similar.

Topical tolnaftate* for athlete's foot

One systematic review has found that tolnaftate versus placebo for 4 weeks significantly reduces treatment failure after 5–8 weeks (NNT 2).

Topical undecenoic acid for athlete's foot

One systematic review has found that undecenoic acid versus placebo significantly reduces treatment failure (NNT 2).

LIKELY TO BE BENEFICIAL

Topical acidified nitrite cream for athlete's foot

One systematic review of one RCT found limited evidence that topical nitrate plus salicylic acid versus salicylic acid alone for 4 weeks significantly improved cure rate.

Topical butenafine for fungal nail infections

RCTs found limited evidence that butenafine cream in combination with either urea or tea tree oil versus placebo significantly improved cure rates at 16–36 weeks (NNT 2).

Topical ciclopiroxolamine for athlete's foot

One systematic review of one RCT found that topical ciclopiroxolamine versus placebo for 4 weeks significantly reduced treatment failure at 6 weeks (NNT 2). ▶

Topical ciclopiroxolamine for fungal nail infections

RCTs found that ciclopiroxolamine lacquer versus placebo significantly improved cure rates at 48 weeks.

Topical griseofulvin for athlete's foot

One systematic review of one RCT found that topical griseofulvin versus placebo significantly reduced treatment failure (NNT 2).

*See table on the CD for a list of allylamines and azoles in common use.

DEFINITION	Athlete's foot is a cutaneous fungal infection that causes the skin to itch, flake, and fissure. Nail involvement is characterised by ungual thickening and discolouration.
INCIDENCE/ PREVALENCE	In the UK, athlete's foot is present in about 15% of the general population,[1] and 1.2 million people have fungally infected toe nails.[2]
AETIOLOGY/ RISK FACTORS	Swimming pool users and industrial workers may have increased risk of fungal foot infection. However, one survey found fungal foot infection in only 9% of swimmers, with the highest incidence (20%) in men aged 16 years and over.[1]
PROGNOSIS	Fungal infections of the foot are not life threatening in people with normal immunity, but in some people they cause persistent symptoms. Others are apparently oblivious of persistent infection. The infection can spread to other parts of the body and to other individuals.

Atopic eczema

Search date September 2001

Dominic Smethurst

What are the effects of preventive interventions and treatments?

BENEFICIAL

Topical steroids

One systematic review has found that topical corticosteroids versus placebo improve the signs and symptoms of eczema after 1–4 weeks and are safe in the short term. We found little good information on their long term adverse effects. One RCT found insufficient evidence about the effects of topical steroids in preventing relapse.

LIKELY TO BE BENEFICIAL

Control of house dust mite

RCTs found limited evidence suggesting that controlling house dust mite significantly reduced severity of symptoms at 6–12 months. We found conflicting evidence about the effects of reducing dust mites in people with atopic eczema and positive mite radioallergosorbent test scores.

Dietary manipulation during lactation in mothers of predisposed infants

Limited evidence from one systematic review suggests that maternal dietary restriction during lactation may protect against the development of eczema at 12–18 months in infants with a family history of atopy.

Emollients

One systematic review has found that emollient plus topical corticosteroid versus topical corticosteroids alone significantly improves clinical signs and symptoms of atopic eczema after 3 weeks.

UNKNOWN EFFECTIVENESS

Avoidance of animal contact; avoidance of vaccination/immunisation; avoidance of all washing detergents

We found no RCTs about the effects of these preventive interventions.

Avoidance of biological washing detergents

One systematic review found no significant difference with washing detergents that contain enzymes versus washing detergents without enzymes in eczema severity at 1 month.

Avoidance of specified clothing textiles

RCTs found limited evidence that, in people with atopic eczema, the roughness of clothing textiles is a more important factor for skin irritation than the type of textile fibre (synthetic or natural). One RCT in infants with atopic eczema comparing cotton nappy/diaper versus cellulose core nappy/diaper versus cellulose core nappy/diaper containing absorbent gelling found no significant difference in eczema scores after 26 weeks.

Dietary manipulation

One systematic review in children and adults with atopic eczema found inconclusive evidence about the effects of dietary manipulation, such as exclusion of egg and cow's milk.

◄ **Dietary manipulation during pregnancy in mothers of predisposed infants**
One systematic review found no significant difference with maternal diet restriction during pregnancy versus no restriction in development of atopic eczema in the infant at 12–18 months.

Prolonged breast feeding in predisposed infants

Limited observational evidence suggests that exclusive breast feeding for at least 5 months reduced the risk of eczema at 1–3 years in infants with a family history of atopy.

Wet wrap dressing and bandaging

One systematic review identified no RCTs on the effects of wet wrap◉ or other forms of bandaging.

UNLIKELY TO BE BENEFICIAL

Topical antimicrobial plus steroid combinations

One systematic review has found no significant difference with topical anti-microbial agents plus steroids versus topical steroids alone in improving the clinical signs and symptoms of atopic eczema.

DEFINITION Atopic eczema (atopic dermatitis) is an inflammatory skin disease charac-terised by an itchy erythematous poorly demarcated skin eruption with a predilection for skin creases.[1]

INCIDENCE/ Atopic eczema affects 15–20% of school children in the UK and 2–3% of
PREVALENCE adults.[2] Prevalence has increased substantially over the past 30 years,[3] possibly because of environmental and lifestyle changes.

AETIOLOGY/ Aetiology is believed to be multifactorial. Recent interest has focused on
RISK FACTORS airborne allergens (house dust mites, pollen, animal dander), outdoor pollution, climate, diet, and prenatal/early life factors such as infections.

PROGNOSIS Although there is currently no cure, several interventions can help to control symptoms. Atopic eczema clears in 60–70% of children by their early teens, although relapses may occur.

Cellulitis and erysipelas

Search date October 2001

Andrew Morris

What are the effects of treatments?

LIKELY TO BE BENEFICIAL

Antibiotics

We found no RCTs comparing antibiotics versus placebo. RCTs comparing different single antibiotic regimens found clinical cure in 50–100% of people at 4–30 days. The RCTs were not designed to detect a clinically important difference between antibiotics.

UNKNOWN EFFECTIVENESS

Different antibiotic regimens; oral versus intravenous antibiotics; short versus long courses of antibiotics

We found no RCTs comparing oral versus intravenous antibiotics, or different durations of treatment. RCTs comparing different antibiotic regimens were not designed to detect clinically significant differences.

Treatment of predisposing factors to prevent recurrence

We found no RCTs or observational studies on the effects of treatment of predisposing factors on recurrence of cellulitis or erysipelas.

DEFINITION   Cellulitis is a spreading bacterial infection of the dermis and subcutaneous tissues. It causes local signs of inflammation such as warmth, erythema, pain, and lymphangitis, and frequently systemic upset with fever and raised white blood cell count. Erysipelas differs from cellulitis in that it tends to be more superficial, with a clearly demarcated edge. The lower limbs are by far the commonest sites, but any area can be affected.

INCIDENCE/   We found no specific data on the incidence of cellulitis. However, in the UK
PREVALENCE   in 1991, cellulitis and abscess infections were responsible for 158 consultations/10 000 person years at risk. In 1985, skin and subcutaneous tissue infections resulted in 29 820 hospital admissions and a mean occupancy of 664 hospital beds each day.[1,2]

AETIOLOGY/   The commonest infective organisms in adults are *Streptococci* (particularly
RISK FACTORS *S pyogenes*) and *Staphylococcus aureus*.[3] In children, *Haemophilus influenzae* is a frequent cause. Several risk factors for cellulitis/erysipelas have been identified in a case control study (167 cases and 294 controls): lymphoedema (OR 71.2, 95% CI 5.6 to 908.0), leg ulcer (OR 62.5, 95% CI 7.0 to 556.0), toe web intertrigo (OR 13.9, 95% CI 7.2 to 27.0), and traumatic wounds (OR 10.7, 95% CI 4.8 to 23.8).[4]

PROGNOSIS   Cellulitis can spread through the bloodstream and lymphatic system. A retrospective case note study of people admitted to hospital with cellulitis found that systemic symptoms such as fever and raised white blood cell count were present in up to 42% of cases at presentation.[5] Lymphatic involvement can lead to obstruction and damage that predisposes to ▶

recurrent cellulitis. Recurrence can occur rapidly or after months or years. One study found that 29% of people with erysipelas had a recurrent episode within 3 years.[6] Local necrosis and abscess formation can also occur. It is not known whether the prognosis of erysipelas differs from that of cellulitis. We found no evidence about factors that predict recurrence, or a better or worse outcome. We found no good evidence on the prognosis of untreated cellulitis.

Chronic plaque psoriasis

Search date September 2001

Luigi Naldi and Bethold Rzany

What are the effects of treatments?

BENEFICIAL

Ingram regimen

One large RCT has found that the Ingram regimen**ⓖ** is of similar effectiveness to PUVA in clearing moderate to severe psoriasis.

Psoralen plus ultraviolet A (PUVA)

One systematic review has found that clearing of psoriasis is more likely with higher versus lower doses of psoralen, and that the mean cumulative dose of UVA required for clearance is significantly reduced. Long term treatment risks include photoageing and skin cancer (mainly squamous cell carcinoma).

Vitamin D derivatives

Systematic reviews and additional long term uncontrolled studies have found that calcipotriol versus placebo improves plaque psoriasis and is at least as effective as topical steroids, coal tars, and dithranol. One review found that calcipotriol monotherapy caused more irritation than potent topical steroids.

LIKELY TO BE BENEFICIAL

Dithranol

Small RCTs have found that dithranol versus placebo improves chronic plaque psoriasis.

Topical retinoids (tazarotene)

RCTs have found that tazarotene versus placebo improves chronic plaque psoriasis in the short term. One RCT has found that tazarotene plus topical steroids versus calcipotriol improves short term outcomes.

Ultraviolet B (UVB)

There is a consensus that UVB is effective, but one systematic review has found insufficient evidence on the effects of UVB versus other treatments, or on the effects of narrow band versus broad band UVB for either clearance or maintenance treatment.

TRADE OFF BETWEEN BENEFITS AND HARMS

Alefacept *New*

One RCT found limited evidence that alefacept versus placebo may improve psoriasis. Adverse effects included dizziness, accidents, chills, and cough.

Ciclosporin

One systematic review has found optimal clearance rates with a ciclosporin dose of 5.0 mg/kg a day. Any advantage of doses greater than 5.0 mg/kg a day may be offset by an increase in dose related side effects, particularly increased renal toxicity.

Etanercept *New*

One small RCT found limited evidence that etanercept versus placebo may improve psoriasis. Reported adverse effects include skin reactions, urticarial manifestations, and upper respiratory tract infections.

▶

◀ **Infliximab** *New*

One RCT found limited evidence that infliximab versus placebo may improve psoriasis. Reported adverse effects include lupus-like syndrome and severe infections.

Oral retinoids (etretinate, acitretin, liarazole)

RCTs found limited evidence that oral retinoids alone may achieve complete clearance in people with plaque psoriasis. The number of people with complete clearance is increased by combination with PUVA or UVB. We found insufficient evidence on the effects of liarozole. We found little reliable evidence on the effects of oral retinoids as maintenance treatment. Adverse effects lead to discontinuation of treatment in 10–20% of people. Teratogenicity renders oral retinoids less acceptable.

Topical steroids

RCTs have found that topical steroids improve psoriasis in the short term. Topical steroids may cause striae and atrophy, which increase with clinical potency and use of occlusive dressings. Continuous use may lead to adrenocortical suppression, and case reports suggest that severe flares of the disease may occur on withdrawal.

Tacrolimus *New*

One RCT found limited evidence that tacrolimus versus placebo may improve psoriasis. Adverse effects are reported to be similar to those of ciclosporin.

UNKNOWN EFFECTIVENESS

Acupuncture; antistreptococcal treatments; balneotherapy; fish oil; heliotherapy; lifestyle changes; oral vitamin D; stress reduction; sunbeds

We found insufficient evidence on the effects of these interventions.

Emollients and keratolytics

We found no clear evidence on the effects of emollients and keratolytics.

Fumaric acid derivatives

One systematic review found limited evidence that oral fumaric acid esters provided short term improvement or complete clearing of psoriasis. Monoethylfumarate on its own has not been found to have a beneficial effect. The incidence of acute adverse effects (flushing and gastrointestinal symptoms) is high; 30–40% of patients discontinue treatment because of adverse effects, non-compliance, or both. We found no evidence on the effects of fumaric acid derivatives as maintenance treatment.

Goeckerman treatment

We found no good evidence on the effects of the Goeckerman treatment𝐆.

Methotrexate

Limited evidence from one small RCT in people with psoriatic arthritis suggests that methotrexate may improve skin lesions in psoriasis. Non-randomised evidence suggests that clearance can be maintained as long as treatment is continued. About half of people relapse within 6 months of stopping treatment. Methotrexate can induce acute myelosuppression. Long term methotrexate carries the risk of hepatic fibrosis and cirrhosis, which is related to the dose regimen employed.

Tars

Small RCTs have found conflicting results on the effects of tars in combination with UVB exposure.

▶

Chronic plaque psoriasis

◄ **DEFINITION**   Chronic plaque psoriasis is a chronic inflammatory skin disease that is characterised by well demarcated erythematous scaly patches on the extensor surfaces of the body and scalp. The lesions may itch, sting, and occasionally bleed. Dystrophic nail changes are found in more than a third of people with chronic plaque psoriasis, and psoriatic arthropathy occurs in 1–3%. The condition waxes and wanes, with wide variations in course and severity among individuals. Other varieties of psoriasis include guttate, inverse, pustular, and erythrodermic psoriasis. This review deals with treatments for chronic plaque psoriasis.

INCIDENCE/ Psoriasis affects 1–2% of the general population. It is believed to be less
PREVALENCE frequent in people from Africa and Asia, but we found no reliable epidemiological data.[1]

AETIOLOGY/ About a third of people with psoriasis have a family history of psoriasis, but
RISK FACTORS physical trauma, acute infection, and some medications (e.g. lithium salts and β blockers) are believed to trigger the condition. A few observational studies have linked the onset or relapse of psoriasis with stressful life events and personal habits, including cigarette smoking and, less consistently, alcohol consumption. Others have found an association of psoriasis with body mass index⑤ and an inverse association with intake of fruit and vegetables.

PROGNOSIS We found no long term prognostic studies. With the exceptions of erythrodermic and acute generalised pustular psoriasis (severe conditions that affect less than 1% of people with psoriasis and that require intensive hospital care), psoriasis is not known to affect mortality. Psoriasis may substantially affect quality of life.[2] At present there is no cure for psoriasis.

What are the effects of treatments?

LIKELY TO BE BENEFICIAL

Insecticide based pharmaceutical products

RCTs have found that permethrin or malathion versus placebo significantly reduce the number of people with head lice at 1 week (NNT 2 for malathion), and that permethrin versus lindane significantly reduces the number of people with head lice.

UNKNOWN EFFECTIVENESS

Essential oils and other chemicals used as repellents; herbal treatments; mechanical removal of lice by combing; removal of viable louse eggs by "nit" combing

We found insufficient evidence on the effects of these interventions.

DEFINITION
Head lice are obligate ectoparasites of socially active humans. They infest the scalp and attach their eggs to the hair shafts. Itching, resulting from multiple bites, is not diagnostic but may increase the index of suspicion. Infestation can be diagnosed only by finding living lice. Eggs glued to hairs, whether hatched (nits) or unhatched, are not proof of active infection, because eggs may retain a viable appearance for weeks after death.

INCIDENCE/ PREVALENCE
We found no studies on incidence and no recent published prevalence results from any developed country. Anecdotal reports suggest that prevalence has increased in the past few years in most communities in the UK and USA.

AETIOLOGY/ RISK FACTORS
Observational studies indicate that infections occur most frequently in school children, although there is no proof of a link with school attendance.[1,2] We found no evidence that lice prefer clean hair to dirty hair.

PROGNOSIS
The infection is almost harmless. Sensitisation reactions to louse saliva and faeces may result in localised irritation and erythema. Secondary infection of scratches may occur. Lice have been identified as primary mechanical vectors of scalp pyoderma caused by streptococci and staphylococci usually found on the skin.[3]

Herpes labialis

Search date August 2001

Graham Worrall

What are the effects of preventive interventions?

LIKELY TO BE BENEFICIAL

Oral aciclovir

Limited evidence from RCTs suggests that prophylactic oral aciclovir versus placebo may reduce the frequency and severity of attacks, but the optimal timing and duration of treatment is uncertain.

Sunscreen

One small RCT found that ultraviolet sunscreen versus placebo significantly reduced herpes recurrence.

UNKNOWN EFFECTIVENESS

Topical antiviral agents

We found no RCTs on the effects of topical antiviral agents used as prophylaxis.

What are the effects of treatments?

LIKELY TO BE BENEFICIAL

Oral aciclovir for first attack

RCTs in children have found that oral aciclovir versus placebo marginally but significantly reduces the duration of symptoms and pain.

Oral aciclovir for recurrent attack

RCTs have found that oral aciclovir versus placebo (if taken early in the attack) marginally but significantly reduces the duration of symptoms and pain.

UNKNOWN EFFECTIVENESS

Topical anaesthetic agents; topical antiviral agents for first attack; zinc oxide cream

We found insufficient evidence on the effects of these interventions.

Topical antiviral agents for recurrent attacks

RCTs found limited evidence that topical antiviral agents versus placebo may significantly reduce healing times, duration of pain and time to crusting of the lesions.

DEFINITION   Herpes labialis is a mild self limiting infection with herpes simplex virus type 1. It causes pain and blistering on the lips and perioral area (cold sores); fever and constitutional symptoms are rare. Most people have no warning of an attack, but some experience a recognisable prodrome.

INCIDENCE/   Herpes labialis accounts for about 1% of primary care consultations in the
PREVALENCE   UK each year; 20–40% of people have experienced cold sores at some time.[1]

◀ **AETIOLOGY/** Herpes labialis is caused by herpes simplex virus type 1. After the primary
RISK FACTORS infection, which usually occurs in childhood, the virus is thought to remain
latent in the trigeminal ganglion.[2] A variety of factors, including exposure to
bright sunlight, fatigue, or psychological stress, can precipitate a recurrence.

PROGNOSIS In most people, herpes labialis is a mild, self limiting illness. Recurrences are
usually shorter and less severe than the initial attack. Healing is usually
complete in 7–10 days without scarring.[3] Rates of reactivation are unknown.
Herpes labialis can cause serious illness in immunocompromised patients.

Malignant melanoma: non-metastatic

Search date October 2001

David Crosby, Thomas Crosby and Malcolm Mason

What are the effects of preventive interventions and treatments?

LIKELY TO BE BENEFICIAL

High dose adjuvant alfa-2$_b$ interferon

RCTs have found that high dose alfa-2$_b$ interferon versus no adjuvant treatment significantly extends the time to relapse and may improve overall survival, but have found that toxicity (myelosuppression, hepatotoxicity, and neurotoxicity) and withdrawal rates are high.

UNKNOWN EFFECTIVENESS

Low dose adjuvant alfa-2$_b$ interferon

RCTs found inconsistent evidence on the effects on survival of low dose alfa-2$_b$ interferon versus no adjuvant treatment. Toxicity occurred in 10% of people.

Other adjuvant treatments(non-specific immunotherapy and chemotherapy)

RCTs found no evidence of improved survival with non-specific immunotherapy (e.g bacille Calmette-Guérin or *Corynebacterium parvum*). RCTs found no difference in survival with single agent cytotoxic agents (especially dacarbazine), chemoimmunotherapy, and multi-agent cytotoxic treatments versus placebo.

Sunscreens in prevention

We found no RCTs about the preventive effects of sunscreens.

UNLIKELY TO BE BENEFICIAL

Prophylactic lymph node dissection

Four RCTs found no significant difference in overall survival with elective lymph node dissection versus surgery deferred until clinical recurrence, but an effect within subgroups cannot be ruled out.

Wide primary excision (no better than less radical surgery)

RCTs have found no difference in survival or local recurrence with wide primary excision (4–5 cm margins) versus narrow incision (1–2 cm margins). Wide excision increases the need for skin grafting.

DEFINITION   Cutaneous malignant melanoma is a tumour derived from melanocytes in the basal layer of the epidermis. After undergoing malignant transformation, it becomes invasive by penetrating into and beyond the dermis.

INCIDENCE/   Incidence in developed countries has increased by 50% in the past
PREVALENCE   20 years. Incidence varies in different populations❶ and is about 10-fold higher in white than in non-white populations. Despite the rise in incidence, mortality has plateaued and even fallen in some populations (e.g. in women and young men in Australia).[1,2] During the same period there has been a sixfold increase in the incidence of melanoma *in situ*, suggesting earlier detection.

AETIOLOGY/   The number of common, atypical, and dysplastic naevi on a person's body
RISK FACTORS   correlates closely with the risk of developing malignant melanoma. A genetic predisposition probably accounts for 5–10% of all cases. Although the risk of developing malignant melanoma is higher in fair skinned white populations ▶

living close to the equator, the relation between sun exposure, sunscreen use, and skin type is not clear cut. Exposure to excessive sunlight and severe sunburn in childhood are associated with an increased risk of developing malignant melanoma in adult life. However, people do not necessarily develop tumours at sites of maximum exposure to the sun.

PROGNOSIS The prognosis of early malignant melanoma (stages I–III)❶ relates to the depth of invasion of the primary lesion, the presence of ulceration, and involvement of the regional lymph nodes, with the prognosis worsening with the number of nodes involved.[3] A person with a thin lesion (Breslow depth❻ < 0.75 mm) and without lymph node involvement has a 3% risk of developing metastases and a 95% chance of surviving 5 years.[4] If regional lymph nodes are macroscopically involved there is a 20–50% chance of surviving 5 years. Most studies have shown a better prognosis in women and in people with lesions on the extremities compared with those with lesions on the trunk.

Non-genital warts

Search date September 2001

Michael Bigby, Sam Gibbs, Ian Harvey and Jane Sterling

What are the effects of treatments? New

LIKELY TO BE BENEFICIAL

Topical treatments containing salicylic acid

One systematic review has found that simple topical treatments containing salicylic acid versus placebo significantly increase the number of people with complete wart clearance, successful treatment, or loss of one or more warts after 6–12 weeks (NNT 4).

Cryotherapy

One systematic review found limited evidence from two small RCTs that cryotherapy is no more effective than placebo in increasing the proportion of people with wart clearance after 2–4 months. However, the review also identified two larger RCTs that found cryotherapy was as effective as salicylic acid in wart clearance at 3–6 months.

Contact immunotherapy (dinitrochlorobenzene)

One systematic review has found that contact immunotherapy❂ with dinitrochlorobenzene versus placebo significantly increases the number of people with wart clearance.

UNKNOWN EFFECTIVENESS

Intralesional bleomycin

RCTs found conflicting evidence about the effects of intralesional bleomycin. Two RCTs found that intralesional bleomycin versus placebo significantly increased the number of warts cured after 6 weeks. One RCT found no significant difference with bleomycin versus placebo in the number of people with wart clearance after 30 days, and another RCT found that bleomycin cured fewer warts than placebo after 3 months. One RCT found no significant difference between different concentrations of bleomycin in the number of warts cured after 3 months.

Carbon dioxide laser

One systematic review identified no RCTs about the effects of carbon dioxide laser.

Cimetidine

Three small RCTs found insufficient evidence about the effects of cimetidine versus placebo in the number of people with wart clearance after 12 weeks, and one RCT found insufficient evidence about the effects of cimetidine versus local treatments.

Distant healing

One RCT found insufficient evidence about the effects of distant healing on wart clearance.

Hypnotic suggestion

We found no RCTs on the effects of hypnotic suggestion in clearance of warts.

Inosine pranobex

One RCT found insufficient evidence about the effects of inosine pranobex on wart clearance.

▶

◀ **Systemic interferon alfa**

We found no RCTs of sufficient quality about systemic interferon alfa.

Levamisole

Two RCTs and one controlled clinical trial found insufficient evidence about the effects of levamisole versus placebo on the clearance of warts. One RCT found that levamisole plus cimetidine versus cimetidine alone significantly increased the number of people with wart clearance.

Photodynamic therapy

RCTs found insufficient evidence about the effects of photodynamic therapy❻ on wart clearance.

Pulsed dye laser

One RCT found insufficient evidence about the effects of pulsed dye laser in number of warts cured.

Surgical procedures

One systematic review identified no RCTs about the effects of surgical procedures on wart clearance.

UNLIKELY TO BE BENEFICIAL

Homeopathy

Two RCTs found no significant difference with homeopathy versus placebo in the number of people with wart clearance after 18 weeks.

DEFINITION Non-genital warts are an extremely common, benign, and usually self limiting skin disease. Infection of epidermal cells with the human papillomavirus results in cell proliferation and a thickened, warty papule on the skin. Any area of skin can be infected but the commonest sites involved are the hands and feet. Genital warts are not covered in this review (see p 274).

INCIDENCE/ There are few reliable, population based data on the incidence and
PREVALENCE prevalence of common warts. Prevalence probably varies widely between different age groups, populations, and periods of time. Two large population based studies found prevalence rates of 0.84% in the USA[1] and 12.9% in Russia.[2] Prevalence rates are highest in children and young adults, and two studies in school populations have shown prevalence rates of 12% in 4–6 year olds in the UK[3] and 24% in 16–18 year olds in Australia.[4]

AETIOLOGY/ Warts are caused by human papillomavirus, of which there are over 70
RISK FACTORS different types. They are most common at sites of trauma such as the hands and feet, and probably result from inoculation of virus into minimally damaged areas of epithelium. Warts on the feet can be acquired from common bare foot areas. One observational study (146 adolescents) found that the prevalence of warts on the feet was 27% in those that used a communal shower room versus 1.3% in those that used the locker room.[5] Hand warts are also an occupational risk for butchers and meat handlers. One cross-sectional survey (1086 people) found that the prevalence of hand warts was 33% in abattoir workers, 34% in retail butchers, 20% in engineering fitters, and 15% in office workers.[6] Immunosuppression is another important risk factor. One observational study in immunosuppressed renal transplant recipients found that, at 5 years or longer after transplantation, 90% had warts.[7]

PROGNOSIS   Non-genital warts in immunocompetent people are harmless and usually resolve spontaneously as a result of natural immunity within months or years. The rate of resolution is highly variable and probably depends on a number of factors including host immunity, age, human papillomavirus type, and site of infection. One cohort study (1000 institutionalised children) found that two thirds of warts resolved without treatment within a 2 year period.[8] One systematic review (search date 2000, 17 RCTs) comparing local treatments versus placebo found that about 30% of people taking placebo (range 0–73%) had no warts after about 10 weeks (range 4–24 wk).[9]

What are the effects of treatments?

BENEFICIAL

Permethrin

One systematic review has found that permethrin versus crotamiton significantly increases clinical and parasitic cure after 28 days. The review suggests that permethrin is as effective as lindane in cure, with fewer adverse effects.

LIKELY TO BE BENEFICIAL

Crotamiton

One systematic review found no significant difference between crotamiton versus lindane in clinical cure, but found that crotamiton is less effective than permethrin.

Oral ivermectin

One systematic review found limited evidence that oral ivermectin versus placebo significantly increased clinical cure, and found no significant difference between oral ivermectin versus lindane in clinical cure. Experience of the use of oral ivermectin in onchocerciasis suggests that it is safe in younger adults, but no such experience exists for children, and there have been reports of increased risk of death in elderly people.

TRADE OFF BETWEEN BENEFITS AND HARMS

Lindane

One systematic review found limited evidence that lindane was as effective as crotamiton, permethrin, or oral ivermectin in clinical cure, but found rare reports of convulsions and other severe adverse effects.

UNKNOWN EFFECTIVENESS

Benzyl benzoate; sulphur compounds

One systematic review found insufficient evidence on the effects of these interventions.

Malathion

One systematic review identified no RCTs on the effects of malathion. Case series have found that malathion cures over 80% of people, but its safety has not been assessed adequately.

DEFINITION   Scabies is an infestation of the skin by the mite *Sarcoptes scabiei*.[1] Typical sites of infestation are skin folds and flexor surfaces. In adults, the most common sites are between the fingers and on the wrists, although infection may manifest in elderly people as a diffuse truncal eruption. In infants and children, the face, scalp, palms, and soles are also often affected.

INCIDENCE/   Scabies is a common public health problem with an estimated prevalence
PREVALENCE   of 300 million cases worldwide, mostly affecting people in developing countries where prevalence can exceed 50%.[2] In industrialised countries, it is most common in institutionalised communities. Case studies suggest that epidemic cycles occur every 7–15 years and that these partly reflect the population's immune status. ▶

Scabies

AETIOLOGY/ Scabies is particularly common where there is social disruption, overcrowding
RISK FACTORS with close body contact, and limited access to water.[3] Young children,
immobilised elderly people, people with HIV/AIDS, and other medically and
immunologically compromised people are predisposed to infestation and have
particularly high mite counts.[4]

PROGNOSIS Scabies is not life threatening, but the severe, persistent itch and secondary
infections may be debilitating. Occasionally, crusted scabies develops. This
form of the disease is resistant to routine treatment and can be a source of
continued reinfestation and spread to others.

Search date January 2002

Adèle Green and Robin Marks

What are the effects of preventive interventions?

LIKELY TO BE BENEFICIAL

Sunscreen (daily versus discretionary use)

One RCT in adults in a subtropical Australian community found that daily versus discretionary use of sunscreen significantly reduced the incidence of squamous cell carcinoma after 4.5 years.

Sunscreens to prevent development of new solar keratoses (better than placebo)

One RCT in people with previous solar keratoses aged > 40 years and living in Victoria, Australia found that daily sunscreen versus placebo sunscreen significantly reduced the incidence of new solar keratoses after 7 months use.

What are the effects of treatments?

UNKNOWN EFFECTIVENESS

Micrographically controlled surgery (unknown benefit compared with standard surgical excision)

We found no RCTs comparing micrographically controlled surgery versus standard excision in primary treatment.

Primary excision (unknown optimal margin of excision)

We found insufficient evidence relating size of primary excision margin to local recurrence rate.

Radiotherapy after surgery (unknown benefit compared with surgery alone)

We found no RCTs comparing the addition of radiotherapy to surgery versus surgery alone.

DEFINITION   Cutaneous squamous cell carcinoma is a malignant tumour of keratinocytes arising in the epidermis, showing histological evidence of dermal invasion.

INCIDENCE/   Incidence rates are often derived from special surveys because few cancer
PREVALENCE   registries routinely collect notifications of squamous cell carcinoma of the skin. Incidence rates on exposed skin vary markedly around the world according to skin colour and latitude, and range from negligible rates in black populations and white populations living at very high latitudes to rates of about 1000/100 000 in white residents of tropical Australia.[1]

AETIOLOGY/   People with fair skin colour who sunburn easily without tanning, people with
RISK FACTORS   xeroderma pigmentosum Ⓖ,[2–4] and those who are immunosuppressed[5] are susceptible to squamous cell carcinoma. The strongest environmental risk factor for squamous cell carcinoma is chronic sun exposure. Cohort and case control studies have found that clinical signs of chronic skin damage, especially solar keratoses, are also determinants of cutaneous squamous cell carcinoma.[3,4] For example, the risk of squamous cell carcinoma in people with the propensity to severe sunburn or with a history of multiple sunburns is three times greater than in people with no such propensity. In people with multiple solar keratoses (> 15), the risk of squamous cell carcinoma is 10–15 times greater than in people with no solar keratoses.[3,4] ▶

Squamous cell carcinoma of the skin: non-metastatic

PROGNOSIS Prognosis is related to the location and size of tumour, histological pattern, depth of invasion, perineural involvement, and whether the person is immunosuppressed.[6,7] A worldwide review of 95 case series, each comprising at least 20 people, found the overall metastasis rate for squamous cell carcinoma on the ear is 11% and on the lip 14%, compared with an average over all sites of 5%.[7] A review of 71 case series found that lesions less than 2 cm in diameter compared with lesions greater than 2 cm have less than half the local recurrence rate (7% v 15%), and less than one third of the rate of metastasis (9% v 30%).[7]

Search date April 2001

Miny Samuel and Christopher Griffiths

What are the effects of preventive interventions? New

UNKNOWN EFFECTIVENESS

Sunscreens; vitamins (vitamin C and vitamin E)

We found no RCTs on the effects of sunscreens or vitamins in preventing wrinkles.

What are the effects of treatments? New

BENEFICIAL

Tretinoin (for fine wrinkles after 6 months)

RCTs in people with mild to moderate photodamage🅖 have found that topical tretinoin versus vehicle cream applied for an average of 6 months significantly improves fine wrinkles. The effect of tretinoin on coarse wrinkles was inconsistent. Common short term adverse effects with tretinoin include itching, burning, and erythema. Skin peeling is the most common persistent adverse effect, which peaks at 12–16 weeks.

TRADE OFF BETWEEN BENEFITS AND HARMS

Isotretinoin

Two RCTs found that isotretinoin versus vehicle cream significantly improved fine and coarse wrinkles after 36 weeks in people with mild to severe photodamage. Severe facial irritation occurred in 5–10% of people using isotretinoin.

UNKNOWN EFFECTIVENESS

Topical antioxidants (ascorbic acid)

One poor quality RCT found limited evidence that an ascorbic acid formulation versus a vehicle cream applied daily to the face for 3 months significantly improved fine and coarse wrinkles. Stinging and erythema were common but were not analysed by treatment.

Carbon dioxide laser

We found no RCTs of CO_2 laser versus placebo or no treatment. One small RCT found limited evidence that CO_2 laser reduced the wrinkle score significantly less than chemical peel at 6 months. Another small RCT found limited evidence that CO_2 laser improved upper lip wrinkles more than yttrium aluminium garnet laser🅖 at 2 months. One small RCT found no significant difference with CO_2 laser plus yttrium aluminium garnet laser versus CO_2 laser alone in improvement in upper lip wrinkles at 4 months. Erythema was common but there were no clear differences between treatments.

Dermabrasion

We found no RCTs of dermabrasion versus placebo or no treatment. Three small RCTs in women with perioral wrinkles found no significant difference with dermabrasion versus CO_2 laser in terms of improvement in wrinkles at 4–6 months. Adverse effects were commonly reported. Erythema was reported in all three RCTs, two of which found that erythema was significantly more common with laser versus dermabrasion. ▶

◄ **Facelift**

We found no systematic review or RCTs on the effects of facelifts.

Oral natural cartilage polysaccharides

One RCT found limited evidence that an oral commercial preparation of cartilage polysaccharide was no more effective than placebo at reducing wrinkles at 3 months. Another RCT found that a different oral commercial preparation of cartilage polysaccharide versus placebo significantly reduced the number of women with moderate or severe wrinkles at 90 days. We found limited evidence that some commercial preparations may be more effective than others.

Topical natural cartilage polysaccharides

One small RCT found that a topical commercial preparation of natural cartilage polysaccharide versus placebo significantly reduced the number of fine and coarse wrinkles at 120 days.

Retinyl esters

We found no systematic review or RCTs of retinyl esters that evaluated clinical outcomes.

DEFINITION Wrinkles, also known as rhytides, are visible creases or folds in the skin. Wrinkles less than 1 mm in width and depth are defined as fine wrinkles and those greater than 1 mm are coarse wrinkles. Most RCTs have studied wrinkles on the face, forearms, and hands.

INCIDENCE/ We found no information on the incidence of wrinkles alone but only on
PREVALENCE the incidence of skin photodamage, which includes a spectrum of features such as wrinkles, hyperpigmentation, tactile roughness, and telangiectasia. The incidence of ultraviolet light associated skin disorders increases with age and develops over several decades. One Australian study (1539 people aged 20–55 years living in Queensland) found moderate to severe photoaging in 72% of men and 47% of women under 30 years of age.[1] The severity of photoaging was significantly greater with increasing age, and was independently associated with solar keratoses ($P < 0.01$) and skin cancer ($P < 0.05$). Wrinkling was more common in people with white skin, especially skin phototypes I and II. One study reported that the incidence of photodamage in European and North American populations with Fitzpatrick skin types I, II, and III☉ is about 80–90%.[2] We found few reports of photodamage in black skin (phototypes V and VI).

DEFINITION Wrinkles may be caused by intrinsic factors (e.g. aging, hormonal status, and intercurrent diseases) and by extrinsic factors (e.g. exposure to ultraviolet radiation and cigarette smoke). These factors contribute to epidermal thinning, loss of elasticity, skin fragility, and creases and lines in the skin. The severity of photodamage varies with skin type, which includes skin colour and the capacity to tan.[3] One review of five observational studies found that facial wrinkles in men and women were more common in smokers than in non-smokers.[4] It also found that the risk of moderate to severe wrinkles in lifelong smokers was more than twice that in current smokers (RR 2.57, 95% CI 1.83 to 3.06). Oestrogen deficiency may contribute to wrinkles in postmenopausal women.[5]

►

◀ **PROGNOSIS**   Although wrinkles cannot be considered a medical illness requiring intervention, concerns about aging that affect quality of life are becoming increasingly common. Such concerns are likely to be influenced by geographical
differences, culture, and personal values. In some cases, concerns about
physical appearance can lead to difficulties with interpersonal interactions,
occupational functioning, and self esteem.[6] In societies in which the aging
population is growing and a high value is placed on the maintenance of a
youthful appearance, there is a growing preference for interventions that
ameliorate the visible signs of aging.

Sleep disorders

Sleep apnoea (OSAHS)

Search date August 2001

Michael Hensley

What are the effects of treatments? New

Nasal continuous positive airway pressure in moderate to severe obstructive sleep apnoea-hypopnoea syndrome (OSAHS)

Systematic reviews and RCTs have found that nasal continuous positive airway pressure (CPAP)☉ versus control or no treatment reduces daytime sleepiness, improves vigilance and cognitive functioning, and reduces depression after 1–3 months.

Nasal continuous positive airway pressure in mild OSAHS

One systematic review has found no significant difference with nasal continuous positive airway pressure versus conservative treatment or placebo tablets in daytime sleepiness, but found significant improvement in some measures of cognitive performance at about 4 weeks.

Oral appliance in mild OSAHS

One RCT found a significant reduction in apnoea/hypopnoea index with oral appliances, but found no significant difference in daytime sleepiness or quality of life at 12 months with oral appliances that produce anterior advancement of the mandible versus uvulopalatopharyngoplasty.

Oral appliance in moderate to severe OSAHS

RCTs have found that oral appliances☉ that produce anterior advancement of the mandible versus no treatment or versus control oral appliances significantly reduce daytime sleepiness and sleep disordered breathing☉ at 1–2 weeks.

Weight loss in moderate to severe OSAHS

One systematic review found no RCTs on the effects of weight loss in people with moderate to severe OSAHS.

Weight loss in mild OSAHS

One systematic review found no RCTs on the effects of weight loss in people with mild obstructive sleep apnoea-hypopnoea syndrome.

DEFINITION   Obstructive sleep apnoea-hypopnoea syndrome (OSAHS) is abnormal breathing during sleep that causes recurrent arousals, sleep fragmentation, and nocturnal hypoxaemia. It is associated with daytime sleepiness, impaired vigilance and cognitive functioning, and reduced quality of life.[1,2] The diagnosis is made when a person with daytime symptoms has significant sleep disordered breathing revealed by polysomnography (study of sleep state, breathing, and oxygenation) or by more limited studies. Criteria for the diagnosis of significant sleep disordered breathing have not been rigorously assessed, but have been set by consensus and convention.[3,4] The criteria are based on the finding of sleep disordered breathing, reported as the number of abnormal breathing events in 1 hour of sleep (for full polysomnography) or in 1 hour in bed for home based monitoring systems that do not include electroencephalography recordings. There are differences in the measurement techniques and the criteria used: the criteria for hypopnoea☉ may or may not include associated hypoxaemia or arousal and the criteria vary for a significant obstructive ▶

◀ event that is not apnoea**ⓖ** or hypopnoea. In OSAHS, apnoeas and hypopnoeas are associated with absent or reduced airflow despite normal or increased inspiratory effort, but may also involve reduced inspiratory effort. However, many healthy people, especially the elderly, can have frequent apnoeas and hypopnoeas. Diagnostic tests are not completely sensitive or specific. For example, an apnoea/hypopnoea index**ⓖ** of 5–20 episodes an hour is often used to define borderline to mild OSAHS, 20–35 to define moderate OSAHS, and more than 35 to define severe OSAHS,[5] but people with upper airway resistance syndrome**ⓖ** have an index below 5 episodes an hour[6] and many healthy elderly people have an index greater than 5 episodes an hour.[7] In an effort to obtain an international consensus, some new criteria were proposed but these have not been widely adopted.[8] The ultimate test for clinically significant OSAHS is to demonstrate clinical improvement in daytime symptoms after correction of sleep disordered breathing by a treatment. Clinically important sleep disordered breathing can also occur without apnoeas or hypopnoeas (upper airway resistance syndrome).[6] In this topic, the criteria for OSAHS include apnoeas and hypopnoeas caused by upper airway obstruction. Central sleep apnoea and sleep associated hypoventilation syndromes are not covered here.

INCIDENCE/ PREVALENCE The Wisconsin Sleep Cohort Study of over 1000 people (mean age 47 years) in North America found a prevalence of apnoea/hypopnoea index greater than five episodes an hour in 24% of men and 9% of women, and of OSAHS with an index greater than 5 plus excessive sleepiness in 4% of men and 2% of women.[9] There are international differences in the occurrence of OSAHS for which obesity is considered to be an important determinant.[10] Ethnic differences in prevalence have also been found after adjustment for other risk factors.[7,10] Little is known about the burden of illness in developing countries.

AETIOLOGY/ RISK FACTORS The site of the upper airway obstruction in the OSAHS is around the level of the tongue, soft palate, or epiglottis. Disorders that predispose to either narrowing of the upper airway or reduction in its stability (e.g. obesity, certain craniofacial abnormalities, vocal cord abnormalities, and enlarged tonsils) have been associated with an increased risk of OSAHS. It has been estimated that a 1 kg/m² increase in body mass index (3.2 kg for a person 1.8 m tall) leads to a 30% increase (95% CI 13% to 50%) in the relative risk of developing abnormal sleep disordered breathing (apnoea/hypopnoea index ≥ 5/h) over a period of 4 years.[10] Other strong associations include increasing age and sex (the male to female ratio is 2 : 1); weaker associations include menopause, family history, smoking, and night time nasal congestion.[10]

PROGNOSIS The long term prognosis of people with untreated severe OSAHS is poor with respect to quality of life, likelihood of motor vehicle accidents, hypertension, and possibly cardiovascular disease and premature mortality.[11] Unfortunately the prognosis of both treated and untreated OSAHS is unclear.[7] The limitations in the evidence include bias in the selection of subjects, short duration of follow up, and variation in the measurement of confounders (e.g. smoking, alcohol use, and other cardiovascular risk factors). The widespread use of treatments complicates the evidence on prognosis for untreated OSAHS. Observational studies support a causal association between OSAHS and systemic hypertension, which increases with the severity of OSAHS (OR 1.21 for mild OSAHS to 3.07 for severe OSAHS).[11] OSAHS increases the risk of motor vehicle accidents three- to sevenfold.[11,12] It is associated with increased risk of premature mortality, cardiovascular disease, and impaired neurocognitive functioning.[11]

Breast cancer: metastatic

Search date September 2001

Stephen Johnston and Justin Stebbing

What are the effects of treatments?

BENEFICIAL

Chemotherapy

Anthracycline based regimens (CAF) containing doxorubicin

RCTs have found that combination chemotherapy🅖 regimens containing an anthracycline, such as doxorubicin, versus other regimens as first line treatment🅖 significantly increase response rates, time to progression, and survival.

Classical combination chemotherapy (CMF)

One systematic review has found that classical combination chemotherapy versus modified regimens as first line treatment significantly increases response rate and survival.

First line chemotherapy plus monoclonal antibody (in people with overexpressed HER2 neu oncogene) *New*

One RCT found that, in women whose tumours overexpress HER2, standard chemotherapy🅖 plus the monoclonal antibody trastuzumab versus standard chemotherapy alone as first line treatment significantly increases the time to disease progression, objective response🅖, and overall survival.

Hormone treatment

Selective aromatase inhibitors🅖 as first line hormonal treatment🅖 in postmenopausal women

RCTs have found that the aromatase inhibitor anastrozole as first line treatment in metastatic postmenopausal breast cancer is at least as effective as tamoxifen🅖 in reducing time to disease progression, and have found that the aromatase inhibitor letrozole was superior to tamoxifen in reducing time to disease progression.

Selective aromatase inhibitors as second line hormonal treatment in postmenopausal women

RCTs in postmenopausal women who have relapsed during or after treatment with tamoxifen have found that the selective aromatase inhibitors anastrozole, letrozole, and exemestane versus progestins significantly increase overall survival at 2–3 years and are associated with fewer adverse effects.

Tamoxifen in oestrogen receptor positive disease

RCTs have found prolonged remission with tamoxifen in the first line treatment of women with oestrogen receptor positive metastatic breast cancer.

For bone metastasis

Radiotherapy plus appropriate analgesia

We found no RCTs comparing radiotherapy versus no treatment or versus bisphosphonates🅖. We found limited evidence from non-randomised studies that persistent and localised bone pain can be successfully treated in over 80% of women with radiotherapy plus concomitant appropriate analgesia (from non-steroidal anti-inflammatory drugs to morphine and its derivatives). RCTs have found no significant difference in pain relief between short and long courses of radiotherapy. One RCT found that different fractionation schedules can be used to effectively treat neuropathic bone pain.

▶

◀ *For central nervous system metastases*

Adding high dose steroids to radiotherapy in spinal cord compression

One small RCT found that adding high dose steroids to radiotherapy improved the chance of walking after 6 months.

Radiotherapy for spinal cord compression

We found no RCTs. Retrospective analyses found that early radiotherapy improved outcomes, but fewer than 10% of people walked again if severe deterioration of motor function occurred before radiotherapy.

LIKELY TO BE BENEFICIAL

Bisphosphonates

RCTs in women receiving standard chemotherapy for bone metastases secondary to metastatic breast cancer have found that bisphosphonates versus placebo significantly reduce and delay skeletal complications. None of the RCTs found an impact on overall survival.

Combined gonadorelin analogues and tamoxifen in premenopausal women

RCTs (in premenopausal women with oestrogen receptor positive metastatic breast cancer) have found that first line treatment with gonadorelin analogues❻ plus tamoxifen versus gonadorelin analogues alone significantly improves response rates, overall survival, and progression free survival❻.

New cytotoxic drugs in anthracycline resistant disease❻ (such as taxanes❻ and semisynthetic vinca alkaloids)

RCTs suggest that second line treatment❻ with the docetaxel or vinorelbine versus standard relapse regimens may improve response rates, especially in women with anthracycline resistant disease.

Radiotherapy to control cerebral and choroidal metastases

We found no RCTs. Retrospective studies suggest that whole brain radiation produces general improvement in neurological function in 40–70% of women with brain metastases secondary to breast cancer and that radiotherapy benefits 70% of women with choroidal metastases.

TRADE OFF BETWEEN BENEFITS AND HARMS

Ovarian ablation in premenopausal women (v tamoxifen)

One systematic review and one subsequent RCT in premenopausal women have found no significant difference in response rate, duration of response, or survival with ovarian ablation (surgery or irradiation) versus tamoxifen as first line treatment. Ovarian ablation is associated with substantial adverse effects such as hot flushes and "tumour flare".

Progestins (v tamoxifen, beneficial in women with bone pain or anorexia)

RCTs have found no significant difference in response rates, remission rates, or survival between progestins❻ versus tamoxifen as first line treatment, but found that progestins increased adverse effects including nausea, weight gain, and exacerbations of hypertension. One RCT found that medroxyprogesterone versus tamoxifen significantly improved bone pain. Observational evidence suggests that progestins may increase appetite, weight gain, and well being. ▶

◀ LIKELY TO BE INEFFECTIVE OR HARMFUL

High dose chemotherapy (v conventional chemotherapy)
One RCT (in women who had complete or partial response🅖 to standard induction chemotherapy) found no significant difference in overall survival at 3 years with additional high dose versus standard dose chemotherapy as first line treatment.

DEFINITION   Metastatic or advanced breast cancer is the presence of disease at distant sites such as the bone, liver, or lung. It is not treatable by primary surgery and is currently considered incurable. Symptoms may include pain from bone metastases, breathlessness from spread to the lung, and nausea or abdominal discomfort from liver involvement.

INCIDENCE/   Breast cancer is the second most frequent cancer in the world
PREVALENCE   (1.05 million people) and is by far the most common malignant disease in women (22% of all new cancer cases). Worldwide, the ratio of mortality to incidence is about 36%. It ranks fifth as a cause of death from cancer overall (although it is the leading cause of mortality in women — the 370 000 annual deaths represent 13.9% of cancer deaths in women). It is the most prevalent cancer in the world today and there are an estimated 3.9 million women alive who had breast cancer diagnosed in the past 5 years (compared e.g. with lung cancer, where there are 1.4 million alive). The true prevalence of metastatic disease is high because some women live with the disease for many years. Since 1990 there has been an overall increase in incidence rates of about 1.5% annually.[1] Metastatic breast cancer causes up to 500 000 deaths worldwide each year (46 000 in the USA and 15 000 in the UK).[2]

AETIOLOGY/   The risk of metastatic disease relates to known prognostic factors in the
RISK FACTORS original primary tumour. These factors include oestrogen receptor negative disease, primary tumours 3 cm or more in diameter, and axillary node involvement — recurrence occurred within 10 years of adjuvant chemotherapy for early breast cancer🅖 in 60–70% of node positive women and 25–30% of node negative women in one large systematic review.[3]

PROGNOSIS   Most women who develop metastatic breast cancer will ultimately die of their disease. Prognosis depends on age, extent of disease, and oestrogen receptor status. There is also evidence that overexpression of the product of the HER2/neu oncogene, which occurs in about a third of women with metastatic breast cancer, is associated with a worse prognosis.[4] A short disease free interval🅖 (e.g. < 1 year) between surgery for early breast cancer and developing metastases suggests that the recurrent disease is likely to be resistant to the drug used for adjuvant treatment🅖.[5] In women who receive no treatment for metastatic disease, the median survival from diagnosis of metastases is 12 months.[6] The choice of first line treatment (hormonal or chemotherapy) is based on a variety of clinical factors🆃.[7–10] In many countries there is evidence of a decrease in death rates in recent years, evident in the USA, Canada, and some European countries. These changes probably reflect improvements in treatment (and therefore improved survival) as well as earlier diagnosis.[1]

Search date June 2001

J Michael Dixon, Kate Gregory, Stephen Johnston and Alan Rodger

What are the effects of treatments for ductal carcinoma in situ?

LIKELY TO BE BENEFICIAL

Radiotherapy after breast conserving surgery (reduces recurrence)

RCTs found that radiotherapy⊕ reduced the risk of local recurrence and invasive carcinoma, with no evidence of an effect on survival.

Tamoxifen plus radiotherapy after breast conserving surgery (reduces recurrence)

One RCT has found that adjuvant tamoxifen⊕ significantly reduces breast cancer events in women who have undergone wide excision and radiotherapy, but found no significant difference in overall survival at 6 years.

What are the effects of treatments for operable breast cancer?

BENEFICIAL

Adjuvant chemotherapy

One systematic review has found that adjuvant chemotherapy versus no chemotherapy significantly reduces rates of recurrence and improves survival at 10 years. The benefit seems to be independent of nodal or menopausal status, although the absolute improvements are greater in those women with node positive disease, and probably greater in younger women.

Adjuvant tamoxifen

One systematic review has found that adjuvant tamoxifen taken for up to 5 years reduces the risk of recurrence and death in women with oestrogen receptor positive tumours irrespective of age, menopausal status, nodal involvement, or the addition of chemotherapy. Tamoxifen slightly increases the risk of endometrial cancer, but we found no evidence of an overall adverse effect on non-breast cancer mortality.

Anthracycline regimens as adjuvant chemotherapy

One systematic review has found that adjuvant regimens containing an anthracycline versus a standard CMF⊕ regimen significantly reduce recurrence, and significantly improve survival at 5 years.

Breast conserving surgery (similar survival to more extensive surgery)

Systematic reviews have found that, providing all local disease is excised, more extensive surgery is not associated with increased survival at 10 years. More extensive local resection in breast conserving surgery gives worse cosmetic results.

Chemotherapy plus tamoxifen

One RCT found that adding chemotherapy (CMF) to tamoxifen significantly improves survival at 5 years.

▶

◀ **Ovarian ablation in premenopausal women**

One systematic review has found that in women less than 50 years of age, ovarian ablation versus no ablation significantly improves survival for at least 15 years.

Radiotherapy after breast conserving surgery (reduces local recurrence; no evidence of effect on survival)

One systematic review has found that the addition of radiotherapy to breast conserving surgery❸ significantly reduces the risk of isolated local recurrence and loss of a breast, but does not increase survival at 10 years. Similar rates of survival and local recurrence are achieved with radiotherapy plus either breast conserving surgery or mastectomy.

Radiotherapy after mastectomy in women at high risk of local recurrence

RCTs in high risk women receiving adjuvant chemotherapy after mastectomy have found that radiotherapy versus no radiotherapy significantly reduces local recurrence and increases survival at 10–15 years.

Total mastectomy

Systematic reviews have found no significant difference between total, supraradical, radical, or simple mastectectomy in survival at 10 years. More extensive surgery results in greater multilation.

LIKELY TO BE BENEFICIAL

Neoadjuvant chemotherapy (reduces mastectomy rates versus adjuvant chemotherapy; no evidence of effect on survival)

RCTs have found that neoadjuvant versus adjuvant chemotherapy reduces mastectomy rates, but found no significant difference in survival at 4–10 years.

Radiotherapy after mastectomy in node positive disease, large tumours, or where lymphovascular invasion is present

One systematic review has found that radiotherapy to the chest wall after mastectomy reduces the risk of local recurrence by about two thirds and the risk of death from breast cancer at 10 years, but found no evidence of effect on overall 10 year survival. One review of retrospective data found that greater axillary node involvement, larger tumour size, higher histological grade, presence of lymphovascular invasion, and involvement of tumour margins reduced the chance of successful treatment.

Total nodal radiotherapy in high risk disease

RCTs have found that in women with high risk disease total nodal irradiation❸ versus no irradiation improves survival. An earlier systematic review found reduced locoregional recurrence, but no evidence of improved survival.

TRADE OFF BETWEEN BENEFITS AND HARMS

Axillary clearance (no evidence of survival benefit and increased morbidity compared with axillary sampling)

RCTs found no significant difference in survival at 5–10 years between axillary clearance❸ versus axillary sampling❸, axillary radiotherapy❸, or sampling plus radiotherapy combined. One systematic review of mainly poor quality evidence found that the risk of arm lymphoedema was highest with axillary clearance plus radiotherapy, lower with axillary sampling plus radiotherapy, and lowest with sampling alone.

▶

◀ **Axillary radiotherapy**

One systematic review has found that axilliary radiotherapy versus axilliary clearance significantly reduces isolated local recurrence, and has found no significant difference in mortality or overall recurrence at 10 years.

Radiotherapy after mastectomy in women not at high risk of local recurrence

One systematic review has found that radiotherapy to the chest wall after mastectomy reduces the risk of local recurrence by about two thirds and the risk of death from breast cancer at 10 years, but found no evidence of effect on overall 10 year survival. Radiotherapy may be associated with rare late adverse effects, including pneumonitis, pericarditis, arm oedema, brachial plexopathy, and radionecrotic rib fracture.

UNKNOWN EFFECTIVENESS

Radiotherapy to the internal mammary chain

One RCT found no significant difference in overall survival or breast cancer specific survival at 2–3 years between radiotherapy versus no radiotherapy to the internal mammary chain. Treatment may increase radiation induced cardiac morbidity.

Radiotherapy to the ipsilateral supraclavicular fossa

We found insufficient evidence about the effects of irradiation of the ipsilateral supraclavicular fossa on survival. RCTs have found that radiotherapy reduces the risk of supraclavicular fossa nodal recurrence.

UNLIKELY TO BE BENEFICIAL

Enhanced dose regimens of adjuvant chemotherapy

RCTs found no significant improvement from enhanced dose regimens.

Prolonged chemotherapy (8–12 months v 4–6 months)

One systematic review found no additional benefit from prolonging adjuvant chemotherapy from 4–6 to 8–12 months.

Radical mastectomy (no greater survival than less extensive surgery)

Systematic reviews have found no significant difference between radical, total, supraradical, or simple mastectectomy in survival at 10 years. More extensive surgery results in greater mutilation.

What are the effects of treatments for locally advanced breast cancer?

LIKELY TO BE BENEFICIAL

Radiotherapy

For locally advanced breast cancer❻ that is rendered operable, small RCTs found that radiotherapy or surgery as sole local treatments have similar effects on response rates, duration of response, and overall survival.

Radiotherapy after attempted curative surgery

One RCT found weak evidence that radiotherapy after attempted curative surgery versus no further local treatment may reduce local and/or regional recurrence.

▶

Women's health

◄ **Surgery**

For locally advanced breast cancer that is rendered operable, small RCTs found that surgery or radiotherapy as sole local treatments have similar effects on response rates, duration of response, and overall survival.

Tamoxifen plus radiotherapy (versus radiotherapy)

One RCT found that hormone treatment plus radiotherapy versus radiotherapy alone significantly improved locoregional recurrence at 6 years and improved median survival at 8 years.

UNLIKELY TO BE BENEFICIAL

Chemotherapy (cyclophosphamide/methotrexate/fluorouracil [5-FU] or anthracycline based regimens)

We found no evidence that the cytotoxic, multidrug chemotherapy regimen (CMF) improves survival, disease free survival, or long term locoregional control.

DEFINITION **Ductal carcinoma *in situ*** is a non-invasive tumour characterised by the presence of malignant cells in the breast ducts but with no evidence that they breach the basement membrane and invade into periductal connective tissues. **Invasive breast cancer** can be separated into three main groups: early or operable breast cancer, locally advanced disease, and metastatic breast cancer (see metastatic breast cancer, p 308). **Operable breast cancer** is apparently restricted to the breast and sometimes to local lymph nodes and can be surgically removed. Although these women do not have overt metastases at the time of staging, they remain at risk of local recurrence and of metastatic spread. They can be divided into those women with tumours greater than 4 cm or multifocal cancers that can be treated by mastectomy, and those with tumours less than 4 cm that are unifocal that can be treated by breast conserving surgery. **Locally advanced breast cancer** is defined according to the TNM staging system of the UICC TNM system **G**[1] as stage III B (includes T4 a–d; N2 disease, but absence of metastases). It is a disease presentation with evidence (clinical or histopathological) of skin and/or chest wall involvement and/or axillary nodes matted together by tumour extension. **Metastatic breast cancer** is presented in a separate topic (see metastatic breast cancer, p 308).

INCIDENCE/ Breast cancer affects 1/10 to 1/11 women in the UK and causes about
PREVALENCE 21 000 deaths per year. Prevalence is about five times higher, with over 100 000 women living with breast cancer at any one time. Of the 15 000 new cases of breast cancer per annum in the UK, the majority will present with primary operable disease.[2]

AETIOLOGY/ The risk of breast cancer increases with age, doubling every 10 years up to
RISK FACTORS the menopause. Risk factors include an early age at menarche, older age at menopause, older age at birth of first child, family history, atypical hyperplasia, excess alcohol intake, radiation exposure to developing breast tissue, oral contraceptive use, postmenopausal hormone replacement therapy, and obesity. Risk in different countries varies fivefold. The cause of breast cancer in most women is unknown. About 5% of breast cancers can be attributed to mutations in the genes BRCA1 and BRCA2.[3]

▶

PROGNOSIS **Primary carcinoma** of the breast is potentially curable. The risk of relapse depends on various clinico-pathological features, including axillary node involvement, oestrogen receptor status, and tumour size. Tumour size, axillary node status, histological grade, and oestrogen receptor status provide the most significant prognostic information. Seventy per cent of women with operable disease are alive 5 years after diagnosis and treatment (adjuvant drug treatment is given to most women after surgery). Risk of recurrence is highest during the first 5 years, but the risk remains even 15–20 years after surgery. Those with node positive disease have a 50–60% chance of recurrence within 5 years, compared with 30–35% for node negative disease. Recurrence within 10 years according to one large systematic review occurred in 60–70% of node positive women compared with 25–30% of node negative women.[4] The prognosis for a disease free survival at 5 years is worse for stage III B (33%) than that for stage III A (71%). Five year overall survival is 44% and 84%, respectively.[5] Poor survival and high rates of local recurrence characterise locally advanced breast cancer**G**.

Breast pain

Search date July 2001

Nigel Bundred

What are the effects of treatments?

LIKELY TO BE BENEFICIAL

Low fat, high carbohydrate diet

One RCT found limited evidence that advice to follow a low fat, high carbohydrate diet versus general dietary advice significantly reduced breast pain (NNT 2) and tenderness (NNT 3) at 6 months.

TRADE OFF BETWEEN BENEFITS AND HARMS

Danazol

One RCT found that danazol versus placebo significantly reduced breast pain after 12 months (NNT 3), but significantly increased adverse effects (weight gain, deepening of the voice, menorrhagia, and muscle cramps).

Gestrinone

One RCT found that gestrinone versus placebo significantly reduced breast pain after 3 months, but significantly increased adverse effects (greasy skin, hirsutism, acne, reduction in breast size, headache, and depession).

Tamoxifen

One RCT found that tamoxifen versus placebo significantly reduced breast pain after 3 months (NNT 3); another found that tamoxifen versus placebo significantly increased the number of women with greater than 50% reduction in mean pain score after 12 months (NNT 3). Tamoxifen increased hot flushes and vaginal discharge.

UNKNOWN EFFECTIVENESS

Antibiotics; diuretics; evening primrose oil; gonadorelin analogues (luteinising hormone releasing hormone analogues); progestogens; pyridoxine; vitamin E

We found no RCTs on the effects of these interventions.

Lisuride maleate *New*

One small RCT found that lisuride maleate versus placebo significantly reduced breast pain over 2 months (NNT 2).

Tibolone

One small RCT found limited evidence that tibolone versus hormone replacement therapy significantly reduced breast pain after 1 year.

UNLIKELY TO BE BENEFICIAL

Bromocriptine

Two RCTs found that bromocriptine versus placebo significantly reduced breast pain but one of these RCTs found that bromocriptine significantly increased adverse effects (including nausea, dizziness, postural hypotension, and constipation; NNH 7).

◀ **Hormone replacement therapy**

One small RCT found limited evidence that women taking hormone replacement therapy had significantly more breast pain at 1 year than women taking tibolone. Hormone replacement therapy has been associated with adverse effects including venous thromboembolism, breast cancer, and endometrial cancer.

DEFINITION   Breast pain can be differentiated into cyclical mastalgia (worse before a menstrual period) or non-cyclical mastalgia (unrelated to the menstrual cycle).[1,2] Cyclical pain is often bilateral, usually most severe in the upper outer quadrants of the breast, and may refer to the medial aspect of the upper arm.[1–3] Non-cyclical pain may be caused by true breast pain or chest wall pain located over the costal cartilages.[1,2,4] Specific breast pathology and referred pain unrelated to the breasts are not included in this definition.

INCIDENCE/   Up to 70% of women develop breast pain in their lifetime.[1,2] Of 1171 US
PREVALENCE   women attending a gynaecology clinic, 69% suffered regular discomfort, which was judged as severe in 11% of women, and 36% had consulted a doctor about breast pain.[2]

AETIOLOGY/   Breast pain is more common in women aged 30–50 years.[1,2]
RISK FACTORS

PROGNOSIS   Cyclical breast pain resolves spontaneously within 3 months of onset in 20–30% of women.[5] The pain tends to relapse and remit, and up to 60% of women develop recurrent symptoms 2 years after treatment.[1] Non-cyclical pain responds poorly to treatment but may resolve spontaneously in about 50% of women.[1]

Dysmenorrhoea

Search date October 2001

Cynthia Farquhar and Michelle Proctor

What are the effects of treatments?

BENEFICIAL

Non-steroidal anti-inflammatory drugs (other than aspirin)

One systematic review has found that naproxen, ibuprofen, and mefenamic acid are significantly more effective than placebo for pain relief over at least one menstrual cycle (NNT 3). The review found some evidence of increased adverse effects with naproxen.

LIKELY TO BE BENEFICIAL

Aspirin, paracetamol, and compound analgesics

One systematic review has found that aspirin is significantly more effective for pain relief than placebo (NNT over at least 1 menstrual cycle 10), but less effective than naproxen or ibuprofen. The review found no significant difference with paracetamol versus either placebo, aspirin, or ibuprofen in pain relief. It found limited evidence that co-proxamol❺ versus placebo significantly reduced pain, but compared to naproxen reduced pain significantly less and was associated with significantly more adverse effects. It also found that co-proxamol reduced dysmenorrhoea related symptoms significantly less than mefenamic acid.

Magnesium

Two RCTs found limited evidence that magnesium versus placebo significantly reduced pain, and another RCT found no significant difference with magnesium versus placebo in pain relief.

Thiamine

One large RCT has found that thiamine versus placebo significantly reduces pain.

UNKNOWN EFFECTIVENESS

Acupuncture

One small RCT found limited evidence that acupuncture versus placebo acupuncture❺ or versus no treatment significantly reduced pain after 3 months.

Behavioural interventions

Two RCTs found insufficient evidence about the effects of behavioural interventions❺.

Combined oral contraceptives

One systematic review found insufficient evidence about the effects of combined oral contraceptives versus placebo for pain relief.

Dietary supplements (other than magnesium or thiamine)

RCTs found insufficient evidence about the effects of fish oil, dietary change, or vitamin E.

Herbal remedies

One systematic review found insufficient evidence of the effects of herbal remedies.

◀ **Surgical interruption of pelvic nerve pathways**

One small RCT found limited evidence suggesting that laparoscopic uterine nerve ablation❻ versus diagnostic laparoscopy significantly increased pain relief at 3 and 12 months. Another RCT comparing laparoscopic uterine nerve ablation versus laparoscopic presacral neurectomy❻ found no significant difference in pain relief at 3 months, but found that laparoscopic presacral neurectomy significantly reduced pain at 6 months.

Transcutaneous electrical nerve stimulation

Small RCTs have found that high frequency transcutaneous electrical nerve stimulation❻ versus placebo significantly increased pain relief. One RCT found no significant difference with low frequency transcutaneous electrical nerve stimulation versus placebo in pain relief. Two RCTs found conflicting evidence about the effects of transcutaneous electrical nerve stimulation versus non-steroidal anti-inflammatory drugs in pain relief.

UNLIKELY TO BE BENEFICIAL

Spinal manipulation

Three of four RCTs found no significant difference in pain relief with spinal manipulation versus placebo manipulation❻ or no treatment.

DEFINITION Dysmenorrhoea comprises painful menstrual cramps of uterine origin. It is commonly divided into primary dysmenorrhoea (pain without organic pathology) and secondary dysmenorrhoea (pelvic pain associated with an identifiable pathological condition, such as endometriosis or ovarian cysts). The initial onset of primary dysmenorrhoea is usually shortly after menarche (6–12 months) when ovulatory cycles are established. The pain duration is commonly 8–72 hours and is usually associated with the onset of the menstrual flow. Secondary dysmenorrhoea may arise as a new symptom during a woman's fourth and fifth decade.[1]

INCIDENCE/ Variations in the definition of dysmenorrhoea make it difficult to determine
PREVALENCE the precise prevalence. However, various types of study have found a consistently high prevalence in women of different ages and nationalities. A systematic review (search date 1996) of the prevalence of chronic pelvic pain, summarising both community and hospital surveys, estimated the prevalence at 45–95%.[2] Reports focus on adolescent girls and generally include only primary dysmenorrhoea, although this is not always specified❼.[3–8]

AETIOLOGY/ A longitudinal study of a representative sample of women born in 1962
RISK FACTORS found that severity of dysmenorrhoea was significantly associated with duration of menstrual flow (average duration of menstrual flow was 5 days for women with no dysmenorrhoea and 5.8 days for women with severe dysmenorrhoea; $P < 0.001$; WMD −0.8, 95% CI −1.36 to −0.24); younger average menarcheal age (13.1 years in women without dysmenorrhoea v 12.6 years in women with severe dysmenorrhoea; $P < 0.01$; WMD 0.5, 95% CI 0.09 to 0.91); and cigarette smoking (41% of smokers and 26% of non-smokers experienced moderate or severe dysmenorrhoea).[9] There is also some evidence of a dose-response relationship between exposure to environmental tobacco smoke and increased incidence of dysmenorrhoea.[10] ▶

Dysmenorrhoea

◄ **PROGNOSIS**   Primary dysmenorrhoea is a chronic recurring condition that affects most young women. Studies of the natural history of this condition are sparse. One longitudinal study in Scandinavia found that primary dysmenorrhoea often improves in the third decade of a woman's reproductive life, and is also reduced following childbirth.[9]

What are the effects of treatments in women with pain attributed to endometriosis?

Hormonal treatment at diagnosis (danazol, medroxyprogesterone, gestrinone, gonadorelin [GnRH] analogues)

Small systematic reviews have found that hormonal treatments (except for dydrogesterone) versus placebo reduce pain attributed to endometriosis, and are of similar effectiveness.

Combined ablation of endometrial deposits and uterine nerve

One RCT found that ablation of deposits plus laparoscopic uterine nerve ablation reduced pain more than diagnostic laparoscopy at 6 months.

Cystectomy for ovarian endometrioma (better than drainage)

One RCT found that cystectomy versus drainage significantly improved pain caused by ovarian endometrioma at 2 years. Complication rates were similar.

Oral contraceptive pill

Two RCTs found no significant difference with combined oral contraceptives versus GNRH analogues in overall pain relief, although one of the RCTs found that oral contraceptives reduced menstrual pain.

Postoperative hormonal treatment

RCTs have found that postoperative hormonal treatment with danazol or medroxyprogesterone versus placebo for 6 months significantly reduces pain and delays the recurrence of pain at 12 and 24 months, but have found that treatment for 3 months does not seem to be effective. One RCT found no significant difference in recurrence of pain with combined oral contraceptives versus placebo at 6 months.

Dydrogesterone

Systematic reviews have found no significant difference in pain at 6 months with dydrogesterone and placebo given at two different doses in the luteal phase.

Laparoscopic ablation of endometrial deposits without ablation of the uterine nerve; laparoscopic uterine nerve ablation

We found insufficient evidence on the effects of these interventions.

Preoperative hormonal treatment

One RCT found no significant difference in ease of surgery with preoperative treatment with GnRH analogues for 3 months versus no treatment. ▶

Endometriosis

What are the effects of treatments in women with subfertility attributed to endometriosis?

LIKELY TO BE BENEFICIAL

Cystectomy for ovarian endometrioma (better than drainage)

One RCT found that cystectomy versus drainage significantly increased pregnancy in women with subfertility caused by ovarian endometrioma. Complication rates were similar.

Laparoscopic ablation/excision of endometrial deposits

One large RCT found that laparoscopic surgery versus diagnostic laparoscopy significantly increased cumulative pregnancy rates after 36 weeks (NNT 8), but a subsequent smaller RCT found no significant difference with laparoscopic surgery versus diagnostic laparoscopy in pregnancy rates at 12 months.

UNLIKELY TO BE BENEFICIAL

Hormonal treatment at diagnosis (danazol, medroxyprogesterone, gonadorelin [GnRH] analogues)

One systematic review and one subsequent RCT found no significant difference with hormonal treatments versus placebo in rates of pregnancy at 4–6 months.

Postoperative hormonal treatment

RCTs found no significant difference with GnRH analogues versus placebo in rates of pregnancy or time to conception.

DEFINITION	Endometriosis is characterised by ectopic endometrial tissue, which can cause dysmenorrhoea, dyspareunia, non-cyclical pelvic pain, and sub-fertility. Diagnosis is made by laparoscopy. Most endometrial deposits are found in the pelvis (ovaries, peritoneum, uterosacral ligaments, pouch of Douglas, and rectovaginal septum). Extrapelvic deposits, including those in the umbilicus and diaphragm, are rare. Severity of endometriosis is defined by the American Fertility Society: this review uses the terms mild (stage I and II), moderate (stage III), and severe (stage IV).[1] Endometriomas are cysts of endometriosis within the ovary.
INCIDENCE/ PREVALENCE	In asymptomatic women, the prevalence of endometriosis ranges from 2–22%, depending on the diagnostic criteria used and the populations studied.[2–5] In women with dysmenorrhoea, the incidence of endometriosis ranges from 40–60%, and in women with subfertility from 20–30%.[3,6,7] The severity of symptoms and the probability of diagnosis increase with age.[8] Incidence peaks at about 40 years of age.[9] Symptoms and laparoscopic appearance do not always correlate.[10]
AETIOLOGY/ RISK FACTORS	The cause of endometriosis is unknown. Risk factors include early menarche and late menopause. Embryonic cells may give rise to deposits in the umbilicus, whereas retrograde menstruation may deposit endometrial cells in the diaphragm.[11,12] Use of oral contraceptives reduces the risk of endometriosis, and this protective effect persists for up to 1 year after their discontinuation.[9]
PROGNOSIS	We found two RCTs in which laparoscopy was repeated in the women treated with placebo. Over 6–12 months, endometrial deposits resolved spontaneously in up to a third of women, deteriorated in nearly half, and were unchanged in the remainder.[13,14]

Search date September 2001

Damian Murphy, Charles Redman and Earlando Thomas

What are the effects of treatments?

UNKNOWN EFFECTIVENESS

Amitryptyline; pudendal nerve compression
We found no RCTs on the effects of these interventions.

DEFINITION Essential vulvodynia is characterised by a diffuse, unremitting burning of the vulva, which may extend to the perineum, thigh, or buttock, and is often associated with urethral or rectal discomfort. Hyperaesthesia over a wide area is usually the only abnormal finding on physical examination. It is found primarily in postmenopausal women.

INCIDENCE/ PREVALENCE We found no data on the prevalence of essential vulvodynia.

AETIOLOGY/ RISK FACTORS The cause is unknown. The role of pudendal nerve compression is not clear; similar symptoms may be caused by pudendal nerve damage.[1-3]

PROGNOSIS Without treatment, the unremitting symptoms of essential vulvodynia may reduce the quality of life. Frequency of micturition, stress incontinence, and chronic constipation may rarely develop,[1-3] but we found no good data on prognosis without treatment.

Fibroids (uterine myomatosis, leiomyomas)

Search date April 2001

Anne Lethaby and Beverley Vollenhoven

What are the effects of medical treatment alone? New

TRADE OFF BETWEEN BENEFITS AND HARMS

Gonadorelin analogues (gonadotropin releasing hormone analogues [GnRHa]) plus combined hormone replacement therapy (oestrogen plus progestogen)

One RCT found that gonadorelin analogues plus combined hormone replacement therapy versus gonadorelin analogues plus progestogen reduced uterine volume compared to baseline, but found no significant difference in fibroid related symptoms over 2 years. Hormone replacement therapy after initial treatment with gonadorelin analogues did not prevent bone loss but relieved some gonadorelin analogue related adverse events.

Gonadorelin analogues (GnRHa) plus progestogen

One RCT found that gonadorelin analogues plus progestogen versus gonadorelin analogues alone significantly reduced heavy bleeding. One RCT found no significant difference in fibroid related symptoms over 2 years with gonadorelin analogues plus progestogen versus gonadorelin analogues plus combined hormone replacement. Hormone replacement therapy after initial treatment with gonadorelin analogues did not prevent bone loss but relieved some gonadorelin analogue related adverse events.

Gonadorelin analogues without hormone replacement therapy

RCTs have found that gonadorelin analogues may reduce fibroid related symptoms, such as heavy menstrual bleeding, and reduce uterine and fibroid volume to half the size. Potential hypo-oestrogenic effects, such as loss of bone density, frequently limit their use to 6 months. Two RCTs found that fibroids returned to previous size after stopping treatment.

UNKNOWN EFFECTIVENESS

Gestrinone; mifepristone

We found no RCTs on the effects of these interventions.

Non-steroidal anti-inflammatory drugs

Limited evidence from two small RCTs found no effect of non-steroidal anti-inflammatory drugs on heavy menstrual bleeding.

What are the effects of preoperative medical interventions? New

LIKELY TO BE BENEFICIAL

Gonadorelin analogues (GnRHa)

One systematic review has found that gonadorelin analogues versus placebo or no treatment for 2–4 months prior to fibroid surgery increase haemoglobin and haematocrit, and reduce uterine and pelvic symptoms. Preoperative gonadorelin also reduces blood loss and the rate of vertical incisions during surgery. Women having hysterectomy are more likely to have a vaginal rather than an ▶

◀ abdominal procedure after gonadorelin pretreatment. However, women are more likely to experience adverse hypo-oestrogenic effects from preoperative treatment.

What are the effects of surgical interventions? New

BENEFICIAL

Laparoscopic myomectomy (compared to abdominal myomectomy)

One RCT found that laparoscopic myomectomy versus abdominal myomectomy resulted in lower postoperative pain and a shorter recovery time (NNT 2 for both outcomes).

LIKELY TO BE BENEFICIAL

Abdominal hysterectomy

We found no RCTs. There is consensus that abdominal hysterectomy is superior to no treatment in reducing symptoms.

Laparoscopic assisted vaginal hysterectomy (compared to total abdominal hysterectomy) in women with uterus with estimated weight of 500 g or less

One RCT found that laparoscopically assisted vaginal hysterectomy versus abdominal hysterectomy reduced the need for analgesia (NNT 2), and reduced postoperative pain and recovery time. These benefits were found to be greater in women with a uterus estimated to weigh 500 g or less.

UNKNOWN EFFECTIVENESS

Laparoscopic assisted vaginal hysterectomy (compared to total abdominal hysterectomy) in women with uterus with estimated weight greater than or equal to 500 g or more

One RCT found limited evidence that laparoscopically assisted vaginal hysterectomy versus abdominal hysterectomy reduced recovery time but increased operating time.

DEFINITION   Fibroids (uterine leiomyomas) are benign tumours of the smooth muscle cells of the uterus. Women with fibroids can be asymptomatic or can present with menorrhagia (30%), dysmenorrhoea, pelvic pain, pressure symptoms, infertility, and recurrent pregnancy loss.[1] However, much of the data describing the relationship between the presence of fibroids and symptoms are based on uncontrolled studies that have assessed the effect of myomectomy on the presenting symptom.[2]

INCIDENCE/   The reported incidence of fibroids varies from 5.4–77% depending on the
PREVALENCE   method of diagnosis (the gold standard is histological evidence). A random sample of 335 Swedish women aged 25–40 years was reported to have an incidence of fibroids of 5.4% (95% CI 3.0 to 7.8%) based on transvaginal ultrasound examination. The prevalence of these tumours increased with age (age 25–32 years: 3.3%, 95% CI 0.7 to 6.0%; 33–40 years: 7.8%, 95% CI 3.6 to 12%).[3] Based on postmortem examination of women, 50% were found to have these tumours.[4] Gross serial sectioning at 2 mm intervals of 100 consecutive hysterectomy specimens revealed the presence of fibroids in 77%. These women were having hysterectomies for reasons other than fibroids.[5] The incidence of fibroids in black women is three times greater than that in white women, based on ultrasound or ▶

Fibroids (uterine myomatosis, leiomyomas)

hysterectomy diagnosis.[6] Submucosal fibroids have been diagnosed in 6–34% of women having a hysteroscopy for abnormal bleeding, and in 2–7% of women having infertility investigations.[7]

AETIOLOGY/ RISK FACTORS
The aetiology of uterine fibroids is unknown. It is known that each fibroid is of monoclonal origin and arises independently.[8,9] Factors thought to be involved include the sex steroid hormones oestrogen and progesterone as well as the insulin-like growth factors, epidermal growth factor, and transforming growth factor. Risk factors for fibroid growth include nulliparity and obesity. There is a risk reduction to a fifth with five term pregnancies compared with nulliparous women ($P < 0.001$).[10] Obesity increases the risk of fibroid development by 21% with each 10 kg weight gain ($P = 0.008$).[10] Factors associated with reduced incidence of fibroids include cigarette smoking and hormonal contraception. Women who smoke 10 cigarettes a day have an 18% lowered risk of fibroid development compared with non-smokers ($P = 0.036$).[10] The combined oral contraceptive pill reduces the risk of fibroids with increasing duration of use compared with never users (users for 4–6 years: OR 0.8, 95% CI 0.5 to 1.2; users for $\geq$ 7 years: OR 0.5, 95% CI 0.3 to 0.9).[11] Women who have used injections containing 150 mg depot medroxyprogesterone acetate also have a reduced incidence compared with women who have never used (OR 0.44, 95% CI 0.36 to 0.55).[12]

PROGNOSIS
There are little data on the long term untreated prognosis of these tumours, particularly in women who are asymptomatic at diagnosis. One small study reported that in a group of 106 women treated with observation alone over 1 year there was no significant change in symptoms and quality of life over that time.[13]

What are the effects of treatments in women with infertility caused by ovulation disorders?

LIKELY TO BE BENEFICIAL

Clomifene

One systematic review has found that clomifene (clomiphene) versus placebo significantly increases the likelihood of pregnancy in women who ovulate infrequently. Four other studies comparing clomifene versus tamoxifen have found no significant difference in ovulation rates or number of pregnancies.

UNKNOWN EFFECTIVENESS

Cyclofenil

One RCT found no significant difference in pregnancy rates with cyclofenil versus placebo.

Gonadotrophins

One systematic review found no significant difference between human menopausal gonadotrophins and urofollitropin (urofollitrophin, urinary follicle stimulating hormone [FSH]) in pregnancy rates. Three RCTs found no significant difference in cumulative pregnancy rates or numbers of live births with follitropin (recombinant FSH) versus urofollitropin. The review found that urofollitropin versus human menopausal gonadotrophins significantly reduced the risk of ovarian hyperstimulation syndrome⊙, although this was confined to women who were not treated with concomitant gonadotrophin releasing hormone (GnRH) analogues. Observational evidence suggests that gonadotrophins may be associated with an increased risk of ovarian cancer and multiple pregnancies.

Laparoscopic ovarian drilling

One systematic review and one subsequent small RCT found no significant difference with laparoscopic ovarian drilling⊙ versus gonadotrophins in pregnancy rates.

Pulsatile gonadotrophin releasing hormone (GnRH)

One systematic review found insufficient evidence on the effects of pulsatile GnRH treatment.

What are the effects of treatments in women with tubal infertility?

LIKELY TO BE BENEFICIAL

Tubal surgery

One systematic review has found that tubal surgery versus no treatment or medical treatment significantly increases the chance of becoming pregnant, and significantly increases the live birth rate. Another review found no significant difference in pregnancy rates between different types of tubal surgery. ▶

◀ UNKNOWN EFFECTIVENESS

In vitro fertilisation

We found no RCTs about in vitro fertilisation (IVF) versus no treatment. One RCT found that immediate⊙ versus delayed IVF⊙ significantly increased numbers of pregnancies and live births. One RCT found no significant difference in numbers of live births with IVF versus intracytoplasmic sperm injection. Observational evidence suggests that adverse effects associated with IVF include multiple pregnancies and ovarian hyperstimulation syndrome.

Selective salpingography plus tubal catheterisation

We found no RCTs on the effects of salpingography plus tubal catheterisation.

What are the effects of interventions in women with infertility associated with endometriosis?

LIKELY TO BE BENEFICIAL

Intrauterine insemination plus gonadotrophins

One RCT found that intrauterine insemination plus gonadotrophins versus no treatment significantly increased live birth rates over three cycles (NNT 6). A second RCT found no significant difference in birth rates with intrauterine insemination plus pituitary down regulation plus gonadotrophins versus expectant management. A third RCT found that intrauterine insemination plus gonadotrophins versus intrauterine insemination alone significantly increased pregnancy rates after the first treatment cycle (NNT 5).

UNKNOWN EFFECTIVENESS

IVF

We found no RCTs in women with endometriosis related infertility undergoing IVF treatment.

Surgical treatment

Two RCTs that compared laparoscopic surgery versus diagnostic laparoscopy found inconsistent results for differences in numbers of pregnancies and live births.

LIKELY TO BE INEFFECTIVE OR HARMFUL

Drug-induced ovarian suppression

One systematic review has found no significant difference in pregnancy rates between drugs that induce ovarian suppression versus either placebo or danazol. The review found that ovulation suppression agents cause adverse effects that include weight gain, hot flushes, and osteoporosis. Danazol causes dose related weight gain and androgenic effects.

What are the effects of interventions in couples with male factor infertility?

BENEFICIAL

Intrauterine insemination

Two systematic reviews have found that intrauterine insemination versus intracervical insemination or natural intercourse significantly increases pregnancy rates per cycle. ▶

◀ **UNKNOWN EFFECTIVENESS**

Donor insemination

We found no good evidence on the effects of donor insemination.

Intracytoplasmic sperm injection plus IVF

One systematic review found insufficient evidence on the effects of intracytoplasmic sperm injection plus IVF.

IVF versus gamete intrafallopian transfer

One RCT found insufficient evidence about IVF versus gamete intrafallopian transfer (GIFT).

What are the effects of interventions in couples with unexplained infertility?

BENEFICIAL

Intrauterine insemination (in couples undergoing ovarian stimulation treatment)

Two systematic reviews and one subsequent RCT in couples undergoing ovarian stimulation treatment have found that intrauterine insemination versus timed intercourse or intracervical insemination significantly increases pregnancy rates. One systematic review has found no significant difference in pregnancy rates with intrauterine insemination versus timed intercourse or versus intracervical insemination, but has found that the addition of ovarian stimulation to any of the three interventions significantly increases the overall pregnancy rate over around three cycles (NNT 11).

LIKELY TO BE BENEFICIAL

Clomifene

One systematic review found limited evidence that clomifene versus placebo significantly increased rates of pregnancy per cycle.

UNKNOWN EFFECTIVENESS

Gamete intrafallopian transfer

We found no RCTs of GIFT versus no treatment. Three RCTs found conflicting results with GIFT versus other treatments (intrauterine insemination, timed intercourse, and IVF) in pregnancy rates.

IVF

Two small RCTs found no significant difference between IVF versus GIFT in pregnancy rates. One RCT found no significant difference in cumulative pregnancy rates with IVF versus intrauterine insemination versus IVF, but found that more couples receiving IVF failed to complete their six cycles of treatment.

DEFINITION   Normal fertility has been defined as achieving a pregnancy within 2 years by regular sexual intercourse.[1] However, many define infertility as the failure to conceive after 1 year of unprotected intercourse. Infertility can be primary, in couples who have never conceived, or secondary, in couples who have previously conceived. Infertile couples include those who are sterile (who will never achieve a natural pregnancy) and those who are subfertile (who could eventually achieve a pregnancy).   ▶

Infertility and subfertility

**INCIDENCE/
PREVALENCE**
Although there is no evidence of a major change in the prevalence of infertility, many more couples are seeking help than previously. Currently, about 1/7 couples in industrialised countries will seek medical advice for infertility.[2] Rates of primary infertility vary widely between countries, ranging from 10% in Africa to about 6% in North America and Europe.[1] Reported rates of secondary infertility are less reliable.

**AETIOLOGY/
RISK FACTORS**
In the UK nearly a third of cases of infertility are unexplained. The rest are caused by ovulatory failure (27%), low sperm count or quality (19%), tubal damage (14%), endometriosis (5%), and other causes (5%).[3]

PROGNOSIS
In developed countries, 80–90% of couples attempting to conceive are successful after 1 year and 95% after 2 years.[3] The chances of becoming pregnant vary with the cause and duration of infertility, the woman's age, the couple's previous pregnancy history, and the availability of different treatment options.[4,5] For the first 2–3 years of unexplained infertility, cumulative conception rates remain high (27–46%) but decrease with increasing age of the woman and duration of infertility. The background rates of spontaneous pregnancy in infertile couples can be calculated from longitudinal studies of infertile couples who have been observed without treatment.[4]

Search date July 2001

Edward Morris and Janice Rymer

What are the effects of medical treatments?

BENEFICIAL

Oestrogens

Systematic reviews and subsequent RCTs have found that oestrogen versus placebo significantly improves vasomotor symptoms, urogenital symptoms, and depressed mood. Important adverse effects include venous thromboembolic disease, breast cancer, and endometrial cancer.

Progestogens (at high doses, in reducing vasomotor symptoms)

RCTs have found good evidence that high doses of progestogens versus placebo, or in combination with oestrogens, significantly reduce vasomotor symptoms. We found no good quality evidence on other outcomes, including quality of life.

Tibolone

RCTs have found that tibolone significantly improves vasomotor symptoms, libido, and vaginal lubrication.

LIKELY TO BE BENEFICIAL

Clonidine

One RCT found that clonidine versus placebo significantly reduced the mean number of flushes at 8 weeks. One crossover RCT found that clonidine versus placebo reduced the mean number of flushing attacks in the 14 days after crossover, but did not analyse the effect prior to crossover.

UNKNOWN EFFECTIVENESS

Antidepressants

We found insufficient evidence on the effects of antidepressants on menopausal symptoms.

Phyto-oestrogens

Limited evidence from small RCTs suggests that soy flour (which contains phyto-oestrogens) versus placebo may relieve vasomotor symptoms.

Testosterone

We found no placebo controlled RCTs or comparisons of testosterone alone. RCTs found that testosterone/oestrogen combinations improve sexual enjoyment and libido.

DEFINITION   Menopause is defined as the end of the last menstrual period. A woman is deemed to be postmenopausal 1 year after her last period. For practical purposes most women are diagnosed as menopausal after 1 year of amenorrhoea. Menopausal symptoms often begin in the perimenopausal years.

INCIDENCE/ PREVALENCE   In the UK, the mean age for the start of the menopause is 50 years and 9 months. The median onset of the perimenopause is between 45.5 and 47.5 years. One Scottish survey (6096 women aged 45–54 years) found that 84% of women had experienced at least one of the classic menopausal symptoms, with 45% finding one or more symptoms a problem.[1]

▶

Menopausal symptoms

AETIOLOGY/ RISK FACTORS Urogenital symptoms of menopause are caused by decreased oestrogen concentrations, but the cause of vasomotor symptoms and psychological effects is complex and remains unclear.

PROGNOSIS Menopause is a physiological event. Its timing may be determined genetically. Although endocrine changes are permanent, menopausal symptoms such as hot flushes, which are experienced by about 70% of women, usually resolve with time.[2] However, some symptoms may remain the same or worsen, for example genital atrophy.

What are the effects of treatments?

BENEFICIAL

Non-steroidal anti-inflammatory drugs

One systematic review has found that non-steroidal anti-inflammatory drugs versus placebo significantly reduce mean menstrual blood loss. One systematic review found no significant difference in menstrual blood loss with mefenamic acid versus naproxen, or with non-steroidal anti-inflammatory drugs versus oral progestogens, oral contraceptives, or progesterone releasing intrauterine devices.

Tranexamic acid

Systematic reviews have found that tranexamic acid versus placebo significantly reduces menstrual blood loss. One systematic review and several additional RCTs have found that tranexamic acid versus other drugs (oral progestogens, mefenamic acid, etamsylate, flurbiprofen, and diclofenac) also significantly reduces menstrual blood loss. Adverse effects of tranexamic acid include leg cramps and nausea in around a third of women. One long term observational study found no evidence to confirm the possibility of an increased risk of thromboembolism with tranexamic acid.

Endometrial thinning before hysteroscopic surgery

One systematic review has found that gonadotrophin releasing hormone analogues versus placebo or versus no treatment significantly reduce the duration of surgery, operative difficulty, and the risk of continuing to have moderate or heavy periods, and significantly increase the rate of postoperative amenorrhoea after 6–12 months. The review has found that gonadotrophin releasing hormone analogues versus danazol significantly increase the rate of postoperative amenorrhoea (NNT 6) and significantly reduce the duration of surgery, but found no significant difference in operative difficulty. We found insufficient evidence on progestogens in pre-operative endometrial thinning.

Hysterectomy (versus endometrial destruction) after medical failure

Systematic reviews have found that hysterectomy versus endometrial destruction significantly reduces menstrual blood loss (NNT 8), significantly increases patient satisfaction at 1 year, and significantly reduces the number of women requiring further operations within 1–4 years. RCTs have found no differences between different types of hysterectomy. One large cohort study reported major or minor complications in about a third of women undergoing hysterectomy.

LIKELY TO BE BENEFICIAL

Endometrial destruction after medical failure

Systematic reviews have found that endometrial destruction versus hysterectomy significantly increases menstrual blood loss, reduces patient satisfaction after 1 year, and increases the number of women requiring further operations within 1–4 years. RCTs comparing different techniques of endometrial destruction found conflicting results. One systematic review and one RCT compared transcervical endometrial resection⊙ versus medical treatment and found conflicting results. RCTs have found complications in 0–15% of women undergoing endometrial destruction.

▶

◄ **TRADE OFF BETWEEN BENEFITS AND HARMS**

Danazol

One systematic review has found that danazol versus placebo significantly reduces menstrual blood loss after 2–3 months. RCTs have found that danazol is as effective or is more effective than luteal phase oral progestogens, mefenamic acid, naproxen, or oral contraceptives. One RCT found that danazol caused adverse effects in 75% of women, of which 40% were considered unacceptable.

UNKNOWN EFFECTIVENESS

Combined oral contraceptives

One systematic review found insufficient evidence on the effects of oral contraceptives in the treatment of menorrhagia.

Dilatation and curettage after medical failure; gonadorelin (GnRH; gonadotrophin releasing hormone) analogues; myomectomy after medical failure

We found no RCTs on the effects of these interventions.

Etamsylate

One RCT found limited evidence that etamsylate versus tranexamic acid or versus mefenamic acid significantly increased menstrual blood loss.

Intrauterine progestogens

We found no RCTs comparing intrauterine progestogens versus placebo. Two systematic reviews and two subsequent RCTs have found conflicting evidence about menstrual blood loss, satisfaction rates, and quality of life scores with levonorgestrel releasing intrauterine devices versus other treatments (endometrial resection, norethisterone, medical treatment, non-steroidal anti-inflammatory drugs, and hysterectomy).

UNLIKELY TO BE BENEFICIAL

Oral progestogens (longer cycle)

We found no RCTs comparing oral progestogens versus placebo. One RCT found no significant difference in menstrual blood loss with 21 days per cycle of oral progestogen (oral noresthisterone) versus a levonorgestrel releasing intrauterine device.

LIKELY TO BE INEFFECTIVE OR HARMFUL

Oral progestogens in luteal phase only

We found no RCTs comparing oral progestogens versus placebo. One systematic review has found that luteal phase oral progestogens versus danazol, tranexamic acid, or a progesterone releasing intrauterine device significantly increase mean menstrual blood loss.

DEFINITION   Menorrhagia is defined as heavy but regular menstrual bleeding. Idiopathic ovulatory menorrhagia is regular heavy bleeding in the absence of recognisable pelvic pathology or a general bleeding disorder. Objective menorrhagia is taken to be a total menstrual blood loss of 80 mL or more each menstruation.[1] Subjectively, menorrhagia may be defined as a complaint of regular excessive menstrual blood loss occurring over several consecutive cycles in a woman of reproductive years.   ►

INCIDENCE/ PREVALENCE In the UK, 5% of women (aged 30–49 years) consult their general practitioner each year with menorrhagia.[2] In New Zealand, 2–4% of primary care consultations by premenopausal women are for menstrual problems.[3]

AETIOLOGY/ RISK FACTORS Idiopathic ovulatory menorrhagia is thought to be caused by disordered prostaglandin production within the endometrium.[4] Prostaglandins may also be implicated in menorrhagia associated with uterine fibroids, adenomyosis, or the presence of an intrauterine device. Fibroids have been reported in 10% of women with menorrhagia (80–100 mL/cycle) and 40% of those with severe menorrhagia ≥ 200 mL/cycle).[5]

PROGNOSIS Menorrhagia limits normal activities and causes iron deficiency anaemia in two thirds of women proved to have objective menorrhagia.[1,6,7] One in five women in the UK and one in three women in the USA will have a hysterectomy before the age of 60 years; menorrhagia is the main presenting problem in at least 50% of these women.[8–10] About 50% of the women who have a hysterectomy for menorrhagia have a normal uterus removed.[11]

Premalignant vulval disorders

Search date September 2001

Damian Murphy, Charles Redman and Earlando Thomas

What are the effects of treatments for lichen sclerosus?

LIKELY TO BE BENEFICIAL

Topical clobetasol propionate (0.05%)
One RCT found limited evidence that topical clobetasol propionate versus topical testosterone propionate or petroleum jelly significantly increased symptom control and reversal of histological changes at 3 months.

TRADE OFF BETWEEN BENEFITS AND HARMS

Oral retinoids (acitretin)
One small RCT found that acitretin versus placebo significantly improved pruritis (NNT 5), atrophic features (NNT 4), hyperkeratotic features (NNT 3), and increased the number of women with a reduction in the extent of lesions (NNT 4), but significantly increased hair loss (NNH 1) and severe skin peeling after 20–22 weeks.

UNKNOWN EFFECTIVENESS

Surgery (vulvectomy⊕, cryosurgery, laser)
We found insufficient evidence on the effects of surgery.

LIKELY TO BE INEFFECTIVE OR HARMFUL

Topical testosterone
Small RCTs found no evidence that testosterone propionate was more effective than petroleum jelly, either as initial treatment or as maintenance treatment after initial treatment with clobetasol propionate. Testosterone propionate is associated with virilisation.

What are the effects of treatments for vulval intraepithelial neoplasia?

UNKNOWN EFFECTIVENESS

Surgical treatments; topical α interferon
We found insufficient evidence on the effects of these interventions.

DEFINITION	There are two recognised premalignant conditions of the vulva. **Lichen sclerosus** is characterised by epithelial thinning, inflammation, and distinctive histological changes in the dermis. It affects all age groups but is typically found in the anogenital region in postmenopausal women. The most common presentation is severe intractable itching (pruritus vulvae) and vaginal soreness with dyspareunia. **Vulval intraepithelial neoplasia (VIN)** is dysplasia of the vulval epithelium, categorised as mild (VIN I), moderate (VIN II), or severe (VIN III). The vulval lesions are often multifocal and are usually associated with itching and pain.
INCIDENCE/ PREVALENCE	We found no data on the prevalence of lichen sclerosus. The true incidence of vulval intraepithelial neoplasia is unknown, but it is being diagnosed with increased frequency in the UK and the USA. This may be because of increased recognition of the disease or a true increase in incidence.[1–3]

AETIOLOGY/ RISK FACTORS The cause is unknown. Vulval intraepithelial neoplasia is associated with human papilloma virus 16.[1]

PROGNOSIS There is currently no cure for lichen sclerosus. The risk of progression to vulval carcinoma ranges from 0–9%.[4] People with concomitant squamous cell hyperplasia are at increased risk of malignancy.[5] Malignant transformation has been reported in 2–4% of women with VIN III but the incidence appears to be lower in women with VIN I and II.[2, 6] About 30% of vulval carcinomas are associated with vulval intraepithelial neoplasia.[1]

Premenstrual syndrome

Search date February 2002

Katrina Wyatt

What are the effects of treatments?

BENEFICIAL

Non-steroidal anti-inflammatory drugs

RCTs found that prostaglandin inhibitors versus placebo significantly improved a range of premenstrual symptoms but did not reduce premenstrual breast pain.

Selective serotonin reuptake inhibitors

One systematic review and subsequent RCTs have found that selective serotonin reuptake inhibitors versus placebo significantly improve premenstrual symptoms (NNT 4–11) but cause frequent adverse events (NNH 3).

Spironolactone/diuretics

RCTs have found that diuretics versus placebo significantly improve symptoms of premenstrual syndrome including breast tenderness and bloating.

LIKELY TO BE BENEFICIAL

Cognitive behavioural treatment

RCTs have found that cognitive behavioural therapy versus control treatments significantly reduces premenstrual symptoms, but the evidence is insufficient to define the size of any effect.

Exercise

One RCT has found that aerobic exercise versus placebo significantly improves premenstrual symptoms; another RCT has found that high intensity aerobic exercise improves symptoms significantly more than low intensity.

Oestrogens

Limited evidence from small RCTs suggests that oestradiol improves symptoms, but the magnitude of any effect remains unclear.

TRADE OFF BETWEEN BENEFITS AND HARMS

Bromocriptine (breast symptoms only)

RCTs have found that bromocriptine relieves breast tenderness, although adverse effects are common.

Danazol

RCTs have found that danazol versus placebo significantly reduces premenstrual symptoms, but has important adverse effects associated with masculinisation when used continuously in the long term.

Gonadotrophin releasing hormone analogues

RCTs have found that gonadotrophin releasing hormone analogues versus placebo significantly reduce premenstrual symptoms. RCTs have found that gonadotrophin releasing hormone plus oestrogen plus progestogen (addback treatment) produces a fall in symptom scores that is intermediate between the fall produced by gonadotrophin releasing hormone analogue alone and by placebo. Treatment with gonadotrophin releasing hormone analogues for more than 6 months carries a significant risk of osteoporosis, limiting their usefulness for long term treatment.

Non-selective serotonin reuptake inhibitor antidepressants/anxiolytics

RCTs have found that non-selective serotonin reuptake inhibitor antidepressants and anxiolytic drugs versus placebo significantly improve at least one symptom of premenstrual syndrome, but a proportion of women stop treatment because of adverse effects. ▶

◀ **UNKNOWN EFFECTIVENESS**

Chiropractic treatment; dietary supplements; endometrial ablation; evening primrose oil; laparoscopic bilateral oophorectomy; reflexology; relaxation treatment

We found insufficient evidence about the effects of these interventions.

Hysterectomy with or without bilateral oophorectomy

We found no RCTs. Observational studies have found that hysterectomy plus bilateral oophorectomy is curative. Hysterectomy alone may reduce symptoms, but evidence is limited because of the difficulty in providing controls. The risks are those of major surgery. Infertility is an irreversible consequence of bilateral oophorectomy.

Oral contraceptives

RCTs found limited evidence that oral contraceptives versus placebo improved premenstrual symptoms.

Progestogens

RCTs found conflicting evidence about the effects of progestogens.

Tibolone

One small RCT found limited evidence that tibolone versus placebo (multivitamins) improved premenstrual symptom score.

Vitamin B_6

One systematic review of poor quality RCTs found insufficient evidence about the effects of vitamin B_6. In the review, an analysis of weak RCTs suggested that vitamin B_6 versus placebo significantly reduced symptoms. Additional RCTs with weak methods found conflicting evidence on the effects of vitamin B_6.

LIKELY TO BE INEFFECTIVE OR HARMFUL

Progesterone

One systematic review of progesterone versus placebo has found a small but significant improvement in overall premenstrual symptoms and no increase in the frequency of withdrawals caused by adverse effects. However, the improvement is unlikely to be clinically important. It remains unclear whether the route or timing of administration of progesterone is important.

DEFINITION   A woman has premenstrual syndrome if she complains of recurrent psychological or somatic symptoms (or both), occurring specifically during the luteal phase of the menstrual cycle and resolving by the end of menstruation❶.[1]

DEFINITION   Premenstrual symptoms occur in 95% of all women of reproductive age; severe, debilitating symptoms (premenstrual syndrome)Ⓖ occur in about 5% of those women.[1]

AETIOLOGY/   The aetiology is unknown, but hormonal and other (possibly neuroendocrine)
RISK FACTORS factors probably contribute.[2,3] There may be enhanced sensitivity to progesterone, possibly caused by a deficiency of serotonin.[3]

PROGNOSIS   Except after oophorectomy, symptoms usually recur when treatment is stopped.

Pyelonephritis in non-pregnant women

Search date July 2001

Bruce Cooper

What are the effects of treatments?

LIKELY TO BE BENEFICIAL

Oral antibiotics (co-trimoxazole, co-amoxiclav, or a fluoroquinolone) for women with uncomplicated infection

We found no RCTs comparing oral antibiotics versus no antibiotics; however, it is unlikely that such an RCT would now be performed. One systematic review and one subsequent RCT in women with uncomplicated pyelonephritis have found no consistent differences between oral co-trimoxazole, co-amoxiclav, or a fluoroquinolone (ciprofloxacin, norfloxacin, levofloxacin, or lomefloxacin) in bacteriological or clinical cure rates.

Intravenous antibiotics (ampicillin, co-trimoxazole) in women admitted to hospital with uncomplicated infection

We found no RCTs comparing intravenous antibiotics versus no antibiotics; however, it is unlikely that such an RCT would now be performed. One RCT in women admitted to hospital with uncomplicated pyelonephritis found no significant difference with intravenous ampicillin versus intravenous co-trimoxazole in clinical response or recurrence of bacteria in the urine. We found no well designed trials comparing newer intravenous antibiotics with older regimens.

UNKNOWN EFFECTIVENESS

Inpatient versus outpatient management

We found no RCTs comparing inpatient versus outpatient management of women with acute uncomplicated pyelonephritis.

DEFINITION   Acute pyelonephritis, or upper urinary tract infection, is an infection of the kidney characterised by pain when passing urine, fever, flank pain, nausea and vomiting. White blood cells are almost always present in the urine and occasionally white blood cell casts are also seen on urine microscopy. Uncomplicated infection occurs in an otherwise healthy person without any other underlying disease. Complicated infection occurs in people with structural or functional urinary tract abnormalities or additional diseases. People with acute pyelonephritis may also be divided into those able to take oral antibiotics and without signs of sepsis who may be managed at home, and those requiring treatment delivered by injection whilst in hospital.

INCIDENCE/   In the USA, there are 250 000 cases of acute pyelonephritis a year.[1]
PREVALENCE   Worldwide prevalence and incidence are unknown.

AETIOLOGY/   Pyelonephritis is most commonly caused when bacteria in the bladder
RISK FACTORS ascend the ureters and invade the kidneys. In some cases, this may result in bacteria entering and multiplying in the bloodstream.

PROGNOSIS   Complications include sepsis, infection that spreads to other organs, renal impairment, and renal abscess formation. Conditions such as underlying renal disease, diabetes mellitus, and immunosuppression may worsen prognosis, with a potential increase in risk of sepsis and death, but we found no good long term evidence about such people.

Search date July 2001

Bruce Cooper and Ruth Jepson

What are the effects of interventions to prevent further recurrence of cystitis?

BENEFICIAL

Continuous antibiotic prophylaxis (trimethoprim, co-trimoxazole, nitrofurantoin, cefaclor, or a quinolone)

RCTs have found that continuous antibiotic prophylaxis lasting 6–12 months with trimethoprim, co-trimoxazole, nitrofurantoin, cefaclor, or a quinolone versus placebo significantly reduces rates of recurrent cystitis, but have found no consistent difference in the risk of infection with different regimens. One RCT comparing continuous daily antibiotic prophylaxis versus postcoital antibiotic prophylaxis found no significant difference in rates of cystitis after 1 year.

Postcoital antibiotic prophylaxis (co-trimoxazole, nitrofurantoin, or a quinolone)

Four RCTs have found that co-trimoxazole, nitrofurantoin, or a quinolone versus placebo up to 2 hours after sexual intercourse significantly reduce the rates of cystitis.

UNKNOWN EFFECTIVENESS

Cranberry juice and cranberry products

One systematic review found insufficient evidence on the effects of cranberry juice and other cranberry products on recurrent cystitis.

Prophylaxis with methenamine hippurate *New*

We found no RCTs on the effects of methenamine hippurate (hexamine hippurate).

Single dose self administered co-trimoxazole

One small RCT found that continuous co-trimoxazole prophylaxis versus single dose self administered co-trimoxazole (started at the onset of cystitis symptoms) significantly reduced the number of episodes of cystitis within 1 year.

DEFINITION Cystitis is an infection of the lower urinary tract, which causes pain when passing urine, and causes frequency, urgency, haematuria, or suprapubic pain not associated with passing urine. White blood cells and bacteria are almost always present in the urine. The presence of fever, flank pain, nausea, or vomiting suggests pyelonephritis (upper urinary tract infection) (see pyelonephritis in non-pregnant women, p 340). Recurrent cystitis may be either a reinfection (after successful eradication of infection) or a relapse after inadequate treatment.

INCIDENCE/ The incidence of cystitis among premenopausal sexually active women is
PREVALENCE 0.5–0.7 infections per person year,[1] and 20–40% of women will experience cystitis during their lifetime. Of those, 20% will develop recurrence, almost always (90% of cases) because of reinfection rather than relapse. Rates of infection fall during the winter months.[2]

AETIOLOGY/ Cystitis is caused by uropathogenic bacteria in the faecal flora that colonise
RISK FACTORS the vaginal and periurethral openings, and ascend the urethra into the bladder. Prior infection, sexual intercourse, and exposure to vaginal spermicide are risk factors for developing cystitis.[3,4] ▶

Recurrent cystitis in non-pregnant women

PROGNOSIS   We found little evidence on the long term effects of untreated cystitis. One study found that progression to pyelonephritis was infrequent, and that most cases of cystitis regressed spontaneously, although symptoms sometimes persisted for several months.[5] Women with a baseline rate of more than two infections a year, over many years, are likely to continue to suffer from recurrent infections.[6]

Search date May 2001

Jason Cooper

What are the effects of preventive interventions?

LIKELY TO BE BENEFICIAL

Postnatal pelvic floor muscle exercises
One RCT found that postnatal pelvic floor muscle exercises plus bladder retraining versus routine postnatal exercises significantly reduced stress incontinence❻ at 12 months (NNT 10).

UNKNOWN EFFECTIVENESS

Antenatal pelvic floor muscle exercises
We found no good quality RCTs of the effects of antenatal exercises in preventing stress incontinence.

What are the effects of treatments?

BENEFICIAL

Open colposuspension
One systematic review of RCTs and observational studies has found that colposuspension versus anterior colporrhaphy improves stress incontinence at 5 years.

Pelvic floor muscle exercises
One systematic review has found that pelvic floor muscle exercises versus no treatment improve objective measures of stress incontinence.

LIKELY TO BE BENEFICIAL

Slings
Small RCTs found no significant difference between slings❻ versus colposuspension in short and long term failure rates.

Tension free vaginal tape
One RCT found no significant difference between tension free vaginal tape versus colposuspension in subjective or objective cure at 6 months.

Weighted vaginal cones
One systematic review has found that vaginal cones versus control treatment significantly improve stress incontinence, and were of similar effectiveness to pelvic floor exercises and electrical stimulation.

UNKNOWN EFFECTIVENESS

α Adrenergic agonists (phenylpropanolamine)
One small RCT found no significant difference between pelvic floor muscle exercises and α adrenergic agonists.

Artificial sphincters; control of fluid intake; implantable devices; weight loss
We found insufficient evidence about the effects of these interventions. ▶

Stress incontinence

Bladder training

One RCT found no significant reduction in incontinence episodes with bladder training plus pelvic floor exercises versus pelvic floor exercises alone.

Biofeedback

One systematic review found no significant difference between biofeedback plus pelvic floor muscle exercises versus pelvic floor exercises alone in the number of women cured.

Electrical stimulation of pelvic floor (less effective than pelvic floor muscle exercises and causes adverse effects)

One RCT found that electrical stimulation was significantly less effective than pelvic floor exercises at improving stress incontinence over 3 days, and caused adverse effects.

Marshall–Marchetti–Krantz urethropexy

One small RCT found that Marshall–Marchetti–Krantz urethropexy❻ versus colposuspension significantly increased the subjective cure rate at 1 year.

UNLIKELY TO BE BENEFICIAL

Addition to pelvic floor muscle exercises of intravaginal resistance devices or biofeedback

RCTs found no significant benefit from the addition of intravaginal resistance devices or biofeedback to pelvic floor exercises.

Endoscopic colposuspension (less effective then open colposuspension)

One systematic review has found that open versus endoscopic colposuspension significantly improves stress incontinence.

Oestrogen

RCTs found no evidence that oestrogen improved stress incontinence.

LIKELY TO BE INEFFECTIVE OR HARMFUL

Anterior colporrhaphy

One systematic review of RCTs and observational studies found that anterior colporrhaphy was significantly less effective than colposuspension at improving stress incontinence at 5 years.

DEFINITION Urinary incontinence is defined as involuntary loss of urine that is objectively demonstrable and is a social or hygienic problem.[1] There are two main types of urinary incontinence: stress incontinence and detrusor instability❻, which together account for more than 80% of all cases of urinary incontinence. Urinary incontinence is eight times more common in women than in men. This review deals specifically with stress incontinence.

INCIDENCE/ PREVALENCE Prevalence is increasing as the population ages. In 1990, the number of women in the UK suffering from urinary incontinence was estimated at 2.5 million❼.[2,3] A community based study in the USA found that the self reported, age adjusted prevalence of female urinary incontinence was 48% (95% CI 45% to 52%).[4] A questionnaire based study in Sweden estimated the prevalence of urinary incontinence to be 3% in women aged 20–29 years old, increasing to 32% in women over 80 years old.[5]

AETIOLOGY/ RISK FACTORS Stress incontinence is made more likely with some genetic alterations in connective tissue, pregnancy and childbirth, menopause, ageing, obesity, some races, chronic constipation, other causes of chronic raised intra-abdominal pressure, and pelvic surgery.[6] Psychological factors, bladder neck ▶

surgery, caffeine, and smoking may aggravate the condition. Other causes of urinary incontinence include urinary tract infection, immobility, loss of physical function and dexterity, dementia, and other conditions causing impaired mental state.

PROGNOSIS Urinary incontinence affects physical, psychological, and social wellbeing, and impairs quality of life. We found no good studies of its natural history. Prognosis after treatment is probably better for stress incontinence than for most other forms of urinary incontinence.

Vulvovaginal candidiasis

Search date November 2001

Jeanne Marrazzo

What are the effects of treatments for symptomatic vulvovaginal candidiasis in non-pregnant women? New

BENEFICIAL

Intravaginal imidazoles

RCTs have found that intravaginal imidazoles (e.g. clotrimazole) versus placebo significantly reduce persistent symptoms of vulvovaginal candidiasis after 1 month (NNT 3). RCTs found no clear evidence that effects differ significantly among the various intravaginal imidazoles. RCTs found no clear evidence of any difference between shorter and longer durations of treatment (1–14 days).

Oral itraconazole

One RCT found that oral itraconazole versus placebo significantly reduced persistent symptoms after 1 week (NNT 4). One systematic review has found no significant difference in persistent symptoms in the short term with oral itraconazole versus intravaginal imidazoles.

LIKELY TO BE BENEFICIAL

Oral fluconazole

We found no RCTs of oral fluconazole versus placebo or no treatment. One systematic review has found no significant difference in persistent symptoms in the short term with oral fluconazole versus intravaginal imidazoles. RCTs have found that fluconazole is associated with increased frequency of mild nausea, headache, and abdominal pain (NNH 11 after 2 wks).

Intravaginal nystatin

One RCT found that intravaginal nystatin versus placebo significantly reduced the proportion of women with a poor symptomatic response after 1 week (NNT 3).

TRADE OFF BETWEEN BENEFITS AND HARMS

Oral ketoconazole

We found no RCTs of oral ketoconazole versus placebo or no treatment. RCTs have found no significant difference in persistent symptoms with oral ketoconazole versus intravaginal imidazoles, but ketoconazole significantly increased the frequency of minor adverse events (mainly nausea). Case reports have associated ketoconazole with a low risk of serious fulminant hepatitis (NNH 12 000).

UNKNOWN EFFECTIVENESS

Treating a male sexual partner

RCTs found no clear evidence that treating a woman's male sexual partner significantly improved resolution of the woman's symptoms or reduced the rate of symptomatic relapse.

◄ *What are the effects of treatments in non-pregnant women with recurrent vulvovaginal candidiasis?* New

LIKELY TO BE BENEFICIAL

Oral itraconazole

One RCT found that oral itraconazole versus placebo significantly reduced recurrence over 6 months (NNT 4).

TRADE OFF BETWEEN BENEFITS AND HARMS

Prophylaxis with intermittent or continuous ketoconazole

One RCT found that oral ketoconazole (given either intermittently or continuously at a lower dose) versus placebo significantly reduced symptomatic recurrences over 6 months (NNT 2–4). Ketoconazole is associated with an increased frequency of gastrointestinal adverse effects, and case reports have associated ketoconazole with a low risk of serious fulminant hepatitis.

UNKNOWN EFFECTIVENESS

Regular prophylaxis with oral fluconazole

We found no RCTs about the effects of fluconazole in preventing recurrence of vulvovaginal candidiasis.

Regular prophylaxis with intravaginal imidazole

RCTs comparing regular prophylaxis with intravaginal imidazole versus placebo found inconsistent effects on the proportion of women with symptomatic relapse. One RCT found that regular prophylactic intravaginal imidazole versus treatment at the onset of symptoms reduced the frequency of episodes of symptomatic vaginitis, but the difference was not significant. The RCTs were too small to exclude a clinically important benefit.

DEFINITION Vulvovaginal candidiasis is symptomatic vaginitis (inflammation of the vagina), which often involves the vulva, caused by infection with a *Candida* yeast. Predominant symptoms are vulvar itching and abnormal vaginal discharge (which may be minimal, a "cheese like" material, or a watery secretion). Differentiation from other forms of vaginitis requires the presence of yeast on microscopy of vaginal fluid. The definition of recurrent vulvovaginal candidiasis varies among RCTs, but is commonly defined as four or more symptomatic episodes a year.[1] This summary excludes studies of asymptomatic women with vaginal colonisation by *Candida* species.

INCIDENCE/ Vulvovaginal candidiasis is the second most common cause of vaginitis (after
PREVALENCE bacterial vaginosis). Estimates of its incidence are limited, and often derived from women attending hospital clinics. At least one episode of vulvovaginal candidiasis occurs during the lifetime of 50–75% of all women. About half of the women who have an episode develop recurrent vulvovaginal candidiasis.[2] Vulvovaginal candidiasis is diagnosed in 5–15% of women attending sexually transmitted disease and family planning clinics.[1]

AETIOLOGY/ *Candida albicans* accounts for 85–90% of vulvovaginal candidiasis infections.
RISK FACTORS Development of symptomatic vulvovaginal candidiasis probably represents increased growth of yeast that previously colonised the vagina without causing symptoms. Risk factors for vulvovaginal candidiasis include pregnancy ►

(RR 2–10), diabetes mellitus, and systemic antibiotics. The evidence that different types of contraceptives are risk factors is contradictory. The incidence of vulvovaginal candidiasis rises with initiation of sexual activity, but we found no direct evidence that vulvovaginal candidiasis is sexually transmitted.[3–5]

PROGNOSIS We found few descriptions of the natural history of untreated vulvovaginal candidiasis. Discomfort is the main complication and can include pain while passing urine or during sexual intercourse. Balanitis🅖 in male partners of women with vulvovaginal candidiasis can occur, but it is rare.

Search date June 2001

Nicky Cullum, E Andrea Nelson and Jane Nixon

Wounds

What are the effects of preventive interventions?

BENEFICIAL

Foam alternatives (v standard foam mattresses)

One systematic review in people at high risk has found that foam alternatives versus standard hospital foam mattresses significantly reduce the incidence of pressure sores after 10–14 days (NNT 4).

Pressure relieving overlays on operating tables

One systematic review in people having elective major surgery has found that pressure relieving overlays on operating tables versus standard operating tables significantly reduce the incidence of postoperative pressure sores.

LIKELY TO BE BENEFICIAL

Low air loss beds in intensive care (v standard beds)

One RCT found that low air loss beds significantly reduced the risk of new pressure sores over the duration of the trial (not specified) (NNT 3).

Medical sheepskin overlays

One RCT in people aged 60 years or over undergoing orthopaedic surgery found that medical sheepskins versus standard treatment significantly reduced the incidence of pressure sores after an unstated period (NNT 5).

UNKNOWN EFFECTIVENESS

Alternating pressure surfaces; constant low pressure supports; different seat cushions; low air loss hydrotherapy beds; repositioning (regular "turning"); topical lotions and dressings

We found insufficient evidence about the effects of these interventions in preventing pressure sores.

LIKELY TO BE INEFFECTIVE OR HARMFUL

Air filled vinyl boots with foot cradle

One small RCT found that air filled vinyl boots with foot cradles versus hospital pillows significantly increased the speed of development of pressure sores.

What are the effects of treatments?

LIKELY TO BE BENEFICIAL

Air fluidised supports (versus standard care)

Two RCTs in people in hospital found that air fluidised supports versus standard care healed more established sores. One RCT in people cared for at home found no significant difference with air fluidised supports versus standard care in healing; this trial had a high withdrawal rate.

▶

◄ UNKNOWN EFFECTIVENESS

Becaplermin (recombinant human platelet-derived growth factor); debridement; electrotherapy; hydrocolloid dressings (v gauze soaked in saline or hypochlorite); low air loss beds; low level laser therapy; nutritional supplements; seat cushions; surgery; topical negative pressure; ultrasound

We found insufficient evidence on the effects of these interventions in healing pressure sores.

DEFINITION	Pressure sores (also known as pressure ulcers, bed sores, and decubitus ulcers) may present as persistently hyperaemic, blistered, broken, or necrotic skin, and may extend to underlying structures, including muscle and bone. Whether blanching and non-blanching erythema constitute pressure sores remains controversial.
INCIDENCE/ PREVALENCE	The most comprehensive data on prevalence and incidence come from hospital populations. Studies have found prevalences of 6–10% in National Health Service hospitals in the UK[1] and 8% in a teaching hospital in the USA.[2]
AETIOLOGY/ RISK FACTORS	Pressure sores are caused by unrelieved pressure, shear, or friction, and are most common below the waist and at bony prominences such as the sacrum, heels, and hips. They occur in all healthcare settings. Increased age, reduced mobility, and impaired nutrition emerge consistently as risk factors. However, the relative importance of these and other factors is uncertain.[3]
PROGNOSIS	The presence of pressure sores has been associated with a two- to fourfold increased risk of death in elderly people and people in intensive care.[4,5] However, pressure sores are a marker for underlying disease severity and other comorbidities rather than an independent predictor of mortality.[4] Pressure sores vary considerably in size and severity.

What are the effects of treatments?

BENEFICIAL

Compression

One systematic review has found that compression versus no compression significantly increases the proportion of venous leg ulcers healed.

Pentoxifylline

One systematic review has found that oral pentoxifylline (oxpentifylline) versus placebo significantly increases the proportion of ulcers healed at 6 months (NNT 6).

LIKELY TO BE BENEFICIAL

Flavonoids

Two RCTs have found that flavonoids versus placebo or versus standard care significantly increase the number of ulcers healed.

Human skin equivalent

One RCT found that human skin equivalent versus a non-adherent dressing significantly increased the proportion of ulcers healed after 6 months (NNT 7).

Peri-ulcer injection of granulocyte–macrophage colony stimulating factor

One RCT found that peri-ulcer injection of granulocyte–macrophage colony stimulating factor versus placebo significantly increased the proportion of ulcers healed after 6 months (NNT 2).

UNKNOWN EFFECTIVENESS

Addition of intermittent pneumatic compression☺; aspirin; foam, film, or alginate (semi-occlusive) dressings versus simple dressings in the presence of compression; low level laser treatment☺; skin grafting; sulodexide; thromboxane α_2 antagonists; topical agents; topical negative pressure☺ *New;* therapeutic ultrasound☺; vein surgery; oral zinc

We found insufficient evidence on the effects of these interventions on ulcer healing.

UNLIKELY TO BE BENEFICIAL

Hydrocolloid (occlusive) dressings versus simple dressings in the presence of compression

One systematic review found no significant difference with hydrocolloid dressings plus compression versus simple, non-adherent dressings plus compression.

Topically applied autologous platelet lysate

One RCT found no significant difference with topically applied autologous platelet lysate versus placebo in time to healing of ulcers after 9 months. ▶

What are the effects of interventions to prevent recurrence?

LIKELY TO BE BENEFICIAL

Compression
One RCT found that compression stockings versus no stockings significantly reduced the risk of recurrence after 6 months (NNT 2).

UNKNOWN EFFECTIVENESS

Rutoside; stanozolol; vein surgery
We found insufficient evidence on the effects of these interventions on ulcer recurrence.

DEFINITION Definitions of leg ulcers vary, but the following is widely used: loss of skin on the leg or foot that takes more than 6 weeks to heal. Some definitions exclude ulcers confined to the foot, whereas others include ulcers on the whole of the lower limb. This review deals with ulcers of venous origin in people without concurrent diabetes mellitus, arterial insufficiency, or rheumatoid arthritis.

INCIDENCE/ PREVALENCE Between 1.5 and 3/1000 people have active leg ulcers. Prevalence increases with age to about 20/1000 in people aged over 80 years.[1]

AETIOLOGY/ RISK FACTORS Leg ulceration is strongly associated with venous disease. However, about a fifth of people with leg ulceration have arterial disease, either alone or in combination with venous problems, which may require specialist referral.[1] Venous ulcers (also known as varicose or stasis ulcers) are caused by venous reflux or obstruction, both of which lead to poor venous return and venous hypertension.

PROGNOSIS People with leg ulcers have a poorer quality of life than age matched controls because of pain, odour, and reduced mobility.[2] In the UK, audits have found wide variation in the types of care (hospital inpatient care, hospital clinics, outpatient clinics, home visits), in the treatments used (topical agents, dressings, bandages, stockings), in healing rates, and in recurrence rates (26–69% in 1 year).[3,4]

Note

When looking up a class of drug, the reader is advised to also look up specific examples of that class of drug where additional entries may be found. The reverse situation also applies. Abbreviations used: CVD, cardiovascular disease; HRT, hormone replacement therapy; IVF, in vitro fertilisation; MI, myocardial infarction; NSAIDs, non-steroidal anti-inflammatory drugs; STD, sexually transmitted disease.

INDEX

Estimating cardiovascular risk and treatment benefit

Adapted from the New Zealand guidelines on management of dyslipidaemia[1] and raised blood pressure [2] by Rod Jackson

How to use these colour charts

The charts help the estimation of a person's absolute risk of a cardiovascular event and the likely benefit of drug treatment to lower cholesterol or blood pressure. For these charts cardiovascular events include: new angina, myocardial infarction, coronary death, stroke or transient ischaemic attack (TIA), onset of congestive cardiac failure or peripheral vascular syndrome.

There is a group of patients in whom risk can be assumed to be high (>20% in 5 years) without using the charts. They include those with symptomatic cardiovascular disease (angina, myocardial infarction, congestive heart failure, stroke, TIA, and peripheral vascular disease), or left ventricular hypertrophy on ECG.

To estimate a person's absolute five-year risk:
■ Find the table relating to their sex, diabetic status (on insulin, oral hypoglycaemics or fasting blood glucose over 8 mmol/l), smoking status and age. The age shown in the charts is the mean for that category, i.e. age 60 = 55 to 65 years.
■ Within the table find the cell nearest to the person's blood pressure and total cholesterol : HDL ratio. For risk assessment it is enough to use a mean blood pressure based on two readings on each of two occasions, and cholesterol measurements based on one laboratory or two non-fasting Reflotron measurements. More readings are needed to establish the pre-treatment baseline.
■ The colour of the box indicates the person's five-year cardiovascular disease risk (see below).

Notes: (1) People with a strong history of CVD (first degree male relatives with CVD before 55 years, female relatives before 65 years) or obesity (body mass index above 30 kg/m^2) are likely to be at greater risk than the tables indicate. The magnitude of the independent predictive value of these risk factors remains unclear—their presence should influence treatment decisions for patients at borderline treatment levels. (2) If total cholesterol or total cholesterol:HDL ratio is greater than 8 then the risk is at least 15%. (3) Nearly all people aged 75 years or over also have an absolute cardiovascular risk over 15%.

Charts reproduced with permission from The National Heart Foundation of New Zealand. Also available on http://www.nzgg.org.nz/library/gl_complete/bloodpressure/table1.cfm

REFERENCES

1. Dyslipidaemia Advisory Group. 1996 National Heart Foundation clinical guidelines for the assessment and management of dyslipidaemia. *NZ Med J* 1996;109:224–232.
2. National Health Committee. Guidelines for the management of mildly raised blood pressure in New Zealand: Ministry of Health National Health Committee Report, Wellington, 1995.

RISK LEVEL Five-year CVD risk (non-fatal and fatal)		BENEFIT (1) CVD events prevented per 100 treated for five years*	BENEFIT (2) Number needed to treat for five years to prevent one event*
Very High	>30%	>10 per 100	<10
Very High	25–30%	9 per 100	11
Very High	20–25%	7.5 per 100	13
High	15–20%	6 per 100	16
Moderate	10–15%	4 per 100	25
Mild	5–10%	2.5 per 100	40
Mild	2.5–5%	1.25 per 100	80
Mild	<2.5%	<0.8 per 100	>120

*Based on a 20% reduction in total cholesterol or a reduction in blood pressure of 10–15 mmHg systolic or 5–10 mmHg diastolic, which is estimated to reduce CVD risk by about one third over 5 years.

Appendix 1

RISK LEVEL: MEN

NO DIABETES

Nonsmoker   Smoker

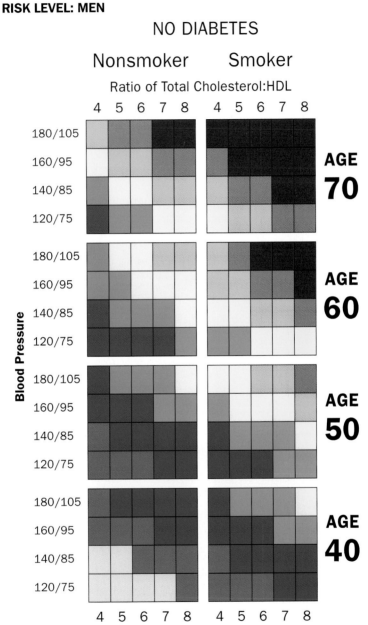

Ratio of Total Cholesterol:HDL

4 5 6 7 8   4 5 6 7 8

180/105
160/95
140/85
120/75

AGE 70

180/105
160/95
140/85
120/75

AGE 60

Blood Pressure

180/105
160/95
140/85
120/75

AGE 50

180/105
160/95
140/85
120/75

AGE 40

4 5 6 7 8   4 5 6 7 8

Ratio of Total Cholesterol:HDL

Estimating cardiovascular risk and treatment benefit

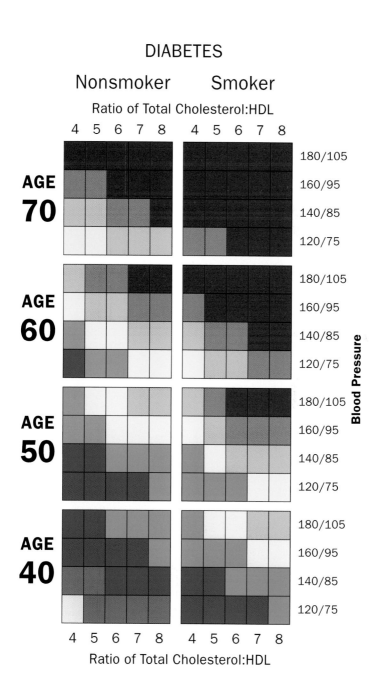

Estimating cardiovascular risk and treatment benefit

RISK LEVEL: WOMEN

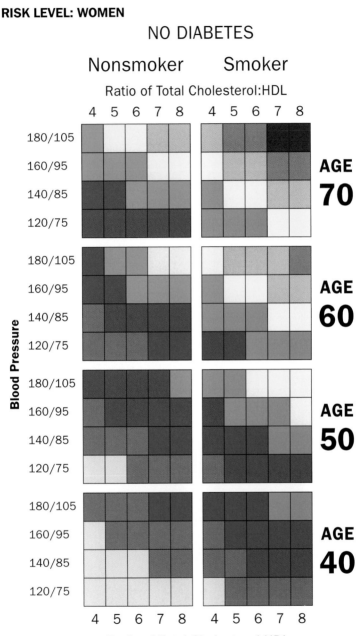

NO DIABETES

Nonsmoker   Smoker

Ratio of Total Cholesterol:HDL

Blood Pressure

Ratio of Total Cholesterol:HDL

AGE 70

AGE 60

AGE 50

AGE 40

Estimating cardiovascular risk and treatment benefit

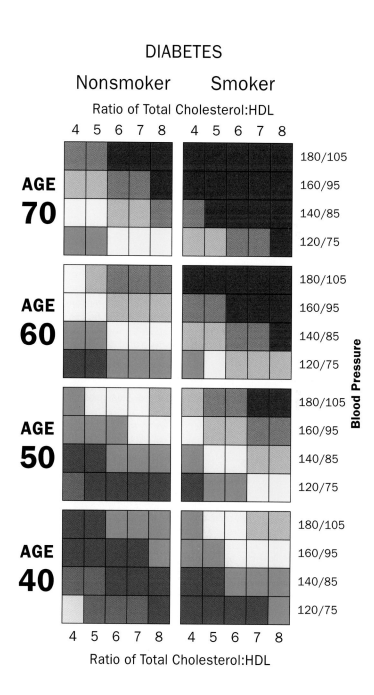

DIABETES

Nonsmoker   Smoker

Ratio of Total Cholesterol:HDL

The number needed to treat: adjusting for baseline risk

Adapted with permission from Chatellier et al, 1996[1]

BACKGROUND

The number needed to treat (NNT) to avoid a single additional adverse outcome is a meaningful way of expressing the benefit of an active treatment over a control. It can be used both to summarise the results of a therapeutic trial or series of trials and to help medical decision making about an individual patient.

If the absolute risk of adverse outcomes in a therapeutic trial is ARC in the control group and ART in the treatment group, then the absolute risk reduction (ARR) is defined as (ARC − ART). The NNT is defined as the inverse of the ARR:

$$NNT = 1/(ARC - ART)$$

Since the Relative Risk Reduction (RRR) is defined as (ARC − ART)/ARC, it follows that NNT, RRR and ARC are related by their definitions in the following way:

$$NNT \times RRR \times ARC = 1$$

This relationship can be used to estimate the likely benefits of a treatment in populations with different levels of baseline risk (that is different levels of ARC). This allows extrapolation of the results of a trial or meta-analysis to people with different baseline risks. Ideally, there should be experimental evidence of the RRR in each population. However in many trials, subgroup analyses show that the RRR is approximately constant in groups of patients with different characteristics. Cook and Sackett therefore proposed that decisions about individual patients could be made by using the NNT calculated from the RRR measured in trials and the baseline risk in the absence of treatment estimated for the individual patient.[2]

The method may not apply to periods of time different to that studied in the original trials.

USING THE NOMOGRAM

The nomogram shown on the next page allows the NNT to be found directly without any calculation: a straight line should be drawn from the point corresponding to the estimated absolute risk for the patient on the left hand scale to the point corresponding to the relative risk reduction stated in a trial or meta-analysis on the central scale. The intercept of this line with the right hand scale gives the NNT. By taking the upper and lower limits of the confidence interval of the RRR, the upper and lower limits of the NNT can be estimated.

REFERENCES

1. Chatellier G, Zapletal E, Lemaitre D, Menard J, Degoulet P. The number needed to treat: a clinically useful nomogram in its proper context. *BMJ* 1996;321:426–429.
2. Cook RJ, Sackett DL. The number needed to treat: a clinically useful measure of treatment effect. *BMJ* 1995;310:452–454.

The number needed to treat

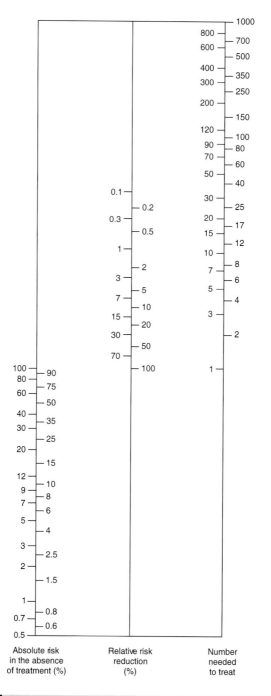

FIGURE Nomogram for calculating the number needed to treat. Published with permission[1]

Clinical Evidence mini CD-ROM

The *Clinical Evidence* mini CD-ROM allows you to:
- Refer to the full *Clinical Evidence* content including clinical questions, summary and background information, evidence detail, figures, tables and appendices
- Choose the method of navigation you prefer, through the table of contents, topic sections or the search engine
- Hyperlink references to abstracts where they appear on PubMed and Cochrane (Internet access required)
- Hyperlink to the glossary, figures, tables and references
- Print the full text of any of the 158 topics

To access *Clinical Evidence* help:
- From within the *Clinical Evidence* CD-ROM, simply click on the link at the top of the screen or from within Windows, select Programs > Clinical Evidence > Help (if you have already installed *Clinical Evidence*)
- For technical help, please go to the FAQs at www.clinicalevidence.com
- For damaged CD-ROMs please contact:
  BMJ Publishing Group • Tel: +44(0) 207 383 6270 • subscriptions@bmjgroup.com (UK/ROW)
  For individual subscriptions • Tel: +1 800 373 2897/+1 240 646 7000 • clinevid@pmds.com (USA)
  For individuals receiving *Clinical Evidence Concise* courtesy of UnitedHealth Foundation:
  ce@unitedhealthfoundation.org

To install *Clinical Evidence*
(i) Exit from any Windows programs you have running.
(ii) Insert the *Clinical Evidence* Installation CD-ROM into the CD-ROM drive. The installation starts automatically (if it does not, select Run from the Start menu and enter d:\setup (where d: is your CD-ROM drive letter).
(iii) Follow the on-screen instructions. As part of this process, you can install Adobe Acrobat Reader so you can efficiently print *Clinical Evidence* topics — this can also be installed later by following the instructions below. An additional 20 Mbytes of hard disk space is required for this.

Minimum system requirements
An IBM compatible PC with at least this specification:
- 60 Mbytes hard disk space
- 90 MHz processor
- 32 MBytes of RAM
- CD-ROM drive
- Modem, if you want to access the Internet for updates, etc.
- SVGA monitor recommended

Operating systems
This software has been tested with the following operating systems:
- Microsoft Windows 95
- Microsoft Windows 98
- Microsoft Windows 2000 Professional
- Microsoft Windows XP Professional
- Microsoft Windows NT SP6
- Microsoft Windows 2000 Server

Please note
Windows XP Home Edition is not a supported operating system. However, please refer to the Windows XP Home section in the Readme file, which is located:
Start > Programs > Clinical Evidence > Readme (if you have already installed *Clinical Evidence*) or contact technical help.

Browsers
Microsoft Internet Explorer 5.5 is the recommended browser, and should be your default browser when installing *Clinical Evidence*.
This software has been tested with the following browsers:
- Microsoft Internet Explorer 5.0 (English)
- Microsoft Internet Explorer 5.5 (English)
- Microsoft Internet Explorer 6.0 (English)
- Netscape 4.7 (English)
- Netscape 6.0 (English)

Please note
Microsoft Internet Explorer 4 is not a supported browser.
Microsoft Internet Explorer 6 is not compatible with Windows 95.
Internet Explorer 5.5 and 6.0 are available on the installation CD-ROM — see below for details.

To install Microsoft Internet Explorer v5.5
(i) With the *Clinical Evidence* Installation CD-ROM in the CD-ROM drive, select Run from the Start menu.
(ii) Type d:\other\ie5.5\ie5setup and click OK (where d: is your CD-ROM drive letter).
(iii) Follow the on-screen instructions. The typical installation requires approximately 17 Mbytes of hard disk space.

To install Microsoft Internet Explorer v6.0
(i) With the *Clinical Evidence* Installation CD-ROM in the CD-ROM drive, select Run from the Start menu.
(ii) Type d:\other\ie6.0\ie6setup and click OK (where d: is your CD-ROM drive letter).
(iii) Follow the on-screen instructions. The typical installation requires approximately 25 Mbytes of hard disk space.

To install Adobe Acrobat Reader v5.0.5
(i) With the *Clinical Evidence* Installation CD-ROM in the CD-ROM drive, select Run from the Start menu.
(ii) Type d:\Adobe\ar505enu and click OK (where d: is your CD-ROM drive letter).
(iii) Follow the on-screen instructions.